MW01505089

FACING
CYSTIC FIBROSIS

A Guide for Patients and Their Families

EDITORS

Yelizaveta Sher, MD

Anna M. Georgiopoulos, MD

Theodore A. Stern, MD

FACING
CYSTIC FIBROSIS

A Guide for Patients and Their Families

Facing Cystic Fibrosis – A Guide for Patients and Their Families

Copyright ©2020 by The Massachusetts General Hospital Psychiatry Academy. All rights reserved. Printed in the United States of America. Except as permitted under the United States Copyright Act of 1976, no part of this publication may be reproduced or distributed in any form or by any means, or stored in a data base or retrieval system, without the prior written permission of the publisher.

ISBN-13: 978-1-951166-11-3 (Print)
ISBN-13: 978-1-951166-10-6 (Ebook)

Cover Design: Falcone Creative Design, LLC
Book Design: Dianne Russell, Octal Productions, LLC
Book Production: Octal Productions, LLC
Copyeditor: Bob Russell, Octal Publishing, LLC
Managing Director: Jane Pimental, MGH Psychiatry Academy
Program Manager: Heather Giza, MGH Psychiatry Academy
Clinical Research Assistant: Julia Chippari, MGH Psychiatry Academy
Printing and Binding: RP Graphics
This book is printed on acid-free paper.

ABOUT THE EDITORS

 Yelizaveta Sher, MD is a Clinical Associate Professor of Psychiatry and an Associate Director of Psychosomatic Medicine/Consult Liaison Fellowship at Stanford. She is also an embedded psychiatrist in the Stanford adult Cystic Fibrosis (CF) program and serves as its first Director of Psychiatric and Psychological Services. In addition, she is a consulting psychiatrist to Stanford Lung Transplantation Program. Dr. Sher is the author of scores of articles and book chapters on mental health in pulmonary disorders, including CF, as well as lung transplantation. She is a co-editor of the book *Psychosocial Care of End-Stage Organ Disease and Transplant Patients*.

 Anna M. Georgiopoulos, MD is Assistant Professor of Psychiatry, Part Time, at Harvard Medical School. Triple board-certified in child and adolescent psychiatry, adult psychiatry, and consultation-liaison psychiatry, she is consulting psychiatrist to the Massachusetts General Hospital Cystic Fibrosis Program and co-creator of the Massachusetts General Hospital Cystic Fibrosis-specific cognitive behavioral therapy intervention, CF-CBT. Dr. Georgiopoulos has published pioneering articles in cystic fibrosis mental health and palliative care, and developed related clinical care guidelines and educational initiatives in North America, Europe, and Australia. She serves in leadership roles on the Mental Health Advisory Committee and Palliative Care Working Group of the Cystic Fibrosis Foundation, and was the 2018 recipient of the Cystic Fibrosis Foundation's Carolyn and C. Richard Mattingly Leadership in Mental Health Care Award.

Theodore A. Stern, MD is the Ned H. Cassem Professor of Psychiatry in the field of Psychosomatic Medicine/Consultation, Harvard Medical School and Chief Emeritus of the Avery D. Weisman Psychiatry Consultation Service, Director of the Thomas P. Hackett Center for Scholarship in Psychosomatic Medicine, and Director of the Office for Clinical Careers, at the Massachusetts General Hospital in Boston, Massachusetts. Dr. Stern has written more than 450 scientific articles and book chapters and edited more than 25 books, including the *Massachusetts General Hospital Handbook of General Hospital Psychiatry* (4/e–7/e), *Massachusetts General Hospital Comprehensive Clinical Psychiatry* (1/e, 2/e), *Massachusetts General Hospital Guide to Primary Care Psychiatry* (1/e, 2/e), *Massachusetts General Hospital Psychiatry Update and Board Preparation*, (1/e–4/e), and *Facing Cancer, Facing Heart Disease, Facing Diabetes, Facing Immunotherapy, Facing Lupus, Facing Osteoporosis, Facing Scleroderma, Facing Psoriasis*, and *Facing Overweight and Obesity*. He is also the Editor-in-Chief of *Psychosomatics*.

DEDICATION

To people living with cystic fibrosis, their families,
our students, our colleagues, our mentors,
and our families . . .

YS, AMG, & TAS

ACKNOWLEDGMENTS

OUR THANKS

This book would not have come into being if not for members of the cystic fibrosis community who expressed their need for information and support navigating the experience of living with cystic fibrosis. They have been generous in including us in their day-to-day triumphs and struggles. Without the contributions of so many dedicated people with cystic fibrosis, their loved ones, and members of multidisciplinary care teams, this book would never have been completed.

We thank our contributors for their thoughtfulness and gifted writing as well as their tolerance of our deadlines and edits. We also thank our teachers and mentors for imbuing in us a sense of responsibility to educate, to write with rigor, and, most important, to provide exceptional care to our patients.

At the Massachusetts General Hospital Psychiatry Academy, we thank Jane Pimental our managing director, Heather Giza and Grace Shanks our program managers, and clinical research assistant Julia Chippari for their assistance and support. At Octal Publishing, LLC, our thanks go to Bob Russell for his yeoman's efforts related to copyediting, and to Dianne Russell at Octal Productions, LLC for overseeing the production of this book, with grace and style.

YS
AMG
TAS

TABLE OF CONTENTS

CHAPTER 3

What Are the Medical and Psychiatric Complications of CF? 19

Xin (Cissy) Si, MD; Yelizaveta Sher, MD; and Paul K. Mohabir, MD

CHAPTER 4

Which Tests and Procedures Assess, Monitor, and Treat My CF? 29

Elika Rad, MS, RN, NP-C; Michelle Stroebe, MS, RD; and Paul K. Mohabir, MD

CHAPTER 5
What Types of Medications Can Help Me Manage My CF?........................... 45
Jaideep S. Talwalkar, MD and Beth A. Smith, MD

CHAPTER 6
What Lifestyle Changes Can I Make to Address My Cystic Fibrosis?.............. 55
Christopher J. Richards, MD; C.J. Bathgate, PhD; Matthew Nippins, PT, DPT, CCS;
Jessica Garton, PT, DPT, OCS, CLT; Gretchen M. Garlow MS, RD, LDN, CNSC; and
Anna M. Georgiopoulos, MD

CHAPTER 7
Which Types of Providers Can Help Me with My CF? 77
Gabriela R. Oates, PhD; Kathryn A. Sabadosa, MPH; Kathleen Quinn Porco, MS; and
Cathy Mims, MS–HQS, BSN

CHAPTER 8
How Can I Manage My CF Care?... 85
Christopher M. Kvam, JD, MPP and Gregory S. Sawicki, MD, MPH

CHAPTER 9
How Does CF Affect My Time in School?... 95
Stephanie Filigno, PhD; Sarah Strong, MEd; Tess Dunn, BA; and Yelizaveta Sher, MD

CHAPTER 10
How Can CF Affect My Work?... 109
Kim Reno, ACSW, LISW-S; Amy E. Mueller, LCSW; and Denis Hadjiliadis MD, MHS, FRCP(C)

CHAPTER 11
What Should I Consider When Thinking About Having a Family?................ 127
Olivia M. Stransky, MPH, BA; Sigrid Ladores, PhD, RN, PNP, CNE; Laura Mentch, EdM, BA;
Molly Pam, BA; and Traci M. Kazmerski, MD, MS

CHAPTER 12
Are My Feelings About Having CF Normal? 147
Desireé N. Williford, MS; Christina L. Duncan, PhD; Tess Dunn, BA; and Yelizaveta Sher, MD

CHAPTER 13
How Can CF Affect My Family and Friends? 159
Ginger Birnbaum, BA; Amanda Bruce, PhD; and Stephanie Filigno, PhD

CHAPTER 14
Which Psychological Interventions Might Help Me Manage My CF? 169
Emily Muther, PhD and Alexandra Quittner, PhD

CHAPTER 15
How Can My Pain Be Managed? 183
Bethany Bartley, MD; Lara K. Dhingra, PhD; Saida Hussain, PhD; Julie Balzano, PhD;
Alexandra L. Quittner, PhD; Elisabeth P. Dellon, MD, MPH; and Anna M. Georgiopoulos, MD

CHAPTER 16
Will I Need a Transplant? 199
Andrea Jonas, MD; Laveena Chhatwani, MD, MSc; Eirik Gumeny, BA; and Yelizaveta Sher, MD

CHAPTER 17

What Is Palliative Care? 215
Elisabeth P. Dellon, MD and Isabel Stenzel Byrnes, LCSW, MPH

CHAPTER 18

What Might Be the Future of CF Prevention and Treatment? 225
Lael M. Yonker, MD; Christine M. Roach, RN, BSN; Frances H. Kiles; and Isabel P. Neuringer, MD

CHAPTER 19
Where Can I Turn for Additional Information on CF and Its Treatment?...... 235
Meg Dvorak, LCSW; Chris Kvam JD, MPP; and Mary Shannon Fracchia, MD

CONTRIBUTORS

Julie Balzano, PhD
Psychologist, Primary Care
Mental Health Integration,
James J. Peters VA Medical Center;
Bronx, NY

Bethany Bartley, MD
Fellow, Pediatric Pulmonology,
Department of Pediatrics,
Massachusetts General Hospital;
Boston, MA

C.J. Bathgate, PhD
Assistant Professor of Medicine,
Licensed Clinical Psychologist
Adult Cystic Fibrosis,
Division of Medical, Behavioral, and
Community Health,
National Jewish Health;
Denver, CO

Ginger Birnbaum, BA
Cystic Fibrosis Patient Advocate and
Mother of a Child with Cystic Fibrosis,
Lookout Mountain, TN

Amanda Bruce, PhD
Assistant Professor of Pediatrics,
Department of Pediatrics and Center for
Children's Healthy Lifestyles & Nutrition,
University of Kansas Medical Center and
Children's Mercy Hospital;
Kansas City, KS

Isabel Stenzel Byrnes, LCSW, MPH
Bereavement Coordinator,
Mission Hospice & Home Care;
San Mateo, CA

Laveena Chhatwani, MD, MSc
Clinical Assistant Professor of Pulmonary
and Critical Medicine,
Stanford University School of Medicine;
Stanford, CA

Zoe A. Davies, PNP, CCRC
Advanced Care Nurse Practitioner,
Pediatric Pulmonary and Cystic Fibrosis Clinic,
Stanford University;
Stanford, CA

Elisabeth P. Dellon, MD, MPH
Professor of Pediatrics,
University of North Carolina School of Medicine;
Chapel Hill, NC

Lara K. Dhingra, PhD
Associate Professor, Department of
Family and Social Medicine,
Albert Einstein College of Medicine;
Director of Health Disparities and
Outcomes Research,
MJHS Institute for Innovation in
Palliative Care;
Bronx, NY

Christina L. Duncan, PhD
Professor of Psychology,
Adjunct Professor of Pediatrics,
Director, Quin Curtis Center for
Psychological Services,
Department of Psychology,
West Virginia University;
Morgantown, WV

Tess Dunn, BA
Musician
Los Angeles, CA

Meg Dvorak, LCSW
Adult Cystic Fibrosis Social Work Clinician,
Department of Social Work and
Case Management,
Stanford Health Care;
Stanford, CA

Stephanie Filigno, PhD
Associate Professor of Pediatrics,
Cincinnati Children's Hospital Medical Center;
Division of Behavioral Medicine and
Clinical Psychology,
University of Cincinnati College of Medicine;
Cincinnati, OH

Mary Shannon Fracchia, MD
Assistant Professor of Pediatrics,
Department of Pediatrics,
Harvard Medical School;
Boston, MA

Gretchen M. Garlow, MS, RD, LDN, CNSC
Senior Clinical Nutritionist,
Cystic Fibrosis/Lung Transplant,
Division of Pulmonary and
Critical Care Medicine,
Massachusetts General Hospital;
Boston, MA

Jessica Garton, PT, DPT, OCS, CLT
Staff Physical Therapist,
Physical Therapy Services,
Massachusetts General Hospital;
Boston, MA

Anna M. Georgiopoulos MD
Assistant Professor of Psychiatry, Part-Time,
Harvard Medical School;
Consulting Psychiatrist, Cystic Fibrosis
Program, Department of Child and
Adolescent Psychiatry,
Massachusetts General Hospital;
Boston, MA

Eirik Gumeny, BA
Author, Cystic Fibrosis Advocate
Albuquerque, NM

Denis Hadjiliadis MD, MHS, FRCP(C)
Paul F. Harron, Jr. Associate Professor of
Medicine,
Pulmonary, Allergy and Critical Care,
Perelman School of Medicine,
University of Pennsylvania;
Director, Adult Cystic Fibrosis Program,
Member, Lung Transplantation Program,
Hospital of the University of Pennsylvania;
Philadelphia, PA

Saida Hussain, PhD
Senior Data Research Associate,
Nicklaus Children's Research Institute;
Miami, FL

Andrea Jonas, MD
Fellow in Pulmonary and Critical Care
Medicine,
Stanford University Hospital;
Palo Alto, CA

Traci M. Kazmerski, MD, MS
Assistant Professor, Pediatrics,
Division of Adolescent and
Young Adult Medicine,
University of Pittsburgh School of Medicine;
Pediatric Pulmonologist,
UPMC Children's Hospital of Pittsburgh;
Pittsburgh, PA

Frances H. Kiles
Research Intern,
Massachusetts General Hospital
Cystic Fibrosis Center;
Massachusetts General Hospital for
Children Pulmonary Division;
Boston, MA

Christopher M. Kvam, JD, MPP
Assistant District Attorney,
Monroe County District Attorney's Office;
Rochester, NY

Sigrid Ladores, PhD, RN, PNP, CNE
Associate Professor of Nursing, Co-Director of
the BSN Honors Program, School of Nursing,
University of Alabama at Birmingham;
Birmingham, AL

Meghan B. Marmor, MD
Fellow, Pulmonary and Critical Care Medicine,
Stanford University;
Stanford, CA

Laura Mentch, EdM, BA
Patient Advocate,
Cystic Fibrosis Reproductive and
Sexual Health Collaborative (CFReSHC);
Seattle, WA

Cathy Mims, MS-HQS, BSN, RN, CPN
Cystic Fibrosis Center Coordinator,
Children's of Alabama;
Birmingham, AL

Paul K. Mohabir, MD
Clinical Professor of Pulmonary and
Critical Care Medicine,
Adult Cystic Fibrosis Program Center Director,
Stanford University School of Medicine;
Stanford, CA

Amy E. Mueller, LCSW
Social Worker/Mental Health Coordinator,
Marie and Raymond Beauregard
Adult Cystic Fibrosis Center,
Hartford Hospital;
Hartford, CT

Emily Muther, PhD
Associate Professor of Psychiatry and Pediatrics,
University of Colorado School of Medicine;
Licensed Psychologist,
Children's Hospital Colorado;
Aurora, CO

Isabel P. Neuringer, MD
Adult Pulmonologist, Co-Director,
Massachusetts General Hospital Adult Cystic
Fibrosis Program, Co-Director, Massachusetts
General Hospital Cystic Fibrosis Therapeutic
Development Center,
Massachusetts General Hospital,
Pulmonary Division;
Boston, MA

Matthew Nippins, PT, DPT, CCS
Associate Clinical Professor of Physical Therapy,
Movement and Rehabilitation Sciences,
Northeastern University;
Senior Physical Therapist,
Massachusetts General Hospital;
Boston, MA

Gabriela Oates, PhD
Assistant Professor of Pediatrics,
Pulmonary and Sleep Medicine,
The University of Alabama at Birmingham;
Birmingham, AL

Molly Pam, BA
Patient Advocate,
Cystic Fibrosis Reproductive and
Sexual Health Collaborative (CFReSHC);
Seattle, WA

Kathleen Quinn Porco, MS
Diabetes Educator,
Attain Health Foundation;
Red Lodge, MT

Alexandra L. Quittner, PhD
Professor of Psychology, Senior Scientist,
Nicklaus Children's Research Institute;
Licensed Psychologist,
Nicklaus Children's Hospital;
Miami, FL

Elika Rad, MS, RN, NP-C
Nurse Practitioner III,
Adult Cystic Fibrosis, Lung and
Heart-Lung Transplant,
Center for Advanced Lung Disease,
Stanford Health Care;
Stanford, CA

Jonathan Rayment, MDCM, MSc, FRCP(C)
Clinical Assistant Professor of Pediatrics,
University of British Columbia;
Pediatric Respirologist,
BC Children's Hospital;
Investigator, BC Children's Hospital
Research Institute,
British Columbia Children's Hospital;
Vancouver, BC, Canada

Kim Reno, ACSW, LISW-S
Manager, Policy and Advocacy
Cystic Fibrosis Foundation,
Compass;
Bethesda, MD

Christopher J. Richards, MD
Instructor of Medicine,
Harvard Medical School;
Adult Cystic Fibrosis Center,
Division of Pulmonary and
Critical Care Medicine,
Massachusetts General Hospital;
Boston, MA

Christine M. Roach, RN, BSN, CCRC
Cystic Fibrosis Research Coordinator
UBMD Pediatrics,
Cystic Fibrosis Center of Western
New York (Buffalo);
Buffalo, NY

Kathryn A. Sabadosa, MPH
Director of Quality Improvement and
Innovation,
Cystic Fibrosis Foundation;
Bethesda, MD

Gregory S. Sawicki, MD, MPH
Associate Professor of Pediatrics,
Harvard Medical School;
Director, Cystic Fibrosis Center,
Boston Children's Hospital;
Boston, MA

Yelizaveta Sher, MD
Clinical Associate Professor of Psychiatry,
Psychosomatic Medicine and Consult-Liaison
Psychiatry,
Stanford University School of Medicine;
Stanford, CA

Xin (Cissy) Si, MD
Pediatric Pulmonary Fellow,
Stanford University School of Medicine;
Stanford, CA

Beth A. Smith, MD
Associate Professor of Psychiatry and
Pediatrics, Executive Vice Chair,
Department of Psychiatry,
Chief, Division of Child and
Adolescent Psychiatry,
Jacobs School of Medicine and
Biomedical Sciences;
Chief of Service, Psychiatry and Behavioral
Medicine, Kaleida Health, Medical Director,
The Children's Psychiatric Clinic;
Buffalo, NY

Theodore A. Stern, MD
Ned H. Cassem Professor of Psychiatry in the
Field of Psychosomatic Medicine/Consultation,
Harvard Medical School;
Chief Emeritus, Avery D. Weisman,
MD Psychiatric Consultation Service,
Director, Thomas P. Hackett Center for
Scholarship in Psychosomatic Medicine,
Director, Office for Clinical Careers,
Massachusetts General Hospital;
Editor-in-Chief, *Psychosomatics;*
Boston, MA

Olivia M. Stransky, MPH, BA
Research Coordinator,
Center for Women's Health Research and
Innovation (CWHRI);
Department of Medicine,
University of Pittsburgh School of Medicine;
Pittsburgh, PA

Michelle Stroebe, MS, RD
Clinical Dietitian,
Adult Cystic Fibrosis Program,
Stanford Health Care;
Stanford, CA

Sarah Strong, MEd
School Liaison Specialist,
Center for School Services and Education,
Research, Division of Pulmonary Medicine,
Cincinnati Children's Hospital Medical Center;
Cincinnati, OH

Jaideep S. Talwalkar, MD
Associate Professor of Internal Medicine,
Associate Director, Yale Adult Cystic Fibrosis
Program, Director of Clinical Skills,
Editor, Yale Primary Care Pediatrics Curriculum,
Yale School of Medicine;
New Haven, CT

Desireé N. Williford, MS
Doctoral Candidate,
Clinical Psychology Doctoral Program
(Child Track),
Department of Psychology,
West Virginia University;
Morgantown, WV

Lael M. Yonker, MD
Pediatric Pulmonologist,
Co-Director, Massachusetts General
Hospital Cystic Fibrosis Center, Co-Director,
Massachusetts General Hospital Pediatric
Cystic Fibrosis Program, Co-Director,
Massachusetts General Hospital Cystic
Fibrosis Therapeutic Development Center,
Massachusetts General Hospital for Children,
Pulmonary Division;
Boston, MA

Jacquelyn M. Zibres, DNP, CPNP, CCRC
Advanced Care Nurse Practitioner,
Pediatric Pulmonary and Cystic Fibrosis Clinic,
Stanford University;
Stanford, CA

FOREWORD

THE BEST INFORMATION SOURCE IN CONFRONTING CYSTIC FIBROSIS

Facing Cystic Fibrosis is for anyone whose life is affected by this diagnosis. Written by leading health care providers in their fields and members of the cystic fibrosis community, *Facing Cystic Fibrosis* combines top-tier medical information and compassionate counsel on the management of cystic fibrosis, with a caring and sensible approach to the physical and emotional aspects of living with cystic fibrosis and its complications. This book provides easily readable and trustworthy information; it is divided into nineteen chapters that ask and answer pertinent questions about cystic fibrosis and its medical and psychiatric/psychological care. A glossary of terms provides important background information to readers (e.g., about nutrition, diet, exercise, risk-reduction); online resources and references are also offered; words italicized in the text are defined in the glossary.

Each of the chapters is accompanied by selected references, internet resources, illustrations, and photographs.

PREFACE

Facing Cystic Fibrosis employs a user-friendly question and answer format to provide practical information on the physical and psychological aspects of cystic fibrosis. Written by experts in pulmonology, pediatrics, nursing, social work, transplantation, physical therapy, critical care medicine, internal medicine, psychology, and psychiatry, as well as people living with CF and their families in an approachable style, this guide is intended for people with cystic fibrosis, their family members, loved ones, and caregivers. We provide a glossary of terms to help you understand the terminology used by medical personnel and have included references and information resources; this will go a long way toward gaining mastery of cystic fibrosis. Although you can read this book straight through, from beginning to end, to learn about all aspects of facing cystic fibrosis, it works just as well if you would prefer to jump around. Feel free to start by turning to the chapter that interests you most. Your questions may change over time, so *Facing Cystic Fibrosis* will remain a useful reference. Above all, we think that this book will provide quick answers to your most pressing questions about how to face cystic fibrosis, helping to prepare you and your family to live well with cystic fibrosis.

YS
AMG
TAS

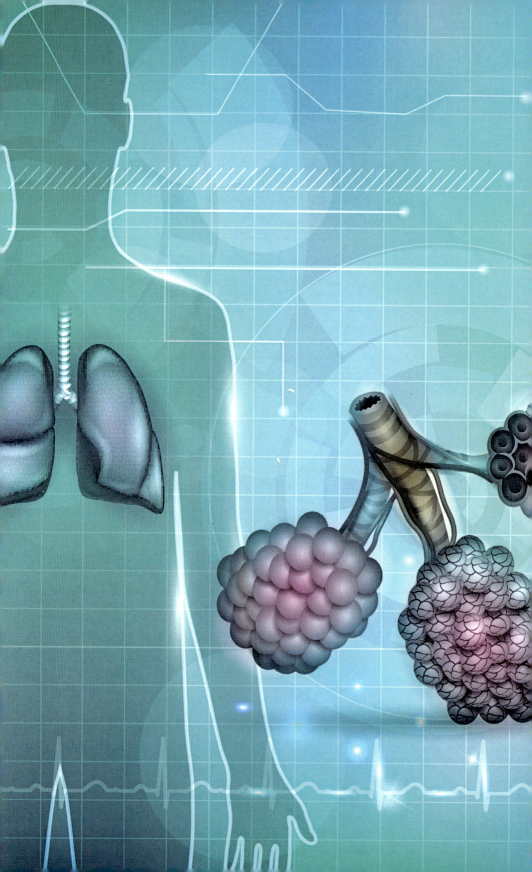

WHAT IS CYSTIC FIBROSIS?

Jonathan Rayment, MDCM, MSc, FRCP(C)

CHAPTER

In This Chapter

- What Is Cystic Fibrosis?
- What Causes CF?
- Is CF an Inherited Condition?
- How Common Is CF?
- Can People from All Racial and Ethnic Backgrounds Have CF?

What Is Cystic Fibrosis?

Cystic fibrosis (CF) is a progressive, genetic disease that affects more than 70,000 people worldwide. It is caused by an inability to regulate the flow of salt and water properly within the body, which adversely affects the function of several organ systems. Even though most people have heard about the *pulmonary* (lung) consequences of CF, many are unaware that it can also negatively affect the function of the pancreas, the *gastrointestinal* (GI) tract, the liver, the upper airways, and the genitourinary tract. Although there is no cure for CF, medical research over the past few decades has led to the development of effective treatments that have improved survival rates and the quality of life of those afflicted with this disease.

What Causes CF?

In a short and simple answer, CF is caused by *genetic mutations* that affect a *protein* that regulates water and salt transport, leading to thick secretions and dysfunction of several organs, whose healthy functioning depends on the right consistency of these secretions. CF is not contagious. The longer answer is provided in the subsections that follow.

Impaired Regulation of Salt and Water in the Body

The amount and location of water and salt in the body are tightly regulated. This seemingly ordinary task is crucial to the maintenance of many basic biologic functions. For example, urine production is controlled by careful balancing of salt and water in the kidneys. Body temperature is regulated by excreting or retaining salt and water (sweating) through the skin. The absorption of ingested salt and water by the body is regulated by the cells of the intestines. And, so it goes for every organ in the body; the ability to efficiently control the movement of salt and water is crucial to the proper functioning of these systems.

In a healthy individual, the movement of salt and water is controlled by various pumps and channels in the surface lining of *cells*. These pumps and channels are *proteins* that are made by the cells and *encoded* by *genes* in our *deoxyribonucleic acid* (DNA). These pumps and channels move salt and water, either actively or passively, in and out of cells to facilitate earlier described functions. Balance between the quantity, location, and activity of the pumps and channels leads to completion of these functions.

At its core, CF is caused by a failure of one of these channels to properly regulate the movement of salt in and out of cells. The name of the malfunctioning channel is the *cystic fibrosis transmembrane conductance regulator* (CFTR). This channel is responsible for allowing one kind of salt, called *chloride*, to flow in and out of cells. CFTR is found in many (but not all) organs in the body, and everybody has CFTR protein. In people with CF, when CFTR is absent or malfunctioning and chloride is unable to move in and out of cells efficiently, the body loses the ability to effectively control the location of salt and water in many organs. This loss of control results in dysfunction of these organs and to the *signs* and *symptoms* of CF.

Consequences of Non-Functional CFTR

Because CFTR is present in many, but not all of our organs, a non-functional CFTR channel adversely affects some parts of the body more than others. The major consequences of CFTR dysfunction stem from the altered salt and water composition of the body's fluids. Most of the treatments that have been developed for CF target these consequences.

In healthy lungs, CFTR is the key to controlling salt and water secretion in the airways. It is crucial that our airways remain well-hydrated, as this allows for the efficient clearance of *mucus*, germs, and debris. In people with CF, this secretion of salt and water into the airways is impaired. As a result, airway mucus becomes dehydrated (Figure 1-1) and difficult to remove with coughing. This sticky, trapped mucus is easily infected by bacteria, thereby leading to a vicious cycle of infection, inflammation, and tissue destruction in the lungs; this is the main cause of disability and death in people with CF. Treatments like *chest physiotherapy*, and inhaled medicines, like *hypertonic saline, dornase alfa*, or *antibiotics*, aim to interrupt this vicious cycle and to maintain lung health for as long as is possible in those with CF.

The pancreas also depends on well-regulated salt and water excretion. Usually, through a system of *ducts*, the pancreas produces and secretes *pancreatic juices* into the intestine. These pancreatic juices contain a variety of *enzymes* that are important for digestion of food. In people with CF, these pancreatic juices don't contain enough water and end up clogging the ducts in the pancreas. In most people with CF (about 85%), this sludging leads to an inability to secrete pancreatic juices into the intestine and the eventual destruction and scarring down *(fibrosis)* of the pancreas. This results in *exocrine pancreatic insufficiency* (EPI) and in a failure to digest food effectively. This inadequate digestion leads to *malabsorption* of fat, oily stools *(steatorrhea)*, abdominal pain and bloating, and ultimately to *malnutrition* in this subset of people with pancreatic insufficiency. Although there is currently no way to reverse this pancreatic insufficiency, people with CF can take capsules that contain *pancreatic enzymes* (by mouth every time they eat) to simulate pancreatic activity. This *pancreatic enzyme replacement therapy* (PERT) allows those with CF to digest and absorb nutrients and vitamins from the food they eat, thus maintaining adequate nutrition.

CFTR is important for the regulation of water in the inside of the intestine (the *lumen*). In the GI tract of people with CF, the secretion of salt and water into the lumen of the intestine is impaired, and the contents of the intestine become dehydrated. Similar to what happens in the lung and in the ducts of the pancreas, this relative dehydration results in an altered consistency of intestinal contents. In a fetus and in the newborn period, this can result in a type of *congenital intestinal blockage* called *meconium ileus*. Sometimes this can be detected on an obstetrical ultrasound and it might require treatment (including surgical repair) immediately after birth. Later in life, people with CF often have difficulties with *constipation* and intestinal blockages, called *distal intestinal obstruction syndrome* (DIOS). Laxatives such as *polyethylene glycol 3350* are typically used to prevent or to treat this GI complication of CF.

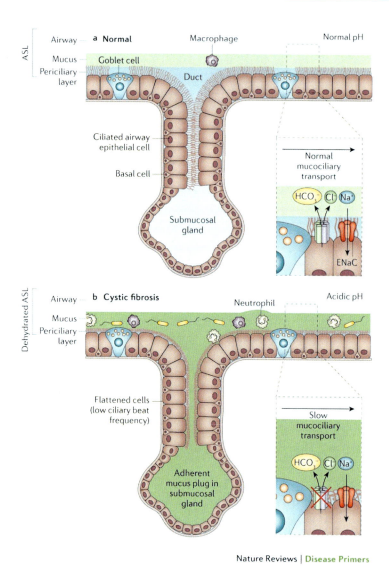

Nature Reviews | Disease Primers

Figure 1-1: Depiction of the effect of the loss of CFTR on the composition of airway surface liquid (ASL) with a normal airway shown in (A) and a CF airway shown in (B) (Ratjen et al, 2015).

One other manifestation of CFTR dysfunction occurs in the *sweat glands*. Sweating is one of the ways in which we regulate our body temperature. Normally, there is very little salt in sweat (10%–15% of the concentration of salt in the blood) because it is reabsorbed into the body within the sweat gland by CFTR. People with CF can't reabsorb salt efficiently during sweating. This leads to the classically described "salty sweat" of people with CF. Indeed, measuring the concentration of chloride with a *sweat test* remains the "*gold standard*" for the diagnosis of CF. The amount of salt in the sweat of people with CF is around three to five times higher than it is in the general population, and this excessive loss of salt can reduce their body stores of salt to dangerous levels. This is especially problematic in young children exposed to very hot weather and is the main reason that *salt supplementation* (i.e., ingesting extra salt, especially when it is hot outside) is a mainstay of CF care.

Later in this book, we discuss other manifestations of decreased CFTR function that are seen in CF.

CFTR Mutations and CFTR Modulators

As we discussed earlier, CFTR is a protein made by the body; like all proteins, it is encoded by a gene in our DNA. The gene encoding the CFTR channel was discovered in 1989 at The Hospital for Sick Children in Toronto, Canada. Since that discovery, scientists have determined that there are many *mutations* in the *CF transmembrane regulatory* (CFTR) gene that can cause the CFTR protein to work improperly (www.cftr2.org). In the CF community, these mutations are called *CF-causing mutations*. The majority of those who have CF carry at least one *mutation*, called *F508del*, but there are many other, less-common CF-causing mutations (e.g., G551D, R553X, G542X).

Scientific research into the ways in which these mutations affect the ability of CFTR to function has led to the development of a new class of medications used for CF, called *CFTR modulators*. Unlike the medications and therapies outlined in the previous section, which target the consequences of CFTR dysfunction, CFTR modulators directly restore the ability of the CFTR to channel chloride into and out of cells. The goal of CFTR modulators is to reverse or prevent the development of the aforementioned consequences. *Clinical trials* of CFTR modulators over the past 10 years have been very encouraging, and new drugs are continuing to be tested and released.

Is CF an Inherited Condition?

CF is an *inherited genetic condition*. We all inherit two copies of each of our genes from our parents; one copy is from our mother and one is from our father. To develop CF, you must inherit a mutated copy of the CFTR gene from each of your parents. There are no adverse health effects caused by having only one copy of the CFTR gene with a CF-causing mutation; this is called being a *carrier*. This means that the parents or siblings of people with

CF are usually unaffected and that there is often no family history of CF. This pattern of inheritance, in which diseases skip generations, is caused by *autosomal recessive* inheritance (Figure 1-2).

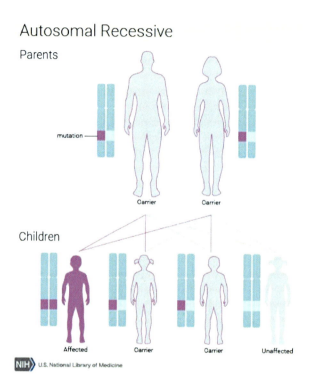

Figure 1-2: A cartoon depiction of an autosomal recessive pattern of inheritance. (Source: https://ghr.nlm.nih.gov/primer/inheritance/inheritancepatterns.)

For a situation in which both parents are known to be carriers of CF-causing mutations, each pregnancy carries a one in four chance of having a child with CF, a one in two chance of having a child who is a carrier, and a one in four chance of having an unaffected child (i.e., a child who neither has CF nor is a carrier). The fact that a couple has had a child with CF does not change the likelihood of having another child with CF. The risk of both parents passing on the mutated gene and thus having a child with CF is always one in four with every new pregnancy. If parents want to know before birth whether a fetus has CF, *prenatal genetic testing* is available; this testing can be performed by *amniocentesis* or by *chorionic villus sampling* techniques. *Carrier testing* is also available for parents prior to conception, but this is not typically done if there is no family history of CF.

How Common Is CF?

According to the United States (Cystic Fibrosis Foundation), approximately 70,000 people worldwide are living with CF; of these, roughly 30,000 are living in the United States. In Caucasians, approximately 1 in 2,500 babies is born with CF, making it the most common life-limiting *genetic condition* in this group.

Can People from All Racial and Ethnic Backgrounds Have CF?

People from all racial and ethnic backgrounds develop CF, but the *prevalence* differs among ethnic backgrounds. The prevalence of CF is directly related to the *carrier rate* of CF-causing mutations in that population; for example, the carrier rate in the Caucasian population is approximately 1 person in 25. Because this carrier rate is higher than in other populations, the prevalence of CF is the highest in this group. The carrier rate of CF-causing mutations in African Americans is approximately 1 in 84; in South Asians it is approximately 1 in 118; and in East Asians it is 1 in 242 (Rohlfs et al, 2011).

Because the prevalence of CF in those from non-Caucasian backgrounds is so low, some health care providers frequently overlook the possibility of CF arising in these people. As such, non-Caucasians with CF often go undiagnosed for several years. A possible diagnosis of CF should not be overlooked in these groups.

HOW IS CF DIAGNOSED?

Meghan B. Marmor, MD; Jacquelyn M. Zibres, DNP, CPNP, CCRC;
Zoe A. Davies, PNP, CCRC; and Paul K. Mohabir, MD

CHAPTER

In This Chapter

- How Is Someone Diagnosed with CF?
- Who Should Be Tested for CF?
- Why Is Newborn Screening for CF Recommended for All Infants?
- What Does Newborn Screening for CF Involve?
- How Are Sweat Chloride Tests Used to Diagnose CF?
- Are There Different Types of Genetic Mutations That Cause CF?
- How Are Genetic Tests Used to Diagnose CF?
- Is the Diagnosis of CF Ever Uncertain?
- What Does It Mean to Be a "CF Carrier"?
- Can CF Be Diagnosed Before Birth?
- What Is a Nasal Potential Difference?

How Is Someone Diagnosed with CF?

A person must meet specific criteria to be diagnosed with cystic fibrosis (CF). We discuss each aspect of this diagnosis in this chapter.

An infant can have a positive *newborn screening test* and/or *genetic test* positive for two *disease-causing mutations*: one mutation from their mother and one mutation from their father. CF is a disease that disproportionately affects Caucasians more than people of other ethnicities. However, CF can occur in people of other backgrounds, though their *cystic fibrosis transmembrane conductance regulator* (CFTR) *mutations* might be ones with which doctors and scientists are not as familiar. More information is needed about different CFTR mutations to improve the accuracy of our diagnoses.

A person with CF should have *symptoms* consistent with the disease. These symptoms involve the lungs (e.g., cough, shortness of breath), the gastrointestinal (GI) tract (e.g., difficulty gaining weight, difficulty digesting fatty foods, severe *constipation*), the reproductive system (e.g., *congenital absence of the vas deferens*, a condition in which men are born without a connection for sperm to travel from the testes to the penis), or the sinuses (e.g., recurrent infections, thick mucus, frequent headaches).

Equally important, a person should show signs of CFTR protein dysfunction. Tests like *sweat chloride* levels or a *nasal potential difference* all measure CTFR protein function, so those with the disease should have an abnormal test; that is, one in which their CFTR protein is unable to perform normally when challenged or stimulated (Farrell et al, 2017). We look at these tests in more detail later in this chapter.

Who Should Be Tested for CF?

Starting in 2010, the *Cystic Fibrosis Foundation (CF Foundation)* made CF screening a mandatory part of the newborn screen in all 50 states. A newborn screen is a series of standardized tests, which can vary from state to state, performed on newborns to detect disease at birth. This means that currently almost everyone in the United States is screened for CF at birth. Screening for a disease is not the same as diagnosing a disease; additional testing and evaluation must be performed to confirm the diagnosis.

Apart from newborn screening, CF is suspected when a baby has respiratory symptoms, has an inability to gain weight, or has a *meconium ileus* (a severe form of constipation) (Accurso et al, 2005). These classic symptoms quickly draw the attention of doctors and prompt testing for CF.

Not all people with CF have the same severity of disease. Although most infants with classic symptoms are diagnosed in the first 6 months of life, some individuals are diagnosed when they are older because their symptoms do not capture a doctor's attention. As many as 7% of individuals with CF are first diagnosed in adulthood (Gilljam et al, 2004).

Now that CF screening is integrated into all newborn screens, the hope is that all individuals with CF will be identified when they are infants, before symptoms occur. In the meantime, when an adult or older child presents to a doctor's office with persistent cough, thick mucus, frequent sinus infections, X-rays or scans with thickened and dilated airways *(bronchiectasis)*, or sputum cultures that grow bacteria that are frequently found in the sputum of individuals with CF, testing for CF should be initiated, even if that individual had a negative newborn screen for CF.

Why Is Newborn Screening for CF Recommended for All Infants?

Regardless of a person's ethnic background, screening for CF is important. Identifying a person with disease at a young age, before they develop symptoms, allows them to receive the care they need early, with the hope that they will live longer and have a more productive life. When scientists look at the effect of newborn screening, they have found that early recognition of the disease helps improve a person's growth and nutrition (Farrell et al, 2001), which can then improve brain development (Koscik et al, 2004). Having a better *nutritional status* in early childhood is associated with improved clinical outcomes and survival with CF (Yen et al, 2013); for some children, early disease identification can improve survival (Grosse et al, 2006). Ideally, newborn screening will help us treat lung disease early and preserve lung function for longer. When researchers have looked at the effect of the newborn screen, there is clear evidence of a nutritional benefit, but there are too many factors that can influence long-term pulmonary outcomes and preserved lung function (Farrell et al, 2003; Southern et al, 2009). Researchers have also found that a late diagnosis of CF has been associated with more respiratory symptoms, higher rates of hospitalization for respiratory illnesses, and worse lung function compared to those diagnosed early via a newborn screen (Coffey et al, 2017).

CF is one of the most common *genetic disorders*, especially in the United States. It is estimated that one out of every 3,000 Caucasians has CF. For other ethnicities, the rate of having CF is lower. For instance, one in every 9,200 Hispanic people, and one in every 10,900 Native Americans will have CF. For African Americans and Asian Americans, the number of individuals who will carry the *genetic mutations* that we know cause the disease is even less common; only one in every 15,000 and one in every 30,000 people, respectively, will have CF (Hamosh et al, 1998).

Doctors and scientists always want to learn more about CF to improve care. By identifying infants with disease, we can enhance our understanding of how individuals with CF are born with relatively healthy lungs and then go on to develop disease at different rates.

What Does Newborn Screening for CF Involve?

The newborn screen involves pricking the heel of a baby for a drop of blood. This small sample is sent to a laboratory for analysis. A protein made in the pancreas, called *immunoreactive trypsinogen* (IRT), is measured from that drop of blood (Castellani et al, 2016).

A baby with CF will usually have a high amount of IRT. Those infants with high levels of IRT will then go on for confirmation testing (discussed shortly) to confirm the suspected diagnosis of CF. The IRT newborn screening test is not perfect; levels of IRT vary significantly among newborns and can be increased when a baby is under stress, meaning that some babies have high IRT levels but do not have CF (Rock et al, 1989). For this reason, a positive newborn screen needs to be followed-up with a confirmation test, like the sweat chloride or *genotype* test (Farrell et al, 2008). Some infants with CF might not present with an elevated IRT; instead, a complete CF evaluation should be performed in suspected cases.

How Are Sweat Chloride Tests Used to Diagnose CF?

The sweat test measures the CFTR protein's function; that is, the ability to move chloride across a membrane, which, in this case, is the skin. Each cell in our body has CFTR protein lining its wall, and, normally, the CFTR protein's job is to move chloride easily and quickly across that *cell membrane* or cell wall.

During a sweat test, a small area of a person's forearm skin is stimulated to sweat. This is done by applying a medication called *pilocarpine* (which stimulates the *sweat glands*), and a gentle electrical current from two electrodes is then applied to the arm. The current does not feel like a shock, but rather like a warm or tingling sensation. A gauze pad or collection disc is used to collect the sweat, which is sent to the laboratory to measure the amount of chloride in the sample.

When sweat is induced for this test, *chloride* is pulled out of cells and into the sweat. Normally, as soon as the electrodes and pilocarpine are stopped, healthy CFTR proteins would move the chloride out of the sweat and back into the cells. However, for individuals with CF, the dysfunctional CFTR protein cannot move chloride back into the cells, and the laboratory will find abnormally high amounts of chloride in the sweat-soaked gauze or collection disc.

Generally speaking, an individual with CF will have a sweat chloride concentration of 60 millimoles (mmols) per liter or more. An accurate test requires that the person administering the test performs the test perfectly and exactly the same each time for each person. The CF Foundation keeps a close eye on how each center performs the test to be sure it is done the same way everywhere, every time, for every person (LeGrys et al, 2007; LeGrys et al, 2009).

The sweat chloride test is not perfect. Different people can have different responses to the test. For instance, if a person has other health problems like a skin disease or *hormone* imbalance, the sweat chloride can be higher than 60 mmols even when a person does not have CF (Cotten et al, 2012). Conversely, swelling of the skin or malnutrition can prevent the skin from secreting chloride into sweat, incorrectly leading doctors to believe that the CFTR protein is normally functioning, even when, in fact, it might not be.

Sweat chloride testing is the most common way doctors and scientists evaluate the function of the CFTR protein (Gibson et al, 1959). This test is certainly helpful but it should always be placed in the context of a person's *symptoms*, health history, physical exam, *pulmonary function tests* (PFTs), and X-rays.

Are There Different Types of Genetic Mutations That Cause CF?

Absolutely! The *genetic mutations* that cause CF are as diverse as are the individuals with the disease.

As a quick review, all people have a *genetic code* that sits at the center of the cells in our body. That genetic code is wrapped into bundles called *chromosomes*; we receive 23 of those chromosomes from our mother and 23 from our father, for a total of 46 chromosomes. The CFTR gene is found in all humans on *chromosome 7*.

A *gene* is a code for a protein. It can be helpful to think of a gene like a set of instruction for the cell to craft a protein; to make a perfect protein, the cell needs a perfect set of instructions from the gene. A mutation is an error in that genetic code and it can take many forms. Some mutations are such that a person does not make any CFTR protein or, if they do, the cell cannot place the protein on its surface to do its job. Often, these individuals have a severe case of CF without any CFTR protein. Other mutations are such that a person makes CFTR protein, but it does not work normally, or they do not make enough. These individuals often have a less severe case of CF.

How Are Genetic Tests Used to Diagnose CF?

Genetic testing is an important part of diagnosing CF. We know that CF is the result of dysfunctional CFTR proteins that come from a mutation in a person's CFTR gene. However, the CFTR gene is huge! Any coding error along this large gene could cause dysfunction of the CFTR protein (Sosnay et al, 2013).

Some genetic mutations are more common and well known, like the *F508del* (also known as delta F508) mutation, but there could be an infinite number of errors along the gene. Some coding errors clearly cause problems—for instance, some coding errors instruct gene processing proteins to just stop early and not make a whole CFTR protein. These are called *premature stop codons*, mutations where no viable CFTR protein is produced. Generally speaking, a premature stop *codon* mutation leads to more severe form of the disease. Other mutations can lead to more subtle changes in the final CFTR protein; it is almost impossible to predict how much of an effect some of these mutations will have on a person's health. Scientists can even sequence a person's entire CFTR gene, which can pick up a large number of mutations, but even this test is imperfect because it can miss mutations outside of the gene proper that regulates or controls an otherwise healthy-appearing CFTR gene (Vaz-Drago et al, 2017).

CF advocacy groups from around the world set out to better characterize the many different disease-causing mutations (CFTR2 Mutation List History, 2015). CFTR2 (www.cftr2.org) is a database that collects information from centers all over the world about CFTR mutations and about the individuals with those mutations. The hope is that with time, we will understand more about all the different CFTR mutations and better understand the degree of disease they cause.

Is the Diagnosis of CF Ever Uncertain?

Because newborn screens, sweat chloride tests, and genetic tests are all imperfect, some individuals have "inconclusive" test results, meaning that doctors are not completely sure whether someone has CF. For instance, a baby might seem perfectly healthy but have a high IRT from their newborn screen and a genotype test with a possible mutation that has never been seen. It can be difficult to determine whether this baby will grow up completely healthy or develop a disease. The CF Foundation has a special category for these infants. *CF-related metabolic syndrome* (CRMS) or *CF screening positive inconclusive diagnosis* (CFSPID) are given to infants with a positive newborn screening (NBS) test and who either have a sweat chloride that is below the diagnostic range or two CFTR mutations, of which at least one is of unclear physical consequence (Borowitz et al, 2009). These infants should have ongoing evaluations performed by CF providers to monitor for symptoms and to intervene early with treatment if CF symptoms develop (Farrell et al, 2017).

Often, doctors need to follow these individuals for many years, evaluating them intermittently over that span to see if they go on to develop problems with their pancreas or lungs, or develop malnutrition. Even though the CF Foundation has created *standardized care guidelines* for individuals with confirmed CF, it is not clear how to best care for individuals for whom we are unsure of their CF diagnosis.

What Does It Mean to Be a "CF Carrier"?

As we mentioned earlier, our genes are a code of instructions for our cells to make proteins. A *mutation* is any error in that genetic code, and it can result in a change to the final protein product.

Because each of us has two copies of every gene, called *alleles* (one from our mother and one from our father), if one CFTR allele has a mutation, perhaps from the father's CFTR allele, but the other allele from the mother is normal, the cell can rely on the mother's copy to always make normal, healthy CFTR protein. In this example, this person is a "*CF carrier*" whereby their genetic code carries the CFTR mutation they received from their father, but they do not have CF because they still make normal CFTR protein from their mother's normal allele. Although a CF carrier does not have CF, their carrier status becomes very important when they want to have children. A CF carrier has a 50% chance of passing their abnormal CFTR gene to their baby, see Figure 2-1.

Let's consider a few examples:

Example 1: A CF-carrier mother has a baby with a father without any CFTR mutations. The baby has a 50% chance of inheriting the abnormal CFTR gene and becoming a CF carrier like their mother, but has a 0% chance of having CF because they will receive only normal, healthy CFTR genes from their father.

How a Person Gets CF

To have CF, you must inherit two copies of the CFTR gene that contain mutations – one copy from each parent. That means that each parent must either have CF or be a carrier of a CFTR gene mutation.

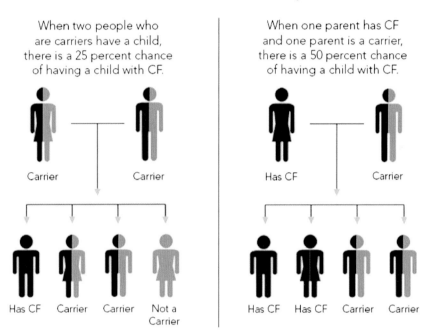

Figure 2-1: How a person gets CF. (Source: Reprinted from the Cystic Fibrosis Foundation website.)

Example 2: A CF-carrier father has a baby with a woman who has CF. The baby will only receive abnormal CFTR genes from their mother and has a 50% chance of receiving an abnormal CFTR gene from their father. This means that the baby has a 50% of having CF and a 50% chance of being a CF carrier.

Example 3: A CF-carrier mother has a baby with a CF-carrier father. The baby will have 25% chance of receiving two abnormal CFTR alleles from each parent and having CF, 25% of receiving only normal CFTR alleles from each parent and being completely normal, and a 50% chance of receiving one abnormal CFTR allele with one normal CFTR allele and becoming a CF carrier themselves.

To determine whether someone is a CF carrier, they must undergo genetic testing. Not all genetic tests are the same: some screen for only the most commonly known mutations, whereas others look at the entire CFTR gene to look for as many errors as possible. For this reason, a *genetic counselor* needs to gauge a couple's level of risk for having a baby affected by CF to select the most appropriate *screening test*. CF genetic screening should be offered for the following (Langfelder-Schwind et al, 2014):

- Those who have a family member with CF.

- Those who are the partner of a person with known CF.

- Couples from ethnic backgrounds known to have high rates of CFTR mutations, including Caucasians of either European or Ashkenazi Jewish descent.

Can CF Be Diagnosed Before Birth?

In some instances, a baby can be diagnosed with CF while inside the mother's uterus. This kind of testing can play a role when one parent has CF and the other parent is a carrier; the only way to determine whether the baby *inherited* the disease is by testing the baby directly. To test the baby, doctors need to obtain a small sample of the baby's cells. This is done two different ways, by taking a sample of either the *amniotic fluid* or the *placenta*. This procedure comes with risk of injury to the baby and, in some cases, the mother can lose the pregnancy.

Ultimately, CF does not affect a pregnancy, meaning that a doctor will treat a pregnant woman the same whether her baby has CF or not. For this reason, it is very important to seriously consider if testing during pregnancy is absolutely necessary and understand how it will affect one's family.

The hope is that scientists will be able to discover a blood test for pregnant women that could isolate the baby's *deoxyribonucleic acid* (DNA) for testing to minimize the risk of testing for the mother and the baby.

What Is a Nasal Potential Difference?

The *nasal potential difference* (NPD) is another way to test the function of the CFTR protein (Rowe et al, 2011). CFTR proteins move chloride across the cell wall; whenever there are different amounts of chloride (or any other ion) separated by a cell wall, this difference on either side of the cell wall results in an electrical charge that can be measured using electrodes. To perform the NPD test, a reference *electrode* is gently inserted just under the skin of the forearm, and an exploring electrode, a tiny plastic tube, is gently placed in the nose. A saline solution is then perfused through the tubing to test the baseline charge in the nose—each person is a little different depending on how inflamed or irritated the nose is that day. Next, several different liquids are passed through the tubing one at a time to block or stimulate the sodium or chloride channels in the nose. The test administrator measures the voltage changes again, with each of the different stimulating or suppressing liquids to see how much that voltage changed from the baseline measurement.

When a person has CF, the CFTR protein struggles to move chloride back and forth across the cell wall. This means that when we measure the NPD at baseline, it is usually higher than normal. Then, when the abnormal CFTR protein is stimulated to move more chloride, it is unable to respond normally; this finding suggests CFTR dysfunction. When paired with classic symptoms, along with a positive *genotype* or newborn screen, it is enough to confirm the diagnosis of CF.

Measuring the NPD is not a perfect test. As mentioned, all people have different voltages in their nose at baseline and this can vary from day to day. First, to perform the test perfectly, the operator needs to have a lot of experience doing the test the same way for every patient, every time. The test can take a lot of time and some people, especially small children, can have a difficult time following the operator's instructions. For this reason, NPD is typically not the first test used to diagnose CF; rather, it is used when other tests, like sweat chloride testing, show ambiguous results (Sermet-Gaudelus et al, 2010).

WHAT ARE THE MEDICAL AND PSYCHIATRIC COMPLICATIONS OF CF?

Xin (Cissy) Si, MD; Yelizaveta Sher, MD; and Paul K. Mohabir, MD

CHAPTER

In This Chapter

- How Can CF Lead to Medical Complications?
- How Does CF Affect My Lungs and Sinuses?
- What Is a Pulmonary Exacerbation of CF?
- What Is a CF "Clean Out"?
- Does Everyone with CF Have Problems Absorbing Food?
- What Other Gastrointestinal Problems Can Be Caused by CF?
- Which Endocrine or Metabolic Conditions Can Be Created or Worsened by CF?
- How Does CF Affect Fertility?
- What Are Other Complications of CF?
- How Can CF Lead to Symptoms of Anxiety and Depression?
- Should I Be Screened on a Regular Basis for Symptoms of Anxiety and Depression?
- Are There Other Mental Health Conditions That Can Affect My CF?

How Can CF Lead to Medical Complications?

Cystic fibrosis (CF) is a *genetic* disease that is passed from parents to child through their *genes*. It is an *autosomal recessive condition*, meaning that the child must have two copies of the abnormal gene (one copy from each parent) to develop the disease. People with CF make abnormal *cystic fibrosis transmembrane conductance regulator* (CFTR) *protein*, which is important in the movement of sodium and chloride ions along with water across cell surfaces (O'Sullivan and Freedman, 2009). When this protein does not work normally, thick, sticky mucus builds up and interferes with the function of many organ systems. In the lungs, the thick mucus obstructs the airways, which leads to lung infections and inflammation, and eventually to a progressive decline in lung function (Flume, 2009). Treatment of exacerbations and the use of long-term therapies have improved the lifespan of patients with cystic fibrosis (CF). In the *pancreas*, the thick mucus clogs the *pancreatic ducts*, leading to malabsorption of vitamins and fats. It can also cause a type of *diabetes* called *CF-related diabetes* (CFRD) (Norris et al, 2019). In the *gastrointestinal* (GI) tract, thick mucus can lead to *intestinal blockage* and back-up of stool (Wilschanski and Durie, 2007). In the liver, thick mucus clogs the *bile ducts*, which can lead to liver damage and *cirrhosis* (Wilschanski and Durie, 2007). In the reproductive tract, thick mucus can lead to infertility in men (by leading to blockage or absence of the sperm canal, known as *congenital bilateral absence of the vas deferens* [CBAVD]) and less commonly in women (due to thicker cervical mucus and lower ovulation rates resulting from poor nutrition) (Ahmad et al, 2013).

How Does CF Affect My Lungs and Sinuses?

The build-up of abnormally-thick mucus in the airways affects the *sinuses* (upper airway) and the lungs (lower airway). The thick secretions lead to inflammation of the lining of the airways and create an environment that allows bacteria to *colonize* and grow.

The function of the nose and sinuses is to humidify and filter the air we breathe (Kang et al, 2015), trapping dust and bacteria from the environment. When chronic inflammation develops in the lining of the nose, *nasal polyps* can form. These polyps are small growths of inflamed tissue (Wang, 2011). If the nasal polyps become large, they can obstruct the nose and sinuses. Mucus in the sinuses that surrounds the nose becomes trapped and leads to chronic sinusitis (Wang, 2011).

Most people with CF develop nasal polyps and chronic sinusitis (Kang et al, 2015). *Symptoms* of this include constant congestion, post-nasal drip, facial pressure, headache, a decreased sense of smell, and bad breath (Wang, 2011). Treatment can include nasal rinses and use of nasal steroids (to decrease inflammation and to clear out mucus) as well as antibiotics for management of acute symptoms. In severe cases, surgery is needed to remove nasal polyps and to clean out the sinuses (Safi et al, 2019).

CF lung disease is present from a young age due to the presence of chronic inflammation and infection of the airways (Flume et al, 2010), manifested by a productive cough, frequent prolonged colds, wheezing, and trouble breathing. Some people with CF experience repeated lung infections that start in early childhood, whereas others remain relatively *symptom-free* until adulthood. CF leads to progressive lung disease, but the trajectory of the decline in lung function has decreased significantly over the past few decades (Sly and Wainwright, 2017).

Bacterial colonization of the airway occurs early in childhood, with certain organisms becoming more problematic during adolescence and adulthood (O'Sullivan and Freedman, 2009). Many people with CF are colonized with multiple bacterial organisms, which are detected by analyzing sputum samples (O'Sullivan and Freedman, 2009).

Over time, with repeated pulmonary exacerbations and development of chronic lung disease, the lungs develop *cystic changes* and scarring. The scar tissue that forms increases the risk of air leaks around the lungs, which is called a *pneumothorax* (Flume et al, 2010). This is treated with observation if the air leak is mild. However, if the air leak is large, a *chest tube* might be needed to remove the air so that the lungs can re-expand (Flume et al, 2010). Having had a pneumothorax increases the risk for having another one.

With chronic lung inflammation, the blood vessels in the lungs become enlarged and abnormal in appearance. During infections, or sometimes even with just forceful coughing, some of these blood vessels can bleed, leading to *hemoptysis*, or coughing up blood. Usually, the bleeding stops on its own. However, in severe cases, treatment can include a procedure called *bronchial artery embolization*, a minimally invasive procedure in which the abnormal *bronchial artery* supplying the lung is blocked through a *catheterization* procedure (Brinson et al, 1998). Dye is injected into the arterial circulation under *fluoroscopy*, or *X-ray guidance*, which locates the abnormal artery. A long thin tube is inserted through catheterization, allowing for a targeted release of small particles into the abnormal vessel to block blood flow to the abnormal vessel, thus stopping the bleeding (Brinson et al, 1998).

What Is a Pulmonary Exacerbation of CF?

A *pulmonary exacerbation* occurs when respiratory symptoms worsen. Symptoms of an exacerbation include increased cough, sputum production, shortness of breath, and a decline in lung function (O'Sullivan and Freedman, 2009). GI symptoms (such as poor appetite and weight loss) can also occur (O'Sullivan and Freedman, 2009). These symptoms can occur in the setting of a viral infection, which still might need antibiotics for treatment due to increased sputum and secretion production in an environment already colonized by bacteria. Although there is no set definition for how much of a decline in lung function is concerning, many providers use a decline in *forced expiratory volume in the first second* (FEV1) of around 10%. Antibiotics and increased airway clearance are the mainstay of therapy for a pulmonary exacerbation to decrease the bacterial burden and mucus production in the airway (Flume et al, 2010). Increasing airway clearance might mean increasing nebulized treatments with chest physiotherapy to as frequent as every four hours. Sometimes, outpatient treatment with oral (by mouth) antibiotics can be used in mild illness. However, in most cases, antibiotics need to be administered *parenterally*, meaning, through *intravenous* (IV) access, such as a *peripherally inserted central catheter* (PICC). This requires a hospital admission. The typical length of antibiotic therapy is around 2 weeks. For most children, this means hospital admission for the duration of the antibiotic therapy. In adults, home IV antibiotic therapy can often be arranged. The goal of treatment is to prevent permanent loss of lung function and to return lung function close to or back to baseline.

What Is a CF "Clean Out"?

A *CF "clean out"* is a colloquial term for a tune-up or treatment that is needed for a pulmonary exacerbation. Usually, a pulmonary exacerbation presents with both increased respiratory symptoms and a decline in lung function. Sometimes, there is a significant decline in lung function without respiratory symptoms. When this occurs, a "clean out" with antibiotics and increased airway clearance might be recommended even without signs of an acute respiratory exacerbation.

Does Everyone with CF Have Problems Absorbing Food?

The pancreas has two functions: its *exocrine* function aids in food digestion by release of *pancreatic enzymes*, whereas its *endocrine* function helps with *insulin* regulation. Abnormal CFTR protein affects fluid flow across the lining of the pancreatic ducts, which results in thick secretions that block release of digestive enzymes into the intestines (O'Sullivan and Freedman, 2009). Instead, the digestive enzymes work on the pancreas itself, leading to pancreatic duct obstruction, *acini* destruction, and overall inflammation and fibrosis (Wilschanski and Novak, 2013).

Pancreatic insufficiency (PI), which refers to pancreatic exocrine dysfunction, exists in most people who have CF. In fact, the pancreas is the first organ to be affected by the abnormal CFTR protein, and these changes start before birth. The newborn screen for CF diagnosis is based on *immune-reactive trypsinogen levels*, which is a direct correlation of the level of enzymatic breakdown that occurs in the pancreas (Wilschanski and Novak, 2013). This exocrine function of the pancreas is important in fat digestion and nutrient absorption, such as the fat soluble vitamins A, D, E, and K (O'Sullivan and Freedman, 2009). When fat is not absorbed appropriately, a person can have abdominal pain and bloating as well as foul-smelling, greasy, white stools, also called *steatorrhea* (fat in stool) (Wilschanski and Novak, 2013).

Although all people with CF have some degree of pancreatic damage, the severity is largely based on *genotype* and the types of *CFTR mutations* that a person has (Wilschanski and Novak, 2013). Treatment for PI includes *enzyme replacement therapy* to help break down fatty foods, as well as *vitamin* supplementation of the fat-soluble vitamins A, D, E, and K.

The *pancreatic beta cells* regulate insulin production, a *hormone* important in carbohydrate metabolism and control of *blood sugar levels*. This endocrine function is usually preserved early in life, but destruction of these beta cells over time can lead to CF-related diabetes (CFRD) (Norris et al, 2019). Approximately half of those with CF develop CFRD in adulthood (Moran et al, 2010). This type of diabetes is treated with insulin injections.

What Other Gastrointestinal Problems Can Be Caused by CF?

Numerous complications in the GI tract can result from CF and its treatments. In the liver, abnormal secretions build up in the bile ducts and can lead to bile duct obstruction. This causes inflammation and scarring of the liver, also called *fibrosis*. When scarring of the liver becomes severe, cirrhosis can develop, although liver failure remains a rare complication (Wilschanski and Durie, 2007). With progressive liver fibrosis, it becomes more difficult for blood to flow properly through the liver and higher pressures are needed in the *portal vein* for blood flow. This is called *portal hypertension*, and it can lead to other severe complications including *ascites* (fluid build-up in the abdominal cavity), *esophageal* and *gastric varices* (enlarged blood vessels in the esophagus and stomach), and *jaundice* (yellowing of the skin). *Gallbladder* disease is also common, including an increased risk of *gallstones* due to the sluggish flow of *bile* (Wilschanski and Durie, 2007).

Acute inflammation of the pancreas, also called *pancreatitis*, is a rare complication of CF. It occurs with acute obstruction of the pancreatic ducts, which leads to breakdown of the pancreas by pancreatic enzymes (Wilschanski and Novak, 2013). Symptoms include severe abdominal pain, nausea, vomiting, and fever. Symptomatic pancreatitis in CF is rare since most people are pancreatic insufficient and do not produce pancreatic enzymes. However, in pancreatic sufficient people, these episodes of acute obstruction and destruction can occur (Wilschanski and Novak, 2013).

In the intestines, *distal intestinal obstruction syndrome* (DIOS) can develop. This is a complete or incomplete obstruction of the small intestines due to blockage by thick stool (Wilschanski and Durie, 2007). Mucus builds within the GI tract leading to sticky intestinal contents that can accumulate. This is different than *constipation*, which occurs in the large intestines *(colon)* that is not complicated by mucus build-up. Symptoms include severe abdominal pain, bloating or distension, vomiting, and a change in bowel movements. Because this complication is usually seen in people with PI, not using pancreatic enzymes as prescribed and dehydration can increase the risk of this condition. Treatment includes *enemas*, laxatives, and hydration (Abraham and Taylor, 2017). Some people need to be on long-term laxatives to prevent a recurrence.

People with CF have higher rates of *gastroesophageal reflux* than do those in the general population. This increased risk can be related to diet, slower gut motility, and positional changes related to *chest physiotherapy*. Severe symptoms of reflux have been associated with decreased lung function. More than half of those with CF are treated with a *proton pump inhibitor* (PPI) to decrease the amount of acid in the stomach (Robinson and DiMango, 2014).

The risk of colon cancer in adults with CF is 5 to 10 times higher than it is in the general population, and it increases substantially after any organ transplant. The reason for this increased risk is not certain, but it is thought to be related to the CFTR gene mutation. Because of this increased risk, colon cancer screening is recommended in the CF population beginning at age 40, which is 10 years earlier than it is in the general population. In people who have undergone an organ transplant, colon cancer screening should start at the age of 30 (Hadjiliadis et al, 2018).

Which Endocrine or Metabolic Conditions Can Be Created or Worsened by CF?

CFRD can occur with progressive *pancreatic beta-cell* destruction (Wilschanski and Novak, 2013). This is a type of diabetes that is different than the more common *type 1* or *type 2 diabetes*, although CFRD shares features of both types (Moran et al, 1998). Insulin is produced and regulated by the pancreatic beta cells and works to convert sugar into fuel for the body. With progressive destruction of these cells, your body becomes deficient in insulin. This is like what occurs in type 1 diabetes, which is an *autoimmune disorder* that leads to beta-cell destruction and a lack of insulin. Unlike type 1 diabetes, people with CFRD rarely go into *diabetic ketoacidosis* (DKA) (Konrad et al, 2013), in which high blood glucose levels lead to dangerously high blood acid levels and electrolyte disturbances. CFRD is not thought of as an autoimmune disease, meaning a disease in which your body's immune cells attack healthy cells. Type 2 diabetes occurs due to insulin resistance and is associated with *obesity* and older age. Similar to type 2 diabetes, CFRD can also have a component of insulin resistance and need for higher levels of insulin to maintain blood glucose control (Moran et al, 1998).

Symptoms of CFRD can also manifest as poor weight gain, fatigue, and unexplained loss of lung function. Management involves dietary monitoring and insulin injections to maintain near-normal blood glucose levels. With chronically high blood glucose levels, complications in various organs, including the eyes, kidneys, and nerves (Moran et al, 2010) can arise.

People with CF also have high rates of low *bone mineral density* (BMD), or brittle bones. This increases the risk of fractures and *osteoporosis*. Factors that contribute to low BMD include poor nutrition, chronic infections, low calcium and vitamin D levels, and CFTR dysfunction that affects bone re-modeling (Marquette and Haworth, 2016). Some people with CF require long-term *steroid* therapy, and this can also be a risk factor for brittle bones. It is important to screen for low BMD with a *dual-energy X-ray absorptiometry* (DEXA) scan, which are X-rays that evaluate the density of bones, as well as annual levels of calcium and vitamin. Sometimes, therapy involves calcium and vitamin D supplementation. If osteoporosis is diagnosed, *bisphosphonate therapy* might be needed, which slows bone loss.

CF-related joint disease is highly variable and can present with joint pain, swelling, or a skin rash (Roehmel et al, 2019). In some people, it can be related to an inflammatory process with imaging that shows signs of bone destruction (Clarke et al, 2019). Symptoms can come and go but can be constant. In contrast, another entity that can occur in those with any chronic lung disease is called *hypertrophic osteoarthropathy*. This presents with *clubbing*, *periostitis* (inflammation surrounding the bone), *synovitis* (inflammation of the fluid around a bone), and pain, which worsens with worsening lung disease (Clarke et al, 2019).

How Does CF Affect Fertility?

Most men with CF are infertile due to congenital bilateral absence of the *vas deferens* (Ahmad et al, 2013). The vas deferens is the sperm canal that carries sperm from the *testes* where they are made, to the *ejaculatory duct*. Men with CF have normal sperm production and can still have biological children through *assisted reproductive technology* (ART) (Ahmad et al, 2013). CF does not affect the ability to have normal sexual relations.

In women, fertility is decreased due to the presence of thick vaginal and cervical mucus that makes it more difficult for sperm to travel into the uterus and for fertilization to occur. However, most women are fertile and able to conceive without assisted technology (Burden et al, 2012).

What Are Other Complications of CF?

Meconium ileus is a common presentation of CF in the *neonatal period*, shortly after birth. This presents as an obstruction of the small and large intestines due to *meconium*, with formed stool *in utero* (O'Sullivan and Freedman, 2009). Dehydration and electrolyte derangement can be major issues, especially during illnesses in infancy. *Rectal prolapse* due to chronic constipation is also common in childhood (O'Sullivan and Freedman, 2009).

As the CF population ages, the *prevalence* of common conditions seen with aging increases. One of these issues is *urinary incontinence*. Although this can affect both men and women with CF, it appears to be more common in women (Frayman et al, 2018). Urinary incontinence is the involuntary leakage of urine, which occurs during activities such as sneezing, coughing, or laughing. In CF, the stress on the bladder muscles from chronic coughing is thought to be a risk factor. Pelvic floor exercises to strengthen the pelvic muscles that support the bladder or *pessaries* used to prevent pelvic organ prolapse can reduce these symptoms. In severe cases, urological surgery can be considered (Frayman et al, 2018).

People with CF have higher rates of *kidney stones* than do those in the general population, and this risk increases with age. This can be due to relatively high levels of *oxalate* and low levels of *citrate* in the urine, defects of calcium handling due to CFTR mutation in the kidney itself, and absence of a particular bacteria called *Oxaclobacter formigenes*, which degrades oxalate in the gut (Gibney and Goldfarb, 2003). These differences can be related to malabsorption, diet, and the need for frequent antibiotics. Symptoms of kidney stones include severe back pain, painful urination, blood in the urine, and nausea.

How Can CF Lead to Symptoms of Anxiety and Depression?

CF affects multiple organ systems and psychosocial areas of your life. Thus, it is not surprising that people living with CF have two to three times the rates of depression and anxiety as compared to those without CF (Quittner et al, 2014). Several reasons might account for this. First, the CFTR gene is widely expressed in the brain (Guo et al, 2009) with yet unknown function, raising a question if there is a direct effect of the mutation in the CFTR gene that contributes to the risk of depression and anxiety. Second, CF affects multiple aspects of life, requires a demanding daily maintenance routine, and often leads to frequent hospitalizations. It is associated with debilitating physical symptoms (such as pain, fatigue, and *dyspnea*). CF can make it difficult to engage in some important areas of life, including going to school, working, or having children. Hospitalizations can be isolating and lonely, creating breaks in life routines, taking a person away from their regular activities and projects. CF is also a life-shortening disease that raises difficult existential questions.

All of these factors can contribute to feeling sad, depressed, and demoralized, and these feelings might grow into full depressive episodes.

Anxiety, on the other hand, might arise to serve an adaptive and helpful function. Having some anxiety might motivate you to do your treatments and keep up with healthy routines. Anxiety might be helpful to anticipate challenges and to troubleshoot. However, too much anxiety can be overwhelming and even paralyzing, significantly decreasing a person's quality of life.

According to the International Depression Epidemiological Study conducted in the CF clinics of nine countries, 10% of adolescents with CF and 19% of adults with CF have depressive symptoms (Quittner et al, 2014). In addition, anxiety symptoms occur in 22% of adolescents and 32% of adults with CF. Moreover, individuals with CF who have anxiety are much more likely to have depression. In fact, adolescents with increased anxiety are 15 times more likely to report depression as compared to adolescents who do not report anxiety; and 6% of adolescents report both depression and anxiety. Similarly, adults reporting anxiety are four times more likely to report depression, with 14% of adults with CF reporting both anxiety and depressive symptoms.

Should I Be Screened on a Regular Basis for Symptoms of Anxiety and Depression?

It is important for you or your child with CF to be screened on a regular basis for symptoms of anxiety and depression given that these symptoms cause suffering, adversely affect quality of life, make it more difficult for you to take care of your medical needs, thereby increasing the risk of medical complications. Moreover, various treatments for these symptoms are available and you don't need to suffer alone. In fact, the *International Committee on Mental Health in CF*, a combined voice of the *Cystic Fibrosis Foundation (CF Foundation)* and the *European CF Society*, recommends at least yearly screening for depression with the *Patient Health Questionnaire-9* (PHQ-9) screening tool, and for anxiety with the *Generalized Anxiety Disorder 7-item* (GAD-7) screening tool (Quittner et al, 2016). If these scores are elevated, indicating increased symptoms of these mental health conditions, screening should be repeated at the next visit (Quittner et al, 2016). If you or your child attend a CF Foundation-accredited center, you will most likely be offered such screens; the results will be reviewed with and explained to you, and recommendations regarding follow-up and treatment will be made according to the results.

Are There Other Mental Health Conditions That Can Affect My CF?

In addition to depression and anxiety, people with CF might have other co-morbid mental health conditions at rates higher than those found in the general population. In one *retrospective study* of children with CF, 9.6% were referred to a psychiatrist and diagnosed with *attention deficit hyperactivity disorder* (ADHD) (Georgiopoulos and Hua, 2011). Out of these children, 61% struggled with non-adherence to CF treatment. In a study of adults in one CF clinic in the United States, 15% had elevated symptoms of ADHD (Georgiopoulos et al, 2018), and 18% of individuals with CF had symptoms of ADHD in a multi-site study from outside of the United States (Cohen-Cymberknoh et al, 2018). In comparison, the prevalence of ADHD in the United States is 4.4% in the general adult population according to the National Comorbidity Survey Replication study (Kessler et al, 2006).

Several factors have been thought to contribute to this increased prevalence of ADHD in people with CF, including chronic inflammation, genetic factors, and increased treatment and organizational demands, which might make symptoms more apparent. If you have ADHD, you are also more likely to have depression and/or anxiety, which can further increase the psychological burden (Georgiopoulos et al, 2018). ADHD is more common in boys with CF as compared to girls with CF (3:1) (Cohen-Cymberknoh et al, 2018); however, the gender difference is no longer present in adulthood (Georgiopoulos et al, 2018; Cohen-Cymberknoh et al, 2018). One study demonstrated that 38% of participants with elevated ADHD screens had to repeat a grade in school (Georgiopoulos et al, 2018), thus demonstrating negative effects of ADHD on social functioning and organization. Concerns remain regarding impaired ability to sustain daily to CF care and downstream effects on medical outcomes in people with ADHD.

Substance use disorders can be co-morbid in those with CF. These are concerning not only due to psychological effects of dependency, but due to detrimental physical effects of substances in individuals who already have a chronic medical condition. Older studies indicate that approximately 11% to 16% of people with CF smoke cigarettes (Ortega-García et al, 2016; Ortega-Garcia et al, 2012; Stern et al, 1987; Evon et al, 2005). This is worrisome given the effects of tobacco smoking on respiratory conditions, immune function, cancer risk, and other medical complications.

According to an older report, between 50% and 60% of individuals with CF, aged 15 to 39 years, consume alcohol on a regular basis (Stern et al, 1987). "Heavy use," defined as having drinks on four or more nights per week with consumption of five or more beers on occasion, increased in this study from 9.5% in the late teens to 13% in those between 20 and 29 years of age, and finally markedly decreased after 30 years of age (Stern et al, 1987). Major social symptoms of alcohol abuse were rarely reported in this study, but patients reported increased pulmonary symptoms following use of alcohol.

Although *autism spectrum disorders* have not been systematically studied in people with CF, co-morbid autism can present additional communication challenges in those affected. Two cases of co-morbid autism spectrum disorder were reported in children with CF and diagnosed with ADHD in one study (Georgiopoulos and Hua, 2011).

WHICH TESTS AND PROCEDURES ASSESS, MONITOR, AND TREAT MY CF?

Elika Rad, MS, RN, NP-C; Michelle Stroebe, MS, RD; and Paul K. Mohabir, MD

CHAPTER

In This Chapter

- What Are Pulmonary Function Tests?
- What Is Spirometry and How Is It Done?
- What Does Spirometry Measure?
- What Other Tests Can Be Used to Evaluate My Lungs?
- What Annual Labs Do My Doctors Order for Me and Why?
- What Are Sputum Cultures?
- Why Is It Important to Know What Kind of Bacteria Are in My Lungs?
- What Are Nebulizers and Why Are They Used?
- When Is Home Oxygen Useful?
- What Are CPAP and BiPAP?
- What Are Peripherally Inserted Central Catheters and Ports?
- What Are the Risks and Benefits of PICCs and Ports?
- Why Does My Medical Team Check My Weight So Often?
- What Are G-Tubes and G-J Tubes?
- What Tests Assess My Digestive System?
- How Are Blood Sugars Measured?

What Are Pulmonary Function Tests?

Pulmonary function tests (PFTs) refer to a variety of non-invasive diagnostic tests that are used to measure how your lungs are working. They include *spirometry, full lung volumes by plethysmography, arterial blood gases, exercise oximetry testing, diffusion capacity, methacholine bronchial challenge testing*, and *pulse oximetry*. Through various methods, they can measure *lung capacity* (such as volume and flow) and *airway reactivity* (or how well the lungs are exchanging oxygen and *carbon dioxide* [CO_2]). Individuals living with cystic fibrosis (CF) are most familiar with spirometry.

What Is Spirometry and How Is It Done?

The word spirometry means "the measuring of breath." The *spirometer* is the machine that records the airflow of your breaths. This test is performed in your doctor's office or in a *pulmonary function lab*. During the exam, you either sit or stand while wearing a clip on your nose to prevent air entry into and exit out of your nose. A tubular mouthpiece is connected to the spirometer in your mouth and your lips are sealed over it to prevent air from escaping from your mouth. During the test, you are asked to breathe in and out several times before taking in a deep breath, which is followed by a full, quick, and forceful exhalation that lasts 6 seconds or longer. This test is technique dependent; therefore, a trained technician/ *respiratory therapist* is pivotal in providing instructions to you during the maneuver. Patients age 6 and older can often follow instructions and complete the maneuver accurately. To ensure accuracy, you will be asked to perform at least three maneuvers in one session.

What Does Spirometry Measure?

Spirometry can be used to evaluate cough, wheezing, shortness of breath, and to help diagnose different types of lung disease, such as *obstructive* or *restrictive lung diseases*. Spirometry might also be ordered before surgery to ensure that *anesthesia* will be safe for you. If you have an established diagnosis of CF, the results will be used to track the degree of obstruction, the progression of lung disease, and/or to diagnose *acute respiratory tract exacerbations* likely due to infection.

Before the test is started, the technician will enter your age, gender, height, weight, and ethnicity into the computer, which is attached to the spirometer. This data is used to generate your expected normal values of lung function, also called the *predicted values*, which can be thought of as the lung function of your clone or twin who does not have lung disease. The two most common values in spirometry that are measured during the exhalation phase of the aforementioned maneuver described, are the *forced expiratory volume in the first second* (FEV1) and the *forced vital capacity* (FVC). FEV1 is the volume of air exhaled by you in the first second into the spirometer, and FVC is the total volume exhaled. In normal lungs, the FEV1 is about 80% of the FVC (West, 1985). Both FEV1 and FVC are looked at as raw measures of volume (in liters) or as a percent of the predicted value.

In obstructive lung diseases (such as *asthma, chronic obstructive pulmonary disease* [COPD], *bronchiectasis*, or CF) airflow is limited and patients often complain of shortness of breath on exhalation. The main contributors to these symptoms are hyper-reactive, swollen, dilated, inflamed, or mucus-impacted airways. Notably, in patients with *restrictive lung diseases* (such as *interstitial lung diseases* [ILDs] and chest wall neuromuscular disorders) the expansion of the lung tissue is reduced and both the FEV1 and FVC are reduced. Patients with this pattern of lung disease often describe shortness of breath as difficulty taking air into their lungs due to the stiffness of their lung tissue. At times, a mixed obstructive and restrictive pattern can be seen (West, 1985).

In CF, an acute infection or exacerbation usually results in a reduction of the FEV1, often without full recovery of lung function (Wagener et al, 2018). This puts you at risk for worsening quality of life and progression to respiratory failure. A decline of 10% to 15% from your baseline FEV1 is considered significant enough to warrant treatment with *antibiotics*, although this is neither an absolute nor a standardized criterion for initiation of therapy (Rabin, et al, 2004; Stenbit and Flume, 2011; Wagener et al, 2018). Baseline FEV1 is determined by the best value 6 months before a pulmonary exacerbation (Sanders et al 2010).

Patients with CF can decrease their chances of exacerbations and experiencing a decline in lung function by adhering to the pulmonary therapies prescribed by their CF provider to clear the obstruction caused by mucus build-up in their airways. These therapies include regular use of inhaled medications (such as *bronchodilators, hypertonic saline, dornase alpha,* and in some cases, inhaled antibiotics) as well as a modality for airway or mucus clearance, including but not limited to manual *chest physiotherapy* (CPT), *positive expiratory pressure* (PEP) *devices* (*Flutter®, Acapella®, Quake®, Aerobika®*), *oscillatory vest, postural drainage* (PD), *huff cough* or an *active cycle of breathing, intrapulmonary percussive ventilator* (IPV), and exercise.

What Other Tests Can Be Used to Evaluate My Lungs?

An X-ray of the chest is one of the oldest non-invasive exams. During the test, a special camera points X-rays (electromagnetic waves of high energy and low wavelength) toward the chest to produce a black and white picture of the structures of the upper body, enabling visualization of the bone structure, heart, lungs, and blood vessels. X-rays pass through the body and give the air in the lungs a dark-gray appearance and other structures a white-ish appearance. Chest X-rays are used to visualize the bones in the chest, the heart, a collapsed lung, mucus-filled airways, dilated airways (bronchiectasis), fluid build-up in the lungs, the position of the *diaphragm* (the muscles the lungs rest on), and a portion of the stomach. In those affected by lung disease, serial X-rays are used to compare progression of disease or new infections that can cause build-up of mucus, sometimes referred to as *pneumonia*.

Computed tomography (CT) scans of the chest are a special type of X-ray taken by a computer that renders more detailed views of the aforementioned structures, especially of soft tissue and blood vessels. Enhanced views are also possible when a *contrast material* is injected into your vein. The images are viewed as *cross-sectional images* of your thorax (chest cavity) and can be re-formatted to display in different planes and even three-dimensional images. They are often more expensive, and they expose you to more radiation compared to chest X-rays; however, because of newer technology the amount of radiation can be adjusted based on your size. CT scans are used widely to evaluate tumors seen on chest X-rays. For CF, this exam is used to determine the extent of bronchiectasis and to look for *cavitary lesions* that can result from certain bacterial and fungal diseases. Both exams are fast, painless, and accurate.

What Annual Labs Do My Doctors Order for Me and Why?

If you are being treated at a CF center, annual laboratory and diagnostic studies will be ordered by your medical provider to track your overall health. Some of the studies overlap with what your *primary care provider* (PCP) might order, but this does not substitute for having your annual check-up with your PCP.

Bloodwork

Blood is drawn by inserting a small needle into a vein (usually in the arm). Some patients have a *centrally implanted catheter* (usually in the chest; i.e., a *mediport*) that can be accessed with a needle for blood draws or for medication infusion (see the section on PICCs and *ports* later in the chapter). Several tubes of blood are drawn for various tests. You might be required to fast for certain tests. If this is required, your CF provider will instruct you to not eat any food for 8 to 12 hours before the blood is to be drawn.

Complete Blood Count

Complete blood count (CBC) looks at the blood cell components to give clues to infection (i.e., white blood cell [WBC] count and its sub-components, [such as *neutrophils*]), *inflammation* (i.e., *eosinophils*), and *anemia* (i.e., *red blood cells* [RBCs]). Anemia can be due to the deficiency of iron stores in the body, active bleeding, or inflammation related to chronic illness. You will not need to fast before your CBC.

Comprehensive Metabolic Panel

Also known as a Chem-14, a *comprehensive metabolic panel* (CMP) gives clues about your body's metabolism by measuring 14 values (including electrolytes, minerals, acid/base balance, the health of your kidneys and liver, and your blood sugar and protein levels). Electrolytes and minerals (including calcium, sodium, potassium, chloride, and bicarbonate) are essential to the functioning of our cells and organs. Magnesium and phosphorus are essential minerals for cell and organ function; they are often ordered separately from the CMP. How well your kidneys are functioning is measured by the *blood urea nitrogen* (BUN) and *creatinine* (Cr); elevated levels of the BUN and creatinine can give clues about dehydration, medications that might be damaging your kidneys (e.g., acute kidney injury [AKI]) or chronic kidney injury, which can be due to prolonged exposure to certain medications or to poorly controlled diabetes. *Albumin* and protein levels give clues about your nutritional status. Several liver function parameters are *alanine amino transferase* (ALT or SGPT), *aspartate amino transferase* (AST or SGOT), *alkaline phosphatase* and *bilirubin;* your provider uses these to monitor for signs of liver disease that can be manifested in CF.

Alkaline phosphatase is also a marker for bone disease, which is also a common manifestation of CF. Your CF provider might order a *basic metabolic panel* (BMP) that includes all CMP parameters except the *liver function tests* (LFTs), albumin, and protein. CMP and BMP do not require fasting.

Fat-Soluble Vitamins

These are vitamins that come from plant and animal food sources or dietary supplements. They are absorbed with fat in the diet and are stored in the body's fat tissue. They include vitamins A, E, D, and K. People living with CF tend to absorb these vitamins poorly due to *pancreatic insufficiency* (PI), even with perfect *enzyme replacement therapy. Fat malabsorption* primarily affects those who have PI; however, due to the negative consequences of vitamin deficiencies, all people with CF are tested annually to ensure that their vitamin levels are within the desired range. Deficiencies of fat-soluble vitamins can lead to the decreased ability to fight off infections, stunted growth, risk of bone fractures, and a poor ability of the body to stop bleeding (Michel et al, 2009). Alternatively, vitamin toxicity can occur when levels of these vitamins are too high, as they are stored in our body, unlike other vitamins. Maintaining normal levels of these vitamins—neither too high nor too low—is vital for people with CF to remain healthy.

Oral Glucose Tolerance Testing

The *oral glucose tolerance test* (OGTT) measures your body's response to *glucose*, which is a simple sugar that our body uses for energy. This test is used to monitor for *type 2 diabetes*, *CF-related diabetes* (CFRD) or *gestational diabetes* (due to pregnancy). You will be asked to fast (no food or drink) for 8 hours prior to this test. It is best to begin fasting at bedtime and schedule the test for early in the morning. The test consists of drawing three to four tubes of blood, starting with a fasting blood glucose level. After this, you will be asked to drink 8 ounces (237 milliliters) of a syrupy glucose drink that contains 75 grams of sugar. This is followed by blood draws at 1-hour and 2-hour marks after finishing the drink; some labs also measure levels at the half-hour mark, but this is not required for testing for CFRD. This test can take up to 3 hours, so it is a good idea to be prepared for the wait; generally, you will not be allowed to walk around because this will give false test results. Aside from diagnosing diabetes, the OGTT can also diagnose *pre-diabetes*, which is a predictor for developing CFRD in the next 3 to 4 years (Schmid et al, 2014). This will prepare you and your CF team to have discussions sooner than later about diabetes management so that you will be well prepared.

Total Immunoglobulin E (IgE-T)

Immunoglobulins are *antibodies* produced by our body's *immune system* and are normally detected in low amounts. They are elevated when there is an immune response to an *allergen*, but it is not specific to any allergen. To determine this, an *allergen-specific IgE* might be ordered. A common allergen in CF lung disease is *aspergillus*, which is a type of *fungus* found in the environment that can colonize the lungs of those with CF. To detect this, *aspergillus IgE* will also be ordered. Along with the IgE-T and symptoms, your CF provider will determine whether the diagnosis of *allergic bronchopulmonary aspergillosis* (ABPA) can be made. It is important to understand that ABPA does not indicate an infection; instead, it suggests an allergic immune-mediated process.

Clotting Factors

Partial thromboplastin time (PTT), *prothrombin time* (PT), and an *international normalized ratio* (PT/INR) evaluate how well your body forms blood clots (i.e., coagulates). The clotting factors are an intricate system of proteins that react to an injury (i.e., bleeding, inflammation). Having too little of these proteins provides clues that your body is taking too long to clot and putting you at risk for excessive bleeding. The risk for bleeding is higher in those affected by CF with a history of severe pulmonary disease and liver disease (Komp and Selden, 1970). A high number of clotting factors, on the other hand, can lead to over-production of blood clots. Liver disease and malabsorption of vitamin K contribute to coagulation abnormalities. Other things that can affect the body's clotting abilities are antibiotics, blood-thinning medications (used to treat clots), and certain blood disorders.

Dual-Energy X-Ray Absorptiometry

Dual-energy X-ray absorptiometry (DEXA [or sometimes just DXA]) scans are non-invasive, low-energy X-rays of your bones, usually of a section of the spine and both hips, used to test your *bone mass*. Bone is constantly being broken down and rebuilt in all healthy individuals. Under certain circumstances (i.e., advancing age, *hormone* deficiencies, malnutrition, or constant inflammation), the rate of bone loss exceeds the rebuilding process, leading to *osteopenia* (decreasing bone mass and strength). This can progress to *osteoporosis* (porous bone) with loss of bone mass and structure, increasing your risk of bone fractures. These fractures can occur with the slightest amount of trauma. This screening test is important because there are no symptoms associated with either osteopenia or osteoporosis. *Primary osteoporosis* is age related, often occurring in later adulthood, and affecting women after menopause more than in men. *Secondary osteoporosis* refers to bone loss related to an underlying disorder; for purpose of our discussion, in CF, it is seen in 15% of people with CF. *CF-related osteoporosis* can be seen much earlier in life compared to that of a primary disease, and the risk increases with lower lung function, a lower *body mass index* (BMI; a marker of malnutrition), higher rates of pulmonary infections, poorly controlled CFRD, higher levels of inflammatory markers in the blood, and female gender. Low *vitamin D* levels are not clearly correlated with an increased risk of osteoporosis (Mathiesen et al, 2018). Another risk factor leading to bone loss is the use of oral *steroids* (e.g., *prednisone*) which is used at times to treat pulmonary exacerbations, overlapping asthma symptoms, and ABPA.

If you are diagnosed with osteoporosis, your CF provider or *endocrinologist* might prescribe bone-building medication that will restore the bone loss. At times, osteopenia might be treated similarly if there are ongoing risk factors or your *DEXA scan* is showing progression toward osteoporosis.

What Are Sputum Cultures?

A *sputum culture* is a test done to look for bacteria or fungus that might be present and infecting the lungs. The sputum can be collected via coughing sputum into a sterile cup, swabbing the throat, or entering the lungs through the mouth with a *bronchoscope*—a thin lighted camera that is attached to a suction tube. With the coughing technique, you are required to cough deeply so that sputum comes up from the lungs instead of just collecting saliva from the mouth or the back of your throat. Throat swabs are usually done on younger children who are unable to cough up mucus, but sometimes this method might not pick up the bacteria that are present in the lungs. Alternatively, sputum can be induced by a *respiratory therapist* who has you inhale 7% or 10% hypertonic saline solution, which draws water to mucus and irritates the lungs, causing coughing. If you produce little sputum, an induction might not be successful. Bronchoscopy is rarely used, because no difference has been found between suctioned samples and those coughed up or found on throat swabs, and the sputum samples have the same types of organisms recovered when compared to bronchoscopy; moreover, those with CF who had bronchoscopy often deteriorated clinically; that is, they experienced an exacerbation within 24 hours of the procedure (Paul, 2017).

After the sputum is collected, it is sent to a *microbiology lab*, where a thin layer of the mucus is spread in a dish containing different materials with nutrients to feed the bacteria. This allows them to grow and enables a trained technician to examine them under the *microscope*. Some bacteria grow slower than others, therefore, it usually takes 3 to 6 days before a bacterial organism can be identified. Fungi and certain bacteria, called *acid-fast bacilli*, can take even longer (up to several weeks) before they are identified. After the organism is identified, different antimicrobials (antibiotics or *antifungals*) are placed on the plate to determine which ones can effectively kill the organism; this is called *antimicrobial sensitivity* or *susceptibility testing*.

Why Is It Important to Know What Kind of Bacteria Are in My Lungs?

In those affected by CF, these bacteria or fungi often *colonize* the lungs, meaning that they can live in the airways without causing infection. At times of high inflammation or too much mucus build-up, the bacteria can become disease-causing. We also know that CF predisposes you to a pattern of colonized organisms over your lifespan, with *Staphylococcus aureus* and *Haemophilus influenzae* in the younger years, followed by *Pseudomonas aeruginosa*, *Burkholderia cepacia complex*, *Stenotrophomonas maltophilia*, and fungi such as *Scedosporium species complex* and *Aspergillus fumigatus*, in the older years (Green and Jones, 2015; Paul, 2017). When a pulmonary exacerbation warrants treatment with an antimicrobial agent, it is important to target the bacteria or fungus with the appropriate antibiotic. Your CF provider will usually use the most recent sputum culture and its sensitivities to guide antimicrobial therapy until a new sputum sample has been cultured, at which point the treatment might be adjusted if you are not improving.

What Are Nebulizers and Why Are They Used?

Nebulizers and *compressors* are devices used to deliver medications into the lungs. The *compressor* is a machine with a small motor that compresses air and pushes it through tubing connected to a nebulizer cup (or nebulizer mask for younger children); this compressed air *aerosolizes* (turns the liquid in the nebulizer cup into a fine mist) for inhalation. There are many types of nebulizers and compressors on the market, and consulting with your CF respiratory therapist is key to using the correct machine given that some medications require specific devices. Medications that are commonly nebulized include *bronchodilators* (*albuterol, ipratropium,* combined albuterol/ipratropium, *levalbuterol*), hypertonic saline, *dornase alpha*, inhaled antibiotics *(tobramycin, aztreonam, colistin), acetylcysteine,* inhaled antifungals. Most people affected with CF are prescribed a bronchodilator, hypertonic saline, and dornase alpha; depending on what is cultured in your sputum, you might also be prescribed an inhaled antibiotic.

When Is Home Oxygen Useful?

A sophisticated network of blood vessels connects your heart and lungs, allowing for normal gas exchange. This involves the delivery of oxygen from the lungs to the bloodstream where it is taken to the heart and pumped to the entire body; the heart then returns *de-oxygenated blood* loaded with CO_2 back to the lungs where the CO_2 is removed through exhalation. Severe bronchiectasis, multiple pulmonary infections, and long-term inflammation eventually leads to *respiratory failure*, a hallmark and terminal stage of CF lung disease. With this change, you might experience *hypoxemia* (low blood oxygen levels) that, if untreated, can lead to further damage to the lungs and to increased pressure in the right side of the heart, with eventual failure of the heart muscle. If you experience hypoxemia, you might develop symptoms, including fatigue, an inability to exercise, chest pressure from reduced muscle strength, shortness of breath, rapid breathing, poor sleep, and frequent headaches, decreased lung function, and, if profound, a blue tint to the lips or fingernails *(cyanosis).*

Two ways to assess hypoxemia are with pulse oximetry (also known as pulse-ox and measured as SpO_2 or SaO_2), and *arterial blood gases* (ABGs). Pulse oximetry is a non-invasive method that uses a computerized light that is shined through one side of the fingertip or earlobe to a sensor that is placed on the opposite side. The computer then calculates this light as a percentage to determine the amount of oxygen in the fingertip or earlobe that is bound to, or saturated, with *hemoglobin*—hence the term *oxygen saturation*—with the normal range expected to be above 95%.

Blood gases are evaluated by drawing a sample of blood from an *artery* (a vessel with mostly oxygenated blood), usually in the wrist, called the *radial artery*; in very young children, a smaller vein or even a *capillary* (a tiny blood vessel) sample can be used. The sample measures the blood *pH* (acidity), and the amounts of oxygen and CO_2 present in the blood, which are maintained by the work of the lungs, heart, and kidneys. Abnormal results tell your provider whether you are not getting enough oxygen, have too much CO_2 in your blood, or there is a problem with the kidneys. The interpretation of this test is complex and can give clues to other abnormalities such as shock, intoxication, chronic vomiting, heart failure, pneumonia, pain, *anxiety*, hyperventilation, or airway obstruction.

For simplicity, hypoxemia is usually referred to as an arterial blood gas *PaO2* of less than 60 mm Hg, and an *SpO₂* by oximetry of less than 90%, for which supplemental oxygen therapy is recommended (Shifren et al, 2017). This can be acute and reversible (i.e., acute respiratory failure in the beginning of a bad CF exacerbation), or chronic, meaning long-term and often signifying worsening CF lung disease. With chronic respiratory failure, you might require oxygen therapy only at night or when you are at high altitude where the atmospheric oxygen concentration is lower, or only when exercising. It is in the end stages of respiratory failure when continuous oxygen, to include use at rest, might be required. Oxygen is usually delivered via a plastic catheter (called a cannula) that is placed in your nose and attached to an oxygen tank. The oxygen, which feels like a cool mist flowing through the tubing, is inhaled through your nose. In certain cases—for example, with severe nasal obstruction or congestion, or if you have a habit of breathing through your mouth—a *facemask* can be used to deliver the oxygen. Humidification of the oxygen is recommended to prevent drying of the *oropharynx* and nasal passages, which can at times cause nosebleeds.

Needing supplemental oxygen is usually a big life change and many people have varying emotions about carrying a large oxygen tank on wheels; there are many types of portable devices that can help with carrying the oxygen in a more inconspicuous manner, which can help alleviate some of the anxiety associated with this.

What Are CPAP and BiPAP?

Because CF is an *obstructive lung disease*, the air inspired through your lungs can be trapped in the airways, causing excess CO_2 gas that cannot be exhaled. This excess in CO_2 is referred to as *hypercarbia* or *hypercapnia* and can be irritating to lung and heart tissues; it can cause headaches and shortness of breath. If left untreated, it can result in flushed skin, rapid breathing, muscle twitching, confusion, and lethargy. Unfortunately, providing more supplemental oxygen is not the treatment for hypercarbia, and studies have shown that oxygen use alone in CF and other obstructive lung diseases can lead to worsening of hypercarbia (Elphick and Mallory, 2013). In the past, patients with hypercarbia needed support with invasive mechanical ventilation to remove excess CO_2 from the lungs, but this is no longer the case, and people can have good quality of life and treat hypercarbia at home with *non-invasive ventilation* (NIV) devices, which consist of a nosepiece, mouthpiece, or facemask connected by a tubing to a machine.

There are two main types of NIV machines: *Continuous Positive Airway Pressure* (CPAP) and *Bi-level Positive Airway Pressure* (BiPAP). CPAP machines apply mild air pressure on a continuous basis to keep the airways continuously open. This is often prescribed to those even without lung disease, in the setting of *sleep apnea*, which can also present in those affected by CF. BiPAP delivers a positive inspiratory pressure in synchrony with your inhalation effort as well as a low level of pressure during expiration, forcing some of the trapped carbon dioxide to be exhaled. NIVs are usually prescribed for sleep or rest and have been shown to allow deeper breaths with less effort, reverse the clinical abnormalities related to hypoxemia and hypercapnia, and improve cardiac function (Brochard, 2003).

What Are Peripherally Inserted Central Catheters and Ports?

Some individuals require antibiotic treatment via infusion to treat pulmonary infections. *Intravenous* (IV) lines are used to infuse the liquid medication into the vein. A slender *peripheral IV* (PIV) is inserted with a needle into a small vein of your forearm or wrist by a nurse; the needle is covered with a plastic sheath or catheter. After your nurse has determined that the needle is in the correct position in the vein, the needle is pulled out and the plastic sheath is the only thing that remains in the vein. Blood can usually be drawn from a PIV only when the needle is initially inserted; however, when only the plastic catheter remains, the PIV can be used solely for an infusion; this is because the catheter is too small to be able to handle the volume of blood needed.

Antibiotic therapy for a CF pulmonary exacerbation can last for 7 to 21 days depending on the severity of the infection or bacterial resistance, and one year or more for certain types of difficult-to-treat infections, such as *non-tuberculosis mycobacterial* (NTM) *infections*. PIVs typically need to be changed every 3 to 4 days to prevent infection; some medications are too strong for the small plastic catheter to last even a couple of days. Frequent blood draws might be required for monitoring of drug levels or lab abnormalities due to the severity of illness. Lastly, if you are stable, you can be sent home to complete your infusions. For these reasons, your CF provider might recommend a *peripherally inserted central catheter* (PICC) or *port* (also called a mediport, *port-a-cath*, or *Hickman*) to be placed. PICC lines can remain in for many months; mediports can remain for several years.

A PICC line is inserted peripherally; that is, the insertion point is in the arm—in most cases the upper arm. A trained nurse or doctor inserts the PICC line into a large vein in the upper arm; the vein is located with an *ultrasound* machine. After disinfecting the skin, the skin is made numb and the catheter is inserted just above the bend of your inner elbow. The catheter is then guided through a larger vein near your heart called the *vena cava*. The needle or guide wire is then removed, leaving the soft, flexible, tube in the vein. After the IV has been inserted, the injection site is covered with antiseptic gauze and a sterile cover, an X-ray of the chest is usually taken to confirm proper placement in the chest. Some hospitals use an *electrocardiogram* (EKG) method instead of an X-ray to ensure appropriate placement; this method has been thoroughly tested and found to be just as accurate as an X-ray, saving time when needing to adjust positioning, limiting radiation exposure, and lowering cost (Moreau et al, 2010).

Ports are inserted in the operating room under X-ray guidance with anesthesia by a trained doctor, nurse practitioner, or physician assistant; you are given a sedating medication for comfort during the procedure. The access point of a port has a central disc called the *septum*, which is usually a nickel- or quarter-sized round, oval, or triangular piece that when inserted through the chest, sits about 1 inch (2.5 centimeters) below your collarbone under the skin. For women, the interventionist can position it to sit under the bra strap. The septum is attached to a catheter that, similarly to a PICC, is guided into the vena cava. Ports can have one *(single lumen)* or two *(double lumen)* access points; most people receive *single lumen ports* because they clog less frequently than do those with double lumens. Some ports are also called *power ports*, meaning that they can be used with high-speed contrast injections that are usually needed during CT imaging. When injections or blood work are needed, a nurse numbs the insertion site of your port and accesses it with a needle that remains in place for duration of the infusion or the blood draw.

Both types of lines need regular maintenance to prevent clot formation around the catheter and to prevent infection at the site. For PICC lines, this includes a sterile dressing, changed weekly, and flushing the line daily with normal saline and in between the use of antibiotics. For ports that are accessed, reaccessing or changing the needle is recommended weekly and a heparin flush (or hep lock) between IV medication doses. When not in use, the port should be cared for with monthly heparin injections.

What Are the Risks and Benefits of PICCs and Ports?

There are several benefits of having centrally placed catheters:

- They can remain in for weeks or months (e.g., PICC) or several years (e.g., mediport).

- They spare your small veins from irritation by some medications.

- Blood can be drawn from both types of lines, sparing your small veins.

- They can be used in the hospital or home settings.

As with any procedure, risks are associated with placement and after, including the following:

- Irritation or discomfort during the insertion and minor bleeding.

- Multiple attempts might need to be made to place the entire length of a PICC line into the correct position.

- Scarring of large veins can occur due to inflammation and after multiple PICC line placements.

- Accidental puncture of an artery, nerve, or tendon can occur.

- Clot can form around the catheter in the vein *(thrombosis)*, causing swelling or pain in the arm; you should report this to your provider right away.

- Infection at the insertion site or in the bloodstream is possible.

- A PICC might become displaced or pulled out partially or completely.

- Blockage of a PICC or port is common, such that medication cannot be infused or blood cannot be drawn from the line; this can happen due a fibrin sheath around the tip of the vein or if the catheter is touching the wall of the blood vessel. An injectable medication can be used to de-clot the catheter. If unsuccessful, the line might need to be exchanged.

Why Does My Medical Team Check My Weight So Often?

Stepping on the scale can be one of several anxiety-inducing check-ups your CF team asks you to complete at each CF clinic visit. Did your weight go up or down? This can be a nerve-wracking experience. As a person with CF, you are at high risk for malnutrition (or poor nutritional status) due to frequent lung infections and increased nutrition needs, which can lead to significant weight and muscle mass loss. Malnutrition in people with CF is associated with slowed growth and cognition, increased lung infections, and overall poor survival (Michel et al, 2009; White et al, 2013). Additionally, research has shown that reaching an optimal weight in CF has a positive effect on lung function (specifically, FEV1) and improved quality of life due to less-frequent exacerbations, increased strength and endurance, and improved body image (Matel, 2012; Truby et al, 2009).

To track your optimal weight, your CF team uses measures that include weight-for-length (for children under 2 years of age), BMI (for children 2–20 years old), and BMI (for adults over 20 years old). BMI is your weight (in kilograms, or kg) divided by your height (in meters squared, or m²). BMI is used to assess nutritional status and growth; it also can be the first indicator of malnutrition or risk for malnutrition. In children with CF, the goal is to reach a BMI over the 50th percentile. For adults with CF, the goal for women is to achieve a BMI of more than 22 kg/m², and for men, more than 23 kg/m² (CF Foundation, 2012).

Frequent tracking of your BMI can ensure proper physical and cognitive growth. It can also help with the development of muscle strength, lean body mass, and improvement in your quality of life and survival measures. In both children and adults with CF, *anthropometric data* (height, length, weight, BMI assessments) are used to track progress toward, or away from, the aforementioned nutrition goals. This allows for early nutritional intervention, including use of nutrition supplements or nutrition support, to prevent malnutrition.

What Are G-Tubes and G-J Tubes?

Maintaining excellent nutrition and weight when affected by CF is critical for numerous reasons; it helps the immune system fight off infections, maintains strength and endurance, and stabilizes or improves lung function (Truby et al, 2009). You might notice that maintaining or gaining weight is more difficult for you or your child with CF than for those without CF. This is because people with CF require 20% to 50% more calories and protein than people without CF (CF Foundation, 2012; Matel, 2012). This increase in nutritional needs can be very challenging due to multiple factors (including malabsorption of fats, poor appetite, increased cough, poor taste or sense of smell, or symptoms of nausea/vomiting associated with exacerbations) that can make weight gain difficult. When other nutrition interventions have failed to help with weight gain or to maintain your weight during an exacerbation—such as the use of calorie-dense foods/beverages and appetite stimulants—your CF team might recommend the placement of a *feeding tube*.

Feeding tubes provide extra nutrition directly into your stomach or small intestine to help with weight gain and to optimize your daily *caloric intake*. Tube feeds can be used as a supplement to a meal when not enough calories are consumed; or, more often, they can be delivered at nighttime when you or your child are/is sleeping. Nighttime feeds (or *nocturnal feeds*) are often recommended; they do not interfere with mealtimes and they allow you or your child to be away from the feeding pump most of the day. Additionally, nocturnal feeds provide an additional 50% to 75% of your estimated nutrition needs while you are sleeping (White et al, 2013). Many parents of children with CF and adults with CF have experienced less stress with meals after a feeding tube is placed, as this can remove the burden of consuming a set number of calories at each meal. This can also help stop weight loss with CF exacerbations because the feeding tube can be used when eating might not be pleasurable or possible.

A *nasogastric* (NG) *tube* is a small tube that is placed through your nose and into the stomach that is used for shorter-term nutrition support. It can be placed by your care team or by yourself or a family member each night and removed the following morning.

A *G-tube*, or *gastrostomy tube*, is a tube that leads directly into your stomach by means of a small valve on your abdomen that is hidden under your clothing. G-tubes are used for longer-term nutrition support; however, they are not permanent. This tube can be used for medications or feeding with formulas or supplements chosen by your CF *dietitian*.

A *gastrostomy-jejunotomy* (G-J) *tube* is also inserted into your abdomen; however, this tube has two ports. The "G" port directly leads to your stomach; the other (the "J" port) leads to the second part of your small intestine, called the jejunum. A G-J tube might be recommended if you have symptoms of *gastric reflux*, a stomach that empties slowly, or with any concern of aspiration into your lungs while you sleep.

What Tests Assess My Digestive System?

Because CF affects the digestive tract, several *gastrointestinal* (GI) complications can arise that might require testing and diagnostics. These include *gastroesophageal reflux disease* (GERD), or *acid reflux*; *gastroparesis*; *pancreatitis*; *exocrine pancreatic insufficiency* (EPI); *gallstones*; liver disease (with or without *cirrhosis*); *constipation*; *bowel obstruction*, also known as *distal intestinal obstruction syndrome* (DIOS); *intussusception*; and rectal prolapse (for a detailed description of these diagnoses, see Chapter 3).

Several tests are available to assess the digestive system, the most common being the *abdominal X-ray* (AXR). This is like the *chest X-ray*, except that the camera is pointed to the abdominal area—the area below the chest and above the pelvic bones. An AXR can visualize the stomach, *gallbladder*, pancreas, liver, spleen, and small and large intestines. At times, excess gas in the bowels can obscure the view of other organs and give limited exam findings. The AXR can be ordered with different views to assess different complaints, and it is generally good at detecting constipation and bowel obstruction in CF. You will be asked to lay down or stand up in different positions for this exam. At times, *oral contrast* is given during a GI exam under X-ray guidance to assess reflux disease, aspiration of food contents into the lungs, or gastroparesis (delay in emptying of the stomach); similarly, G and J tube blockages and complications can be analyzed using oral contrast or contrast injected into the tubes.

More detailed views of the abdominal organs require a CT scan. Like the CT scan of the chest, contrast injected into your vein can be used for even more detailed viewing of the abdominal and pelvic structures and their blood supply. Abdominal CT scans are great for detecting pancreatitis, liver disease, constipation, bowel obstruction, intussusception, and *volvulus*. Patients lay down for this procedure; at times, your provider will ask you to refrain from eating or drinking before this exam.

Another widely used test is the ultrasound, which is favored for its general accuracy, safety, cost effectiveness, and lack of radiation exposure to the patient. This type of imaging uses sound waves from a probe that reflect off organs to produce an image through a computer. It is used widely to diagnose pancreatitis, gallstones, liver disease (including abnormalities in the size of the liver and spleen), and bowel obstruction. You are asked to lay down for this exam, usually in a dimmed room. A technician sits next to the patient, places a small amount of clear gel on the ultrasound probe, and guides the probe on and around the abdomen, while capturing images on the computer.

Acid reflux and stomach ulcers can be assessed with an *endoscopic exam* in which the physician guides a lighted scope through the mouth and into the stomach; you are sedated for this procedure and samples can be taken from the stomach. This is a moderately invasive test; thus, conservative medical management is usually tried first, unless bleeding in the GI tract is suspected. Similarly, a *colonoscopy* is used to evaluate the intestinal tract. In this procedure, a lighted scope is passed into the large intestine from the rectum. This test is the standard test for ruling-out *colorectal cancer* and it can also detect *polyps* that can be pre-cancerous inflammatory lesions. You are asked to perform a bowel preparation prior to this exam, which consists of drinking a significant volume of laxatives the day before the test. You are sedated for your comfort.

Stool elastase testing is used to diagnose PI. A pancreas not affected by CF secretes an enzyme called *elastase* as well as other digestive enzymes when we eat. These are transported to the small intestine to digest fats, protein, and carbohydrates in the food. In CF, the cells of the pancreas, called *exocrine glands*, that secrete elastase are destroyed, preventing digestion. The test is simple and does not require fasting. You are asked to collect stool in a cup in a laboratory; if collected at home, the sample will need to be placed on ice and kept cold. The stool should be formed and not be mixed with urine or water. The stool is assessed in the lab and the amount of elastase is measured. Low levels of elastase are diagnostic of PI, which can be mild, moderate, or complete. All severities will require *pancreatic enzyme replacement therapy* (PERT), which your CF dietitian will recommend, and your CF provider will need to prescribe. This will aid in the digestion of food.

How Are Blood Sugars Measured?

If you or your child is diagnosed with CFRD based on the OGTT described earlier in this chapter, you will be asked to test your blood sugars at home. Keeping blood sugars within the desired range that your physician recommends is important to maintain weight as well as to prevent infections, renal failure, retinal damage, blindness, and vascular disease—all *side effects* and end-organ damage related to poorly controlled diabetes. *Glucometers* are machines that detect the level of glucose in the blood.

Traditionally, *home glucose monitoring meters*, require you to prick your fingers, arm, forearm, base of your thumb or thigh using a thin needle lancing device to release a small drop of blood. The *glucometer* holds a test strip and the drop of blood is placed on this strip, after which the machine quickly reads the level of glucose in the blood. Because a blood-sugar measurement can be prescribed several times a day, it can become cumbersome and painful to continually prick these parts of the body. For this reason, advances have been made to develop *continuous glucose monitoring* (CGM) *devices*, which are small devices that often work on the arm or lower stomach; they have a small sensor and are attached to a transmitter. The device detects the blood glucose level in real time and transmits it to a receiver; some devices can store the data on a smartphone that can be sent to your provider. This gives patients better control of their blood sugars. If you use an *insulin pump*, you can link the CGM to the pump. It is not as accurate as the traditional glucometer, so your provider might still ask you to check your blood sugar in the traditional fashion from time to time. It is often difficult to obtain approval for continuous meters through insurance companies, so you might need to work with your provider or be referred to an endocrinologist—a diabetes specialist—to help obtain this if it is deemed right for you.

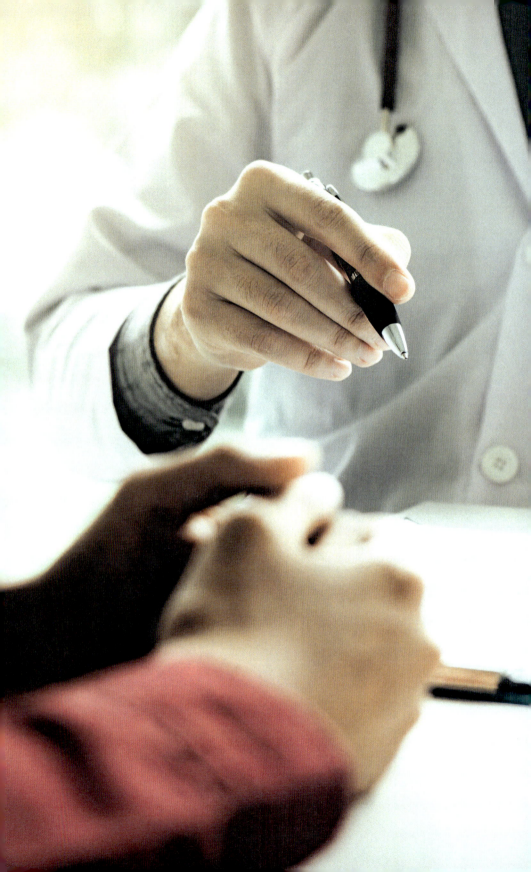

WHAT TYPES OF MEDICATIONS CAN HELP ME MANAGE MY CF?

Jaideep S. Talwalkar, MD and Beth A. Smith, MD

CHAPTER

In This Chapter

- Which Medications Might Improve My Pulmonary Function?

- What Are Nebulized Medications?

- Which Medications Affect the Function of My Gastrointestinal Track?

- Which Medications Are Used for CF-Related Diabetes?

- What Is Gene-Modifying Therapy?

- What Are the Side Effects of Medications Used for CF?

- Which Over-the-Counter Medications Can I Take, and Which Ones Should I Avoid?

- Which Medications Might I Take to Manage My Anxiety or Depression?

- Which Side Effects of Antidepressants and Anti-Anxiety Agents Should I Be Mindful of?

- Will Medications That I Take for ADHD Interact with My CF Medications or Affect My Weight?

- Which of My Drugs Used for CF Interact with Other Medications (and How)?

Which Medications Might Improve My Pulmonary Function?

The *Cystic Fibrosis Foundation (CF Foundation)* maintains a Drug Development Pipeline, which is an online list of medications available to individuals with cystic fibrosis (CF) (CF Foundation, 2019). The list contains treatments at various stages of the research and approval process. Several treatments are available for maintenance of lung health, which we can divide into categories based on how they work. These medications work best when used on an ongoing basis to keep your lungs healthy.

Three commonly used inhaled medications help to clear thick mucus from the lungs. In 1993, *nebulized dornase alpha (Pulmozyme®)* became the first medication to receive specific approval for use in individuals with CF. It remains a standard part of treatment for individuals 6 years of age and older with lung disease due to CF (Mogayzel et al, 2013). Part of what makes the mucus in CF so thick is that it is full of long strands of *deoxyribonucleic acid* (DNA). Dornase alpha contains an enzyme that breaks the DNA into small fragments, which thins the mucus and makes it easier to cough up. Mucus in CF is also thick because the airways are dehydrated. Surfers with CF in Australia realized that their lungs felt better the more they surfed; this led to the development of inhaled 7% *hypertonic saline* as a medication. This treatment is essentially medical-grade salt water that is inhaled via a nebulizer to improve lung health. Because it can be irritating, hypertonic saline is usually prescribed along with *albuterol*, an inhaled medication that reduces muscle spasms within the lungs. Finally, *mannitol (Bronchitol®)* is a powder administered by inhaler that is available in Australia and parts of Europe and might soon be available in the United States (Brown, 2019). Mannitol draws water into the airways by *osmosis*, which makes the mucus thinner. Because it is administered via an inhaler, it can be easier and quicker to use than 7% hypertonic saline. However, the strength of the research in support of using mannitol is not as strong (Nevitt, 2018), and it is not on the current list of medications recommended by the CF Foundation (Mogayzel et al, 2013).

Next, *antibiotics* can be used on a long-term basis to treat chronic lung infections. Infections with bacteria, such as *Pseudomonas aeruginosa*, are commonly seen in individuals with CF. *Tobramycin* and *aztreonam* are antibiotics recommended for use in individuals with CF who are 6 years of age and older and who have persistent growth of *Pseudomonas aeruginosa* (Mogayzel et al, 2013). Tobramycin is available in both a nebulized solution (*Tobi®, Bethkis®*) and inhaler (*Tobi Podhaler®*) forms, whereas aztreonam (*Cayston®*) is delivered by a nebulizer. Though tobramycin and aztreonam were initially designed to be used separately (i.e., you would be on only one of them), they are increasingly being prescribed in alternating cycles called "*continuous alternating therapy*" (Talwalkar and Murray, 2016). *Colistin* is another inhaled antibiotic that can be used for chronic lung infection from *Pseudomonas aeruginosa*. It is used more regularly in Europe than it is in the United States. Several other inhaled antibiotics have been developed, though these are used less commonly and are used only in very specific circumstances.

Azithromycin is an antibiotic, but in CF it is used to combat *inflammation* more than to kill bacteria. Inflammation is a normal process that occurs when the immune system is trying to fight infection. In CF, chronic infection leads to constant inflammation in the lungs. Over time, this inflammation can damage the lungs. When used over the long term, oral azithromycin decreases inflammation in the lungs, specifically in individuals with persistent growth of *Pseudomonas aeruginosa* in sputum cultures (McArdle and Talwalkar, 2007). Its use is recommended by the CF Foundation for individuals age 6 years and older with chronic *Pseudomonas aeruginosa* infection. Azithromycin might have less benefit for those who are not infected with this bacterium (Mogayzel et al, 2013).

Other anti-inflammatory treatments commonly used in people without CF are sometimes used to treat lung disease in individuals with CF. High-dose oral *ibuprofen*, administered with careful monitoring with blood tests, can preserve lung health. The effect is most pronounced in those between 6 and 17 years of age; in fact, this is the only age group in which the CF Foundation recommends this treatment (Mogayzel et al, 2013). Even though use of oral *corticosteroids*, such as prednisone, helps with lung function, long-term use is not recommended because of worrisome side effects (e.g., slowed growth, weak bones, cataracts, diabetes) (Mogayzel et al, 2013). There are fewer side effects from inhaled corticosteroids, but these medicines are not helpful (Balfour-Lynn and Welch, 2009) unless individuals have other problems with their lungs (e.g., *asthma, allergic bronchopulmonary aspergillosis*) in addition to CF.

A new category of medications called *CFTR modulators* are available to those with certain *CF transmembrane conductance regulator* (CFTR) mutations. These medicines are discussed in more detail later in this chapter.

Finally, lung health in CF is affected by your general health and adherence to other aspects of treatment. Maintaining your goal weight, using airway clearance devices, and treating common complications of CF (e.g., *exocrine pancreatic insufficiency* (EPI), *sinus disease, CF-related diabetes, anxiety, depression*) are critical to preserving lung health.

What Are Nebulized Medications?

Because lung disease is the biggest health problem most individuals with CF face, decades of research has gone into developing treatments that are delivered directly to the lungs. Nebulized medications are derived from small quantities of liquid that are placed into nebulizers that turn the liquid into a mist that can be inhaled over a few minutes. Similarly, some medicines can be inhaled more quickly by using an inhaler (a *"puffer"*), a device designed to turn the medicine (usually a liquid or powder) into an aerosol that is breathed into the lungs. Through nebulizers or inhalers, high doses of medicines can be delivered directly to the lungs, leading to fewer side effects because the medicine acts directly where it needs to rather than having to go through the rest of the body before it arrives at the lungs.

Several issues should be kept in mind when using nebulized medicines. You must use the appropriate nebulizer machine for each nebulized medicine because the medicines will not work properly unless they are properly paired. Additionally, when you use multiple nebulized or inhaled medicines, follow this specific sequence: *bronchodilator* (e.g., albuterol), hypertonic saline, dornase alpha, and inhaled antibiotic (Mogayzel et al, 2013). The rationale for using the antibiotic last is that it will not be washed out or diluted by other treatments. Finally, nebulizers and related tubing can collect germs, so you must disinfect the equipment regularly using established methods, such as those described by the CF Foundation (CF Foundation, 2019).

Which Medications Affect the Function of My Gastrointestinal Tract?

CF causes a variety of problems in the *gastrointestinal* (GI) tract, primarily because "tubes" in the *pancreas*, *intestines*, and *liver* can become plugged with thick secretions, similar to how the lungs become plugged with mucus. EPI occurs when small ducts in the pancreas become plugged with *digestive enzymes*, leading to destruction of the pancreas. In some people with CF, this happens before birth, whereas in others it develops later in life. In people with EPI, the use of oral *pancreatic enzyme replacement therapy* (PERT) is critical to ensure proper digestion. PERT is taken before or during meals and snacks to help your body absorb the calories and nutrients in food. Without PERT, individuals with EPI develop diarrhea, oily stool, cramping, poor growth, and vitamin deficiencies. Given that vitamin deficiencies are so common, most individuals with EPI will also be prescribed supplements of vitamins A, D, E, and K, all of which depend on proper pancreatic function for absorption.

The intestines can become plugged with hard stool in some individuals with CF. When severe, this can lead to a life-threating blockage called *distal intestinal obstruction syndrome* (DIOS), a condition that occurs only in people with CF (Munck et al, 2016). More commonly, individuals with CF suffer from constipation; however, constipation can quickly progress to DIOS in some people. To treat constipation and prevent DIOS, at-risk individuals are prescribed *laxatives* on a regular basis. *Polyethylene glycol (MiraLAX®)* is commonly used for this purpose. Those with more severe constipation might receive other medications, such as *lubiprostone (Amitiza®)*.

The liver also has a complex network of ducts that can become plugged with *bile*. Because these plugged ducts can lead to inflammation damaging the liver, many individuals with CF-associated liver disease will receive *ursodiol (Actigall®)* to improve bile flow and reduce inflammation. However, whether ursodiol leads to prevention of serious liver disease in CF is unclear (Cheng et al, 2017), and more research is needed.

Individuals with CF commonly experience *gastroesophageal reflux disease* (GERD), with studies revealing GERD in 35% to 91% of individuals, many of whom do not have the typical symptoms of heartburn seen in GERD in those without CF (Robinson and DiMango, 2014; Assis and Freedman, 2016). Unlike the other GI problems that we just described, GERD does not occur because of thick secretions. Instead, it can be a result of lung disease, vigorous coughing, frequent meals, and *chest physiotherapy* (Robinson and DiMango, 2014). GERD in individuals with CF is treated with medications that suppress stomach acid—either *proton-pump inhibitors* (PPIs) (e.g., *dexlansoprazole, esomeprazole, lansoprazole, omeprazole, pantoprazole*) or *histamine2 receptor antagonists* (e.g., *famotidine, ranitidine*). The acid suppression provided by these medicines can also make PERT more effective for EPI, though with newer PERT formulations, acid suppression is not necessary solely for this purpose (Assis and Freedman, 2016).

Which Medications Are Used for CF-Related Diabetes?

CF-related diabetes (CFRD) is different from *type 1* and *type 2 diabetes* in terms of cause and treatment. It is caused by destruction of the pancreas due to plugged ducts, inflammation, and eventual scarring. Insulin is the only medication recommended by the CF Foundation (Moran et al, 2010) and the *International Society for Pediatric and Adolescent Diabetes* (Moran et al, 2018) for CFRD. There are many types of insulin available, and because control of CFRD depends on so many factors (e.g., diet, activity, lung health, other medications), a personalized approach to each individual is determined by your CF care team. Apart from insulin, there are dozens of medications available to treat other types of diabetes, though none are recommended for individuals with CFRD. There has been some recent enthusiasm for using the oral medication *repaglinide (Prandin®)* early in the treatment of CFRD, but experts caution that more research is needed (Moran et al, 2018).

What Is Gene-Modifying Therapy?

CF is a *genetic disease* caused by *mutations* in a *gene* called CF *transmembrane conductance regulator* (CFTR). This gene makes a protein that does not function correctly in individuals with CF. There are nearly 2,000 known mutations in CFTR that can lead to CF. New medications called CFTR modulators have become available to treat people with dozens of specific CFTR mutations. These medications are taken by mouth, enter the blood stream, and find their way into the cells of an individual with CF. After they are in the cells, they help correct the function of the defective CFTR protein. This has led to dramatic health improvements in some people, and more modest improvements in others. Currently available CFTR-modulators include *ivacaftor (Kalydeco®)*, *lumacaftor-ivacaftor* in combination (Orkambi®), *tezacaftor-ivacaftor* in combination (Symdeko®), and most recently approved by US Food and Drug Administration (FDA) triple combination of *elaxacaftor-tezacaftor-ivacaftor (Trikafta®)*. Many other CFTR-modulators are in various stages of development as well (CF Foundation, 2019).

What Are the Side Effects of Medications Used for CF?

Because CF is a complex disease that affects many parts of the body, there are dozens of medications that can be used, and these medications all have side effects (Table 5-1). In general, inhaled medications can be irritating to the throat and lungs, leading to hoarseness, cough, and chest tightness. In many people, the side effects of inhaled medications improve after a short period of use; however, some people need to discontinue these medicines because of the side effects. It is important for those with CF to discuss specific side effects of these and other medications with prescribing clinicians at their CF care centers. Many CF centers include CF-specialty *pharmacists* as members of an interprofessional care team to help anticipate, avoid, and recognize side effects and medication interactions (Talwalkar et al, 2017).

Table 5-1: Selected Side Effects of Medications Commonly Used to Treat People with CF

Medication	Common or Serious Side Effects
Inhaled	
Dornase alpha (Pulmozyme®)	Cough, hoarse voice, sore throat
Hypertonic saline	
Mannitol (Bronchitol®)	
Tobramycin (TOBI®, Bethkis®)	
Aztreonam (Cayston®)	
Colistin	
Albuterol	Cough, tremor, racing heart
Oral	
Azithromycin	Nausea, diarrhea, QT prolongation, abnormal LFTs*
Ibuprofen	Stomach upset, GI bleeding, kidney injury
Prednisone	High blood sugar, increased appetite, heightened emotions, infection, osteoporosis, cataracts
Pancreatic enzyme replacement therapy	Abdominal discomfort, fibrosing colonopathy (scarring of the colon)
Polyethylene glycol (Miralax®)	Diarrhea, nausea, abdominal cramping
Lubiprostone (Amitiza®)	Diarrhea, nausea, bloating, gas
Ursodiol (Actigall®)	Diarrhea, nausea, abdominal discomfort
Proton pump inhibitors (PPIs)	Vitamin deficiencies, pneumonia
Histamine2 receptor antagonists	Headache, drowsiness, low platelets
Repaglinide (Prandin®)	Low blood sugar, weight gain
CFTR-modulators	Abnormal LFTs, cataracts
Selective serotonin re-uptake inhibitors (SSRIs)	Nausea, constipation, diarrhea, sleep problems, headache, problems with sexual functioning
Lorazepam	Drowsiness, sleepiness, dizziness
Injection	
Insulin	Low blood sugar, weight gain

* LFTs = liver function tests

Which Over-the-Counter Medications Can I Take, and Which Ones Should I Avoid?

Anyone with a chronic medical condition on *prescription medications* use should speak to prescribing clinicians before using *over-the-counter* (OTC) medications. This general rule applies to individuals with CF. However, given the complexity of CF, the different organs that can be involved, the range of disease severity seen in different people, and the fact that it is a relatively rare disease, close communication with the CF care team is especially important before individuals with CF use OTC medications, herbs, supplements, or even medications prescribed by non-CF specialists.

Certain OTC medications can be particularly problematic for individuals with CF. Antidiarrheal agents such as *loperamide* can lead to constipation and DIOS. Because cough and cold preparations are unlikely to help with symptoms of CF, they could delay the use of more effective treatments and you should not use them. As noted earlier, certain antacids can have important medication interactions, and you should use them only with full knowledge of the CF care team. You should avoid OTC reusable nasal sprays because these can become contaminated with germs such as *Pseudomonas aeruginosa*.

OTC pain and fever medications like *acetaminophen (Tylenol®)* and ibuprofen (Advil®, Motrin®) will typically be safe in CF, though discussion with the care team is still advisable to ensure that your liver and kidney function are good enough to use these products. Even vitamin supplements can be confusing in CF because OTC multi-vitamins typically do not contain adequate amounts of the specific vitamins (A, D, E, and K) that individuals with CF need. The CF Foundation provides some guidance on its website to help those with CF and their families learn more about vitamins and supplements in CF (CF Foundation 2019; Casey et al, 2010).

Which Medications Might I Take to Manage My Anxiety or Depression?

The International Committee on Mental Health in Cystic Fibrosis recommends using a *selective serotonin re-uptake inhibitor* (SSRI) as a first-choice medication to treat depression and anxiety in adolescents and adults living with CF (Quittner et al, 2016). Sometimes, individuals living with CF struggle with their mood, which can make it difficult to take care of themselves or to enjoy daily life. Getting treatment can help with these problems. SSRIs are the most commonly prescribed *antidepressants*. For individuals living with CF, *citalopram (Celexa®), escitalopram (Lexapro®), fluoxetine (Prozac®)*, or *sertraline (Zoloft®)* are good first choices in most cases when medication is needed to help you overcome depression or anxiety. SSRIs are the first choice because they are effective for both depressive disorders and anxiety disorders, are well studied (even in those with serious medical illnesses), and very rarely need to be withheld in individuals living with CF due to any potential harm they might cause. SSRIs work by increasing levels of *serotonin* in the brain. Serotonin is a chemical messenger in the brain that carries signals between brain cells. These medications keep more serotonin available to signal between brain cells, helping to regulate your mood and anxiety. These medications can also help you solidify any new skills you learn on your own or in therapy to fight your depression or anxiety and to maintain your health.

Some individuals living with CF experience anxiety in anticipation of or during medical procedures. Avoidance of these procedures can have negative consequences to your health. The International Committee on Mental Health in Cystic Fibrosis has recommended the medication lorazepam (Ativan®) as a useful short-term treatment for procedure-related anxiety when psychological techniques (e.g., deep breathing, distraction, breaking down the steps, coping-promoting behavior) and other strategies (e.g., using fast-acting topical creams, or using optimum positioning for comfort) are ineffective (Quittner et al, 2016). Lorazepam is an example of a *benzodiazepine*, a group of medications that work by blocking overactive nerve firing in your brain and other areas of your *central nervous system* (CNS). For procedure-related anxiety, these medications reduce anxiety quickly and/or cause sleepiness, allowing you (or your child living with CF) to tolerate and complete procedures required for the treatment of CF.

Which Side Effects of Antidepressants and Anti-Anxiety Agents Should I Be Mindful of?

All SSRIs work in a similar way and, in general, all can cause similar side effects. Side effects of SSRIs include nausea, constipation, diarrhea, sleep problems, headache, and problems with sexual functioning; however, you might not experience any side effects. These side effects are most likely when you start the medication and they often disappear over time or when the dose is decreased. If you have side effects that worry you, call your doctor. Simple changes, such as taking the medication after a meal to help with nausea or before bed if you are too sleepy, could be all you need to do to minimize side effects. If you cannot tolerate one SSRI, you might be able to tolerate a different one. Although SSRIs are not addictive, you can develop side effects (flu-like symptoms; e.g., nausea, dizziness, fatigue) if you suddenly stop them or miss several doses. Your doctor can provide guidelines for slowly coming off an SSRI to avoid these symptoms.

The most commonly reported side effects of benzodiazepines, such as lorazepam, are drowsiness, sleepiness, or dizziness. Benzodiazepines require close monitoring in individuals living with CF, especially those who also have a history of substance misuse, depression, or lung disease. Typically, these medications are used briefly because they can lead to misuse and addiction.

Will Medications That I Take for ADHD Interact with My CF Medications or Affect My Weight?

Medications for children and adults with *attention-deficit hyperactivity disorder* (ADHD) are categorized as *stimulants* (*amphetamine* or *methylphenidate*) or non-stimulants (e.g., *atomoxetine* or *alpha-2 agonists*). Stimulants are commonly considered the first-choice treatment, with non-stimulants used for individuals who do not benefit from a stimulant or who cannot tolerate a stimulant. If you or your child with CF has ADHD, studies show there's more than an 80% chance of responding to medications; however, there are a few things specific to CF that you should know. Having ADHD can make it more difficult to sustain your daily care; therefore, you should work with your team early on for possible solutions. The potential for medication interactions exists and doses might need to be increased or decreased based on your other medications. Additionally, your dose might need to be lower if you have problems with your kidneys or liver. *Stimulant medications* can have side effects (e.g., headaches, loss of appetite, trouble sleeping). One study of individuals with CF found that stimulants were more likely to be associated with significant weight loss than were non-stimulants (Georgiopoulos and Hua, 2011). Your team might proactively work to boost calories or even consider a medication to help stimulate your appetite. *Atomoxetine (Strattera®)* is a non-stimulant treatment that can cause GI side effects and your doctor might monitor your LFTs. You should use this medication cautiously if you have CF-related liver disease. The other non-stimulant medications are alpha-2 agonists (e.g., *guanfacine, clonidine*). These can cause fatigue, headache, dizziness, and constipation, and your doctor might monitor your blood pressure. Medications like guanfacine and clonidine should not be withdrawn suddenly, because this can cause dangerous increases in your blood pressure.

Which of My Drugs Used for CF Interact with Other Medications (and How)?

Even though individuals with CF are often taking many medications, dangerous interactions between medications used to treat CF are uncommon. CF care teams have a high awareness about possible interactions and make adjustments to medication doses and schedules to minimize the risk of interactions. Medications that are known to interact with one another can often still be used together under appropriate medical supervision.

Many medications are broken down *(metabolized)* by *enzymes* in the liver called *cytochrome P450 (CYP450)*. Although most medications have no effect on the activity of CYP450 enzymes, some medications result in *induction* (speeding up) or *inhibition* (slowing down) of CYP450 enzymes. Induction of CYP450 can make other medications less effective because they are broken down too quickly. In contrast, inhibition of CYP450 can cause other medications to have more side effects because they raise drug levels in the body. The CF care team will do a careful drug interaction check when prescribing medications that induce or inhibit CYP450 enzymes (such as *rifampin, azole antifungals*, PPIs, *ciprofloxacin*, SSRIs, and CFTR-modulators).

Other medications can have overlapping side effects. These side effects can be inconsequential when a medicine is used alone. However, when used together, the side effects of these medicines can be additive. For example, many medications have subtle effects on the electrical activity of the heart (i.e., cause prolongation of the *QT-interval*). CF care teams exercise caution when prescribing multiple medications that can affect the QT-interval and might check an *electrocardiogram* (EKG) to ensure that the interval remains in a safe range. Some medications commonly used in CF care that can affect the QT-interval include azithromycin, *levofloxacin*, ciprofloxacin, azole antifungals, and SSRIs. A specific interaction between SSRIs and the antibiotic *linezolid (Zyvox®)* deserves mention. These medications all increase levels of serotonin in the body; when these levels climb dangerously high, they can cause *serotonin syndrome*, which is characterized by fever, agitation, tremor, sweating, and diarrhea (Jordan et al, 2016).

WHAT LIFESTYLE CHANGES CAN I MAKE TO ADDRESS MY CYSTIC FIBROSIS?

Christopher J. Richards, MD; C.J. Bathgate, PhD;
Matthew Nippins, PT, DPT, CCS; Jessica Garton, PT, DPT, OCS, CLT;
Gretchen M. Garlow MS, RD, LDN, CNSC; and
Anna M. Georgiopoulos, MD

CHAPTER

In This Chapter

- How Can the Risk of Infection (and Being Infected) Affect My Lifestyle?

- What Equipment and Medication Should I Bring with Me If I Plan to Travel by Car, Train or Plane?

- What Type of Diet Should I Follow (and Why)?

- Should I Avoid Certain Foods?

- What Kind of Exercise Should I Do?

- How Can CF Affect My Sleep?

- What Can I Do to Improve My Sleep?

- How Can I Learn to Clear Secretions from My Lungs?

- How Can I Cut Down or Stop Drinking Alcohol and Smoking Cigarettes?

- Should I Stop Smoking Cannabis? (and Other Drugs?)

- Should I Use Edible Cannabis?

How Can the Risk of Infection (and Being Infected) Affect My Lifestyle?

Keeping yourself healthy and avoiding infections is a lifelong concern; moreover, it can be overwhelming. Fortunately, the *Cystic Fibrosis Foundation (CF Foundation)* has compiled guidelines that can help those with cystic fibrosis (CF) keep themselves healthy without sacrificing their lifestyle. These guidelines were last updated in 2014 to reflect changes in our knowledge about how to best lower one's risk of getting an infection (Saiman et al, 2014). Although these guidelines were designed to help keep people with CF stay healthy, it is important to remember that there is nothing about your illness that prevents you from engaging in activities of everyday life. Interactions with others who have CF is where you need to take extra steps to avoid transmitting infections to one another; these guidelines are often referred to as the "*6-foot rule.*"

Good hygiene practices outside of the hospital or clinic should always include regular hand washing when using public bathrooms, handling food, or when interacting with those who might be ill. Everyone with CF, regardless of their age, is strongly encouraged to complete their routine pediatric *vaccine* series for *measles, mumps, and rubella* (MMR), *tetanus, diphtheria, and pertussis* (TDap), as well as receiving the pneumococcal vaccination ("*pneumonia vaccine*") and the vaccine for seasonal *influenza* (Malfroot et al, 2005). Although many people develop mild symptoms of aches, cough, and runny nose after receiving the flu vaccine, it does not cause the flu. For families in which there might be more than one member with CF, there are some unique considerations. There is no need to restrict interactions among siblings with CF or with other members of their family. This includes contact in the home, at school, at after-school activities, or at summer camps. However, the CF Foundation recommends that airway clearance occurs with only one family member in the room at a time. This is intended to limit exposure to any germs that might be coughed out during the therapy; in addition, you should not share your equipment with other members of your family (Saiman et al, 2014).

For school-aged children, there is no legal requirement that you disclose your CF status or your respiratory culture information to your school or to anyone else; however, it is important that certain precautions are taken to keep you and other students with CF at your school healthy. These precautionary measures include making sure that two children with CF are not assigned to the same classroom and developing strategies to limit contact during common activities such as lunch time, gym, recess, and assemblies. Even though there is a theoretic risk of acquiring *methicillin-resistant Staphylococcus aureus* (MRSA) while participating in sports, there has not been a confirmed case of someone with CF acquiring MRSA in this way (Barrett et al, 2004). There is no reason for you to avoid participating in group activities, after-school programs, or sports teams, because this is a normal part of life; nothing about your illness prevents you from being a regular participant.

Summer camps are an area of specific concern. You might have heard of outbreaks of *Pseudomonas cepacia*, now referred to as *Burkholderia cepacia complex*, at CF-specific summer camps in the 1990s (Pegues et al, 1994). Because of these experiences, views on how those with CF interact with one another outside of school have changed. The CF Foundation now recommends that those with CF not attend summer camps if there are other children with CF present (this excludes your siblings with CF). Individuals with CF, their families, and providers should understand the importance of you making friends and developing a community that can share the challenges of CF. Fortunately, with the advent of social media and live-streaming events on the internet, those with CF can now interact in ways that were not possible in the past.

When you are hospitalized, all CF Foundation–accredited programs and most hospitals have strict infection-control polices to keep you safe. These policies include hand washing by staff as well as wearing contact precaution gowns and gloves when they enter your hospital or exam room. The surfaces in exam rooms should be cleaned after every patient who comes through to limit transmission of bacteria from one person to the next. This includes common equipment, such as blood pressure cuffs and pulmonary function machines, among others (Zuckerman et al, 2009). Because there have been confirmed cases of transmission of infection between those with CF in outpatient clinics, you might find that when you arrive at the clinic, you will be brought back to the exam room right away; this is to limit your contact with other people with CF at your appointments (LiPuma et al, 1990; Biddick et al, 2003). While admitted, most individuals can leave their rooms and walk around the hospital without restrictions, although you will be reminded to wear a mask. Because policies between hospitals can differ, you should ask about any restrictions early into your admission.

What Equipment and Medication Should I Bring with Me If I Plan to Travel by Car, Train, or Plane?

Travel for work, family, and vacation is important and should not be avoided just because you have CF. However, to make your trip as safe and enjoyable as possible, you might need to undertake extra preplanning while you make travel arrangements and pack. Here are some recommendations:

- Make sure that you bring more medication than you need in case you lose some while you are away or stay longer than anticipated. If traveling by air, keep your medication in your carry-on luggage in case your checked baggage is lost or delayed.

- Consider how you can continue your health care routines while traveling and when you arrive. When traveling by car, for example, allow time for additional breaks to carry out *nebulizer* treatments or *airway clearance*. When flying, choose the timing of your flights carefully so that you can fit in treatments.

- Discuss with your CF team whether it would be appropriate to have a supply of oral *antibiotics* while you travel to help provide a sense of security and to treat an exacerbation early on.

- To fly with your equipment, you will need a letter from your CF team to bring with you to the airport. This letter should verify your need to transport certain items (such as your vest, nebulizer, liquid medications, a cooler for refrigerated medications, syringes and oxygen in addition to your regular luggage). Speak with the airline and CF team well in advance, as different carriers have different requirements for what needs to be documented. Bring multiple copies of your letter because you might need to present it during security checks, departures, connections, and arrivals.

- Think about what will help you adapt to the conditions at your destination. With documentation, amusement parks might allow priority access so that you aren't standing in hot, sunny, and humid conditions for long periods.

- Bring extra sunscreen; many of the medications that you might be taking cause *photosensitivity* and can make you sunburn more easily.

Traveling with oxygen has specific considerations. As altitude increases during flight, the oxygen pressure in the atmosphere decreases. Most commercial flights fly at an altitude of 30,000 feet. At this altitude all people would become *hypoxemic* if the cabin were not pressurized. However, although the cabin of the aircraft is pressurized, it is only pressurized to an altitude equivalent of 5000 to 8000 feet, not to sea level (Ergan et al, 2018). When exposed to the lower oxygen tension (available oxygen) during flight, most people without lung disease will experience a 3% to 5% drop in their *oxygen saturation*. For those with lung disease, this change can be even more pronounced. Blood flow might not be efficiently redistributed within the lung, and increases in heart rate and blood pressure can worsen *shunting* of blood toward damaged parts of the lung thereby lowering oxygen levels. Additionally, elevated *pulmonary arterial pressures* from hypoxemia can cause *right heart dysfunction*. For people with lung disease, sleeping on airplanes can result in further declines in oxygen saturation during the flight. Although some individuals with CF may not notice these changes, others will develop symptoms of breathlessness, lightheadedness, and *palpitations* unless they use supplemental oxygen while flying.

If you don't regularly use oxygen, it can be challenging to determine whether you need it when you fly, and you might need additional testing before your trip. Simple predictors such as resting oxygen saturation or *pulmonary function testing* (PFT) might not be reliable indicators of your in-flight oxygen requirement (Robson et al, 2009). A *6-minute walk test* and clinical judgment are the most common assessments. The most accurate test is a *High-Altitude Simulation Test* (HAST), in which a person breathes the reduced amount of oxygen found at altitude through a tight-fitting mask for 15 to 20 minutes, while oxygen saturation, vital signs, and symptoms are monitored (Mohr, 2008).

For people with CF who already use oxygen therapy, the rule of thumb is to double the oxygen flow rates to keep oxygen saturation above 92% while flying. For those using portable concentrators, this will decrease the battery life of the device, so having sufficient back-up is essential. When you arrive at your destination, having access to supplemental oxygen will be necessary. Contact your oxygen supply company as soon as possible before your trip and let them know your dates of travel and where you will be staying. They will be able to tell you which subcontractors they work with in different areas and what equipment you will need to bring. Unfortunately, there are occasions when you might need to bear these costs yourself, but with advance notice, it still might be possible to obtain insurance coverage.

What Type of Diet Should I Follow (and Why)?

The nutrition goals for anyone with CF are to achieve and to maintain an *optimal nutritional status*. According to data from the *CF Foundation Patient Registry* as well as population-based studies, optimal nutritional status is associated with better lung function and longevity for children and adults. For infants, children, and adolescents, optimal nutritional status is defined as a *body mass index* (BMI) at or greater than 50% of people of the same age and gender. Adult nutrition goals are a BMI of 22 for women, and 23 for men (CF Foundation Registry, 2017).

There is no special diet for those with CF; instead, there are nutritional goals. Many people think of a CF diet as a high-calorie diet because most people with CF require more calories each day to achieve and maintain their growth and weight goals (Schindler et al, 2015). The increased calories required by those with CF vary from 10% to 100% above what would be needed by an individual without CF (Stallings et al, 2008). The actual calorie requirement is influenced by activity level, age, developmental stage, pancreatic sufficiency, lung function, infections, and blood sugar control (Turck et al, 2016). Caloric needs increase during periods of growth and during pulmonary exacerbations.

Of the three major macronutrients—protein, fat, and carbohydrate—fat is the most calorie dense. Many people refer to a CF diet not just as a high-calorie diet, but as a high-fat diet because the easiest way to increase the calorie content of meals is by increasing the fat content of your diet (Schindler et al, 2015). Diets without calorie-dense foods will require a meal pattern with a higher volume of food to achieve the needed calorie goals. People who prefer lower fat intake often find eating three meals plus three or more snacks each day is a preferred meal pattern.

Despite eating a high-calorie, high-fat diet that is complete with three meals and regular snacks, some people might need to use nutritional supplements to meet their goals. These supplements are often in the form of calorie-rich beverages (such as Ensure®, Boost®, or Pro-Stat®) or, in some cases, supplements supplied via *gastric tube*. Gastric tubes, or "G-tubes," are surgically placed catheters that enter the stomach (or in some cases, the small intestine, referred to as "*J-tubes*") and allow people to take medications and nutrition without swallowing. These are sometimes placed when an individual is losing a concerning amount of weight, is unable to meet their caloric goals, or prior to a lung transplant. These tubes are meant to be placed for long periods, often years, but might not need to be permanent (Schwarzenberg et al, 2016).

Along with higher calorie needs, CF patients with *pancreatic insufficiency* (PI) have higher requirements for *vitamins* and *minerals*. The most important of these are Vitamins A, D, E, and K. There are specially formulated vitamin and *mineral* supplements for CF that contain unique forms of these fat-soluble vitamins that can be more easily absorbed by someone who is *pancreatic insufficient* (Schindler et al, 2015). These special CF formulations also contain higher doses of vitamins than are found in typical over-the-counter products and include a wider range of minerals.

Sodium (salt) is usually not thought of as a mineral or supplement, but people with CF need much more sodium than those without CF. In general, the use of added salt should be encouraged and consumption of foods that are higher in sodium content should be allowed. In fact, infants should be supplemented with one-eighth of a teaspoon of salt from birth to 6 months of age, and have this amount increased to one-fourth of a teaspoon of salt for those aged 6 to 12 months (Schindler et al, 2015).

Many families struggle with balancing the high-calorie needs of an individual with CF with the need for a prudent heart-healthy diet for the rest of the family. To manage this, consider an approach referred to as *layering*. For example, the family might serve turkey sandwiches on whole-wheat bread for lunch. The individual with CF can layer on a slice of cheese, a few slivers of avocado, some bacon and mayonnaise to add an extra 390 calories to their sandwich. Instead of just having an apple as a snack, you could add peanut butter or cheese slices for some extra calories. If this practice is followed with two or three items at each meal or snack, the basic menu for the family can remain consistent for everyone while enhancing with layered extras for the individual with CF. The changes and additions do not need to be complex.

For a person with *CF-related diabetes* (CFRD), it can become frustrating to decide what to eat. Suddenly, you go from a practically unrestricted diet to one for which you need to pay attention to the sources of nutrients, amounts of carbohydrates, protein, and fat in your diet. At the same time, you still need to achieve or maintain an optimal nutritional status. How can someone gain or maintain weight if they are now limiting their intake of certain nutrients? In CFRD, rather than severely limit carbohydrates, we suggest a more moderate restriction. You should still strictly avoid sugar-sweetened beverages (such as soda, sweet iced teas, and juice [even 100% fruit juice]) because these items rapidly raise your blood glucose. You should also avoid very high sugar content foods (such as candy, syrups, and frosting).

Foods with added sugar (such as desserts) will elevate your blood sugar less if you eat them as a part of a meal. This is because the protein and fat from the other foods in the meal will slow the rate at which the carbohydrates are digested. Snacks should include foods that contain protein, fat, and some carbohydrate. As an example, an apple with peanut butter or cheese and crackers would make a very good snack if you have diabetes. A meal pattern of three meals with two or three snacks is the easiest way to meet your calorie needs. The meals and snacks do not need to be enormous, just consistent day to day so that your intake is stable. Following these strategies will help modulate your blood glucose.

Some people with CFRD try to avoid the need for *insulin*, so they limit their diet, sometimes severely. This is discouraged in the strongest possible terms. Insulin is a *hormone* that is needed to move glucose from your blood into your cells. In the absence of enough insulin, such as in CFRD, even though your blood glucose is high, the cells think they are starving because glucose cannot enter your cells. Therefore, a consequence of CFRD can be difficulty maintaining weight or experiencing unintentional weight loss. Insulin has another role in protein metabolism that contributes to difficulty maintaining weight and lean muscle mass when CFRD is uncontrolled. Not everyone with CFRD will require insulin, but you will need to work closely with an *endocrinologist* to see what is best for you. CFRD is different from *type 1* or *type 2 diabetes*. If you know someone with either of those types of diabetes, do not follow their diet or advice for managing your blood sugar. By taking your insulin regularly and by tightly controlling your blood sugars you can look forward to an easier time gaining muscle mass and achieving weight goals, with a positive effect on your lung health (Moran et al, 2014).

Should I Avoid Certain Foods?

There is no food so horrible that you can never consume it. Conversely, there is no food so wonderful that you need to eat it even though you do not enjoy it. There are some foods that people with CF commonly have concerns about eating in excess, but with some additional information, you might be able to allay those fears.

Dairy

Some people believe that they should avoid dairy products because dairy can increase their mucus production; however, research does not support this (Wuthrich et al, 2005; Thiara and Goldman, 2012). This myth might have started because when someone drinks milk, the *particulates* in it become trapped within saliva, creating the sensation of new mucus. Milk and milk products provide calcium, protein, phosphorous, iodine, vitamin A, vitamin D, riboflavin (vitamin B_2), and vitamin B_{12}. If milk products are unnecessarily excluded from your diet, it could make achieving adequate intake of these minerals and vitamins more difficult.

Fats

A common question is: "Can I eat too much fat?" Individuals who have PI do not digest and absorb fat normally. Even with pancreatic enzyme replacement medications (Creon®, ZenPEP®, and others), there will still be some loss of fat in the *stool*. In addition to *fat malabsorption*, there is an alteration in *fatty acid metabolism* in CF (Moukarzel et al, 2017). This means that we do not see changes in serum *triglycerides* and *cholesterol* normally expected after fat consumption. Therefore, there is no absolute restriction on the amount of fat that you should consume. Individuals with PI are encouraged to follow a diet with enough calories and fat to meet their weight goals. If a pancreatic-sufficient person is at normal weight or is overweight, the same guidelines exist for those with or without CF; eat a healthy diet without extra fat.

Sugar

Individuals with CF often need extra food in their daily diet to meet their calorie needs. Sometimes, people choose foods (e.g., candy, juices, desserts) with a high added-sugar content. Although these foods are not expressly excluded, consuming a large portion of your daily diet from foods with low *nutrient* value is not encouraged (Moran et al, 2014). If you can ingest enough servings of fruit and vegetables, whole grains, dairy, and protein, and still need more calories, you might add some additional "other foods," such as a dessert. Consider having these "other" foods within a meal rather than as snacks to minimize the impact on your appetite at the next meal. See special considerations for people with CFRD earlier in this chapter.

What Kind of Exercise Should I Do?

Exercise is an essential component to a healthy lifestyle for any individual. In people with CF, physical activity and exercise have been shown to promote improved quality of life, endurance, strength, posture, body image, and appetite; to delay the onset of osteoporosis; and to enhance airway clearance (Nixon et al, 1992; Bradley et al, 2008; O'Neil et al, 1983; Peebles, et al 1998; Wolman et al, 1999). In addition, individuals with CF report regular exercise and activity enhance their ability to perform essential and recreational activities throughout the day.

When choosing exercise, there are three different options to choose from: *aerobic exercise*, *resistance* or *strengthening exercise*, and *flexibility exercises*. Aerobic exercise uses large muscle groups for prolonged periods. Walking, biking, running, swimming and rowing are several examples of aerobic exercise. These exercises can be done over longer periods (greater than 15–20 minutes), or done in shorter intervals with frequent rests to accumulate those longer periods. The current aerobic exercise recommendation for both children and adults with CF is 30 to 60 minutes of moderate to vigorous activity per day for at least 150 minutes per week (Swisher et al, 2015; Nippins, 2014). Moderate to vigorous activity would be considered exercising at 70% or more of your maximal predicted heart rate (which can be approximated by subtracting your age from 220) over that period. This is well within the parameters of the current evidence to gain the benefits of exercise, especially the aforementioned airway clearance.

Resistance or strengthening exercises are exercises targeted to an individual muscle or group of muscles to increase their size and strength. Resistance training can use free weights, weight machines, resistance bands, or even one's own body weight to increase the size and strength of the targeted muscle. The current recommendation for children with CF for resistance training is to use any age-appropriate body-weighted activities, such as jumping, climbing ropes or trees, swinging on bars. In adolescents, teens, and adults with CF, formal resistance training is recommended two or more times per week and should include all major muscle groups (chest, back, core, upper and lower extremities) (Swisher et al 2015; Nippins, 2014). Resistance should be at least 70% of the weight at which you can perform only one repetition, or at an intensity that allows for one to three sets at 8 to 15 repetitions (Nippins, 2014). Resistance training can be combined in circuits (sequences done with little rest) to provide an aerobic benefit, as well.

Flexibility exercises are exercises to promote range of motion throughout the joints of the body. These can include stretching or yoga activities. Although there is no formal evidence or recommendation in people with CF, the American College of Sports Medicine recommends adolescents, teens, and adults perform stretching of all major muscle groups at least two times per week. Special attention should be paid to the muscles in the front of the chest such as the pectoralis major. These muscles tend to shorten and enlarge with chronic coughing over the lifespan of a person with CF. This can lead to a forward-slouched posture, which can negatively affect lung function and lead to musculoskeletal pain. Stretching of these muscles can prevent musculoskeletal pain from postural abnormalities over time while preserving your lung function.

Overall, the best types of exercise are those that are fun, engaging, and can be done with others. Try a variety of different types of exercise to find which one best suits you. The exercises should fit you, your lifestyle, and the equipment and facilities available to you. Use the recommendations given above (e.g., 150 minutes of aerobic activity per week, with resistance and flexibility training at least two times per week) as a guide. Unfortunately, there is no single exercise program that is right for everyone with CF. Some activity is better than no activity, and a moderate amount of activity is better than a little activity. Gradually increasing your activity level results in sustainable changes that tend to last longer than quick fixes. You and your health care team should determine what activities are best for you and your health status. Seek out your CF center's physical therapist or your pulmonologist for specifics of what might work best for you.

How Can CF Affect My Sleep?

Sleeping well is crucial for everyone. It facilitates mental and physical health and is essential for cell growth and repair. Disrupted sleep is common in those with CF, especially in those with a *forced expiratory volume in the first second* (FEV1) below 70% (Fauroux et al, 2012; Perin et al, 2012; Sawicki et al, 2008). Poor sleep also contributes to daytime sleepiness, decreased daytime performance, fatigue, alterations in mood and behavior, and changes in appetite and food choices (Edinger and Carney, 2015; Greer et al, 2013; Katz, 2014).

Having a low oxygen level *(hypoxemia)*, a higher carbon dioxide (CO_2) level *(hypercapnia/ hypercarbia)*, coughing, or difficulty breathing can cause you to wake up frequently and decrease the amount of deep, restorative, sleep. Although you can experience low oxygen levels during the day, these dips in oxygenation can and do worsen with sleep. Nocturnal low-oxygen levels commonly occur in those with an FEV1 less than 70% (Fauroux et al, 2012) and in those with daytime oxygen saturations less than 94% (Perin et al, 2012). *Obstructive sleep apnea* (OSA), which is characterized by recurrent pauses in breathing during sleep, is quite common in children with CF, whereas adults with CF experience these pauses less often (Katz, 2014). Among children (between 6 months and 11 years) with mild CF lung disease, 70% have at least mild symptoms of OSA (Spicuzza et al, 2012). Despite being clinically stable, children with CF sleep less and have poorer sleep quality than do other children.

Excessive worrying, spending too much time in bed, and napping frequently during the daytime can lead to *insomnia*, which is difficulty falling asleep, maintaining sleep, or waking up too early. For some individuals, there is a mismatch between when they feel sleepy (their "internal body clock") and when they are expected to sleep and wake. If this pattern persists and interferes with daytime functioning, a *circadian rhythm disorder* might be present.

What Can I Do to Improve My Sleep?

There are a lot of things you can do to improve your sleep. If you suspect that your sleep problems are related to physical causes (e.g., low oxygen levels, higher CO_2 levels, pauses in breathing at night), talk with your health care provider. They can recommend an *overnight sleep study* or *nocturnal oximetry* study. If a physical cause is found, your health care providers will often suggest a trial of using *supplemental oxygen* via a *nasal cannula* or *non-invasive ventilation* such as a *continuous positive airway pressure* (CPAP) or *bi-level positive airway pressure* (BiPAP) machine.

If physical causes of poor sleep are ruled out, making changes in your *sleep hygiene* might help. You can establish a bedtime routine to reduce pre-sleep worry and prepare for sleep. To do this, you can create a wind-down composed of relaxing activities, (e.g., reading a book, journaling, engaging in a deep-breathing exercise). Watching television or using electronics before bed can have the opposite effect and stimulate you just before you try to sleep. Be sure to wake up at the same time every day and to keep this schedule the same on weekends by avoiding the "stay up later, sleep in later" cycle. This can throw off your healthy sleep schedule during weekdays. Limit your time in bed to sleeping (and having sex). Engaging in other activities in bed such as watching television, planning, worrying, reading, working on your computer, or using other electronics can create unhelpful associations that train your body to do things other than sleep after you are in bed. If possible, also try to limit your daytime napping because it can reduce your body's natural drive to fall asleep at night. If you do take daytime naps regularly, adjust your nighttime sleep expectations accordingly.

There are several common drugs that you should avoid in the evening, including alcohol, caffeine, and nicotine. Even though alcohol can make you drowsy, it also fragments your sleep, resulting in less *restorative sleep* and morning grogginess. Caffeine and nicotine are stimulants, which can make it difficult to fall asleep. Drinking a cup of coffee many hours before bed can still cause you to be awake and alert late into the evening. Exercising regularly in the morning or in the late afternoon and eating well with foods rich in *tryptophan*, magnesium, calcium, and/or vitamin B_5 can promote good sleep.

There are many simple things that you can do to create a comfortable environment that helps you to fall and stay asleep. Keep your room dark by blocking out excess light with curtains or an eye mask. Noise can also interfere with sleep, so try to eliminate unnecessary sounds by using earplugs or "white noise" from a sound machine or fan. Try to make your bed as comfortable as possible, using an appropriately supportive mattress and pillow. Over time, mattresses become less supportive and may contribute to pain; if your mattress is more than 9 years old, consider replacing it with a newer one with more support. Lastly, try to expose yourself to natural light shortly after you wake up. Sunlight sends a signal to your brain to "turn off" *melatonin*, a natural hormone that promotes sleep, and to "turn on" wakefulness. If you are unable to access natural light (based on your living situation, time of year, or the time of day you are waking), you can use a special bright-light box designed to simulate natural light as an effective alternative.

It is important to recognize that changes in your sleep hygiene alone might not be effective if you are experiencing persistent insomnia, a circadian rhythm disorder, or having difficulties adhering to their non-invasive ventilation treatments. Instead, you might consider addressing underlying cognitive and behavioral causes for your poor sleep with a *behavioral sleep medicine specialist*. The therapist you select can use *evidence-based treatments* to improve your sleep, such as *Cognitive-Behavioral Therapy for Insomnia* (CBT-I), *chronotherapy* (in the case of circadian rhythm disorders), or CPAP/BiPAP desensitization to improve adherence. They will provide you with tools to measure and track your sleep and create an individualized plan to achieve better sleep. They can also help address underlying worries, concerns, and fears that might get in the way of sleep.

How Can I Learn to Clear Secretions from My Lungs?

We all make mucus to protect against dirt, dust, debris, and germs reaching the furthest parts of our lungs. Mucus—secretions that are retained in the lungs—can cause airway obstruction and airway injury in CF. Clearing secretions is vital to maintaining your health and lung function, and people with CF should perform regular *airway clearance* to help mobilize and expectorate these secretions.

Various *airway clearance techniques* are available for people with CF. Currently, no strong evidence supports one method over another, but there is strong evidence suggesting that all of these forms of airway clearance have significant benefits (Wilson et al, 2019). These techniques differ in terms of their need for assistance or equipment, time, and cost. The most appropriate method of airway clearance varies from person-to-person and from situation to situation. It is often advantageous to learn about and try multiple techniques so that you can find something that works best for you and that fits your lifestyle. Your airway clearance method works only if you are willing and able to do it regularly and properly.

Studies have found that adherence to regular airway clearance in those with mild lung disease is poor, but it is difficult for everyone regardless of their lung function (Oermann et al, 2000). Ideally, finding the technique that fits easily into your day and that is most productive in removing secretions from your lungs will result in improved utilization of airway clearance. The following subsections present an overview of various airway clearance techniques used in CF. Table 6-1 provides a comparison of these techniques and devices, including a description of the activity, the time required to perform it, and the estimated cost of the required devices.

Table 6-1: Comparison of Different Airway Clearance Techniques

Airway Clearance Technique	Description/Mechanism of Action	Time Required	Cost Range
Percussion and *vibration* in postural drainage positions i.e., traditional *chest physical therapy*	Percussion is a technique of clapping the chest wall. Vibration applies shaking of the chest wall usually during exhalation. Percussion and vibration can be done in postural drainage positions.	30–60 minutes	No cost if done by a family member
Forced expiratory technique (FET)	Sometimes called huff coughing and consists of 1–2 huffs from mid-to-low lung volumes with the back of the throat open. This is followed by relaxed *diaphragmatic breathing*.	2–5 minutes	No cost
Active cycle of breathing techniques (ACBT)	This technique includes *breathing control, thoracic expansion exercises* and forced expiratory technique. Can be combined with PEP device or percussion and vibration.	10–45 minutes	No cost
Positive expiratory pressure (PEP)	This technique uses a device that you breathe out through against a pressure of 10–20 cm H_2O.	10–25 minutes	$25–45
Airway oscillating device (oscillatory PEP)	This technique uses a pneumatic, oscillating positive expiratory pressure device that you breathe out through.	10–25 minutes	$35–85

Cough

None of the forms of airway clearance covered in this chapter will be effective without a strong cough. Although the other forms of airway clearance work to mobilize mucus more centrally out of the smaller airways, the cough clears the central larger airways including the *trachea* (Button and Button, 2013). This is why no form of airway clearance is effective without a good cough.

An effective cough consists of three phases:

1. Deep inhalation.

2. Closure of the back of the throat, or *glottis*, with contraction of the abdominal muscles. This results in an increase in *intrathoracic pressure*. This phase can be lengthened with a 3-second breath hold to allow air to get behind any secretions.

3. Upon re-opening of the glottis, air will flow out more quickly helping to shear mucus from the outer airways inward and subsequently out (Irwin and Tecklin, 2004).

An effective cough requires a delicate balance between having enough force to mobilize secretions and not creating too much airway irritation and *bronchospasm*. One way to increase the force of your cough is to lean slightly forward, with your forearms supported on a table. This will allow you to use your chest muscles to help produce a more forceful cough.

Percussion and Vibration in Postural Drainage Positions

Traditionally referred to as *Chest Physical Therapy* (CPT), *percussion* and *vibration* is performed by an individual trained in the technique. To take advantage of gravity, percussion and vibration are performed in different positions with the area of the lungs being cleared being most upright. Percussion involves clapping the chest wall with a cupped hand for 2 to 5 minutes in different areas of the chest then immediately followed by vibration or shaking of the chest wall during exhalation. Percussion and vibration of the chest wall loosen accumulated secretions and help to move them to more central airways before coughing to clear them (Irwin and Tecklin, 2004). A health care provider (e.g., *physical therapist*, *respiratory therapist*, nurse) can perform this technique or a family member or caregiver can be trained to do this at home. This technique can be time and effort intensive because it requires the assistance of another person. You can find a more detailed description with pictures on the CF Foundation website (https://www.cff.org/Life-With-CF/Treatments-and-Therapies/Airway-Clearance/Chest-Physical-Therapy/).

Forced Expiratory Technique

The *forced expiratory technique* (FET), also known as *huff coughing*, consists of high-velocity airflow with an open *glottis* to move mucus from the smaller peripheral airways up to the larger, more central ones. This allows you to clear more secretions, with less effort, when followed with a good cough.

To perform this technique, you first take in a medium-sized breath, then tighten the abdominal muscles firmly while *huffing* (forcefully expiring while keeping the back of the throat (and glottis) open. This can be performed by making an "H" sound in the back of the throat, as if you were fogging a mirror. The huff should be maintained long enough to mobilize secretions without triggering a *spasmodic cough*. It is then important to follow this with relaxed *diaphragmatic breathing* for 15 to 30 seconds followed by another one to two huffs. This period of relaxed breathing allows mucus to move to the larger, uppermost airways, where a huff or cough should expel the mucus (Irwin and Tecklin, 2004).

Active Cycle of Breathing

Active cycle of breathing techniques (ACBT) can be used independently or in combination with other techniques. ACBT has three phases:

1. Breathing techniques to relax the airways.

2. Thoracic expansion to get air behind mucus and to mobilize the secretions.

3. FET to help get the mucus out of your lungs.

You should do the first phase in a relaxed and supported position, such as sitting in a chair or lying propped up on pillows. You should breathe in easily through your nose and breathe out through your mouth. Be sure to relax your upper chest wall and shoulders while focusing on breathing gently through your lower chest. You can do this by placing your hand on your abdomen and focusing on gently raising it when you inhale. Then, exhale fully through pursed-lips (like blowing out birthday candles); this helps to splint open the airways, thereby allowing more air to flow out. This phase relaxes your airways and opens them. Repeat this for 30 to 90 seconds before moving on to the *thoracic expansion exercises* (TEE).

In this second phase, you utilize thoracic expansion exercises to get air behind the mucus; this is followed by a return to breathing control to mobilize that mucus. To perform thoracic expansion exercises, start by taking a deep breath, then follow that with a 2- to 3-second breath hold. This breath hold allows air to move behind the mucus. You then want to breathe out slowly without forcing out air. You can do this phase in conjunction with manual or mechanical percussion and vibration. You might also include chest expansion exercises during this second phase. This phase loosens the secretions and it is followed by another round of relaxed breathing before moving onto the third and final phase.

The third phase is the forced expiratory technique described earlier, which helps to clear the mobilized secretions. A full breathing cycle with this technique begins with *breathing control* (BC) followed by TEE, a return to BC, and then the FET. The active cycle of this breathing pattern can be modified to include an additional round of TEE to help mobilize more secretions before clearing them with the FET. Figure 6-1 illustrates both patterns. One of the main benefits of this technique is that it does not require any assistance or a device. This means that you can do it anywhere and anytime that you feel the need to mobilize secretions.

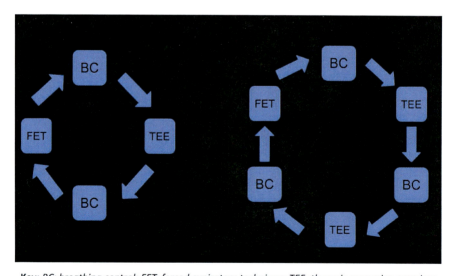

Key: *BC: breathing control; FET: forced expiratory technique; TEE: thoracic expansion exercises*

Figure 6-1: The active cycle of breathing.

Positive Expiratory Pressure

Positive expiratory pressure (PEP) involves exhaling through a device via a mask or a mouthpiece against pressures of 10 cm to 25 cm H_2O. Breathing out against this slight resistance both dislodges the secretions and splints the smaller airways open, which prevents collapse and allows more mucus to be mobilized centrally (McIlwaine et al, 2013). A PEP device has adjustable resistance to help achieve the 10 to 25 cm H_2O of pressure. A breath hold of 2 to 3 seconds after inhalation and before blowing it out through the device helps air get behind mucus to further mobilize secretions. A cycle of 10 to 20 breaths with the PEP device is then followed by the FET and cough to clear the mobilized secretions. Typically, you perform this technique while sitting, but you also can do it in postural drainage positions. There are many different PEP devices on the market; some can be combined with a nebulizer via facemask or mouthpiece, which allows you to use your nebulized medicines at the same time as airway clearance.

Airway Oscillating Device

An airway oscillating device (oscillatory PEP) works in a fashion similar to the PEP device, with the addition of a vibratory force. When exhaling through the device, the oscillatory force vibrates the airway walls, which helps to loosen secretions. This adds to the benefits of the PEP device. The same sequence is used for the oscillatory PEP device as for the regular PEP: 5 to 20 breaths with a 2- to 3-second hold and exhalation through the device followed by the FET and cough. The most common oscillatory PEP devices are the *Acapella®*, *Aerobika®*, and the *Flutter device®*. Only the Flutter® device is position dependent and needs to be done in an upright position. You can use the Acapella® and Aerobika® in postural drainage positions as well as upright (Morrison and Agnew, 2009).

Autogenic Drainage

Autogenic drainage (AD) means "self-drainage," and it involves a series of breathing techniques at different lung volumes to mobilize mucus. Progressing from breathing at low lung volumes to higher lung volumes facilitates movement of the mucus from the deep peripheral airways to the larger central airways. Because this is a progressive technique, it is important to hold coughing until you complete the entire sequence. This is broken down into three phases: the unsticking phase, the collection phase, and the evacuation phase, which you should repeat until all secretions are cleared (approximately 20 to 45 minutes).

Let's take a closer look at each phase:

Unsticking

Moves secretions from the small airways:

1. Start with relaxed breathing.
2. Take a large breath and breathe all the air out of your lungs.
3. When there is no air left, take a small, 1-second breath through your nose.

4.   Hold for 3 seconds and then exhale.

5.   Repeat two times.

Collection

Moves secretions along to the medium airways:

1.   Take a medium 2-second breath through your nose.

2.   Hold for 3 seconds and exhale fully.

3.   Repeat three times.

Evacuation

Moves secretions along to the large airways and then coughs them out:

1.   Take a large 3-second breath through your nose.

2.   Hold for 3 seconds and exhale fully.

3.   Repeat 3 times and do not cough until the third breath.

4.   Perform a strong huff and cough to clear the secretions.

You can customize the number of breaths in each phase and the number of cycles, based on the location of your secretions and your lung function at a given time (Lapin, 2012). You can work with a *respiratory therapist* or *physical therapist* to determine the correct number of breaths and cycles for you. Figure 6-2 demonstrates this technique in further detail.

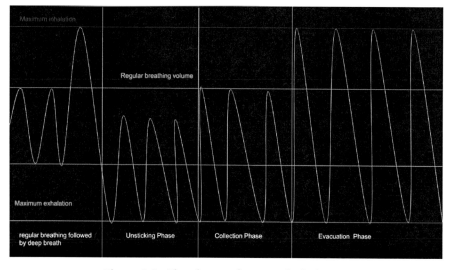

Figure 6-2: The phases of autogenic drainage.

High-Frequency Chest-Wall Oscillation

High-frequency chest-wall oscillation (HFCWO) or *"vest" therapy* consists of wearing a vest that inflates and provides external chest-wall compressions and vibration. The increased pressure on your chest wall causes an increase in the flow of air out when you exhale, and the vibration creates shearing forces that help shake mucus from the lining of the airways (Fink and Mahlmeister, 2002). There are multiple brands of HFCWO devices on the market, and settings for the devices are specific to each manufacturer. In general, you will want to progress from lower to higher frequencies while adjusting the pressure to your comfort. It is essential to pause the device every 3 to 5 minutes to perform a huff cough to clear any secretions that are mobilized; treatment times vary from 15 to 30 minutes and are conducted one to two times per day. This strategy is frequently referred to the Minnesota Protocol (Kempainen et al, 2007). To decrease treatment burden, HFCWO devices can be used with nebulizer treatments.

How Can I Cut Down or Stop Drinking Alcohol and Smoking Cigarettes?

Tobacco

Smoking cigarettes is an unhealthy behavior for everyone, but those living with CF are particularly vulnerable to its adverse effects. It is estimated that about 3% of all individuals with CF smoke; that compares favorably to the 17% of all Americans who smoke (CF Foundation Patient Registry, 2017). Smoking is harmful because it decreases lung function, increases the rate of decline of lung function, increases sputum production, and leads to respiratory infections. Those who are exposed to second-hand smoke at home are more likely to be hospitalized and to have lower lung function than those who are not (Hassanzad et al, 2018).

Quitting smoking can be difficult; fortunately, there are many proven therapies that can help you quit. Studies have shown that *nicotine replacement therapy*, such as patches, gums, and lozenges, all have high rates of success, especially when combined with counseling (Rigotti et al, 2013). Nicotine replacement products are widely available and are easily purchased without a prescription. There are also *prescription medications* that can help you to quit smoking. These include *varenicline (Chantix®)*, *bupropion (Zyban®)*, and *nortriptyline*. Because these medications have the potential to cause side effects and interact with other medications, it is important to speak with your doctor and to let your CF team know whether you are taking these. Non-pharmacologic methods include *cognitive-behavioral therapy* (CBT) and *motivational interviewing*. We cover these topics in more depth in the upcoming section on alcohol misuse treatments.

Before you attempt to quit smoking, you should do an inventory of how you are feeling about quitting. If you seek the assistance of a medical, mental health, or social work professional, they might find it helpful to identify at which *stage of change* you are to help motivate you along the path to quitting (Diclemente et al, 1991).

Here are those stages:

Pre-contemplation

Unaware or unwilling to quit. At this stage, you might be asked to identify how you feel about your smoking or identify the pros and cons of continuing.

Contemplation

Ambivalent but considering quitting in the next 6 months. You might be asked to identify why you want to quit and what is making you continue.

Preparation

Getting ready to quit in the next 30 days. At this stage, you might need help to identify the method you would like to use to assist you in quitting and help identifying barriers to quitting.

Action

You have begun your quit attempt. You might need motivation and encouragement to continue.

Maintenance

You have successfully stopped smoking and need assistance and encouragement to continue to refrain from smoking.

Regardless of which technique you choose to help you quit and where you are in the stages-of-change model, keep in mind it often takes people three to four quit attempts before they are successful at stopping smoking. There is no need to be hard on yourself. The more you try, the more successful you are going to be.

E-cigarettes and vapes have been growing in popularity; almost 12% of all teenagers have tried *vaping* by the time they graduate from high school (Wang et al, 2018). There have been studies suggesting that when combined with counseling, e-cigarettes can be effective for quitting smoking (Hajek et al, 2019). This can lead to confusion about the actual health effects of e-cigarettes. The liquid in e-cigarettes contains trace amounts of lead and benzene, toxins that can reduce lung function, damage the cells that line the lung, and increase your cancer risk (Canistro et al, 2017). There is also evidence that common e-cigarette brands contain small amounts of fungal and bacterial material as well as toxic aldehydes, which can have adverse effects on your lung function (Lee et al, 2019; Klager et al, 2017).

Alcohol

Although alcohol use is common, excessive consumption that interferes with your daily life and obligations is a major problem. Alcohol use can also negatively affect your adherence to your daily CF treatments (Weitzman et al, 2015). To see how significant your drinking is, you can ask yourself the following questions:

- "Do I drink more or longer than I intend to?"
- "Have I tried to cut back or stop but can't?"
- "How much time am I spending drinking or thinking about my next drink?"
- "Is my drinking causing trouble with my friends and family?"
- "Is my drinking causing problems taking care of my health, school, or work?"
- "Do I ever crave or just need a drink?"
- "Has my drinking made me feel depressed or anxious?"
- "Have I ever blacked out? Have I ever done anything dangerous while I have been drinking?"
- "Have I ever felt anxious, depressed, agitated, nauseous, or shaky when I stop drinking?"

If you answered yes to two or more of these questions, you might have a problem with alcohol, also known as *alcohol use disorder* (American Psychiatric Association, 2013). Seeking professional help is essential for dealing with this issue. Treatments include various forms of counseling as well as several pharmacologic options. Behavior treatments include the following:

CBT

This involves a therapist who can help you to identify the emotional and physical feelings that precede the decision to drink and help you to build alternative behaviors for coping (Laude et al, 2017).

Motivational interviewing and intervention

During this treatment, a counselor assists you to identify a list of pros and cons of your drinking and desire to stopping drinking, to help you create a plan for cutting back or maintaining abstinence (Engle et al, 2019).

Pharmacologic options

This includes the use of *naltrexone*, which can decrease the amount of alcohol consumed and prevent a return to heavy drinking; *disulfiram (Antabuse®)*, which induces nausea and vomiting when you drink alcohol, and *acamprosate*, which helps to continue abstinence (Akbar et al, 2018).

Regardless of the treatment methods you use, it is important to seek the help of your physicians and support systems and to remind yourself that achieving abstinence or control of your drinking is a process with ups and downs. Change will not come instantly; however, with the help of others and persistence many people change their habits for the better.

Should I Stop Smoking Cannabis? (and Other Drugs?)

In recent years, many states have passed laws establishing the use of *medical marijuana*, decriminalizing its use, establishing legal recreational use and creating sanctioned dispensaries. This trend in public policy and attitudes can send a confusing message about what is healthy, especially for people living with CF. The health effects of cannabis for those with CF are unknown. It is recommended that, just as with tobacco, everyone with CF should refrain from smoking marijuana or any other drug due to potential harm to the lungs (Tetrault et al, 2007). In addition, marijuana carries the risk of invasive infection from the *fungus aspergillus* and can cause severe asthma-like complications (Verwejj et al, 2000).

A survey-based study of patients with obstructive lung disease showed more symptoms of cough, mucus production, and chest tightness in those who smoke both marijuana and tobacco compared to those who smoke only tobacco, but no additional symptoms in those who smoke only marijuana compared to non-smokers (Tan et al, 2009). However, people included in this and similar studies had only mild reductions in FEV1 (Tan et al, 2009), or were from the general population (Kemper et al, 2014), so the findings could be different for many individuals with CF.

Should I Use Edible Cannabis?

People who use edible marijuana (i.e., *edibles*) cite the effect on *anxiety* and relaxation as a major reason for its use, but also frequently complain about the duration and unpredictable intensity of the high as a downside to its use (Giombi et al, 2018). One thing to consider is that the dosing of *tetrahydrocannabinol* (THC) in various cannabis products is inconsistent and is often found in greater quantities than expected. There is no data to inform the long-term health effects of these high doses of THC (Steigerwald et al, 2018); however, some of the complications of marijuana use include impaired driving, withdrawal symptoms (e.g., agitation, insomnia, restlessness, anxiety), as well the possibility for overdose, especially in children (Sachs et al, 2015). In addition, there is concerning evidence that using cannabis, especially in larger amounts, is associated with development of *psychotic symptoms* (i.e., having beliefs that are not true, experiencing *hallucinations*, and having problems with logical thinking) (Marconi et al, 2016).

Marijuana is often viewed as an appetite stimulant and anti-nausea agent, which could improve the quality of life of many people with CF who struggle with maintaining their weight. Unfortunately, frequent use is associated with the development of *hyperemesis syndrome*, a condition of frequent and uncontrollable nausea and vomiting. It is important to remember that there are prescription versions of THC (e.g., dronabinol, nabilone) that have been approved by the United States Food and Drug Administration (FDA) to treat these very symptoms and they have been studied to treat *cannabis use disorder* (Levin et al, 2015).

WHICH TYPES OF PROVIDERS CAN HELP ME WITH MY CF?

Gabriela R. Oates, PhD; Kathryn A. Sabadosa, MPH;
Kathleen Quinn Porco, MS; and Cathy Mims, MS-HQS, BSN

CHAPTER 7

In This Chapter

- Do I Need a Specialized Center to Manage My CF?

- What Might a CF Center Expect from Me?

- Who Is on a Multidisciplinary CF Team and What Are Their Roles?

- What Other Types of Medical Specialists Might I Be Referred to?

- How Can I Improve Communication with My CF Team?

- Should I Anticipate That My Health Care Team and I Will Engage in Shared Decision Making?

- What Is It Like to Transition from a Pediatric CF Center to an Adult Center?

- How Can I Prepare for Transitions in My Health Care Team?

Do I Need a Specialized Center to Manage My CF?

Cystic fibrosis (CF) is a complex condition that affects multiple organs and systems, so it is best for you to receive care at a specialized CF center where you will be treated by a team of experts trained in different specialties. In the United States, such specialized disease management is provided at CF centers accredited by the *Cystic Fibrosis Foundation (CF Foundation)*. To maintain accreditation, each center undergoes an annual review and periodic re-accreditation visits to ensure that high standards of care are implemented. Currently there are more than 120 accredited CF centers and 50 affiliate programs at teaching and community hospitals across the country. To find the one closest to you, you can visit the CF Foundation's website for an up-to-date listing at https://www.cff.org/Care/Care-Centers.

An accredited CF center follows standards of care that are based on the latest research, medical evidence, and consultation with experts. There are age-specific standards of care for infants (Borowitz et al, 2009), preschoolers (Lahiri et al, 2016), school-aged children, adolescents, and adults with CF (Yankaskas et al, 2004). There are also evidence-based guidelines for CF diagnosis (Farrell et al, 2017), infection prevention (Saiman et al, 2014), treatment of pulmonary exacerbations (Flume et al, 2009a), respiratory care (Mogayzel et al, 2013; Flume et al, 2009b), nutrition (Stallings et al, 2008), *CF-related diabetes* (CFRD) (Moran et al, 2010), and mental health care (Quittner et al, 2016), among others. Accredited CF care centers follow guidelines for routine monitoring of lab values and *pulmonary function testing* (PFT), and have requirements for *sweat testing*, *imaging*, and *microbiology tests*. An accredited CF center is required to have a transition plan for moving individuals with CF from pediatric to adult care and a referral plan for transplantation services.

Accredited CF centers participate in clinical research to improve CF treatments and to find a cure for the disease, and help educate doctors, nurses, and health care teams about CF care. Collaboration among centers in the CF center network allows CF teams to learn from one another and optimize care through quality improvement endeavors. Accredited centers also participate in the *CF Foundation Patient Registry*, which follows the health of people with CF who agree to share their information to improve CF care. To receive the best possible CF care, you should attend an accredited CF center even if you must travel to get there.

What Might a CF Center Expect from Me?

You will be asked to visit your CF center at least four times per year, and more often if necessary. During these visits, your CF care team will work with you to develop or to revise your treatment plan and to monitor your health. You will be asked to do pulmonary function tests (PFTs), give sputum samples, or do other tests. These tests can detect germs in your lungs, small decreases in lung function, or other health problems before you can feel them.

As an individual with CF or as a parent of a child with CF, you are an integral component of the CF care team. You will be expected to follow treatment recommendations and report honestly if these recommendations are not being met. Transparency is essential for optimal care. For example, if you report that your child is not seeing much improvement from *antibiotics*, but he or she is doing only two out of three prescribed doses per day (and the team does not know this), their doctor might assume that the antibiotics are not working and look into more aggressive next steps. This confusion can be easily prevented by acknowledging that your child was not following the recommendations. Similarly, your team cannot offer you tips for keeping up with treatments if they do not know that a specific treatment is a hurdle for your family. To achieve the best possible outcomes, it is vital to be forthcoming about your needs and limitations.

The team sees your child with CF only a few times each year, so it's important that you describe your child's *symptoms* accurately and honestly. Remember that your CF clinic is most effective in making recommendations when the care team knows the complete picture. The team will rely on you as a caregiver to provide information about the nuances of your child's life and your observations and concerns. Living with a disease as multifaceted as CF often puts parents in a position to question their own judgment or to feel like a burden to their care team. The truth is, your team wants you to communicate your concerns with it. If you are not reaching out to the team, the team members will assume that all is well.

When you reach out to the team, try to be as specific as possible and withhold emotions from your description; for example, "My child is experiencing an increase in coughing. It is wet and productive (or dry and hoarse). She has woken up due to coughing twice this week. She seems lethargic and is struggling when exercising. Her appetite is definitely decreased from her normal." Clinicians know how to respond to that information. Offering that your child "seems sick" does not paint a detailed picture for the team to make a specific recommendation. Above all, remember that you and the clinicians are a team and your hoped-for outcomes are the same—the best health for your child.

Who Is on a Multidisciplinary CF Team and What Are Their Roles?

The core members of a multidisciplinary CF team include a *pulmonologist*, a nurse, a *registered dietitian* (RD), a *respiratory therapist* (RT), and a *social worker*. A *mental health coordinator*, a *pharmacist*, a *physical therapist* (PT), and a *psychologist* or *psychiatrist* might also be part of the team. Because CF care should be age appropriate, the team is either pediatric or adult focused. Although the roles of team members can vary from center to center, there are common roles, which we describe in the following paragraphs.

The pulmonologist is responsible for physical exams, review of lab results and imaging tests, and providing care during routine visits, sick visits, and hospital admissions. The pulmonologist is also responsible for *bronchoscopy* procedures and interpretation of PFTs. The pulmonologist recommends treatments and prescribes medications.

The *CF nurse* works closely with the pulmonologist and might be responsible for coordinating labs and tests, implementing treatment protocols, and educating the patient and their family about CF care. The nurse might also serve as the CF center coordinator who works with the team to ensure that guidelines are followed to maintain CF center accreditation. The nurse is typically the point of contact at the CF center, taking patient calls regarding changes in symptoms or exacerbations that require intervention. The nurse will then coordinate a treatment plan with the pulmonologist and other team members.

The RD is responsible for dietary guidance and education, to ensure that you receive the proper caloric, protein, vitamin, and mineral content in your diet. The dietitian works closely with the pulmonologist to provide adequate enzyme dosing and to assess and treat GI manifestations and endocrine complications.

The RT is another very important member of the multidisciplinary team. The RT has expertise in PFTs and coaching, inhaled medications and delivery systems, *airway clearance techniques* and devices, and the proper cleaning and care of equipment. The RT evaluates the effectiveness of respiratory therapies and techniques and educates the individual with CF and their family about respiratory care.

The social worker is an integral part of the CF team. They provide access to resources, coordinate services to help with the financial and legal aspects of living with a chronic illness, assess the psychological impact of the disease on the patient and their family, help with parenting issues, and promote self-management and quality of life.

A mental health coordinator (MHC) can complement the CF social worker by screening individuals with CF for depression and *anxiety* and providing counseling services or referrals to appropriate services. MHCs can be a social worker, a nurse, or a nurse practitioner, a psychologist, or a psychiatrist. In some centers, MHCs might recommend or refer to a psychologist or psychiatrist for needs not met by the MHC within the CF center.

A pharmacist with experience in CF care is a recommended member of the multidisciplinary team. To ensure safe, appropriate, and cost-effective medication therapy, the pharmacist obtains an accurate medication history, provides drug information, and offers adherence counseling. The pharmacist also monitors drug levels for certain medications. For inpatient care, the pharmacist also makes recommendations for drug dosing and management of therapeutic drug levels.

A PT is another recommended member of the CF team. The PT can provide useful assessment of the *musculoskeletal, cardiovascular,* and *pulmonary systems,* including muscle fitness, balance and coordination, and *aerobic capacity.* The PT can coach individuals with CF regarding posture, exercise, and physical activity to improve their outcomes and overall physical health.

What Other Types of Medical Specialists Might I Be Referred to?

You might be referred to specialists outside of the CF care center. For example, adults with CF might face a bevy of challenges (such as fertility issues, problems with bone health, CFRD, increased risk of colorectal cancer, or challenges with balancing work, life, and chronic illness). The most frequent referrals are to an *otorhinolaryngologist* (an ear, nose, and throat doctor) to help diagnose and manage sinus problems. An *endocrinologist* can help treat CF-related endocrine issues, such as delayed growth or CFRD. A *gastroenterologist* is called to diagnose and treat stomach, *pancreatic,* or *liver* problems. Other medical specialists that might provide care or consultation for people with CF include *allergists* and *immunologists, geneticists* or *genetic counselors, infectious disease specialists, obstetricians/gynecologists, radiologists,* and various types of *surgeons.*

How Can I Improve Communication with My CF Team?

When you begin receiving care at a CF center, talk to your team about communicating with it between visits. Discuss when you should contact team members; for example, should you call when your child has a cold, when there is an increase in cough, when you hear about a new potential therapy? Determine which practitioner is your point of contact, and find out their preferred method of communication—should you call them or can you use email, instead? Be sure to know the protocol for weekends, after-hours, and acute situations, as well. Find out how soon after you have contacted your team it is reasonable to expect a response, and what to do if you have not heard from the team in that time. Ensure that your CF center has current contact information for you, including mailing address and phone numbers. It is important to have handy the contact information for your preferred pharmacy, as well.

Before a clinic visit, you might want to make a list of questions or concerns that you would like addressed during the visit. This will help your team to provide care that is timely and personally relevant. It is also helpful to keep track of your symptoms and CF-related observations between visits so that you can give your team accurate information about your health status and help it to make best treatment recommendations. It is important to be honest and forthcoming: if you have difficult time doing your treatments, taking your medicines, exercising, or following a diet, it is best to tell your team so it can work with you to find a better solution. A problem not communicated is a problem not resolved, so make sure to bring up all the concerns that you have, even if they might not seem all that important.

Do not hesitate to ask as many questions as you need. If in doubt, repeat back to your practitioner what you think they told you to make sure your understanding is correct and clarify any potential misunderstandings. If your center does not provide a written treatment plan or summary of recommendations, ask for one at the end of your visit. Then, make sure to follow it, and also bring it with you to your next visit.

Finally, teams are like families: there are a lot of individuals involved, and a lot of personalities. It is not possible for everyone to be a perfect fit, but it is critical to understand how to work together. If you have a strong personality conflict with a member of the team, let another team member know that you do not work well together, and ask how to resolve this for the best interest of you or your child.

Should I Anticipate That My Health Care Team and I Will Engage in Shared Decision Making?

If you are a person with CF, the care team relies on your first-hand experience with your symptoms, side effects, and overall well-being. If you are a parent of a child with CF, the team relies on your caregiver expertise. In both cases, the team needs to know about your personal goals and limitations so that it can recommend treatments that align well with your preferences and you are more likely to follow. This is only possible through a process of shared decision making. There are times when the next step, such as a hospital admission, is clear. There will be other times when the situation is a little more nuanced, and you might play a larger role in the decision-making process.

On the occasion when the care team feels strongly about proceeding with a specific plan, its decision is supported by either clinical experience or research evidence. If the recommendation is not in alignment with your vision, be sure to engage in a partnering dialogue. You are an advocate for yourself and a voice for your child. Feel confident to ask to see the study results or to hear about the clinical experience that is guiding them.

Sometimes in the CF journey you will be faced with making decisions or accepting recommendations that require you to be stronger than you can imagine possible. If you meet these moments with receptiveness and in a collaborative spirit, you will find support and reassurance in working together with your team to develop a plan rather than feeling that you are on the opposite sides of a decision. You hold the power to make the decisions for yourself or your child, but your team is your best resource for making these decisions. Forging a partnership with your team is the best policy for your or your child's health and longevity.

What Is It Like to Transition from a Pediatric CF Center to an Adult Center?

Transitioning from a pediatric to an adult CF center is a lot like moving—you need a good checklist, people to help you pack and transport your stuff, time to say goodbye to old friends, and the courage and confidence to meet new ones. At the top of your checklist is finding an adult center that would be a good fit for what is most important in your life. For example, if going off to college is the goal, you should start a conversation in your high school years with your team about striking the right balance; for example, how much should CF care dictate your college options? Should you visit schools and centers at the same time so that you can meet potential CF teams as you tour prospective college campuses? Should you stay close to your current center or consider places further away where you might need to navigate care on your own? Making these decisions can take several months and many family conversations, sifting through online resources, and talking to a lot of people, including others with CF, their families, and CF clinicians.

The rest of the checklist will also take time. Some of the tasks that you will need to complete include signing proxies to access records, creating new electronic medical record accounts, navigating insurance coverage, and setting up medication deliveries. Typically, your pediatric CF center will provide a transfer packet to your receiving adult center. This packet should include a letter of introduction with a summary of your current state of health as well as your summary report from the CF registry, confirmation of diagnosis including sweat test results and genetics report, your last hospital discharge summary with your *aminoglycoside* dose, your last clinic note, your current medication list, your last annual lab results, your last imaging reports (*DEXA scans*, liver *ultrasound*, chest and sinus scans), your last operative notes from bronchoscopy or sinus surgery, your last hearing screen, your last multidisciplinary notes, your PFTs for the past year, and results of your past 3 years of sputum culture results. Most centers will offer a tour of the transitioning facility and an opportunity to meet some members of the adult team before the transition.

For a smooth care transition, you can use the help of the program coordinators at both your current pediatric and your future adult center. You can reach out to the adult care coordinator and ask what would be helpful for their team to have for your first visit. You can then relay this information to your pediatric team and exchange contact information between all parties. If you have cultivated a trusting relationship with your pediatric team, it can provide to the adult team not only the necessary medical information but also make personally relevant care recommendations. It can be difficult to say goodbye to your pediatric team as you transition to adult care. But if you had put time into the first item on our check list—the people to help you—you or your child will have the courage and confidence to build a similar relationship with your adult team.

How Can I Prepare for Transitions in My Health Care Team?

To prepare for transitions in health care, several items are critical: knowledge, self-care skills, awareness of your preferences and values, and practice of behaviors that convey confidence. Even though health professionals have many opportunities to share their knowledge about CF during clinical encounters, you as a parent or an individual with CF might need to establish your own authority as an expert in your disease. You need to know how medications work and why it is important to do your therapies, to maintain your weight, and exercise, and to lead a healthy lifestyle. Being knowledgeable about your disease will boost your or your child's confidence, allowing you or your child to connect with the care team on a level playing field.

Skill-building from an early but appropriate age will prepare your child for the transition. You can do much of this through games and role playing. You can role-play checking into the clinic: asking your child for their name, date of birth, and home phone number. Through elementary and middle school, you can use the same approach to teach your child how to sterilize *nebulizers*, keep a calendar for appointments, and refill medications. You can make treatments and exercise a family activity to help build daily habits and routines in your child.

With any transition, it is important to know what matters to you and not to lose sight of that as you go through the process. It will take time to adjust to a new setting and new care team, and it is natural to experience pauses or to miss old connections as you form new relationships. Knowing your values and preferences and sharing them honestly with your new care team will build stronger care connections.

Just as it is important for parents to advocate for their child, it is equally important that they encourage their child to use their own voice and to advocate for themselves. This experience will help your child develop confidence and take the lead when interacting with their team. As a young adult, they will be equipped to approach transitions with confidence in their knowledge and self-care and their ability to speak up about what matters to them.

In addition to independence, other developmental milestones that help adolescents transition smoothly to adult care include knowledge of nutritional challenges and changes during the transition to young adulthood, knowledge of airway clearance techniques and how to incorporate them into a new routine, knowledge of reproductive issues associated with CF, and an understanding if insurance changes and challenges during the transition years. There is also the realization that the adult care center will likely not be as aesthetically pleasing as the pediatric center. CF centers can offer varying degrees of support for adolescents to meet these milestones, but you can help your own transition to adult care if you work toward this goal with the help of your family and others close to you.

HOW CAN I MANAGE MY CF CARE?

Christopher M. Kvam, JD, MPP and Gregory S. Sawicki, MD, MPH

CHAPTER

In This Chapter

- Introduction
- Why Is It So Difficult to Keep Up with My CF Treatments?
- How Can I Improve My Support Systems and Know When to Ask for Help?
- How Can I Enhance My Ability to Care for Myself?
- What Might I Expect If I Am Admitted to the Hospital?
- How Can I Pay for My Treatments?

Introduction

Overall, treatments for cystic fibrosis (CF) can be quite complex and burdensome. In this context, sustaining daily care regimens can be challenging. In this chapter, we discuss the reasons for treatment complexity and identify strategies that people with CF can adopt to help manage their daily care. We discuss how people with CF can maintain and develop support systems within their families, peer groups, and communities, and discuss ways to improve relationships that people with CF have with their clinical care teams. Finally, we describe the challenges and options related to health insurance and access to high-quality care for your CF.

Why Is It So Difficult to Keep Up with My CF Treatments?

Fundamentally, treatments for CF focus on the range of issues (e.g., *inflammation*, thick mucus, and chronic infections of your sinuses, airways and lungs, gastrointestinal [GI] tract, and reproductive tract) that stem from dysfunction of the *cystic fibrosis transmembrane conductance regulator* (CFTR) *protein*. As a result, the complexity of chronic therapy, particularly the time burden of daily care, is quite high (Sawicki and Tiddens, 2012). Not a day goes by that a person with CF does not have at least some treatments to complete. Even on a good day, it can be difficult to keep up with daily treatments.

For your airways, treatments include use of *bronchodilators*, *mucolytics*, *airway hydrators*, and *anti-inflammatories*. These therapies are generally prescribed in combination, and often with airway clearance/*chest physical therapy* techniques. Many people with CF need to take *antibiotics*, either on a regular basis or episodically, to treat chronic infections. For GI treatments, *pancreatic enzyme replacement* (PERT) with every meal and snack is common, as are nutritional supplements, high-calorie diets, and vitamins. For some people with CF who develop additional complications, including *diabetes* or liver disease, additional treatments are often required. All told, it is common for a person with CF to have up to 15 to 20 different treatments prescribed by their care team, and most adults with CF require nearly 2 hours every day to complete their prescribed therapies. Studies have shown that early, aggressive care and treatment can improve health outcomes. Thus, this degree of treatment burden often begins during childhood and peaks during adolescence; by the time a person with CF reaches adulthood, they have been prescribed a complex, time-consuming, regimen for many years.

It is not simply the number of therapies that makes treatment challenging, but also the varying modalities and time needed to administer treatments. Inhaled therapies often require *nebulizers*, and each therapy takes a varying amount of time to complete. Some inhaled therapies are taken daily, whereas others are taken up to three times a day. Some antibiotics are prescribed on an alternating month schedule, which can lead to additional challenges when it comes to creating a consistent schedule for daily therapies. Nebulizers also need to be cleaned, and equipment needs to be maintained. Airway clearance also requires time, whether through exercise, *manual chest percussion*, or using specialized devices.

How Can I Improve My Support Systems and Know When to Ask for Help?

Growing up well with CF is a team sport. Some of those team members are picked by default: families, the first care team. As people with CF become older, they get to choose who their friends are, who participates in their CF care, what kind of people they enter relationships with, and how they interact with the broader CF community. Recognizing what types of support someone needs in their life and how to seek it out is an important skill, for people with CF and for their families. Many people with CF fear that they are the ones dragging down their family or friends, and thus they avoid or undermine relationships that could be supportive. Thoughts of future sickness, disability, expense, and stress can erode self-worth. These thoughts must be recognized and actively dispelled. Everyone has their part to play, and there are plenty of examples of people with CF being dragged down by those who surround them. People with CF should recognize that they are worth being in a relationship with those family members and friends who hold them up and desire to actively support them.

The role of parents in providing support changes over time. During childhood, a person with CF is wholly dependent on their parents or guardians for every aspect of their daily care. Every dose of enzymes, every nebulizer treatment, every round of airway clearance, every prescription refill and doctor visit must be facilitated by others. This is a huge responsibility. Over time, that treatment burden must be gradually shifted onto the person with CF. This shift is neither automatic nor immediate. The first step is establishing a care regimen that becomes so routine that it happens smoothly. Developing habits around a care routine facilitates shifting responsibilities. However, it cannot be a passive process. It also requires educating the young person with CF and gaining hands-on assistance. Part of that effort should include teaching how to ask for help and learning what aspects of care can be maintained by others, if necessary.

Support groups for people with CF also change over time. For example, transitioning to college is a huge milestone. The decision whether to live at home, live in a dorm, and whether to have roommates or to live in a medical single are each significant and must be weighed carefully. Being able to disclose CF to potential roommates is important. Do they smoke? Will they be tolerant of medical equipment and therapy taking up time in shared space? These are important questions that need to be answered beforehand, not later. Being comfortable with sharing your CF diagnosis and expressing needs is an important part of being able to navigate these challenges.

As people with CF grow through adolescence and into adulthood, dating and romantic relationships often become a part of their lives, and those partnerships often become an important source of support in adulthood. Teens and adults with CF are not precluded from these relationships. Being able to discuss CF honestly within the vulnerable context of dating or committed relationships is important. People with CF often discover that relationships can end due to CF being too difficult for partners to accept or to handle, but it is better to figure that out earlier than later. No one with CF should want to be in a relationship with someone who can't handle the fact that they have CF; they should truly appreciate how a relationship with someone with CF can be more intentional and meaningful than others. People with CF are lovable and worthy of that love from others and should never let their diagnosis make them feel otherwise.

Regardless of the personal support system that surrounds a person with CF, knowing when to ask for help is a critical part of managing life with CF. This help can take a variety of forms. A change in physical symptoms might require a call to your clinic for evaluation and conversation about current levels of treatment. Asking for help also includes evaluating how well one is coping with the weight of living with CF. Life with CF can be difficult emotionally, and it is key to recognize that is not a personal weakness or deficiency. Feelings can include deep sadness, being overwhelmed (as if trying to juggle too many balls in the air), or being ambivalent about life and things that once brought joy. Depression and *anxiety* occur at astonishingly high rates within the CF community, among those with CF and their parent caregivers. Recognizing increased *symptoms* of anxiety or depression and acting on them is as important to your self-care as is recognizing the beginning of a pulmonary exacerbation. Being able to talk openly with members of the CF care team and close supporters about these changes is an important skill to foster.

Living with CF can be isolating. Many people find it easy to wrap themselves in the "otherness" that being diagnosed with a serious illness provides. Finding solidarity and support in others shifts some of that burden away and erodes the barriers and walls that living with CF can create. Ultimately, individuals with CF are people, and everyone experiences challenges. Choosing to traverse them with others is a testament to that common humanity.

How Can I Enhance My Ability to Care for Myself?

At any stage, there are some steps that you can take to improve your own ability to manage your daily CF care. First, you should identify and assess the things that get in your way. For some, making time during each day for therapy is a challenge. For others, lack of routine or normal schedules can be a barrier. Some might find it difficult to remember medications or therapies regularly, and others might experience side effects that make therapies more difficult to take. Additionally, some can have trouble obtaining or paying for certain therapies. After you identify your individual barriers and challenges, be sure to start a conversation with your clinical care team about ways to reduce them. For instance, if scheduling is a challenge, a reminder system such as an app might be of benefit to you. However, if that is not a challenge you consider for yourself, the same system that helps another person might not be at all helpful to you. Honest, two-way conversations with your care team will allow you to partner with them to develop appropriate interventions for your own barriers to CF care.

Motivation for completing one's treatment changes over time, particularly given that completing daily therapies is not always obviously linked to one's overall perception of health during times of stability. During early childhood, "because Mom said so" or "because the doctor said so" might be enough to motivate adherence to care. However, while developing as a normal teenager, it is not likely to be enough. Adherence for the sake of adherence is usually not going to be a strong enough motivator given that CF remains a progressive and chronic condition. Although daily therapies are intended to maintain lung function, there is no guarantee that adherence to care will ensure longevity or a high *forced expiratory volume in the first second* (FEV1), and that reality can make adherence challenging for many. However, connecting adherence to a passion can be motivating. A person with CF can make the jump from the rule of "Do it because I said so" to having individually motivated adherence. For many, understanding that adherence to treatment facilitates other activities is an important milestone. Everyone with CF can be passionate about something and can learn to use that passion to drive their adherence to care and develop health promoting habits.

What Might I Expect If I Am Admitted to the Hospital?

In any given year, more than one-third of everyone with CF experience a period of increased respiratory symptoms, often called a *pulmonary exacerbation* (Waters and Ratjen, 2014). In general, worsening respiratory symptoms that occur during an exacerbation include increased cough, more sputum production or a change in sputum production, new or worsened shortness of breath, or coughing up blood *(hemoptysis)*. Other signs and symptoms include weight loss, fatigue, fever, and loss of appetite. These symptoms can arise abruptly, triggered by a cold or viral infection, or they could be occurring over a longer period. Your clinical care team might recommend hospitalization to treat a pulmonary exacerbation, particularly if your symptoms are associated with a decline in lung function or are not responsive to outpatient-based therapies.

The goal of a hospitalization is to relieve the symptoms and improve lung function, such that you can return to your baseline state of health. Many hospitalizations last for 2, or even 3 weeks, although the length of time varies based on an individual's baseline state of health and response to therapies. The backbone of hospital treatment includes *intravenous* (IV) antibiotics, usually administered via a *peripherally inserted central catheter* (PICC). In addition, you will continue to receive your daily inhaled and oral medications, and often airway clearance regimens are augmented during a hospital stay.

Infection prevention and control guidelines have recently been updated by the *Cystic Fibrosis Foundation (CF Foundation)* and recommend private rooms for those with CF; these guidelines also can limit your movement outside of your hospital room except for necessary tests, therapies, or procedures (Saiman et al, 2014). Many CF programs have developed programs for home administration of IV antibiotics, and such options can be discussed with your clinical care team.

Being hospitalized can be a lonely and disruptive experience; it can interrupt school, work, and other community and family obligations. In addition, your doctors, nurses, and other staff might not be the same people that you see in the outpatient CF clinic. Rest assured that communication about treatment goals and plans is ongoing, even if "behind the scenes," but always remember that you are your own best advocate in terms of understanding your treatment plan or decisions.

How Can I Pay for My Treatments?

Meeting the undeniably high medical costs of living with CF is a significant but predictable challenge to every person with CF and their families. People with CF and their families must understand the pathways to health insurance, and the barriers that stand between them and affordable, comprehensive coverage, to navigate a complex and challenging system.

Health insurance coverage in the United States comes from several sources. Individuals with CF might receive their own health insurance as employees, purchase it on their state's health care exchange, or receive it if they are eligible for *Medicaid* and/or *Medicare*. Those who are under the age of 26 might be dependents on their parent's employer-based health insurance plans, if they have a parent enrolled in such a plan. Adults with CF can obtain health insurance coverage on their own or, alternatively, might qualify for coverage through their spouse if their spouse has health insurance through an employer. Children with CF can access coverage through their parent's health insurance via their parents' employer, purchased on a health care exchange, or through Medicare/Medicaid if the child has been deemed disabled, or if they have a parent who is Medicaid eligible. This chapter will not focus on the intricacies of these groupings or variations. Instead, a brief overview will present the three main pathways that single adults with CF face: employer-based health insurance, individual health care exchanges, and Medicaid/Medicare.

Employer-Based Health Coverage

Access to health insurance has long been closely tied to full-time employment. Employers might offer health care plans to their full-time employees, and, in doing so, they act as gate keepers to health insurance for many people. Employers decide which plans they offer to their employees, and how much cost-sharing (e.g., premiums, deductibles, co-insurance, co-pays) their employees will be responsible for. Enrollment occurs at the time of initial employment, and changes can be made annually during open enrollment periods. Employer-offered plans must cover a minimum of federally defined health services. Whether plans go beyond those federal minimums is determined by the employer. Employers may not deny an employee access to the health insurance plans it offers to all of its other employees. However, people with CF should be cognizant of the potential for illegal discrimination during the hiring process based on their CF status. People with CF should also be aware that employers are not required to offer health insurance to part-time employees, even if they offer it to full-time employees. People with CF need to understand and to appreciate how their access to employer-based health care can be limited by career decisions. For example, working part time, as an independent contractor, or freelancer will likely exclude that individual from employer-based plans. Similarly, choosing a high-deductible plan versus a traditional *health maintenance organization* (HMO) or *preferred provider organization* (PPO) plan from an employer's offerings can have unforeseen financial consequences. There are many types of health care insurance plans, and people with CF and their families should carefully consider the costs and benefits of each plan they are offered by their employer. It is critically important to predict annual medical costs (such as hospitalizations, monthly prescription drug co-pays, and quarterly CF clinic visits) when selecting which plan works best for your health care needs and budget. Individuals with CF who have employer-based plans might also be candidates for prescription drug manufacturers' co-pay assistance programs. These programs reimburse co-pays/co-insurance for specific CF prescriptions, but do not affect how much the plan pays for prescription drugs. These reimbursement programs are very important when controlling out-of-pocket costs for those with CF and their families.

Individual Health Care Exchanges

Created under the *Affordable Care Act* (ACA), also known as *ObamaCare*, the individual health care marketplace was created to provide a platform for insurance companies to compete with one another in offering health plans to individuals who could not access them through their employment, and who do not qualify for Medicaid. This provides critical access for those who might not be able to work full time and do not qualify medically as disabled or meet Medicaid asset and income requirements. Each state is responsible for the maintenance and regulation of their individual exchanges. The ACA required every plan offered on the exchange to cover a defined *Minimum Essential Coverage Standard*, and eliminated *pre-existing condition clauses*, meaning that no one could be denied coverage for previously being uninsured or losing coverage in the past. Although this paints an optimistic picture for access to care, the effectiveness of the exchanges has been compromised by inconsistent commitment and offerings across states. Whereas some states actively fostered robust exchanges with multiple insurers that offered competitively priced insurance products and tax incentives for participation, others have not, resulting in few options that could be considered both affordable and comprehensive. People with CF who are looking to purchase health care insurance through an individual exchange should not be afraid to compare offerings across states.

Medicaid and Medicare

Medicare eligibility for people under the age of 65 years requires a disability determination by the *Social Security Administration*, and a 2-year waiting period before Medicare coverage begins. Those who are eligible for Medicare should understand the limits of services for which they are entitled, and the cost-sharing requirements involved. Medicaid is more complex but it does not involve any cost sharing on the part of patients. Each state must extend Medicaid eligibility to defined groups of individuals and provide a defined minimum level of health care services. However, every state is also permitted to go beyond those minimum standards, both in terms of eligibility requirements and optional services provided. As a result, every state's Medicaid program is different. Some cover clinical services, and some do not. Eligibility rules also vary. For example, under the ACA, states were permitted to expand Medicaid eligibility to all adults with incomes under 138% of the federally defined poverty level. However, only 26 states elected to fully implement this expansion. This means that in those states with the ACA expansion, any adult with CF whose household income falls under 138% of the federal poverty level qualifies for health care through Medicaid, regardless of disability status. In those states that did not implement the ACA expansion, adults with CF must be qualified as medically disabled and meet their state's income and asset requirements to qualify for Medicaid. As a brief aside, if an individual receives a disability determination, fulfills the 2-year waiting period, and meets the income and asset conditions of Medicaid, they are dually eligible for Medicaid and Medicare, and can receive services from both.

Access to affordable and comprehensive health insurance is one of the most daunting issues for adults with CF. This issue affects decision making about pursuing higher education, career choice, what state to live in, and whether you should apply for disability. Even if an adult with CF is currently able to work and has found an employer with adequate health insurance, the effort to maintain that access is significant and not entirely within your control. Employers can change their health insurance offerings, or disease progression can result in people with CF being presented with the difficult choice of giving up employer-based care and impoverish themselves to qualify for health care through

Medicaid. This is especially true of those living in states that have not fully implemented or supported the ACA, and do not have well-functioning health care exchanges. Do not take health care access for granted. Every person with CF should work toward building an understanding of what their choices are and what they can do to give themselves the best chance to obtain comprehensive, affordable, and quality health care.

HOW DOES CF AFFECT MY TIME IN SCHOOL?

Stephanie Filigno, PhD; Sarah Strong, MEd; Tess Dunn, BA; and Yelizaveta Sher, MD

CHAPTER

In This Chapter

- What Should I Tell (or Should My Parents Tell) Teachers About My CF?

- When Should I (or My Child) Talk to Classmates About CF?

- What Supports Are Available for Me (or My Child) at School?

- What Can I Do If I Miss a Lot of School?

- How Can I Manage My CF If I Go Away to College?

What Should I Tell (or Should My Parents Tell) Teachers About My CF?

Every family has the right to decide what information they share, whom they share information with, and when they share the information. There is no perfect formula or approach to "disclosure," which means sharing information with others. As you make decisions about sharing information about your cystic fibrosis (CF), keep in mind that there is a balance between how much privacy versus disclosure you want. The balancing considers advantages (possible positive things that can come from sharing) and disadvantages (possible negative things that can occur), and your child's stage of development. For example, when CF is disclosed, other people can provide emotional, physical, and practical support (Borschuk et al, 2016), including reminders to engage in daily CF care. When you share information about your child's CF with the school system, the system is designed to help support your child through accommodations and understanding of symptoms, treatment needs, and the impact of CF on their school performance.

When your child is young, you will be making the "who, what, where, when, why, and how" decisions about how much information to share. However, as your child grows older, he or she will have more thoughts and feelings about the decisions regarding disclosure that can affect all aspects of life. Eventually, as an adult, he or she will be making all the decisions about sharing information with friends, coworkers and bosses, and in any educational settings with which he or she is involved. Colleges, universities, and trade-school programs often have disability offices that provide support to students with conditions that affect their educational performance; becoming connected with these resources early in the process is very important.

Family Meetings

When your child reaches school age, you can begin to have family meetings to be sure that all family members have the chance to express their thoughts and to contribute to family decision making, including discussions and decisions on school. Family meetings are facilitated by having a clear purpose, a manageable time frame, a list of content areas to be discussed, and an organized process (see Table 9-1).

Table 9-1: Strategies for Holding Family Meetings

Establish the purpose	Common goals are to:
	• Keep the lines of communication open. • Foster a greater sense of responsibility within children. • Diffuse sibling rivalry. • Encourage discussion and cooperation. • Build family unity. • Develop listening and positive communication skills.

Set aside a time for discussion	Set aside time each week or month for the entire family to spend constructive, quality time together discussing concerns and issues. Common topics include announcements, positive recognition, complaints, conflict resolution, the family budget and allowances, rules, chores, plans for upcoming events (e.g., vacations, birthdays), scheduling, and logistics.
	Tape a piece of paper marked "agenda" to your refrigerator or family work space at the beginning of the week. As the week progresses, any family member can add any issues or complaints to the agenda.
Set the frame	You can use these family meetings to exchange positive feedback! This exchange will bring out good feelings, identify behaviors that you want to see, and teach family members the importance of "building up each other."
	And, you don't need to use family meetings solely for problem solving. It can be also a great way to get together regularly as a family and to talk about other family issues, like planning fun activities—vacations, game nights, and special dinners. It is essential that family members understand that the focus of the meeting is to resolve problems. It is not to scapegoat, criticize, punish, or complain.
	Keep the meeting short and sweet. Consider making the site for your family meeting somewhere new and fun if needed.
	Discuss the roles and expectations of each family member; announce plans for upcoming outings, vacations, or events; delegate chores to each family member; and discuss family rules and the consequences for breaking them. It often helps to set aside some time to play a game together after the meeting.
Set the agenda	Review the two rules that family members must follow during the meetings: be respectful of others (through words and actions), and wait your turn to speak (i.e., no interrupting). You might want the person talking to hold an object (e.g., a potholder) that symbolizes the speaker role.
	Identify who is going to do what during the meeting. Assigning roles (secretary/note-keeper) can help children be excited about the meeting.
Run the meeting	Go around the table and make a list of topics that everyone wants to discuss. Have family members write them down and put them in a bowl. You can draw them out or plan for how to address them before you begin.

continued

Develop the rules	Establish rules (i.e., "Family Meeting Rules") at your first meeting. Write them down and follow them during each meeting. Have rules specifically against disrespectful behaviors, such as interrupting, insulting, or yelling. Have the family meeting at the same time and place each week, allowing for emergency time changes as necessary.
	• Make sure all family members are present and have a chance to be heard.
	• Keep the meeting positive.
	• Start your meeting with everyone sharing appreciations.
	• Put all decisions made during the meeting in writing.
	• Avoid distractions; turn off cell phones and make sure there are no TVs or radios on in the vicinity.
	• Discuss "Looking forward to" which could include upcoming activities like events or meals.
	• End the meeting with announcements that require no planning.
	• Have each family member sign the sheet when the meeting ends.
Parental responsibilities	• Enforce the two very important rules (catch people being good and praise listening).
	• Follow the agenda.
	• Facilitate the problem solving and brainstorming process by allow each family member to talk about possible solutions and then consider voting on the best solution.
	• Keep the meeting on task.
	• Maintain a positive, solution-focused atmosphere by reflecting on what family members say and acknowledging listening, patience, forgiveness, and family values.
	For example: "Good job sharing! I like the way you were able to state the problem clearly and in a respectful way. You are frustrated because someone has been going into your room without your permission. Your room is messier than when you left it. You are also missing items from your room and can't find things when you need them."

Sharing with the School

You should consider sharing several things with the school. You can begin with these ideas and you can discuss them with your CF care team. Parents often need support and coaching about how to advocate for their child in the school setting (Filigno et al, 2017; Filigno et al, 2018) and your team can provide that support.

You and your child can benefit when the school understands how your child's daily routine is different because of CF.

It can be helpful to explain to your child's teachers how CF affects your child's body, the many different systems that are involved (e.g., gastrointestinal, respiratory, sinus, endocrine, mental health) and how CF affects your child's entire daily routine. Some school systems might know certain things about CF, whereas others might know nothing. It is important for schools to know that CF is different for every person; CF is variable and unpredictable. You can describe the steps that you take during your 24-hour schedule so that they understand the treatment demands of staying healthy (including that your child needs to do more treatments and take in more energy from food and drink when ill). You can share with them how you get up early to do treatments and that sometimes treatments require going to bed later than you would like. You can also talk about how doing certain types of homework is not possible when your child is shaking from wearing the vest. That's a big deal! Along the way, you can share changes in medications, diagnosis, and your child's treatment plan, especially if you think they're having emotional, academic, or behavioral concerns in the classroom related to these changes. Your child might also need to take medications or do treatments at school.

You and your child can benefit from your school's understanding of your fears and concerns based on past experiences.

It can be helpful to have school staff understand your child's medical history since birth, including hospitalizations, and why this might contribute to you wanting to be extra cautious when your child is near other children who are ill in the classroom. You can also share how it can be extra stressful for you and your child when you have not been able to get make-up work, making you try even harder to plan to avoid falling behind. You can inform schools that your child might be absent one day at time, a few days in a row, or weeks at a time. Given that parents and medical teams are not always able to predict the length of absence, it will be important to have a plan in place to be sure that you keep up with school work. Each school can have different processes and procedures for how and when teachers give make-up work, and so it is important to ask the school about its usual practices. For example, some schools do not require make-up work unless a child misses three days. When children are away from school for more than a few days, it can help them when the teacher finds ways to keep them connected to their classmates so that your child avoids feeling "forgotten" when absent. Some children with CF are teased for having CF or having symptoms of CF, which can be due to peer misunderstanding. Educating peers can help reduce your child feeling neglected, rejected, or self-conscious when peers ask questions about CF (that might make them uncomfortable). Ask your team about books or other resources that could be used in the classroom if this is of concern.

You can also talk to the school about the things that worry you about your child's health in the school setting and how that affects their school performance. You can talk about times when it was difficult to advocate for your child and what you learned from that experience. Sometimes, parents become frustrated when the school cannot do all of the things that parents would like when it comes to steps to prevent the spread of infection; however, efforts to find ways to compromise are very important.

You and your child can benefit from your school understanding how CF symptoms can be visible or invisible during the day, but still affect your child's school performance.

When someone has CF, some symptoms (e.g., headaches, bellyaches, chest tightness) cannot be seen by others. It can be helpful for the school to understand how CF affects your child's sleep quality because of coughing, having body aches and pains, and receiving tube feedings. In fact, some children who have nightly tube feedings feel physically uncomfortable and full in the morning. Having CF can make children feel fatigued even when they get the proper amount of sleep because the quality of sleep can be poor, causing problems with paying attention, which can be perceived as intentional. Some medicines, when taken in the morning, can affect childrens' ability to concentrate or to sit still. Schools benefit from knowing that when people with CF have a cough, it does not always mean that it is contagious. In addition, the school will benefit from knowing that some people with CF throw up mucus, which is different than vomiting that requires children to be sent home from school. If your child has *CF-related diabetes* (CFRD), it will be important for the school to know how this is different from other forms of *diabetes* with which they might be more familiar. In addition, having a *port* and *g-tube* can require further accommodations. As your child grows older, you can help them learn skills to talk to the school about these symptoms and advocate for what they need to be successful in the classroom with these symptoms and experiences.

Schools can help parents and families when children develop an avoidance of school.

When children have negative experiences at school or have a strong desire to be at home during the day, they can develop *school avoidance*. School avoidance is manifested by children stalling and delaying getting to school, or staying at school, and refusing to go to school at all. When kids begin to avoid school, it might not be obvious at first, and it can build over time. It is important to understand the child's reasons for avoiding school and make sure that the CF team, schools, and parents work together to promote appropriate school attendance. For example, children with CF might have worries about using public bathrooms, being away from their parents, and getting sick at school. It is crucial for you to understand that school avoidance is common and there are effective tools to problem solve and make it better. The earlier that you ask for help, the easier it is to address the problem. You can find some resources to get you started at the website of the *American Academy of Pediatrics* (AAP) (2019).

Having a plan for communication among parents, medical teams, and the school is very important.

One of the key elements of communication among families, medical teams, and schools is the plan for re-integration of the child to school when they return from an absence, especially if several days were missed. In addition to annual *Individualized Education Plan* (IEP)/*504 Plan* meetings (more on this in a moment), it is okay to ask for quarterly meetings or feedback, including specifics about your child's performance in the school setting. Each school and teacher will likely have a preferred way to be reached and have ongoing communication. Feel free to ask schools and team members the preferred ways to communicate with the teacher, counselor, nurse, and principal. It is important to keep in mind that some schools have procedures for communication that they might need to follow, and these can be different than what parents might want, or are used to, and from the medical team (which often responds within 1–2 days).

When Should I (or My Child) Talk to Classmates About CF?

It is up to you when and to which classmates you disclose that you have CF or guide your child through such disclosure. However, several factors can help you make this decision. Think about how close your relationships with classmates are, how often you see them, and what supports (emotional and practical) you can receive from your classmates if they understand that you have CF, and what it means for you. In the book (based on her diaries), *Salt in My Soul: an Unfinished Life* (Smith, 2019), Mallory Smith shares how before each school year, her mother would read a book "Mallory's 65 Roses" that she had created to educate children (Shrader Smith, 1997). Mallory felt that it put other kids and herself at ease because her symptoms and need for care would be apparent during school (Smith, 2019).

When you are the one going to school with CF, you should decide whether disclosure seems appropriate to you. If there is a classmate whom you see on a rather regular basis, it might be helpful for them to understand what you are going through. You might feel less self-conscious about the coughing spells or needing to take enzymes before your meals if you know that your classmates understand that this is a part of self-care for your chronic condition. In fact, some people with CF take this as a good opportunity to explain to others that they have CF and what it means for them (Lail, 2015). After you cough, and your classmate is concerned, you might explain that you have CF and coughing is a frequent symptom of CF and that it is not contagious.

Your classmates might also understand why it is so important for you to stay away from germs and to be more thoughtful and careful about not coming to class or being close to you when they are sick and could spread their germs. You or your child can also show themselves as a thoughtful friend teaching how to disinfect their surroundings. In addition, your classmates and peers might help you to keep up with important resources (e.g., class notes, homework information) if you must miss school because you don't feel well or were hospitalized. They might also offer emotional support during the more difficult times or visit you at home or in the hospital. Or, they might understand why you prefer to stay home on some nights to do your treatments instead of going out with others, and they might join you the next time. Classmates are an important source of friendship and support, and many people find that disclosing something as important as your chronic medical condition allows you to become closer and to be more understanding and to provide support for one another.

If you don't want to disclose information about CF to your classmates, it is important to reflect on the reasons why. Is it because this is private information that you would like to protect (which you have a right to do)? Do you worry about being teased or treated differently because of CF, or do you feel ashamed about having CF and needing treatments to stay healthy? If you have negative thoughts, beliefs, and emotions about sharing information about your CF, you should know that it is very common; it is important to talk with someone who can help prevent these beliefs from negatively affecting your self-esteem, relationships, mental health, or adherence to your treatments. For some students who choose not to disclose to their classmates due to a fear of negative reactions, this can be a barrier to their adherence because they are more reluctant to take enzymes before their meals at school or engage in anything else health related out of worry of seeming different from their peers (Bishay and Sawicki, 2016). Experiencing *stigma*, which includes internalized feelings of shame and anticipation of stigma from others leading to social isolation, has been associated with lower pulmonary function and quality of life, poorer self-esteem and body image, and decreased quality of life and optimism in adolescents and young adults with CF (Oliver et al, 2014).

Although it is understandable that your child might not want their peers to know, consider informing their teachers and administrative staff of their concern so that they can help to monitor your child's mental, physical, and emotional health.

Disclosure is your decision. Working through the possible benefits and drawbacks with someone you trust can help you reach an informed decision about disclosure versus privacy that works best for you.

What Supports Are Available for Me (or My Child) at School?

There are various ways in which supports could be made available for your child at school. Several aspects can affect these supports, such as attending a private or public school. If you are considering a private school, request information on what services and accommodations would be available for your child. Most private schools are not bound by the same laws as public schools; however, some receive federal funding that allows students to have access to resources available in public schools.

If your child attends a public school, there are two ways that they can access support. Because your child has been diagnosed with CF, he or she qualifies under the Section 504 of the *Rehabilitation Act of 1973* for a *504 Plan*. This law was put into place to stop discrimination against people with disabilities. This detailed plan outlines accommodations to ensure that persons with disabilities have the same access to the general education curriculum as their peers. It helps to ensure that access to the learning environment is not affected by a person's disability or chronic medical condition and they are able to achieve their academic success. To qualify, you will need a written statement that demonstrates how the student's condition "substantially limits" their ability to access, receive, and benefit from learning or school activities. There is typically a form from the school district for your medical team to complete, and the school might ask for additional medical documentation from your child's doctor.

Each child's needs differ, and needs can change over time. The plan is updated yearly and the re-evaluation for eligibility occurs every 3 years. Table 9-2 lists frequently requested and realistically recommended accommodations for children with CF. However, be aware that these plans are flexible and that the needs of your child can change as they become older or as the academic demands increase (see Table 9-2).

Table 9-2: Recommended Accommodations for Children with CF

Have unlimited access to restrooms.
Have extra time between bells or switching of classes for restroom use.
Obtain permission to carry a water bottle.
Obtain permission to have snacks and/or ability to get up to reduce fatigue (e.g., stand in the back of the classroom).
Have extra time to get enzymes from nurse or designated personnel before lunch.
Carry enzymes. Know that your state might have a law that allows students to carry only emergency medications that are characterized as a seizure medication, EPIpen®, or an inhaler. If the state has a law that requires this, and your district follows the law, your medical team will need to follow the school's policy.
Be first in line at lunch for more time to eat.
Have tissues and a trash can near your desk.
Have preferential seating near the door for easy access to bathrooms.
Have the ability to change seats if nearby students are ill or look sick.
Receive notification of increased cases of colds, flu, and whooping cough.
Wipe down high touch areas and ability to wipe down own areas with sanitizing cloth.
Obtain permission to carry your own hand sanitizer.
Have extra time for tests and quizzes (for standardized testing, as well).
Have small group settings for testing.
Have extra time to make-up missing assignments.
Prioritize and, potentially, reduce class and homework to achieve quality of learning over quantity of work.
In high school, the integrity of the class might need to be maintained, which can limit the amount of such reduction. If needed, make accommodations for ports and G-tubes or nasogastric (NG) tubes, such as no dodgeball, and speaking with parent about physical education curriculum. If swollen or warm, call the parent immediately; if the G-tube falls out, have an extra button to replace (shows need for a medical professional); extra time for feeds not in the nurse's office.

Another support plan is an IEP, which falls under the *Individuals with Disabilities Education Act* (IDEA), which means it is a federally mandated document. For a student to receive services under this plan, they must be found eligible under one of the 14 categorical designations through an evaluation process. The evaluation will determine academic area of needs. From this, the school will create the IEP to address their unique educational needs. The child's progress will be monitored to ensure that they are making adequate gains on their goals and objectives. The document does allow for the same accommodations for their CF to be added in (see the section on the 504 Plan earlier in the chapter for recommended accommodations). Overall, this document provides specialized intervention to meet the unique educational needs of the student. Figure 9-1 presents a chart of the IEP process.

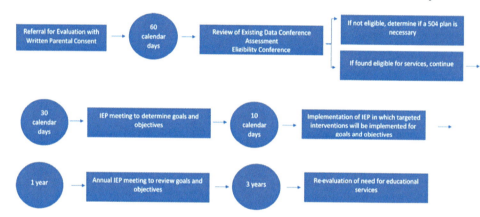

Figure 9-1: A graphic depiction of the Individualized Education Program (IEP).

If the child is found ineligible, there will still be substantial information learned through the evaluation process. This could help to develop a 504 Plan with accommodations to meet the child's needs.

Note that the foundations of these plans are federally mandated, but each state, county, and district might have their own additional laws that could affect the implementation of these plans. If you have additional questions, your state's Department of Education website could be a helpful resource in navigating their processes.

What Can I Do If I Miss a Lot of School?

Having accommodations in place with either a 504 Plan or an IEP is very beneficial when your child is absent from school. Specific benefits that these accommodations can provide to students who must miss school include extended time on assignments, prioritized work, reduction of assignments or number of questions on an assignment, and access to copies of student or teacher notes.

One of the most important ways to support the needs of children who face increased absences is to have a plan in place to address attendance with the school team. It is reasonable to meet with the teachers or send an email requesting to create a plan. The age of your child plays a role in the creation of this plan. As your child grows older, he or she should be encouraged to develop self-advocacy and independence in getting their work. Some good questions to ask are, "Is there a point person who can tell others that a child is out?" "Can all the work be provided to that person?" and "What is the best form of communication and way to gather work (fax, email, parent or sibling pick up)?"

If your child is admitted to the hospital, ask your team or inpatient staff what school resources are available. Determining whether a bedside teacher is available to aid in gathering work and assist in instruction is an important first step. If a certified teacher is not available, check to see whether a volunteer is available. Each hospital offers a different level of educational support and it is helpful to let your school know.

For older children, it is reasonable to work with their school to add a study hall into their schedule (or pursue adding an additional one if they already have one). This can mean that they will not have access to electives they want or might need to wait for another year to fit it into their schedule. In upper grades, peer-tutoring sessions might be available to help all students learn the material. If this is available, you can work with your child's school to determine the group that would be the best fit.

Online classes have been used during the school year (sometimes even for electives), which allows for more flexibility and access to the curriculum. Online classes have pros and cons, so it is important to talk with your child to determine their level of engagement. If a child has difficulty staying on task, is disinterested, or finds the online format difficult, they might not be as motivated to complete the course and find it more frustrating than rewarding.

Any student enrolled in public school has access to *Homebound Instruction* (HBI) if they meet the criteria. HBI allows a student to earn a certain number of hours of instruction (to be provided by a certified teacher) after they have been absent for a specific number of consecutive days. The number of hours a student can earn varies per state as well as how many consecutive days they are absent. This information can be found in your state's Department of Education website. Each district might also implement the law differently from how it is written. For example, some districts will allow for a child to miss 5 days and then implement HBI due to the child having a chronic illness. Overall, the state is required to meet the minimum number of hours if a child continues to miss school after 10 consecutive days of absence.

It is also important to speak with the school about the *anxiety* that some children with CF feel about being sick. At times, teachers feel like they are being helpful by not sending work because they want the child to focus on feeling better. Although this seems kind and helpful, especially at the beginning of an admission, it can cause more anxiety in the child. Let the teachers know when your child is feeling better and that they might have some time (between treatments, physical therapy, and medication administration) to work on their assignments. It is also reasonable to ask if there is a different way of inputting missed assignments online so that they do not negatively affect your child's grade. It can be helpful to engage in this process with your child's input. This helps your child to understand that the grade on the screen is not reflective of their hard work or academic success; it simply reflects their understandable absence from school.

How Can I Manage My CF If I Go Away to College?

Going away to college is an enormous accomplishment. However, it also comes with a great deal of responsibility for those with CF. It is crucial to remain diligent with your medical regimen. Even though this might mean heading home early from a party, bringing enzymes with you everywhere, and no social smoking, you don't need to completely sacrifice a college lifestyle.

First and foremost, get in contact with your school's disability office. Before going in, be aware that the accommodations you can access in college are different than high school. You can always talk to your high school counselor before applying or with the disability office when you arrive to school. Advisors can provide you with plenty of accommodations, ranging from priority registration to extra time on assignments, to living in a single dormitory room. Meet with your advisor before each semester to review the classes you'll be taking and the accommodations that are needed for each class.

If you are living with a roommate, try connecting with them prior to the start of the semester. Because you will be sharing a living space with this person, you will need to make compromises to take proper care of your health. Establish times when you can do your respiratory therapy without waking up your roommate. If your roommate becomes sick, make sure you have your own essentials and food as well as antibacterial wipes around, to help keep their sickness isolated. By establishing "rules" prior to the start date, it will be easier to coexist.

You will be experiencing many wonderful things and time can slip away. Although it can be easy to skip medications and respiratory therapy when you're tired or busy, it's crucial to stay on top of your medication and therapy. Previous support systems will not be present—the upkeep of your health will be dependent on you. And even though it can be tempting to neglect your health, remember that multiple missed treatments can lead to a downward spiral. Be accountable to yourself. If you tend to forget a certain medication, make a checklist and keep it close to you so that you can mark every time you take the medication, or set a constant reminder on your phone.

You might need to plan your classes around taking care of your physical and emotional needs. Don't downplay the importance of good sleep. In fact, you might need to schedule your classes in the later morning or afternoon to ensure that you get enough sleep, are not forced to wake up too early, and have plenty of time for your morning treatment (Buck, 2015).

Of course, you are not required to tell people details. If you'd rather keep your CF from unfamiliar acquaintances, you are under no obligation to disclose. If you are transparent with your disability advisor and your teachers, as well as any potential roommates, your CF is your own. Although you should never feel as though it's a burden, you can keep it private.

HOW CAN CF AFFECT MY WORK?

Kim Reno, ACSW, LISW-S; Amy E. Mueller, LCSW; and
Denis Hadjiliadis MD, MHS, FRCP(C)

CHAPTER

In This Chapter

- What Should I Consider When I Am Choosing a Career?

- When (and Why) Should I Discuss My CF with My Employer or Coworkers?

- What Should I Consider When I Am Deciding Whether to Cut Down or to Stop Working?

- When Should I Consider Disability Benefits and How Would I Apply for Them?

- What Resources Are Available to Help Me Make Informed Decisions?

What Should I Consider When I Am Choosing a Career?

Choosing a career when you have cystic fibrosis (CF) can be both challenging and rewarding. Working can provide a sense of purpose, increased financial stability, and health insurance. Although the treatment burden in CF remains high, medical advances are making it possible for people with CF to reconsider their opportunities for employment and career options. For the first time, there are more adults than children living with CF; this number will continue to grow. Those with CF can attend college, complete technical training, or join the workforce after completing secondary schooling. Your choice of a career does not need to be limited by your CF; you can choose a career that is molded by your interests and goals.

Career development typically begins in adolescence and continues well into adulthood as your interests, needs, and circumstances change. During high school, many people begin to think about what they see themselves doing in the future, identify what they are good at, and consider what skills they are beginning to develop. It is important for teenagers to discuss their career and life goals with trusted family members and friends, school guidance counselors, and employment or education professionals. There are also opportunities to benefit from vocational assessments that can help to identify interests, likes and dislikes related to joining the workforce, as well as to help identify career goals. A good resource for career and vocational information is O*Net Online (aka Occupational Network Online). This is a government website *sponsored* by the Department of Labor where you can search for specific job titles and get a wealth of career information, such as level of education needed, salary data, specific job tasks, related job titles, job growth projections, and more. Also, there is a free "career interest inventory" on the website that can help you identify what types of careers might fit with your interests. As with most big decisions, it is a good idea to talk with family members, friends, guidance or vocational counselors, and members of your health care team, such as the *social worker*, physician, nurse, nurse practitioner, or *mental health coordinator* (MHC), as they are familiar with your health needs as well as the impact of CF.

Though many people plan to attend college, other programs (e.g., vocational school, training programs) might be more in line with your skills and interests. Vocational high schools or programs can focus on a skill or trade like computer technology, engineering, or culinary arts. After high school, technical school certificate programs or trade education programs are typically a shorter-term option than college degree programs and can lead directly to employment. Some individuals might choose to work directly after high school and not pursue higher education. These decisions are very personal, so it is important to think about your options with the help of family members, friends, guidance or vocational counselors, and members of your health care team.

The cost of college is a growing concern for everyone, not just for those with CF. It is important to do a *"cost/benefit" analysis* when considering whether and where to attend college and to think about the amount of debt you will be able to pay off after completing higher education. Several factors will affect this; for example, the type of student loans you are considering and/or qualify for, how much financial aid or scholarship awards you might qualify for, the affordability of the particular college, and the time needed to complete the education required for a particular career. It is also critical to know that private student loan debt cannot be forgiven based on a disability, whereas federal student loans can be excused due to a medical condition. The type of job and income level you can expect after college must also be weighed against the financial investment you make in your education.

In addition to the potential financial ramifications of continuing your education, it is also important to think about the potential impact that CF will have on your education and overall career. There might be times when your health needs will require you to miss school or to take time off from work. For teens with CF, while in middle and high school, it is important to develop a plan for when a significant amount of school is missed due to CF. Parents often work with their child's school to make a formal plan to ensure that their child with CF receives the same education as others, even though they might miss school due to illness. This is usually done through a *504 plan* or an *Individual Education Plan* (IEP) that is created to allow a child to have accommodations in school to ensure that they can complete requirements for the school year successfully. Some accommodations include an ability to make up a missed test or to have extra time to complete homework assignments or tests/exams.

If you are planning to attend college, it makes sense to contact the college disability resource center before beginning school to develop a similar plan, depending on what accommodations are anticipated. These plans are intended to help students with a medical condition succeed even with an illness that can disrupt a busy college class schedule and workload.

While reviewing opportunities for a specific job or career, it will also be important to consider the distance you live from your employer, and your transportation needs. You should consider whether you can drive yourself to work or whether you will need to use public transportation (with its increased risk of exposure to illnesses). Additionally, because there will be stress with any sort of employment you should realize that job stress has the potential to negatively affect your health. At each stage of your career, it is important to be flexible, to adhere to your medical routine to avoid undue illness, and to practice self-care to enhance your ability to cope with stress at work as well as within your personal life.

In addition to self-care, when identifying employment or career opportunities, you should consider health insurance, potential occupational exposures (e.g., cleaning products, chemicals), scheduling flexibility, proximity to a CF care center, and a full-time versus part-time schedule.

What Types of Health Insurance and Other Benefits Are Available?

When finding employment and interviewing for a job, the natural question to ask is usually related to annual salary. Salary is an important factor; you want to be able to afford housing, utilities, and food, and to have money available for social engagements with friends. It is also important, if not more so, to ask about the benefits package you will receive. Other things to consider include the policy for sick leave, flexible work schedules, and telecommute or work-from-home options, if available. Often, depending on the size of your company, the benefit package will include health insurance, dental benefits, vision benefits, a 401K retirement plan, short-term disability insurance, and long-term disability insurance. While interviewing or negotiating with a potential employer, you might want to consider the value of having a lower annual salary but a complete benefits package. These benefits, particularly the short- and long-term benefit plans, can be quite valuable in the future should you need to apply for *Social Security Disability Income* (SSDI). That is, short- and long-term insurance could provide the financial bridging you might need until you are approved for disability by Social Security and while you are awaiting Medicare coverage.

You should also consider the size of your company. In general, companies with many employees might provide better benefits, including health insurance, whereas smaller companies tend to provide more individualized work schedules yet offer fewer benefits. Both characteristics are important to consider. You will need to evaluate your health status, financial needs, and long-term and future needs related to your health and finances when choosing an employer.

As you review the benefit package, particularly health insurance, you should evaluate the employer group plan(s) that will be provided by the human resources department and be aware of enrollment deadlines. If you are insured through your employer, your employer decides when you can enroll in its coverage or when you can make changes to your current health care plan. Most employers hold open enrollment in the fall, and coverage often begins on January 1 and ends on December 31.

Be mindful of all the health insurance coverage options available to you. Depending on your employment status, household size, and income, you might be able to select from a variety of insurance types.

Insurance Types

- *Private or commercial insurance* is health coverage purchased directly from a health insurance company, either with a group, such as an employer, labor union, university, or it can be purchased as an individual.

- The *Health Insurance Marketplace*, also known as the *Health Insurance Exchange*, was created by the *Affordable Care Act* (ACA) to help residents of the United States pay for health care. If you do not have access to group-based employer plans or do not qualify for *Medicare* or *Medicaid*, the marketplace provides an online tool to purchase a health insurance plan to ensure that you have coverage.

- *Government health care programs* are government-funded and provide health care assistance to qualifying individuals and their families. The largest of these programs are Medicare and Medicaid, but government health care programs also include the Veterans Health Administration (VHA), the Children's Health Insurance Program (CHIP), Children with Special Health Care Services (each state program has a unique name) the Department of Defense TRICARE and TRICARE for Life programs (DOD TRICARE), and the Indian Health Service (IHS).

- The *Consolidated Omnibus Budget Reconciliation Act* (COBRA) is a form of employer-based coverage that gives employees and their families the option to extend their insurance should you lose your job-based health coverage. This benefit is available for up to 18 months; however, you will be responsible for paying the entire monthly premium, which could be expensive. You can choose not to use COBRA benefits and instead enroll in a marketplace plan (COBRA Coverage and Health Insurance Marketplace Options. HealthCare.gov, www.healthcare.gov/unemployed/cobra-coverage/).

Each plan type mentioned above will have specific rules for eligibility and enrollment. You should consult with a member of your health care team or with *CF Foundation Compass* (844-COMPASS; compass@cff.org) to help you identify which plan is right for you.

Due to the ACA you can remain on your parents' insurance until you are 26 years of age. This extra time with parental insurance coverage allows you to review options for a career and health insurance coverage. In addition, with the ACA, you can be insured immediately (when you start or transition to a new job) without worrying about *pre-existing condition clauses.*

When you are insured by Medicaid and start working, you will likely lose your Medicaid coverage due to the increase of your household income. It will be important to find a job with health insurance when you risk losing your Medicaid coverage. The income guidelines for Medicaid vary from state to state and can change over time, so you should be aware of your options to avoid gaps in insurance coverage.

Medicare is available for those who meet certain health requirements; typically, those who qualify for Medicare before retirement age are sicker. When considering your employment and career options, you should think carefully about your future needs related to Medicare. Medicare is available for those who meet the health requirements and have worked long enough to be vested into the program. This means that you must have worked long enough and paid taxes into the program. Sometimes, people are tempted to work for cash or "under the table"; however, because you are not paying taxes into the Medicare program, you might not qualify for Medicare or the monthly payment included with SSDI later, when it is needed. In addition, when you do qualify for social security benefits, the amount of your monthly check will be dependent upon what you paid into the system.

What Services Does Your Insurance Plan Cover?

The next step in understanding your insurance is knowing what your plan covers. When we use the word "covered," it means that your insurance company is willing to pay for some, or all, of the costs of using medical services or prescribed medications.

The easiest way to get a full picture of what your plan covers is by reviewing the *summary of benefits and coverage* (SBC). This document and a glossary of terms that must be provided by insurance companies and job-based health plans. The SBC includes details on costs, coverage, and examples of what the plan would cover in two common medical situations (i.e., diabetes care and child birth).

What Medications are Covered?

The best way to determine whether a plan covers your medications is by looking at the *drug formulary* (or prescription drug list). A drug formulary is a list of prescription medications that is covered by your plan. The formulary is a document readily available from your insurance company or on your insurance provider's website.

It is important to search for restrictions to medication coverage (e.g., quantity limits, prior authorizations, pharmacy restrictions). When the time comes to access your medications, your health insurance policy might require *prior authorization* or pre-authorization for certain services or medications before you can receive them. Prior authorization is a formal review and approval process conducted by your insurance company before it will agree to cover a service, medication or prescription refill. If you have a drug that needs prior authorization, be sure to let your doctor know.

What Doctors Are Covered?

Not all health care providers are contracted under an insurance plan's provider network. A health insurance network consists of the facilities, medical providers, and suppliers that the health insurance plan has contracted with to provide health care services at a pre-negotiated rate. Provider networks depend largely on the type of health insurance plan you have. The plan you choose will ultimately determine the size of your provider network, the rules for seeing a specialist, and how much you will pay each time you receive care.

In addition, you will need to understand in-network benefits and what the health plan policies are regarding out-of-network coverage before enrolling in a plan. An in-network provider is contracted with the health insurance plan to provide services to policy holders for specific pre-negotiated rates while also meeting quality standards. Out-of-network providers are those who are not contracted with the health insurance plan. Typically, the insurance company pays either less or nothing at all for services received from out-of-network providers. You will want to make sure your CF care center and all your medical providers, hospitals, and pharmacies are in-network for the plan; that is, you can ask whether your health care providers are able to bill, and be paid by, your health insurance.

Costs

You should understand your out-of-pocket expenses (including monthly insurance premiums, *co-pays*, co-insurance, annual deductibles, and out-of-pocket maximums) of your health insurance.

A *premium* is the monthly amount you pay, as the policy holder, to purchase a health plan. A premium must be paid to keep the coverage active, regardless of whether you seek medical care. If you do not pay the premium, your plan will be canceled.

A co-pay is a fixed dollar amount (for example, $15) that the policy holder pays for covered health care service. For example, if you go to the doctor for a visit and your co-pay is $30, you would pay $30, and your insurance company would pay the remainder of the bill.

In most cases, co-pays do not count toward the *deductible*, but do count toward the out-of-pocket maximum. Co-pays vary between plans and might apply to different health care services (e.g., urgent care, office visits, prescription medications).

A *co-insurance* is the cost that the policy holder shares with the insurance company for covered services, calculated as a percentage. For example, if the policy holder has an office visit that costs $100 before insurance and the plan's co-insurance requirement is 20%, the policy holder would pay $20. The health insurance plan would then pay the remaining 80%, or $80.

A deductible is a fixed dollar amount that the policy holder must pay before the insurance company begins to make payments for covered medical services. Some insurance plans have both individual and family deductibles, whereas some family plans have only a family deductible. They also might have a separate drug deductible. Deductibles might apply only to specific services and might not apply to office visits or prescription medications. Under the Affordable Care Act, deductibles do not apply to preventive care (e.g., annual exams, immunizations) and routine gynecological visits.

Out-of-pocket (OOP) *maximum* is the maximum amount that the policy holder can spend for covered services in a set coverage period. A coverage period is typically defined as a plan year or calendar year. You will need to review your plan to know the exact dates. After the out-of-pocket maximum is reached, the insurance plan pays for all covered services for the remainder of the coverage period. Some plans have a separate OOP maximum for medications.

Two key aspects of understanding your insurance are knowing the different types of insurance plans and the types of available plans. Health insurance can be both complicated and expensive; however, learning more about the type of insurance you qualify for and the details of various plans can help you make the most of your coverage and evaluate your options. Case managers with *Compass* are available to assist with this endeavor.

One final option to consider when choosing a job is whether your employer is large enough to offer the protections offered by the *Family Medical Leave Act of 1993* (FMLA). The FMLA provides protections for you to have a leave from work for your own health needs or to help care for a spouse or child with an illness. You are eligible for FMLA when you work for an employer with 50 or more employees within a 75-mile radius, you have worked for the organization for 12 months, and you worked at least 1,250 hours during the previous 12 months (Wage and Hour Division). The FMLA allows a person with CF to take up to 12 weeks off from work at one time, or intermittently throughout the year, when medically necessary, maintain health insurance benefits, and maintain employment with the same job or an equivalent job. It is important to note, that the FMLA requirement is for unpaid leave; however, it is possible to be paid with your accrued sick time or vacation time. A provision to the FMLA allows up to 26 weeks of unpaid leave; although it does not ensure access to the same job or position in the company, health insurance is maintained during the leave.

Will Occupational Exposures Be a Concern?

Although CF affects many organs, it most frequently interferes with lung function leading to exacerbations and hospitalizations. With this in mind, you should consider the potential effects of different occupations on your lung health.

Professions that expose you to lung pollutants or irritants are not ideal jobs for those with CF. This is especially true if there are limited options for job modifications or accommodations to preserve your lung health. In addition, for those occupations that require personal protective equipment (e.g., masks), the environment at work could make it difficult for you to breathe (e.g., working in a chemical plant, working with harsh cleaning solutions, welding, construction, stone cutting, plumbing, electrical trades, landscaping, ceramics work). If you are thinking about working in any of these trades, you should consult with your health care provider before accepting a position. With any job you have, you should always use the personal protective equipment that is required by your employer to minimize any harmful exposures.

Other occupations frequently chosen by those with CF are in health care. This career choice is not surprising due to experiences in the medical field because of frequent doctor visits or hospitalizations. In medical professions, exposures to illness are most often related to infections that are transmitted from those who are treated in medical facilities. Hand hygiene and diligence with following all policies and procedures required by the employer to limit exposure to illnesses are necessary. In general, choice of work areas where there is less exposure to illness (e.g., outpatient surgery rather than in an emergency room) would be preferable. In addition, many people who work in health care are required to work long hours under difficult and stressful conditions. At times, this environment makes it difficult to maintain health for those who have a chronic health condition like CF. Due to unpredictable schedules and break times in health care, managing *CF-related diabetes* (CFRD) and nutrition requirements can be a challenge. It is important to have a thorough discussion with your health care provider to review the potential risks and exposures that you might have when choosing a career in health care.

Will Work Hours Be Flexible?

When exploring different careers or jobs, you should consider whether the type of career, the employer, or the nature of the work will place rigid demands on you and on your time. Some careers are not well suited to part-time or flexible scheduling, whereas others are quite flexible, so long as your work is completed. Working in an education field, for example, might be appealing to some because of time off during the summer, although work and time demands during the school year can be quite high. You can get a better idea of the demands of any career simply by talking to someone who is working in that career or, better yet, by shadowing them during a typical workday to experience what it is really like.

Most employers offer paid time for holidays, personal time, sick time, and vacation, and they usually provide that information as part of the benefits package. Knowing this allows you to plan for expected, scheduled "well visits" to your CF center and other routine appointments. But what about additional time needed for unexpected "sick visits" or a hospitalization? For some, CF exacerbations are common at certain times of the year and can be somewhat "predictable," but for others it is more difficult to predict when an exacerbation might occur. If an employer allows you to reduce work hours for a period of time, you should investigate the FMLA and learn whether your health insurance and other benefits might be affected and how they can be protected.

Options of Full-Time versus Part-Time Work or Self-Employment

Deciding whether to work full time or part time, or perhaps to be self-employed, like all work–life balance decisions, is very personal and is based on several factors (including health, financial status, availability of insurance, and paid time off). Many people with CF work full time. According to the 2017 CF Foundation Patient Registry Data Report (2017 Cystic Fibrosis Foundation Patient Registry Highlights), 38.6% of adults with CF work full time, 12.4% work part time, whereas 17.3% are disabled. Working full time for a large company or organization usually ensures availability of employer-based health insurance (that the employer helps pay for), accrued paid time off, and, depending on the type of work, enough income to save for the future. "Future" you say? Yes, you should save money for when you might decide to retire! Let's break it down and consider each of these factors:

Health status, stamina, and daily health routine

On one end of the spectrum, you might have overall good, stable health, plenty of energy throughout the day, only need to see your health care team the recommended four times per year, and have a care routine that takes an hour or two each day. In this case, working full time and maintaining good health might not conflict and it is manageable to work full time for the satisfaction it brings, not to mention the long-term financial stability it can offer. On the other end of the spectrum, some people have more severe CF symptoms, tire more quickly, have greater illness complexity to manage, and require more time for daily treatments to keep exacerbations or hospitalizations to a minimum. For these people, the time for additional appointments to other specialists, more frequent sick visits to the CF center, and home intravenous (IV) antibiotic treatment or hospital admissions can add up very quickly just to maintain and to slow the progression of the disease. If you know that you are in the latter group, consider working part time to keep a work, life, and health balance, if at all possible. Everyone needs time for family and friends, enjoyable activities, and a satisfying and manageable workload to feel like they are contributing and living a life that they value. This leads to the next point as financial needs vary and affect these decisions.

Financial status

If you have financial support from family or a spouse, you might be able to decide between working part time or full time. In general, using a spouse's insurance provides you with more flexibility for working part time. (The same is also true if you work for a smaller company or family-owned business that does not offer health insurance.) Even with this choice, many individuals want to work because it feels good to use and to contribute your skills, talents, and interests to something that you find meaningful, beyond daily self-care. Others want to work because they are concerned about feeling like a "burden" to their loved ones and they want to contribute to the household income. However, keeping this emotion in check is key, so that your health does not suffer. And, for some, engaging in part-time versus full-time employment can be more of a necessity due to health, than a choice. Working part time can also be challenging because you could be at risk of working more hours than is healthy for you at the time. This can culminate in deciding to pursue disability as a source of income.

Insurance, paid sick time, and other benefits

Often, working part time means having limited or no health insurance coverage. If, however, you are able to be covered under a spouse's or parent's insurance plan and an employer allows you to earn some paid time off, a part-time job is not out of the question, if your health and the satisfaction of working are both important to you. There are also jobs that offer some benefits for part-time employees, but this is rare. It is often best to work full-time and to move to part-time status with the same employer, if possible, to maintain continuity and access to benefits.

Self-employment

Many people believe that self-employment offers the greatest degree of flexibility for making a living and taking care of a chronic illness like CF. It can seem like the ideal situation to avoid the hassle of negotiating time off, changing hours, and not having to justify taking time off for doctor appointments or answer to someone each time you do not feel well. To some extent, this is true, but it is rare that the work we do (or don't do) will not have any affect on others. We all must meet some expectations for a job, whether you are self-employed or are an employee in a large company. How the work gets done, how you maintain a steady income, and what happens to that income when you're "out sick" are important questions. Having other people coordinate with you to get a job done within an organization can be less stressful in the long run than being self-employed. Remember, when you work for yourself, all of the responsibility falls to you to run that business (e.g., paying the cost of insurance, keeping track of the financial aspects, generating adequate income) regardless of your health. To learn more about self-employment opportunities, some organizations offer support and information such as the national network of Small Business Development Centers.

Living and Working Near a CF Center

"Location, location, location!" The all-important question when deciding where to buy real estate is also a consideration when deciding where to work and to live when you have CF. Living and working hours away from your care center when you are reasonably healthy might be manageable for well-visits four times a year.

However, as you age with CF, your symptom severity, frequency of exacerbations, and health care needs change over time, even for those who remain adherent to all therapies. Hopefully these changes occur slowly, allowing you to manage new routines of daily care, follow-up appointments, and your employment. It is okay, of course, to follow your passion and your dreams; however, planning for how to manage your health is important when considering the distance from your care center.

When (and Why) Should I Discuss My CF with My Employer or Coworkers?

Many people want to be honest with their employer, even before they have been offered a job, whereas others want to keep this information private. In either case, you should know that you are not obligated to share medical information with your employer, either before or after you are hired. In fact, if you tell the employer you have CF before you are offered the job and then the job offer is not made, it would be very difficult to prove that the employer discriminated against you because of your CF. On the other hand, if you are offered the job, and then share that you have CF and the job offer is taken back, you might have a basis for a discrimination complaint. Just to be clear: There are no laws requiring you to share your diagnosis of CF with an employer either during the interview process or after being hired. In fact, there are laws that prevent an employer from asking you whether you have a disability or requiring that you to have a medical exam before making a job offer. There are some exceptions to this. During the interview process, an employer can ask if, and how, you can perform the job. If the employer asks all new employees, in the same job or position to answer medical questions or to take a medical exam, the law does allow the employer to offer or to not offer the job or position to people based on those answers. For this reason, it is helpful to talk with your health care team or an attorney knowledgeable in employment law who can help guide you to resources to explain your rights.

A diagnosis of CF should not affect your accepting a job offer or performing on the job if you are confident you can meet all of the job requirements. You should be able to review a job description during the application or interview process to decide whether the job is the correct fit for you.

It is also important to familiarize yourself with the laws of the *Americans with Disabilities Act* (ADA) and the *Equal Employment Opportunity Commission* (EEOC). The ADA requires employees to be provided with "reasonable accommodations" to perform the functions of a job, as long as there are 15 or more employees. The EEOC is the agency responsible for enforcing federal laws regarding discrimination or harassment against a job applicant or an employee in the United States. A resource for understanding these laws and many employment issues is the *CF Legal Hotline*, a legal service that specializes in the needs of those with CF.

One situation in which you must tell your employer about your CF is if you anticipate needing to use FMLA benefits. As a reminder, the FMLA provides protections for you to obtain a leave from work due to your own health needs or to help care for a spouse or child with an illness. To access FMLA, you and your physician will be required to complete paperwork. All the completed forms need to be returned to Human Resources. Your physician is required to indicate how long you will need to be off work, whether the time off will be intermittent or taken at one time, and when (approximately) you can return to work.

If you choose to disclose and your employer is looking for accurate information about CF, you can provide them with the CF Foundation website (www.cff.org) for accurate, up-to-date information. Being open and honest with trusted colleagues can be very helpful when their social and professional support is needed during an exacerbation or when you are not feeling well and need time off or assistance during the workday.

Disclosing your diagnosis to an employer or to coworkers is a personal decision. It is important to talk through the pros and cons of disclosing your CF diagnosis with trusted friends, caregivers, or an attorney before discussing CF with your supervisor, employer, or colleagues. As a reminder, if you know that you will require accommodations to perform your job, or if you need to plan for using intermittent FMLA, you will need to share your diagnosis with your employer (Human Resources).

What Should I Consider When I Am Deciding Whether to Cut Down or to Stop Working?

People often begin to wonder about reducing or stopping work altogether when they notice that their symptoms are worsening, when they are having more frequent exacerbations, and when they are having more difficulty "bouncing back" from illnesses or exacerbations. The progression of CF involves gradually more difficulty breathing, more frequent episodes of illness, increased number of hospitalizations, less energy, greater illness complexity (including CFRD, more time spent on daily self-care and appointments, and spending less time and energy for day-to-day tasks). These issues can lead to reduced rest or a decreased ability to do all therapies, both of which are needed to remain well. The stress of managing your health while trying to work full time can, in and of itself, lead to worse physical symptoms, and so the negative health impact of working full time might outweigh the benefits of continuing to do so.

The timing of deciding to work less or not at all depends on your health and circumstances. Optimally, experimenting with different strategies that help you maintain your usual activity and workload early on, rather than waiting until your health becomes acutely worse, will keep you more in control and help you to decide when and how much to adjust your work hours. "Early on" might mean that you recognize feeling more tired more days a week, needing more time to rest and recover over the weekends, more visits or calls to your CF care team requesting oral antibiotics to avoid the need for IV antibiotics or a hospitalization, exacerbations close together, and noticing this trend in your health over a period of a few months.

Another "sign" that may point you toward deciding to work fewer hours or to make a plan to stop working could be your CF care team's recommendation to be referred for *lung transplantation*. Sometimes, stopping work and focusing on your health might stabilize the condition and delay end-stage lung disease and lung transplantation. But only you know what will work best for your health and overall sense of well-being. The transplant referral and evaluation process are complex on many fronts, from the emotional to the practical, and involve numerous appointments and tests and financial planning while still enjoying your life and the activities you value. Cutting back on work, even gradually, might allow you to better manage a shift to this new phase of your health, more time to make thoughtful decisions, and time to prioritize important relationships, family time, and doing what you enjoy.

How much flexibility and choice you have in the matter of working less is tied to practical considerations of financial stability, resources for support, maintaining health insurance, and how you've strategized for the possibility of not working. For those who have a good income, who have been able to save money, who live financially within their means, who have good health insurance, and who have paid into short- and long-term *employer-based disability* plans, decreasing work hours will be a manageable financial transition. Stable employment can also allow for developing a strategy to gradually work less, including working some hours from home rather than from an office, having flexible hours, negotiating a job re-entry plan after transplant, and having stable health. Still others might have an employed spouse, an extended family or other supports (e.g., to lend financial, logistical, emotional and decision-making support) to help in planning to work less, whereas some are not so fortunate in this regard.

Another important factor when deciding how much to work, is maintaining a sense that you are living a life with meaning, regardless of your actual employment. The concern for some is that working less might mean losing a sense of purpose. Also, if you are not earning a living you might feel as if you are not contributing to society, and you might worry about others viewing you this way. People might also worry about becoming more isolated and losing connection to activities that bring satisfaction while having to focus more and more on illness and basic self-care. Although work can serve the purpose of being an "anchor," knowing what other activities and relationships are important to you and what you value most in life can actually hold even greater meaning for you. Worthwhile questions for anyone to ask themselves include: "What do I truly care about? What do I want my life to stand for? What do I want other people to know about me or my life, now and after I'm gone?" You might discover that what you care about, and enjoy learning and doing, lies outside of your job or career, within it, or perhaps in both.

When Should I Consider Disability Benefits and How Would I Apply for Them?

It is important to understand several factors when trying to decide when and how to apply for disability benefits. Specific medical criteria need to be met, medical records need to support the medical criteria (even with regular treatment), finances need to be considered, and, of course, your health insurance needs to be maintained while disabled. Also, there are different types of disability.

Having a diagnosis of CF does not by itself automatically qualify you for any disability benefits. Many people believe they will qualify simply by having the diagnosis, but this is not the case. Though there are physical impairments associated with CF recognized by the Social Security Administration, there are specific criteria that must be met to be deemed "disabled." It is extremely helpful to review these criteria with someone, such as an attorney, who is skilled in social security benefits and CF.

On the other end of the spectrum, some people think they can pursue disability benefits only when they are "truly sick" and they cannot work at all because of their health. People can wait far too long to consider applying for benefits, but taking care of your health while working part time might be an approach to consider, so it is a good idea to know what the criteria are, to discuss the options with people close to you, and to review different strategies with your health care team.

The first type of disability is for those who are employed by a company or organization that offers short- and/or long-term disability benefits. This type of *"employer-based" disability* is paid into by both the employer and the employee with every paycheck, and it can be accessed based on that plan's criteria and application process, usually explained in an employee benefits package. Some people do not take advantage of these plans or simply overlook it. Even if you have CF, you can opt into this type of plan. It is important to consider enrolling into this benefit because it will provide you with a percentage of your salary, for a period of weeks or months, should you require to take time off from work due to your health needs. It is typical to access this after you have first used all accrued paid time-off and your unpaid FMLA time. Consult with your human resources department to learn more about your benefits and how to enroll and apply for benefits when you need it.

The next two types of disability are government-based programs. If you are still unable to return to work after you have used both short- and long-term disability or if you did not have the employer-based disability to begin with, you are able to apply for SSDI.

Social Security Disability Income

Social Security Disability Income (SSDI) provides a monthly check and Medicare insurance. You can apply and qualify for SSDI if you have a work history (which means you've earned work credits that essentially pay into the fund over time) and you meet specific criteria for a medical condition that prevents you from any "substantial gainful activity." The amount of SSDI you would receive in a monthly check is calculated from the work credits you've earned: the more years of full-time work you have done, the greater your work credits and the greater amount you could receive in monthly SSDI payments. SSDI is a federal government program overseen by the *Social Security Administration* (SSA). You can apply for SSDI if either your employer does not offer or you haven't signed up for employer-based short- and/or long-term disability (remember, this type is specific to your employer and has nothing to do with the government), when you cannot work due to your health, and when your health needs meet the requirements as recognized by social security.

Supplemental Security Income

Supplemental Security Income (SSI) also provides a monthly check and health insurance, though the health insurance is provided through your state's Medicaid program, not through Medicare, which is managed by the federal government. Also, just like SSDI, it is a government-based program managed by the SSA and requires that you meet specific medical criteria. However, it is a completely separate and different program from SSDI. This type of disability is based on your need due to low-income, minimal or no work history, and having a disabling medical condition. To repeat: Although SSI and SSDI are both managed under the SSA and both involve medical criteria that determine you are unable to work, they are completely different programs, with the main difference being that to qualify for SSDI, you must have a work history. The opposite is true for SSI: to qualify for SSI you cannot have a significant work history and you must have low income.

Lastly, you should seek guidance from an attorney with CF-specific knowledge in applying for disability. When people apply on their own without professional guidance, it is common for the application to be denied; when this happens, it is very difficult to appeal the decision, and it sometimes takes several months or years to successfully obtain benefits. The Cystic Fibrosis Legal Information Hotline is one resource available for people thinking about applying for disability benefits. In addition to consulting with the CF Legal Information Hotline, you should also discuss your thoughts with your health care team. Your application will require the support of your physician, and he or she will need to submit medical records. You can contact the CF Legal Information Hotline by email at CFLegal@sufianpassamano.com or you can call 1-800-622-0385.

Your medical records are an important part of this process. You should talk with your physician and your CF center social worker to ensure that your medical records include the following:

- Pulmonary function tests (PFTs)

- Sputum culture results/lab work

- Hospital admission and discharge summary information

- Emergency room visit records

In addition to these medical records, it is important that you make sure you are being seen by your physician on a regular basis. It will be difficult to prove your deteriorating health and disability status if you have few visits during the year prior to your application.

There are specific criteria that help determine whether you qualify for disability. Poor lung function is one of them, but many other factors are important, including the number of times you get sick; the number of hospitalizations you have had in the last year; the number of days you've had IV antibiotics in the past year; the development of a collapsed lung *(pneumothorax)* or bleeding from the lungs *(hemoptysis)*; requiring *bi-level positive airway pressure* (BiPAP) or mechanical ventilation or oxygen. In addition, other conditions, including weight loss, need for using supplemental feeding by *G-tube*, and development of CFRD can all be considered when determining disability. Close contact between you, your attorney, and the health care team will be needed during this process.

In general, the application review and processing for SSDI can take several months, and payments usually start five months after approval. Therefore, it is important to plan, beginning with stopping work, because you cannot initiate the application process if you are still actively working. Also, you cannot work while waiting to qualify for disability, but you will still need health insurance during this time. Though you will receive Medicare insurance after qualifying for SSDI, Medicare coverage does not begin until 24 months after you begin receiving the monthly benefit checks. This means you will not have Medicare until 29 months after the date you are approved for disability, so you need to have a plan for insurance coverage and financial stability while waiting for Medicare to begin. One option for insurance coverage is to use your employer-based health insurance through COBRA. If you choose to use COBRA, you will be responsible for paying the monthly premium and this is a short-term solution. COBRA benefits are available for only 18 months.

If you are applying for and are approved for SSI, you will qualify for Medicaid the first month you receive an SSI payment. It is important to note that some states require you to complete a separate application for Medicaid after you have been approved for SSI. In those states, the notice of SSI approval will also include an instruction for how to do this.

Many people wonder how long they will continue to receive disability and whether they can return to work. After you qualify for disability, there is a periodic review of your health status. If your condition changes, for example after a lung transplant, you will need to have careful documentation of changes in your health included in your medical record. At times, following a transplant, you may develop other health issues that still require you to maintain disability. Finally, if you also have long-term disability through your work or another entity in addition to SSDI, it is important to know that these programs can also review your health status. Sometimes disability companies will look closer and scrutinize your need to remain on disability. If you receive notice that your health status is being reviewed, it is very important for you to be in close contact with an attorney who specializes in disability and CF.

Many people wonder if it is possible to work, receive disability payments, and have health insurance. Again, there are different situations depending on the type of disability you are receiving. Careful consideration to individual circumstances is warranted before deciding to return to work. Work incentive programs might be available for you; however, it is extraordinarily important to consult with an attorney or the CF Legal Hotline to review your options.

What Resources Are Available to Help Me Make Informed Decisions?

- *State Vocational Rehabilitation Agencies*—https://www.askearn.org/state-vocational-rehabilitation-agencies/

- *O*NET OnLine*—www.onetonline.org/

- *Americans with Disabilities Act and the ADA Amendments Act*—https://www.ada.gov/ Prohibits employers

- *Equal Employment Opportunities Commission* (EEOC)—https://www.eeoc.gov//

- *CF Foundation Compass*—https://www.cff.org/Assistance-Services/Insurance/Your-Insurance-Plan/Find-Resources-CF-Foundation-Compass/

- *Family Medical Leave Act of 1993* (FMLA)—https://www.dol.gov/whd/fmla/fmla-faqs.htm

- *Ticket to Work and Work Incentives Improvement Act of 1999*—https://yourtickettowork.ssa.gov/about/history.html

- *Health Insurance Portability and Accountability Act of 1996* (HIPPA)—https://www.hhs.gov/hipaa/index.html. This act insures the availability of health insurance should you change jobs, it illuminated preexisting condition clause which would for a waiting period prior to being insured

- *Division of Labor*—https://www.dol.gov/

- *US Small Business Administration*—https://www.sba.gov/local-assistance/find/?type=Small%20Business%20Development%20Center&pageNumber=1

- *"Six Tips for Managing CF While Working Full Time" blog*—https://www.cff.org/CF-Community-Blog/Posts/2015/Six-Tips-for-Managing-CF-While-Working-Full-Time/

- *"Your Insurance Plan"*—https://www.cff.org/Assistance-Services/Insurance/Your-Insurance-Plan/

- *Understanding Long-Term Disability Insurance vs. Social Security*—Disability https://www.disability-benefits-help.org/blog/long-term-disability-benefits-and-social-security-disability

WHAT SHOULD I CONSIDER WHEN THINKING ABOUT HAVING A FAMILY?

Olivia M. Stransky, MPH, BA; Sigrid Ladores, PhD, RN, PNP, CNE;
Laura Mentch, EdM, BA; Molly Pam, BA; and
Traci M. Kazmerski, MD, MS

CHAPTER

In This Chapter

Introduction

Deciding to become a parent is an important life decision. As people with cystic fibrosis (CF) grow into adulthood, they often think about starting a family. Perhaps you are wondering what it would be like to have children while living with CF.

If you are thinking about having children, it would be wise to talk with those in your support system—your partner, family, and/or friends. Additionally, your CF care team will be an important resource as they are familiar with what you need to maintain your health and can offer you guidance. Although people with CF face specific challenges when starting a family, an increasing number pursue pregnancy and parenthood. Pregnancy rates for women with CF continue to climb (CF Foundation Registry Report, 2018), and European studies have demonstrated that one-fourth of women with CF and 6% of men with CF are parents. A 2005 Australian survey found that 84% of men with CF wanted children (Sawyer et al, 2005), whereas a 2018 survey found that 78% of adolescent and young adult women with CF in the United States intended to have children (Kazmerski et al, 2018).

It can be helpful to think about the people close to you and consider how they help you now and how that might change if you have one or more children. Having a conversation about their availability and their willingness to assist you will help you determine how much support you will have and what else you might need. It is normal to have concerns and questions about having a child, including worries about how your health will affect your new role as a parent and how parenthood might affect your health. In this chapter, we provide information to help you navigate these questions and concerns.

What Should I Consider If I Am Thinking About Becoming a Parent?

Becoming a parent changes your life, even if you don't have CF. Most people who are thinking about becoming a parent, especially those who live with CF, can benefit from assessing their support system (including their partners, family, and friends), financial situation, career, and lifestyle when deciding whether to start a family.

People with CF should consider additional factors when thinking about becoming a parent. Some parents with CF have mentioned that it can be difficult to balance taking care of themselves and taking care of a child, making them feel as if they need to prioritize one over the other (Barker et al, 2017). You will need to consider how you will balance taking care of yourself and your child, finding time to do your treatments, and getting the sleep you need to stay healthy. You will also need to plan for who will care for your children if you become sick or are hospitalized. Thinking about how you might strike this balance ahead of time can be very helpful.

It's also important to think about the ways that having a child would affect you, your partner, and your support system (Table 11-1). You might also want to think about the emotional and practical aspects of raising a child while facing a reduced life expectancy with medical complications. You might also want to consider how you feel about the possibility of having a child who has CF. Your feelings on this can affect how you choose to build your family.

Table 11-1: Things to Consider When Deciding Whether to Become a Parent As a Person with CF

Support System	
Partner	• Their willingness to participate in some, most, or all of the parenting responsibilities, at different times • Parental leave policies at their place of employment • Impact on your relationship • Their willingness to be a single parent during times of illness or after you pass away
Family	• Impact on the relationship with your family (as grandparents or aunts/uncles) • Potential need for relocation to be closer to your support system • Their willingness and ability to provide care for a child when you are sick or hospitalized • Potential need to take care of aging relatives in addition to parenthood, CF care maintenance, and inpatient hospitalizations for exacerbations and other complications
CF Care Team	• Ability to collaborate on a plan of care for conception, fertility, pregnancy, and parenting • Level of trust and honesty with your care team • Experience with CF pregnancies or ability to collaborate with Maternal Fetal Medicine or a high-risk obstetrician
Other Support	• Need for additional childcare and support (like a nanny, babysitter, or daycare)
Lifestyle	• Effect of obtaining new identity as a "parent" • Social benefits of connecting with your peers who might be building families • Impact on sleep and self-care • Impact on ability to travel or engage in personal hobbies or interests • Impact on social life

continued

Support System	
Financial Considerations	• Costs of child-rearing and childcare
	• Cost of ART (if applicable)
	• Cost of adoption or *surrogacy* (if applicable)
	• Increased household expenses (health insurance, food, supplies, travel costs, increased cost of a larger living space)
	• Potential changes in employment status
	• Potential increased health care costs for you and/or a child
	• Financial impact of partner or support system needing to take off work to care for you and/or a child
Career	• Balancing work and childcare
	• Impact on career opportunities
	• Parental leave policies at your place of employment
	• Potential need to stop working entirely or go on disability status to take care of yourself and/or a child
CF	• Increased exposure to infection from a child
	• Effect of decreased sleep and self-care
	• Impact of parenting on treatment regimen and compliance
	• Impact of your CF on a child (potentially less-active parenting, less time spent with child, early passing, emotional stress)
	• Potential for child to have CF

How Does CF Affect My Birth Control Options?

Women

Women with CF have access to the usual range of contraceptives or birth control options; however, there is little information about birth control use and its effectiveness in CF (Roe et al, 2016). The interplay of CF-specific risk factors, such as medication interactions, CF-related liver disease, *cholelithiasis* (*gallbladder disease* and *gallstones*), CF-related diabetes (CFRD), bone health, and *implantable vascular access devices* (such as *Mediports®*), complicates *contraception* decisions (Whiteman, et al, 2016). Table 11-2 further explores contraception options for women with CF.

In addition to preventing pregnancy, hormonal contraception (e.g., birth control pills, shots, implants), *vaginal rings*, patches, hormonal *intrauterine devices* [IUDs] like the Mirena®, can also be used for other reasons (e.g., irregular periods, menstrual cramps, acne). Some women with CF report that using a hormonal form of contraception can help with symptoms of CF that worsen during their periods (Chotirmall et al, 2012).

Table 11-2: Contraceptive Methods and CF-Specific Considerations

Contraceptive Method	Success Rate (Typical Use; Perfect Use*)	General Summary	CF-Specific Considerations
Intrauterine Device (IUD) • Copper (Paragard®) • Hormonal (Mirena®, Kyleena®, Liletta®, Skyla®)	99%; 99%	• Highly effective, reversible, and long acting • Copper IUDs are effective for 12 years; hormonal IUDs are effective for 3 to 7 years • Copper IUDs can have side effects, such as spotting between menstrual periods, increased cramping, and heavier flow • Hormonal IUDs can lessen or cease menstrual flow and can be used to treat menstrual abnormalities	• *Lumacaftor–ivacaftor (Orkambi®)* may make hormonal IUDs less effective. If you are taking Orkambi, non-hormonal contraceptive methods are recommended. • Copper IUDs (Paragard) are not affected by Orkambi.
Hormonal Implant (Nexplanon®, Implanon®)	99%; 99%	• Highly effective, reversible, and long acting; implants are effective for 3 years • Can lessen or cease menstrual flow, can cause irregular menses or spotting between menstrual periods	• Lumacaftor–ivacaftor (Orkambi®) can make this method less effective. If you are taking Orkambi, non-hormonal contraceptive methods are recommended.

continued

Contraceptive Method	Success Rate (Typical Use; Perfect Use*)	General Summary	CF-Specific Considerations
Depot medroxy-progesterone acetate (DMPA) injection (the shot; Depo-Provera®)	94%; 99%	• Each injection provides 3 months of contraception • May decrease or cease menstrual flow or cause irregular menses • Requires a doctor's visit every 3 months	• DMPA may cause increased loss of *bone mineral density*, such as osteopenia or osteoporosis (Curtis et al, 2016). • Lumacaftor-ivacaftor (Orkambi®) may make hormonal IUDs less effective. If you are taking Orkambi, non-hormonal contraceptive methods are recommended.
Combined hormonal contraceptive pills (the pill)	91%; 99%	• Can provide non-contraceptive benefits, such as treatment of dysmenorrhea (menstrual cramps) or acne • Must be taken daily at the same time • Can decrease menstrual flow and can help regulate your period	• Must be taken around the same time every day and can add onto your CF care routine. • For women who are pancreatic insufficient, not taking enzymes as directed can make the pill less effective. Major issues with malabsorption can also reduce the pill's efficacy (*Contraception: an Australian Clinical Practice Handbook*, 2016). • Lumacaftor-ivacaftor (Orkambi®) may make hormonal contraceptives less effective. If you are taking Orkambi, non-hormonal contraceptive methods are recommended.

Contraceptive Method	Success Rate (Typical Use; Perfect Use*)	General Summary	CF-Specific Considerations
Combined hormonal contraceptive pills (the pill) (*continued*)			• Some antibiotics (e.g., rifampin) and other drugs used to treat *HIV*, certain anti-seizure and antifungal medicines, and some herbal medicine (St. John's wort) will make hormonal contraceptive methods less effective. A second contraceptive method, such as condoms, should be used to prevent pregnancy while you are taking these medications. • Hormonal birth control that contains estrogen can increase the risk of blood clots and might not be a good option if you have CF-related liver disease or have an implanted device such as a port (Deerojanawong, et al, 1998).

continued

Contraceptive Method	Success Rate (Typical Use; Perfect Use*)	General Summary	CF-Specific Considerations
Combined hormonal contraceptive patch (the patch) and Combined hormonal contraceptive vaginal ring (the ring; NuvaRing®)	91%; 99%	• Can provide non-contraceptive benefits, such as treatment of dysmenorrhea (menstrual cramps) or acne • The patch adheres to the skin for 3 weeks, then no patch is worn for a week, then a new patch is applied • The ring is inserted into the vagina for three weeks, then no ring is used for a week, then a new ring is inserted	• Lumacaftor-ivacaftor (Orkambi®) may make hormonal contraceptives less effective. If you are taking Orkambi, non-hormonal contraceptive methods are recommended. • Some antibiotics (e.g., rifampin) and other drugs used to treat HIV, certain anti-seizure and antifungal medicines, and some herbal medicines (St. John's wort) will make hormonal contraceptive methods less effective. A second contraceptive method, such as condoms, should be used to prevent pregnancy while you are taking these medications. • Hormonal birth control that contains estrogen can increase the risk of blood clots and might not be a good option if you have CF-related liver disease or have an implanted device, such as a port.
Tubal Ligation (female sterilization)	99%	• Permanent • The fallopian tubes are cut and tied or cauterized through one or two small incisions in your abdomen • May cause temporary cramping, nausea, and abdominal pain	• After a sterilization procedure, it is important to manage any pain or cramping so that it does not interfere with your airway clearance routine. • Sometimes *anesthesia* is used during a sterilization procedure. People with CF can experience respiratory complications when anesthetized (Deighan et al, 2014).

Contraceptive Method	Success Rate (Typical Use; Perfect Use*)	General Summary	CF-Specific Considerations
Condoms Male condom Internal/Female condom	82%; 98% 79%; 95%	• Must be used during every instance of sexual intercourse	
Internal Barrier Methods *Diaphragm* or cervical cap Sponge	84%; 94% 88%; 91%	• Used in conjunction with spermicide • Must be used during every instance of sexual intercourse • The sponge is less effective for women who have already given birth	• Thicker cervical mucus might make it more difficult for diaphragms, cervical caps, and sponges to stay in place over the cervix.
Emergency Contraception (EC) Levonorgestrel oral form (Plan B, Ella; the morning-after pill) Copper IUD (if inserted within 120 hours of unprotected intercourse)	89%–95%	• The sooner EC is administered after unprotected intercourse, the more effective it is (up to 95% effective if taken within 24 hours of unprotected intercourse) • Side effects are usually mild and may include nausea and early or late menstruation • EC will not affect a pregnancy that has already begun	• If you are pancreatic insufficient, not taking your enzymes as directed can make the pill form of EC less effective.

continued

Contraceptive Method	Success Rate (Typical Use; Perfect Use*)	General Summary	CF-Specific Considerations
Abortion Medication Abortion Surgical Abortion	99%	• Can cause temporary cramping, spotting, or bleeding • Access varies by state and length of gestation	• Medication abortion uses mifepristone, which can reduce the efficacy of long-term corticosteroid therapy. The physician providing the abortion can determine whether medication abortion is contraindicated for you (Guiahi and Davis, 2012). • After an abortion, it is important to manage any pain or cramping so that it does not interfere with your airway clearance routine.

*Perfect use indicates how well a method works when used exactly as directed; typical use indicates how well a method works based on how people use it on average.

If you are taking lumacaftor-ivacaftor (Orkambi®), you should not use a hormonal method of contraception, because this method of contraception could be less effective (Vertex pharmaceuticals, 2017). Instead, you can use a copper intrauterine device (Paragard® IUD), barrier methods (e.g., a condom, female condom, diaphragm, cervical cap), the fertility awareness method, or abstinence. *Ivacaftor (Kalydeco®)* and *tezacaftor-ivacaftor (Symdeko®)* do not have these same interactions, and hormonal birth control is safe to use while on those drugs (Vertex pharmaceuticals, 2018; Roe et al, 2016).

Common CF medications (such as *Cayston®*, Tobi®, Pulmozyme®) and *hypertonic saline* are not known to interact with any forms of contraception. If you are participating in a study for a new medication for CF, you might have additional limitations around the type of contraception that you can use during the study. Talk with your CF care team or study investigator about your contraceptive use.

If you do not want to become pregnant, it is important to use effective contraception that meets your needs because most women with CF are fertile and a healthy pregnancy is supported by careful planning. An unplanned pregnancy can have a big effect on your health. Some CF medications are *teratogenic*, meaning that they can cause problems for the developing fetus; therefore, it is very important for you to prevent pregnancy if you are taking these medications and to have a plan to stop them before trying to become pregnant so that you avoid having a child with birth defects.

Men

Condoms are 85% to 98% effective in preventing pregnancy and they also help avoid *sexually-transmitted infections* (STIs) (Centers for Disease Control and Prevention [CDC], 2018). Men with CF should consider themselves *fertile* unless they know, through testing, that there is no sperm in their *ejaculate*. Condoms benefit all men with CF in reducing the chance of getting an STI during oral, anal, or vaginal sex. *Vasectomy* (a procedure that blocks or severs the vas deferens) is a permanent option for men with CF who do not have absence of the vas deferens (see below under Fertility). A vasectomy can sometimes be reversed with surgery.

Regardless of your fertility and whether you are using birth control, condoms will protect you from STIs like *gonorrhea, chlamydia, syphilis, Hepatitis B,* and *HIV.*

What Are My Options for Building a Family?

If you are thinking about starting a family, talk with your CF care team to help determine your safest and best approaches. Pregnancy can be an option for women with CF. For those with fertility concerns, *assisted reproductive technology* (ART) can help (see below). Other options for starting a family include being a foster parent, adopting, and using surrogacy.

Fostering is when you provide a home for one or more children while their own family is temporarily unable to care for them. The amount of time a child stays with a foster family can vary and can lead to adoption. *Adoption* is when you assume the legal parenting responsibilities for a child whose parents or legal guardians are unable to care for them. If you decide to adopt, you will need to research the options available to you, such as domestic adoption (when you adopt a child from the United States) or international adoption (when you adopt a child from another country). Each has its advantages and disadvantages, and different adoption agencies might have their own guidelines and requirements for placing children with families. Importantly, each state and country has its own regulations, processes, and costs for fostering or adopting children.

Surrogacy is when someone else becomes pregnant and carriers a child specifically for you. There are two types of surrogacy: *gestational* and *traditional*. *Gestational surrogacy* is what people usually refer to when they say "surrogacy." In gestational surrogacy, *in-vitro fertilization* is used, and one or more eggs from the female partner (or an *egg donor*) is fertilized with sperm from the male partner (or a sperm donor), and the developing *embryo* is implanted in the surrogate. In traditional surrogacy, the surrogate is inseminated with semen from the male partner or a donor. *Traditional surrogacy*, which relies on the surrogate's egg, can have additional legal complications because the surrogate is the biological mother of the child; however, this option can be good for same-sex male couples, single men, or women who cannot produce healthy eggs. Surrogacy can be a good option for you, depending on your health, fertility, or your partner's carrier status. It is important to realize that there are different regulations and laws around surrogacy that vary by state and country. International surrogacy can be a less expensive option than domestic surrogacy; however, it comes with its own legal and emotional challenges.

Does Having CF Affect My Fertility?

Women

Women with CF have the same female anatomy (i.e., ovaries, fallopian tubes, uterus, cervix, vulva, vagina) as women without CF and they usually have normal menstrual cycles. However, the mucus in and around your cervix can be thicker than in a woman without CF, which can make it more difficult for sperm to travel through it to reach an egg (Schoyer et al, 2008). Thicker cervical mucus can also change the fertilization ability of sperm (Muchekehu and Quinton, 2010). Additionally, poor nutrition or low weight affect a woman's fertility (Hodges et al, 2008).

New *CF modulator therapy*, like ivacaftor, addresses the basic *cystic fibrosis transmembrane conductance regulator* (CFTR) defect and can thin cervical mucus in women with CF (Ladores et al, 2017) and improve mucus viscosity (Jones and Walshaw, 2015). The effects of these medications on female fertility have not been formally studied and the effects on the fetus are unknown, but case studies have reported on the perceived positive effects of such therapies on fertility in women with CF.

If you have stopped using birth control and have been trying to become pregnant without success, you might want to learn more about fertility awareness, a natural method of learning about the fertility signs during the menstrual cycle and tracking ovulation to increase your odds of conception. If you have been unable to become pregnant for some time, you can talk to your CF team about obtaining a referral to see a *fertility specialist* (Lyon and Bilton, 2002). Typically, fertility testing isn't done until a woman and her partner have been trying to get pregnant for about a year.

Men

Although men with CF have most of the same anatomy (i.e., penis, scrotum, testes) as men without CF, 97% to 98% of men with CF do not have *vas deferens*, the tubes that carry sperm from the testes toward the penis. This is called *congenital bilateral absence of the vas deferens* (CBAVD; Bombieri et al, 2011). Because of CBAVD, the ejaculated semen does not contain any sperm. However, men with CF still produce sperm in the testes and are not technically considered infertile. There are ART methods to help men with CBAVD conceive (see the following section). CBAVD does not affect sexual function or cause impotence or erectile dysfunction. Men with CF and CBAVD can have less ejaculate than men without CF when they achieve orgasm.

What Is Assisted Reproductive Technology (ART)?

Women

The process of addressing fertility concerns is the same for all women. Different techniques of reproductive technology include the use of the following:

Fertility medications

These agents stimulate the ovaries to release eggs. Sometimes, these medications can cause *ovarian hyperstimulation syndrome*, which can cause you to have difficulty breathing (Neill and Nelson-Piercy, 2001). Your fertility specialist and CF care team should monitor you closely when you are taking fertility medication.

Intrauterine insemination (IUI)

This technique involves placing sperm directly inside of a woman's uterus in conjunction with her ovulation cycle. This can increase the number of sperm reaching the egg and increase the chance of pregnancy. Sometimes IUI is done in conjunction with use of fertility medications.

In-vitro fertilization (IVF)

This technique involves retrieval of sperm and eggs and fertilization outside of a woman's body in a laboratory. Fertilized eggs (*embryos*) are then transferred into the uterus to continue to develop and then implanted into the uterus, thus beginning a pregnancy. IVF can be a good option for women with CF whose partners have been identified as carriers of CF, as fertilized eggs that do not have two CF gene mutations can be selected for implantation (aka *pre-implantation genetic diagnosis* [PGD]; Mahmoud et al, 2013). With IVF, more than one embryo can be implanted, which can result in multiple pregnancies (twins or triplets). Women with CF who are interested in IVF can talk with their IVF team about the number of embryos to insert in the uterus to reduce the chance of a multiple (high risk) pregnancy, and the added stress of caring for more than one baby. With pregnancy initiated by IVF, there is a higher chance that embryos will split, creating two embryos. Insurance companies in the United States might not cover the costs of IVF and/or PGD, so it is important to consult with your fertility specialists' financial office to determine ways to pay for the procedure(s) and related medications, which can be very expensive.

Men

Men with CF can father healthy children through ART. Typically, sperm is retrieved from the *testes* or *epididymis*, after which IVF is used. Studies have shown a 60% to 65% success rate of ART among men with CF (Hubert et al, 2006). In the general population, there can be an increased risk of poor outcomes in newborns conceived from ART and of a specific risk of increased *genetic malformations* (Kurinczuk, 2003).

An alternative option for men with CF and their partners is *artificial insemination* using donor sperm. In this approach, men and their partners will work with a sperm bank to select a sperm donor. Their partners will then be inseminated with donor sperm. Artificial insemination has a success rate of around 15% per cycle, and it can take several cycles to be successful (Chavkin et al, 2012). Some sperm banks require individuals and couples to undergo counseling prior to the procedure to address any potential emotional, psychological, and ethical concerns with using donor sperm.

Can CF Be Prevented?

CF is a *genetic condition* that occurs when both parents carry a copy of the gene mutation for the CFTR protein which is a *chloride channel* in your body. Although there is no way to prevent these genes from being inherited, there are ways to screen for CF. Your partner or sperm donor can have a *carrier test* to determine whether they carry a copy of the CF mutation gene.

What Is Carrier Testing for CF?

About 1 out of every 31 Americans is a carrier of a CF gene mutation. Genetic testing is available to find out whether your partner is a carrier for CF. This is done using a blood sample or by scraping cells from the inside of a person's mouth. There are three possible tests that can be done. The most common is a panel of the 23 most common CF gene mutations. If this test comes back negative, there is still a small chance a person is a CF carrier, but it carries a less common CF gene mutation. Another panel tests the 85 most common CF mutations. Rarely, you can elect to test for the full panel of CF gene mutations. Contact your insurance provider to find out what tests are available and covered by your insurance plan.

It is a personal decision to have genetic testing done to find out whether your partner is a CF carrier. In addition to your family and friends, there are many people you can talk to about whether this is the right choice for you. As someone with CF, you should consider consulting with a *genetic counselor*, who is a great resource (to ask questions and to help you understand the testing options). The *Cystic Fibrosis Foundation (CF Foundation)* website has more information on genetic testing (https://www.cff.org/What-is-CF/Testing/Carrier-Testing-for-CF/). You can also visit the website for the *National Society of Genetic Counselors* (https://www.nsgc.org/).

Will My Baby Have CF?

CF is a genetic disease that requires two copies of a CF gene mutation (one from each parent) to occur. A person with one CF gene mutation is a *carrier* for CF. CF carriers do not have CF symptoms but could pass the CF gene on to their children. If you have CF and are thinking about getting pregnant and having children, it is important to think about finding out whether your partner is a CF carrier and what the chances of passing CF on to your children might be. If you become pregnant through IVF, your fertilized eggs can be tested for CF mutations using PGD before implantation in the uterus (Biazotti et al, 2015). With this method, you and your doctor can select embryos that have only one CF mutation, ensuring that they will be a carrier for CF, but will not have the CF disease.

If you have CF and your partner is a carrier for CF, there is a 50% chance that your child will have CF and a 50% chance that your child will be a carrier for CF (Figure 2-1). If your partner is not a carrier for CF, there is a 100% chance your child will be a carrier of CF and a 0% chance that your child will have CF. If you and your partner have CF, there is a 100% chance your child will have CF. If your partner is a carrier for CF and you are using a donor egg or sperm from someone who is a carrier for CF, there is a 25% chance your child will have CF and a 50% chance they will be a carrier of CF. If you have CF and your partner is not screened and their status is not known, your child will have a 1 in 50 risk of having CF.

If you or your partner is already pregnant you can take a test to find out whether the fetus has two mutations for CF. *Chorionic villus sampling* (CVS) can be done as early as 10 weeks of pregnancy, and *amniocentesis* can be done starting at 15 weeks (American College of Obstetricians and Gynecologists, 2017). If the test indicates that the fetus has two mutations for CF (your child will have CF), you will have three options: continue the pregnancy and make preparations to have a child with CF, continue the pregnancy and make plans for adoption, or terminate the pregnancy through an abortion.

How Will CF Affect My Chances of Having a Healthy Pregnancy?

Pregnancy is increasingly common in women with CF (*Cystic Fibrosis Foundation Annual Patient Registry Report*, 2014). Despite the increased respiratory, cardiovascular, metabolic, and endocrine demands of pregnancy, many women with CF deliver healthy infants with little effect on their own health. Overall, women with CF who become pregnant have better pulmonary function and nutritional status and fewer CF complications than those who do not become pregnant (McMullen, et al, 2006). However, women with CF who are pregnant also undertake more treatments for their CF and have more outpatient clinic visits (Goss et al, 2003; Gillet et al, 2002). During pregnancy, you might experience temporary decreases in your pulmonary function, develop diabetes, or require more antibiotics or hospitalizations (Boyd et al, 2004; Hilman et al, 1996).

For some women with CF, pregnancy poses significant risks. If you have *pulmonary hypertension*, *cor pulmonale* (failure of the right side of your heart), or respiratory failure, it is unsafe for you to become pregnant (Budev et al, 2005). Women with CF who have CF-related liver disease or infection with *Burkholderia cepacia* should be cautious about becoming pregnant (Edenborough et al, 2008). Pregnancies have been reported in women awaiting and after *lung transplantation* (Thorpe-Beeston et al, 2013; Cheng et al, 2006). However, women with CF who have had lung transplants have an increased risk of *organ rejection*, decreased survival, and complications in their babies (Gyi et al, 2006). Furthermore, many transplant *anti-rejection medications* are teratogenic (Table 11-3). Current recommendations are to wait for a period of stable health of at least 2 years after transplantation before modifying your medication regimen and trying to become pregnant. Please talk with your transplant team before attempting to become pregnant.

Table 11-3: Teratogenic CF Medications (Categorized by Drug Type)

Antimicrobials (Antibiotics, Antivirals, and *Antifungals*)
Acyclovir
Chloramphenicol
Ciprofloxacin
Clarithromycin (avoid in first trimester of pregnancy)
Colistin (intravenous and inhaled/nebulized forms)
Doxycycline
Fluconazole
Gancyclovir
Gentamicin (intravenous form)
Imipenem
Itraconazole
Meropenem
Metronidazole
Posaconazole
Rifampin
Tobramycin (intravenous form)
Trimethoprim-sulfamethoxazole (Bactrim®)
Vancomycin
Voriconazole
Other Medications
Bisphosphonates
Ranitidine (Zantac®)
Ursodiol (avoid in first trimester of pregnancy)
Vitamin A supplements

Children of women with CF are generally healthy but can be *premature* (i.e., born more than three weeks before their due date) (Edenborough et al, 2000).

If you are thinking about becoming pregnant, it's always best to plan ahead with the help of your support system. It is also very important to talk with your CF team, who can help you think about your health and any risks that pregnancy could pose for you. Your CF team will consider your lung function, nutritional status, whether you have diabetes or liver disease, and other important health factors. Careful planning for pregnancy at a time when you are as healthy as possible can lead to the best outcomes for you and your baby.

Women with CF who become pregnant are often referred to a *high-risk obstetrician* (also known as a *maternal-fetal medicine* or *MFM specialist*). Safe, successful pregnancies require care from both the CF team and from specialized women's health providers. You and your partner will most likely be referred for genetic and mental health counseling with attention to the emotional and practical aspects of pregnancy and raising a child. Optimizing your health before becoming pregnant, and maintaining your CF care through-out pregnancy, delivery, and in the *postpartum period* will help you be as healthy as possible to take care of your baby. Maintaining good airway clearance, nutrition, and being screened for diabetes will support a healthy pregnancy. The *prevalence* of *postpartum depression* and *anxiety* in women with CF is not known, but all women, regardless of whether you have CF, should be monitored carefully.

You will need to consider where your high-risk obstetrician is located and the potential need and impact for inpatient CF treatment before or after birth. In addition, after delivery, all women experience changes in their brains that support positive adaptation to mother-hood (Kim, 2017). As you become more focused on your baby and less on yourself, it will be important to create a plan that enables you to continue your CF treatment regimen.

Can I Take My Regular CF Medications If I Plan on Becoming Pregnant?

Some CF medications are teratogenic, or dangerous for a developing fetus, and can cause birth defects. That's why it's very important for you to tell your CF team when you are thinking about becoming pregnant and to use birth control correctly when you want to avoid pregnancy. Your CF care team will help you figure out any changes to your medica-tions and therapies that might be required beforehand. If you have had a transplant, your transplant team will help you do the same. Your provider(s) will also likely have you take *prenatal* vitamins and folic acid before you try to become pregnant. See Table 11-3, for a list of CF medications that can be teratogenic. If you are taking any of the listed medications and are considering becoming pregnant, you should consult with your CF team.

Can I Take a CF Modulator During Pregnancy?

The effects of ivacaftor (Kalydeco®), ivacaftor-lumacaftor (Orkambi®), and tezacaftor/ivacaftor (Symdeko®) when used during pregnancy and breastfeeding are being studied (Heltshe et al, 2017). Several women on modulators have had healthy pregnancies, and some research has shown that stopping a modulator can have negative effects on your CF health (Trimble and Donaldson, 2018). Talk with your CF care team if you are taking these medications and are pregnant or thinking about becoming pregnant.

How Does CF Affect My Chance of Complications During Pregnancy?

During pregnancy, some women experience more CF exacerbations, whereas others feel healthier while pregnant. You might also experience *constipation* and issues with nutrition and gaining enough weight for your baby's growth. Just like women without CF, you can also develop a form of *diabetes* called *gestational diabetes* during pregnancy that usually improves after your baby is born. *Anemia* is common in CF and in pregnancy; thus, testing for blood iron levels is important in prenatal care for women with CF. Because of these health concerns, it is important to work closely with your CF care team and obstetrician throughout your pregnancy.

Complications that can occur during pregnancy include the following:

Pulmonary exacerbations

Women with CF experience more CF exacerbations during pregnancy. Your CF care team will review your medications that have treated your exacerbations. Because many antibiotics are unsafe to take during pregnancy, the antibiotics you are prescribed might need to be changed. It's important to work with your CF care team to continue your daily therapies to prevent exacerbations.

Pre-term or premature delivery

Some women with CF deliver their baby early. A *pre-term* or premature delivery is a birth that takes place more than 3 weeks before the baby is due. Babies born early often have a low birth weight and have heart problems, gastrointestinal issues, breathing problems, and feeding difficulties. Depending on how early a baby is born, they might have to spend time in the *neonatal intensive care unit* (NICU).

Gestational diabetes

This is a type of diabetes that a woman develops during pregnancy that usually improves after giving birth. Women with CF who do not have CFRD are at a higher risk of developing gestational diabetes than women without CF. Women with CFRD can expect their insulin needs to change during pregnancy.

Constipation

Almost all women experience some constipation during pregnancy. Women with CF have a higher risk of constipation while they are pregnant. This can be treated with stool softeners and/or laxatives. Talk with your obstetrician about which medications you can use when you are pregnant.

Nutritional deficiency

A woman should gain about 25 to 35 pounds during pregnancy. Because many women with CF struggle with maintaining an optimal weight, it can be more difficult to gain enough weight during pregnancy. Women with CF can consider taking nutritional supplements during pregnancy to gain the right amount of weight. Prenatal vitamins and folic acid should be started before conception and taken throughout your pregnancy.

Hypertension

Women with CF have a higher risk of hypertension (high blood pressure) during pregnancy. If you become pregnant, your CF team and your obstetrician will monitor your blood pressure closely. Hypertension during pregnancy can be treated with medications.

Can I Breastfeed?

Women with CF can breastfeed their babies safely. However, there are some considerations for women with CF when deciding whether or how long to breastfeed. Early in your pregnancy, you might want to talk with your dietitian to decide on a threshold for weight loss because of breastfeeding, which can use a lot of calories. You will need to work with your CF team to make sure you are maintaining a healthy weight. Your CF team will also let you know which of your medications might be unsafe if you are planning on breastfeeding. Breastfeeding also interrupts sleep. If you choose to pump ahead of time or supplement with formula, even if only at night, your partner can feed the baby, allowing you to get a full night's rest. Remember that taking care of yourself is taking care of your baby and that you can feed your baby with breastmilk, formula, or a combination of both.

How Can I Talk to My Children About My CF?

Including your child in your CF care routines from a young age can be a great start to introducing them to your disease. At early ages, your child will have questions about your treatment and care with CF. Answer each question clearly and simply, and then ask "Is that what you wanted to know?" It might be helpful to think about how CF was explained to you as a child and adapt it to explain your CF to your child. You might also find it useful to look at resources for parents of children with CF for suggestions on how to explain the disease. As they grow older, children can be involved with your routine by helping with your *airway clearance technique* or exercising with you. The CF Foundation has published videos and articles on parenting as someone with CF that might be helpful for you (www.cff.org/Life-With-CF/Transitions/Family-Planning-and-Parenting-With-CF/Parenting-as-an-Adult-With-CF).

Conclusions

Regardless of whether you plan to have a family, your sexual and reproductive health is an important part of your well-being. This chapter discussed how CF interacts with your reproductive and sexual health. Your CF can affect your birth control options, your fertility, and/or your parenting, and you might want to talk more with your CF team about your sexual health and reproductive goals.

ARE MY FEELINGS ABOUT HAVING CF NORMAL?

Desireé N. Williford, MS; Christina L. Duncan, PhD; Tess Dunn, BA; and Yelizaveta Sher, MD

CHAPTER 12

In This Chapter

- Introduction

- Is There a Normal Way to Feel About Having CF?

- Why Might I Feel Guilty That My Child Has CF?

- Why Might I Feel Helpless or Angry?

- Is It Normal to Feel Sad, Discouraged, Frustrated, or Hopeless?

- Is It Normal to Feel Overwhelmed by Dealing with CF?

- Are My Feelings About My Body Normal?

- How Do I Deal with My Feelings When Friends with CF Become Sicker or Die?

- How Can I Learn to Cope Better with My Emotions?

Introduction

In this chapter, we explore the relation between cystic fibrosis (CF) and emotions, the coping strategies that individuals might use, and how those coping strategies can interact with the acceptance and management of CF. Our mental and physical health are intimately linked, so understanding your emotions and how you deal with them, whether you are a parent of a child with CF or an individual with CF, is important for maintaining and improving overall well-being.

Is There a Normal Way to Feel About Having CF?

Parents

Providing care for someone with a chronic illness like CF can be emotionally challenging, particularly if that someone is your child. There is no "right" or "normal" way to feel about CF. You might experience one or more emotions while learning about and coping with CF, living with its day-to-day management, and dealing with related medical, social, and financial concerns. Some important and common negative emotions include guilt, helplessness, anger, sadness, discouragement, frustration, and hopelessness. You might feel multiple emotions at the same time, and they can change over time, potentially making it difficult to identify how or what you are feeling. This is okay, as different emotions can arise based on your personal experience and ways of coping (Wong and Heriot, 2008). Learning to recognize and to attend to what you are feeling is what is most important.

Although feeling negative emotions is quite common, persistent emotional distress such as overwhelming *anxiety* and depression warrants a discussion with your doctor, a mental health professional, or your child's care team. In fact, studies have shown that high rates of anxiety and depression occur among those caring for a child with CF (Besier et al, 2011; Quittner et al, 2014). Your care team can direct you to various resources and support, such as information produced by the *Cystic Fibrosis Foundation (CF Foundation)*, or referrals to a behavioral or mental health specialist. The bottom line is that taking steps to care for yourself and these symptoms helps you and your family, including your child with CF.

Adolescents/Adults

Similarly, when it is you who is living with CF, you might experience a variety of emotions. Although there might be some similarities and themes across populations with CF, there is no one "normal" way to feel about dealing with CF. You might have spent many days processing your thoughts and feelings and by now have accepted your diagnosis. Or you might have avoided thinking about what it means for you to live with CF beyond how it intrudes on your life and forces you to deal with your treatments or hospitalizations. Or, your acceptance of CF might change with a new medical complication. As someone living with this disease each day, at times you might feel angry, sad, hopeless, frustrated, or overwhelmed. Alternatively, you might feel hopeful and look forward to new scientific and clinical advancements, appreciating and enjoying the good things in your life. You also might feel that meticulously planning your life allows you to feel most in control; or, you might feel that being spontaneous and living for today creates your best opportunities to experience the joys of life. At times, you might feel isolated and different from others, worried that others might not be able to understand or relate to what you are going through. Or you might feel deeply appreciative of special connections and bonds that you have developed outside of and within the CF community and feel grateful that you get to be a part of this vibrant community. Finally, as Mallory Smith, a young woman with CF, describes in *Salt in My Soul: An Unfinished Life* (Smith, 2019), you might feel that having CF has allowed you to gain wisdom that it takes others many more years to appreciate, and that although CF is a burden, you are also grateful for this opportunity.

These feelings might change depending on how you are doing emotionally and physically. There is no one "normal" way to feel about CF, and hopefully you feel comfortable with your feelings, learn to express them in a healthy way, and develop coping skills to manage overwhelming feelings that get in the way of taking care of yourself. This chapter aims to help you explore these feelings and identify strategies that might work for you.

Why Might I Feel Guilty That My Child Has CF?

Parents

Guilt is frequently felt by parents and caregivers of a child with CF. Given the *genetic* underpinnings of the disease, parents might experience guilt and sadness around their positive *carrier status*, particularly at the time of diagnosis (Salm et al, 2012). Parents can feel responsible for their child having the illness and might have misunderstandings about its causes (e.g., my child has CF because of something I did during or before pregnancy), leading to negative feelings (Cunningham and Taussig, 2013). Problematic or misinterpreted communication from health care providers at the time of initial screening and diagnosis (e.g., during discussions of the causes and genetic risk of CF) can also contribute to guilt, which can be further complicated by later struggles of deciding when, how, and what to tell their child about the diagnosis, associated genetic risks, and prognosis (Metcalfe et al, 2011; Cunningham and Taussig, 2013; Ulph et al, 2015).

Simultaneously managing CF-related demands with tasks of everyday life (such as caring for all children, maintaining employment, and running a household) can create stress and guilt for parents and caregivers. Caregivers might feel they are not "good enough" or "doing enough" for their child with CF and/or others in the home. Parents might describe guilt around spending different amounts of time with the child with CF (e.g., due to hospitalizations; time involved with medical routines; changes in attention, routines, resources available for healthy siblings) as compared to the time spent with their healthy children. These themes are described in Myra Bluebond-Langer's 1996 book, *In the Shadow of Illness: Parents and Siblings of the Chronically Ill Child* (Blubond-Langner, 1996), which highlights the experiences of real families living with CF. As highlighted in such resources, these feelings are a normal part of adjusting to a chronic illness. However, strategies and supports are available to help you cope successfully with negative feelings.

Why Might I Feel Helpless or Angry?

Parents

Helplessness and anger arise commonly. For example, contemporary artists have visually-illustrated personal anger and its relationship to feeling marginalized, isolated, and depersonalized due to CF (Milliken, 2018). CF community blogs have also discussed experiences of family members who feel helpless and angry. In a blog post by Kimberly Houston (2017), a mother of two children with CF, she describes her anger and frustration regarding the rigorous nature of CF care, which then resulted in her directing frustrations and sadness toward her children. Or, as described by Lisa Greene, a mother of two teenagers with CF, the demands of managing her child's CF makes her feel like "a doctor, nurse, lawyer, pharmacist, accountant, and child psychiatrist all in the same body" (Greene, 2016).

Facing mental health concerns like anxiety or depression can also contribute to helplessness and anger. Effectively addressing these mental health concerns (e.g., entering *psychotherapy*) and engaging in self-care is often crucial. Though it can feel selfish to attend to yourself and to your well-being, it is not; rather, it is an ideal way to show your child or adolescent with CF that mental health and wellness are as important as is physical health. Taking care of yourself is also essential to helping you care more effectively for your family and for building resilience (i.e., the ability to "bounce back" from these stressful life experiences) for yourself and your family. Research has even suggested that there are significant links between parental mental health and outcomes of their children with CF (such as adherence to CF care and disease self-management) (Quittner et al, 2014; Barker and Quittner, 2016).

Adolescents/Adults

When you are the one living with CF, as an adolescent or an adult, feelings of anger can surface as a reaction to your chronic illness, to the multiple demands CF imposes on your life, to the compromises that you might need to make, and to the challenges inherent in communicating with and navigating through the health care and insurance systems, just to name a few. You might feel angry having to juggle multiple needs (such as taking in necessary nutrition, doing treatments, undergoing procedures, and attending doctors' appointments). You might also feel angry when comparing your life to those who don't have CF. These feelings are described in a two-part blog post titled "CF is an Inherently Angry Disease, but We Can't Let it Win," by a man living with CF, Brad Dell (Dell, 2018). He describes how anger was one of his main emotions expressed while processing what it meant to grow up and live with CF. He felt angry at himself for having been born with mutations, angry at his parents for "having let him be born," angry at his healthy siblings, and angry at the world. As he grew up and faced his mortality, he realized that although his anger was warranted, there was a better way to express his passion for life. He astutely concluded, "We need to ensure the anger is used to motivate us to fight the disease, rather than fight those around us" (Dell, 2018).

Anger is an understandable emotion. However, it is important to ensure that you use anger to fuel you and not destroy you. If you are feeling overwhelmed by your anger, make sure to talk to your CF doctors or a mental health professional to find ways to cope and channel your anger more effectively.

Is It Normal to Feel Sad, Discouraged, Frustrated, or Hopeless?

Parents

Feelings of sadness, discouragement, frustration, and hopelessness about CF are normal. Demands associated with the illness are ever present; concerns, fears, and uncertainty about your child's health are persistent; the chronic course of the disease is draining; and the potential for infections, hospitalizations, and other complications are daily fare. As a parent or caregiver of a loved one with CF, you might find yourself asking questions such as, "Why is this happening to my child and my family?" and feeling discouraged about the life-limiting nature of CF (Cunningham and Taussig, 2013). You might also feel frustrated by or resentful about thoughts that your life is consumed by CF, due to the time, money, and other nonfinancial resources committed to participating in your child's treatment plan (e.g., avoiding germs, attending appointments, and managing hospitalizations) (Cunningham and Taussig, 2013). You might have difficulty feeling gratitude or hope that your family's life can be "normal." Or, you could feel lonely and isolated from others because many people you interact with each day are unable to understand your family's experience or your child's illness (Cunningham and Taussig, 2013).

Adolescents/Adults

Similarly, when you are living with CF as an adolescent or an adult, it is normal to have these feelings due to how CF consumes so much of your time, energy, and finances. It is normal to feel sad when you realize that CF can reduce your longevity, your overall health, and affect a host of life decisions because you have CF. Feelings of sadness, discouragement, frustration, and hopelessness might soar during the times of pulmonary exacerbations and/or hospitalizations. A study from one center described that during pulmonary exacerbations people with CF are more likely to experience peaks of illness-related feelings of threat and loss of control (Schmid-Mohler et al, 2019). This study highlights how symptoms and treatment during the exacerbations consume energy and restrict physical activity and roles of daily life. In turn, emotional distress was also the major driver for patients' improved self-management; personal goals and illness beliefs influenced their self-management decisions.

In the aforementioned book, Mallory Smith described all of these feelings, especially when coming into close contact with new complications and barriers to her previously made goals, repeated hospitalizations, multiple exacerbations, all while dealing with the infuriating inefficiencies of the medical system (Smith, 2019). She also focused on her immense gratitude and appreciation when she felt well, when she was able to do meaningful things, when things went right, and when she felt the love for, and of, those around her.

It is, however, important to distinguish transient symptoms of sadness from persistent symptoms of *depression*. Depression is diagnosed when someone continues to feel depressed and/or have lost interest or pleasure in their everyday activities, more days than not, for 2 or more weeks, in addition to having changes in their appetite or weight, changes in their energy and activity level, feelings of worthlessness or guilt, having difficulty with decision making, or thoughts of death or suicide; these *symptoms* affect functioning and roles of this individual (APA, 2013). If you think that you have developed *major depressive disorder* (MDD) and not just transient sadness, reach out to your health care team or professional mental health provider for further evaluation and treatment (see Chapters 3, 5, and 14 to learn more about depression and anxiety and how you can treat and manage them).

Is It Normal to Feel Overwhelmed by Dealing with CF?

Parents

Having a child with CF creates a wide range of challenging emotions that vary in their intensity and nature depending on the timing (e.g., initial diagnosis, "typical" adolescent struggles) and situation (e.g., exacerbation or hospitalization, transition in care, waiting for lung transplant). Caring for anyone with a long-term health condition can be overwhelming. Indeed, having a young child with CF is accompanied by tremendous responsibility, as parents bear the burden of providing all or most of the direct care, which can create parental stress (Bourdeau et al, 2007). Responsibilities are wide ranging (e.g., taking their child to clinic; navigating insurance coverage; obtaining and organizing medications and equipment; setting up, administering, and cleaning up after treatments; preparing and overseeing proper nutrition; taking time off of work and other responsibilities when their child has an exacerbation or is hospitalized). As a result, incorporating CF into daily family life and routines is unquestionably taxing. Parents might unknowingly find themselves focusing so much on caring for their child that they no longer attend to their personal and health needs and can lose a sense of their own identity (Hodgkinson and Lester, 2002). Consequently, it is vital that parents develop their own supports, including family members and friends who can help with responsibilities from time to time (Hodgkinson and Lester, 2002), and who might have a more objective view of recognizing when a parent is overwhelmed.

In addition, transitions that are stressful for parents of healthy children, like sending a child to daycare or school for the first time, become even more emotionally charged when the child has a chronic health condition, like CF. Parents need to be assertive when reaching out and partnering with school staff, so that accommodations can be made for the specific needs of their child (Grieve et al, 2011). Though youth with CF take on more responsibility for CF care as they grow older, parents never fully disengage, emotionally. Parents often report struggles in how to transfer responsibility to their child in a confident and effective manner. Not surprisingly, some parents have heightened concerns when their adolescent or young adult transitions to adult health care (van Staa et al, 2011), goes to college, or moves out of the home to start a new job or to marry.

Adolescents/Adults

As an adolescent or an adult, it is also normal to feel overwhelmed when dealing with CF and knowing you are living with a disease that has no cure. Although there is hope on the horizon as new therapies receive United States *Food and Drug Administration* (FDA) approval, the disease is still variable and progressive. There are no days off from having CF; the lows that accompany the disease are daunting, with intravenous antibiotics, time spent in the hospital, and declining lung function all too common. It is no surprise, then, that CF creates an emotional roller coaster, full of ups and downs. On days when you are feeling good, you can be confident and grateful; on days when you are feeling physically down, it is easy to feel anxious or depressed. It is also overwhelming to manage your CF and do all the treatments and self-care necessary to maintain your health. Even on the days when you are feeling okay, the idea that you might relapse can be terrifying and overwhelming. Again, these feelings are normal, though they might require some strategies or support to manage effectively. With effective self-care and coping mechanisms, it is possible to manage symptoms of depression and anxiety.

Are My Feelings About My Body Normal?

CF affects the body's appearance in several ways. In particular, youth with CF tend to be smaller and thinner than their peers, and they can go through puberty later than other teens (Aswani et al, 2003). These effects can also make adolescents look younger than their age. Although many adults value a younger appearance, adolescents generally do not like it and would rather "look normal" and be like their peers (Withers, 2012). Even though this has the potential to reduce self-confidence, youth can be comforted in knowing that puberty and appearance will catch up in time. In fact, some healthy teenagers weather this same angst, as puberty is a trying process for many—coming too early for some and late for others.

As adolescents and adults with CF, you are not immune to the culture that surrounds all of us and its focus on having the "perfect body" (i.e., in terms of size and shape). Body image is an issue for everyone, but it is particularly meaningful for those with CF because of its potential association with disordered-eating behaviors (e.g., food avoidance), which in turn can negatively affect health status and prognosis. For example, some individuals with CF become accustomed to their smaller body and might feel some social acceptance when peers compliment their thinness. This can contribute to conflicting goals regarding physical functioning (e.g., disease status) and physical appearance. Indeed, one study showed that those with CF are at increased risk for body image concerns relative to healthy peers or peers with other chronic health conditions (Pinquart, 2013). Body image concerns increase noticeably during adolescence and young adulthood (Truby and Paxton, 2001), consistent with Western cultural ideals that emphasize thinness in females and muscularity in males.

In general, women with CF seem to be happier with their bodies, which are usually slim, as compared to those without CF because this fits with the general society's expressed socio-cultural stereotypes about the attractiveness of the female body (Tierney, 2012). Of note, women receiving nutritional supplementation (i.e., tube feedings) are more likely to want to be bigger, whereas those without a nutritional intervention would like to be thinner, similar to healthy people (Tierney, 2012). On the other hand, men with CF are more likely to be dissatisfied with their slender frames and want to be bigger and more muscular, again to conform to society's ideals of male bodies. Cultural pressure for women to remain thin and for men to gain muscle mass likely contribute to body dissatisfaction in people with CF.

In contrast, others with CF can experience frustration, worry, and a sense of helplessness when not gaining weight or sustaining a recommended body mass index (BMI) at or above the 50th percentile, particularly knowing how important it is for lung function and *prognosis* (Stephenson et al, 2013). If this describes your circumstance, you might feel substantial pressure from your family and your CF care team to increase your *caloric intake* and weight, even when your appetite is low. Given the unique nutritional needs of individuals with CF (see Chapters 3 and 6), chasing a "normal BMI" is demanding. When other people say how lucky you are to eat anything you want and not gain weight, you recognize how your real struggles can be truly misunderstood by those around you. Related to this strain, individuals with CF often experience common gastrointestinal (GI) problems, such as GI upset, food intolerances, constipation, and, at times, frank *distal intestinal obstruction syndrome* (DIOS), which can be very painful and emotionally traumatizing. Food—even though necessary for survival—can provoke fear and anxiety. Individuals might develop beliefs that "food can hurt me" and feelings that food is no longer meant for pleasure, but instead is merely a lot of hard painful work.

Although people with CF do not have elevated rates of eating disorders, disordered eating patterns can occur more frequently in individuals living with CF (Shearer and Bryon, 2004; Abbott et al, 2007). In fact, one study of adolescents with CF demonstrated that one-fourth of those in the study sample had some disturbed eating behaviors, the most common of which was restraint (Shearer and Bryon, 2004). In addition to dieting and restricting nutritional intake, individuals with CF can control their weight and body shape in a variety of ways, including omitting enzymes or insulin, over-exercising, taking weight-loss supplements, or increasing the amount of laxatives or diuretics, which can be dangerous.

On the other hand, post-transplant, people with CF are likely to gain weight due to burning fewer calories on *respiration* with their new healthy lungs, having improved nutritional status, and taking high-dose steroids. There can be also changes in facial and body shape secondary to steroids, such as *moon facies* (which is a rounded appearance due to fat deposits on the sides of the face) and increased abdominal girth. This can be especially troubling to young women who were used to and enjoyed their thinness prior to transplantation. Their new body with greater weight might be unsettling and people might go to extreme attempts to lose post-transplant weight, which can jeopardize their health.

CF affects your body in several ways; however, it is important to recognize that your body does not define you as an individual. You might not have control over what others say and think, but you do have control over your reactions to them and to your body. Surround yourself with people who support and value you for your inner worth, not your outer appearance. Talk openly with your CF care providers about your body image. According to one study (Helms et al, 2017), adolescents and young adults with CF want to discuss their body image as a "distinct topic" with their CF care providers, rather than in the context of physical health or weight-based conversations (including conflicted views on weight goals, *G-tubes*, and medical care goals). Providers also feel that body image concerns should be discussed as part of routine CF care (Helms et al, 2017). Hence, it is important to recognize that body image can be a "touchy subject," but that opening lines of communication between providers and people with CF should get matters moving in a positive direction.

How Do I Deal with My Feelings When Friends with CF Become Sicker or Die?

As someone living with CF, you will likely watch CF progress and even end the lives of your friends with the disease. This can spur many emotions; fear, guilt, and grief are extremely common. Watching a friend struggle is difficult for anyone, let alone someone who shares the same disease. It can be all the more frustrating when you can't be physically present for someone you care for. Guilt is a normal reaction, especially when you are feeling healthier than your friend(s). You might wonder why you are doing fine while your friend is struggling. You can feel helpless, as if there is nothing you can do to change your friend's situation. However, you can turn your guilt into something more positive by reaching out to your friend and supporting this person in the unique ways that you can because of your perspective and insights as a result of sharing CF. Your friend most likely does not hold your good health against you and instead will appreciate your effort to help them. Fear is also common. Seeing what CF can do to a person you care about can make you wonder about your own future health and mortality. Seeing a friend struggle gives you a glimpse into a world you are trying to avoid, and sickness and death might feel inevitable. Again, caring for your friend by listening and providing validation and joy can help lessen your fear and instead lead you to live in the present.

Sometimes, friends become sick and they pass away. Such loss can cause survivor's guilt, make you wonder why they died when you are still alive, worry that you are next, and simply feel overwhelming grief. In her book, Mallory Smith discussed how medical struggles and deaths of her friends with CF affected her (Smith, 2019). She shared, "When someone dies, we all feel the effects, rippling through the network, upsetting the sense of calm that was always an illusion to begin with" (page 133). It is necessary to acknowledge and process these emotions rather than to run from them, no matter how tempting it is to push them aside. Talking with a therapist is key when this occurs; it provides an opportunity to voice your fears, guilt, and sadness with someone who understands your emotions and allows you to explore how you are feeling in a safe space. They can also offer and teach you effective coping skills to use when you feel yourself slipping into anxiety or depression.

How Can I Learn to Cope Better with My Emotions?

Although having a range of difficult emotions is normal, some people living with CF or their parents and caregivers might not be aware of ways to manage and resolve these feelings. Living with CF or caring for a loved one with CF is stressful, as are negative emotions like sadness, discouragement, frustration, hopelessness, helplessness, anger, and guilt. If you are feeling these emotions, seeking support is vital. Although the amount and type of support that might work best for you can vary, support can take many forms; for example, family members, co-workers, and friends, church or other social activities, a support group, a doctor or mental health provider, and/or online resources, like other parents with children with CF. Self-care is also important for managing the demands and stressors of CF and building personal resilience. Self-care activities, including healthy eating and exercise (physical); engaging in preventative medical care (physical); staying connected to others (emotional); scheduling time for fun activities (emotional); and making time for the practice of religion, spirituality, or simple reflection and gratitude (spiritual), can take a variety of forms, so it is best to find the options that work best for you. Outlets such as music, art, and reading are also all healthy ways to identify and express your negative emotions.

Time spent with family, friends, and other social supports can also provide encouragement and connection in addition to promoting self-care behaviors and overall wellness. It is key to find a support system that can reassure you and help you when your anxiety and depression take over. It is useful to recruit a close group of friends and family who can care for you in the midst of your depression and anxiety and provide you with comfort and reassurance.

Face-to-face and online support groups (and community blogs) are additional options to those living with, or caring for, someone with CF. These provide similar benefits to the other social supports noted earlier. Online support groups and blogs, specifically, can be a convenient way of receiving information, encouragement, and advice while reaching out to other parents and young people from a larger geographical region, yet maintaining your chosen degree of privacy and anonymity. These options are particularly helpful if you do not yet feel comfortable with the idea of face-to-face groups or are someone with CF and therefore unable to attend in-person meetings. Some of these resources also include technology-facilitated face-to-face components, such as video chat. A few examples of online support and communities that are available to you include the CF Community Blog and *CF Peer Connect* program through the CF Foundation; the *Support Families Program* through *Claire's Place Foundation Incorporated*; Facebook and email-based groups, such as *CF Connect and CYSTIC-L*; and psychosocial support programs and classes available through *Cystic Fibrosis Research Incorporated* (CFRI) (for additional resources, see Chapter 19).

Discussing your personal journey and connecting with others who are also faced with the challenges of CF can provide support, comfort, hope, and encouragement during times of stress, worry, and other negative emotions. It also can provide a safe space to ask questions and to elicit information and advice from others on important CF-relevant topics such as coping with the diagnosis; balancing the demands of CF with everyday life; managing ongoing challenges, concerns, and negative emotions; handling treatment options and CF-related complications; establishing social and educational connections (e.g., interpersonal relations, school accommodations), and managing the hospital experience (Kirk and Milnes, 2016). However, if these support systems alone are not helpful to you and/or you feel your negative emotions are persistent and overwhelming, discuss these difficulties with your doctor or a mental health professional because professional *psychosocial intervention* can be what you need to feel better (see Chapter 14 for more details). *Therapy* is a safe space; you can vent about your feelings and frustrations without worrying about being a burden, disappointing someone, or being "strong." Therapy can also give you room to feel your emotions without completely "spinning out." A therapist is there to help you move forward without losing yourself to feeling overwhelmed.

HOW CAN CF AFFECT MY FAMILY AND FRIENDS?

Ginger Birnbaum, BA; Amanda Bruce, PhD; and
Stephanie Filigno, PhD

In This Chapter

- How Should I Talk to My Children About Their CF?

- How Can I Help My Children Who Do Not Have CF As They Grow Up with a Sibling with CF?

- How Might My Family and Friends Respond to Me and My CF?

- How Will I Know Whether My Family or Friends Are Not Dealing Well with My CF?

- Is It Wrong for My Family Members to Resent Me and My CF?

- How Can I Help My Children with CF (or My Family When I Have CF) Handle Living with CF More Effectively?

- How Might My Coping Be Influenced by My Family and Friends?

- Are There Support Groups for My Family Members?

- When and How Might I Tell My Romantic Partner About My Having CF?

How Should I Talk to My Children About Their CF?

Talking to children about important topics can be difficult. Preparing for conversations that could bring up strong feelings for you and your child can help to make the conversation easier. One way to prepare is to think through potential questions and answers ahead of time to give your conversation direction. The *Cystic Fibrosis Foundation (CF Foundation)* website provides information to help you to prepare for the conversation (CF Foundation, 2019). Keep in mind that an important goal for raising children with cystic fibrosis (CF) is to help them begin to recognize the importance of their treatments to stay healthy at a young age so that they can do all their favorite things throughout childhood and later in life.

The conversation can take different forms depending on whether your child has come to you with a request to discuss CF or if you have decided to initiate the conversation. Some important topics to cover at some point are listed here; they will not apply to everyone living with CF and at every stage of development, so choose what is pertinent to your situation:

- The pitfalls of not adhering to treatment recommendations
  - Why is *airway clearance* helpful?
  - What is an exacerbation?
- The importance of nutrition
  - Why is nutrition important for you?
  - Do you need to take your enzymes consistently?
  - Are there other ways that you can live with CF and stay healthy?
- Becoming acutely ill
  - Why is good handwashing important?
  - Why is it important to adhere to contact precautions and infection-control guidelines?
- Life, death, and in between
  - Will you be able to live a "normal" life?
  - Will you be in the hospital all of the time?
  - Will you die from this disease?
- Curing CF
  - Is there a cure for CF?
  - Will this be your life forever?
  - Are there good treatments available and are there potential treatments on the horizon? A drug development pipeline is available on the CF Foundation website (CF Foundation, 2019).

Many times, after your child begins to ask questions, he or she will become even more curious. Do not be surprised if "CF Ins and Outs" becomes the hot topic! This is a positive and healthy way to express curiosity. Like adults, children might have been thinking about questions related to their CF for quite some time and feel relieved to get them out into the open. If your child senses that you are willing to be open and honest with them, they will be more likely to ask you questions.

Remember: it is better for you to admit that you do not have an answer than to make one up. Many things about CF are complicated, cannot be planned, or come up unexpectedly. You have every reason to reveal your uncertainties. It is great role modeling for you to say to your child, "That is a great question. Let me ask our care team the answer to that. They love your questions, too."

How Can I Help My Children Who Do Not Have CF As They Grow Up with a Sibling with CF?

Much like your child who is living with CF, the previously listed information will be important for your other child(ren). Siblings of a child living with CF will have unique concerns and needs. When children are either chronically or acutely ill, normal routines often go by the wayside to make room for hospital stays and doctors' visits. This can affect your child, caregivers, and brothers and sisters; siblings might become confused, upset, afraid, numb, or worried (Center for Pediatric Traumatic Stress at the Children's Hospital of Philadelphia: https://www.chop.edu/conditions-diseases/pediatric-traumatic-stress).

A sibling to a child living with CF must deal with many things that other children cannot understand. As they become older, these feelings and experiences can become more stressful. In times of acute illness for the child living with CF, emotions will often be heightened for their siblings. Even with this stress, many siblings want to be supportive and will react positively.

Although these concerns might not apply to every situation, they apply to many. It is also important to keep in mind that typical sibling dynamics, such as rivalry and competing for your attention, apply to your situation, as well.

As for your child without CF, their questions and concerns might include the following:

- They might be interested in their sibling's disease.

- Does their sibling have a life-threatening condition?

- What medications are being used?

- Is their own life is going to change due to their sibling's illness?

- Will others treat them differently because their sibling is ill?

- Will they receive less attention because of their sibling's CF?

- Will you love their sibling more?

Keep in mind the amount of attention your child living with CF requires. As referenced in a study assessing differential treatment in siblings, it was shown that younger children with CF are given more positive attention than an older sibling without CF. The two groups studied were 1) the younger sibling had CF and the older child was healthy and 2) both siblings were healthy. The study took the hours spent on CF medical care into account when quality time was compared between the two groups. As part of the study, playtime was compared between the two groups. It was shown that mothers in the "CF group spent 34% more time in play with younger versus older siblings" (Quittner and Opipari, 1994). It is very important that you plan ways to spend one-on-one quality time with your child without CF. However, it is likely that your child who is not living with CF will note the difference in focused attention given to each child. This is typical response to the situation. You can take this opportunity to listen and allow your children to share their feelings. Expressing your love through words and actions can help to reassure your child of your love.

How Might My Family and Friends Respond to Me and My CF?

People respond to situations in different ways depending on their life experiences and their relationship to the specific situation. Individual differences are important to keep in mind when considering the way people respond to you. You might be able to manage most responses by having meaningful conversations with people important to you and ensure they have or know how to access information about living with CF. There are many excellent resources online where you can find credible information that is fit for sharing.

The following list presents some places where you can find credible information about CF (and your CF Care Center is always an excellent resource):

- **Cystic Fibrosis Foundation:** www.cff.org

- **Boomer Esiason Foundation:** www.esiason.org

- *Cystic Fibrosis Research, Inc.:* cfri.org

- **Cystic Fibrosis News Today:** cysticfibrosisnewstoday.com

Family and friends might express their concern by telling you that they feel bad for you. For many people living with CF, especially as they become older, this can be uncomfortable. Perhaps knowing ahead of time that this is a potential reaction can help you to be better prepared. This could provide an opportunity to respond with information regarding life with CF and the fact that people with CF are living longer than ever before.

Many times, siblings respond positively to your diagnosis by supporting you and by sharing in hopefulness. However, they are likely to become jealous of the attention that they perceive you're receiving. Try to remember that they are also living with CF, in their own way, and might have a difficult time understanding why you get such focused attention so often. Perhaps you can share that you appreciate their support and help, and that you understand (as best you can) that it is also difficult for them to live with CF.

Many people want to help you "get well." Your family and friends can become involved with your care in a variety of ways. How they get involved is entirely up to you and what you are comfortable with.

Here are some ways to help family and friends become involved:

- Share treatment time with them.

- Have them help you with one of your daily care tasks (like set up or cleaning or picking up medications from the pharmacy).

- Invite family and friends to be a part of fund-raisers.

- Invite family and friends to care center appointments.

- Keep family and friends up-to-date on recent advancements in CF research.

- Host education days at school or work.

Some people may respond with disbelief that you have an illness because many people who are living with CF do not show outward signs of the disease. Many older people living with CF say that this is one of the most difficult things that they deal with. Educating others about the disease and what is happening inside your body is a good way to educate them about your condition. You can tell them that on many days you go about your life just as they do, but with the addition of completing necessary medical therapies. In fact, it is these medical therapies that allow you to go about your business when you are feeling well.

You might find that some family and friends become overwhelmed by your living with CF. They worry about your health, feel sad when you miss fun things because of treatments or when you are sick, and feel stressed about your medical appointments and medical bills. The guilt and burden can be difficult to manage for many who are living with CF. In fact, in the International Depression Epidemiological Study (TIDES), the largest international trial focused on *anxiety* and depression in CF, anxiety was two to three times more likely in adolescents and adults with CF as well as their caregivers (Quittner et al, 2014).

Additionally, depending on what is currently going on in your life, people will respond to you differently. It is entirely possible that many of your family members and friends will not understand your life with CF until something serious happens. Setting your expectations and preparing for these conversations will make a tremendous difference in how you are able to handle these conversations.

It is important for you to be surrounded by people who support your health. Unfortunately, some members of your family and your friends might not initially understand the importance of avoiding smoke, staying away from them when they are unwell, and practicing good hand washing. As soon as people know the reasons why these things affect your life with CF, they might be more likely to make important changes to help you stay healthy. It is also appropriate to set boundaries with those who are not doing what you ask them to do so that you can stay healthy.

How Will I Know Whether My Family or Friends Are Not Dealing Well with My CF?

There is no perfect, ideal, or "right" way to cope with the challenges that come with caring about someone who has CF. People often struggle with thoughts and feelings about CF for different periods of time. Some say and do different things because of these thoughts and feelings. At times that are known to be more difficult than other times (e.g., when the CF diagnosis is first made, hospitalizations, discussion about transplant), stress is often high. When people with CF are ill and need more intensive treatments, their family and friends can be more stressed. Stress can also be more noticeable when CF progresses or an additional diagnosis is made (like *CF-related diabetes* (CFRD) or *CF-associated liver disease* (CFLD). If your family or friends have frequent, persistent, and uncontrollable sadness, worry, or anger for more than two weeks, they might need to address these experiences. You can contact your CF care team or your primary care provider for support making these connections. It is important to appreciate that the stress of a chronic illness can affect our day-to-day lives, and the sooner that others get help for that stress, the faster and easier it will be for them to feel better.

Increased stress can lead to more conflict and arguments. Alternatively, when people are struggling to cope, they often avoid the person, conversation, or situation because it feels overwhelming. If you feel like your loved ones are avoiding you, not having conversations with you, or no longer supporting you in your daily care, this can also be a sign that they need more support.

Is It Wrong for My Family Members to Resent Me and My CF?

People sometimes feel resentment when they think that something is "unfair." Thinking that CF is "not fair" is common, for those with CF and those who care about them. The thought that CF is unfair can be linked to other thoughts, behaviors, and feelings that might make how people talk and treat each other challenging. Common feelings include jealousy, bitterness, anger, annoyance, unhappiness, and feeling dismissed and mistreated. Common behaviors (what people do) when people feel resentment can include arguing with you, saying mean things to you, saying things that make you feel guilty, avoiding spending time with you, and treating you in a way that is hurtful. These thoughts, feelings, and behaviors are natural from time to time because of the stress that CF can cause for everyone. However, if the thoughts and feelings make it consistently more difficult to treat each other well, talk to each other with respect, and have fun together; it is time to make things better. It is important to address stress as it happens because when stress builds, communication and partnership can be difficult. When it comes to help, the rule is: the sooner the better. One strategy is to talk about how even though it might feel like CF is "pulling" you away from one another, everyone can "come together" and agree on one thing: everyone would like CF to be cured so that things would feel "fair." Siblings often experience these feelings most intensely because they are often evaluating "fairness" within the family. Involving siblings without CF in daily CF care and providing them with their own one-on-one attention and opportunities to talk about how CF is affecting their life is also important. As parents, you might also have these thoughts and feelings related to how CF affects your ability to work, invest in the parenting or marital relationship, manage finances, engage in self-care, operate the family, and have an active social life. You can talk to your CF team and see whether a referral to another provider who can help you to work on communication would benefit you and your family.

How Can I Help My Children with CF (or My Family When I Have CF) Handle Living with CF More Effectively?

Many people with CF strive to balance daily CF care with doing things that they value. This can include things like working, going to school, exercising, spending time with friends and family, reading, playing video games, attending sporting, music, and/or art events. One key factor in finding this balance is to find and follow a daily routine that works to keep you healthy, so that you can do the things that you love doing. Many people write out a daily schedule or use technology (e.g., smart phone apps) to help remind them of daily care tasks. The more that you follow a routine, the easier it will feel to find this balance, even when you are very busy!

You can also ensure that the lines of communication are open to keep positive momentum, or, when things are not going well, to find new ways to obtain support and to work together. For example, when children are young, pointing out to them when they complete a CF care task right away can help to highlight and enforce that behavior in the future. In the teenage years, it is easy to talk to teens only when they miss daily care; however, it is more important to again point out when care is completed to provide the support and acknowledgment of this effort to stay healthy. Problem-solving when daily CF care is missed is also important, especially when done with the help of teamwork. It is also important to point out when you are grateful for someone's help (whether that is a friend or a family member).

Finally, it is commonly said that managing CF well "takes a village" and getting consistent support from friends, family, the medical team, and other meaningful people can help you manage your CF, feel less overwhelmed, and achieve more. Feel free to talk with the CF team when sustaining daily care and health is challenging so that you can get support and recommendations. Wanting and needing this support is natural; asking for help shows your team how much you care about yourself, your health, and living your very best life.

How Might My Coping Be Influenced by My Family and Friends?

Receiving social support from those who care about you is important for anyone with a chronic disease; CF is no exception. Social support comes from family and friends, and even from your medical team. Because being physically close to others with CF is discouraged, face-to-face social support typically comes from those who do not have CF. Important social support from individuals who are living with CF comes through communicating via social media or other forms of technology.

In other chronic diseases, researchers have studied how social support is important for better mental health (e.g., anxiety, depression) (Aslund et al, 2014), improved physical health (Uchino, 2004), and increased adherence to a variety of treatment regimens (DiMatteo, 2004; Gallant, 2003). Not surprisingly, having good social support can positively affect your outcome. A recent study found that in a large sample of patients with CF, more social support was associated with a variety of positive outcomes, including fewer physical symptoms, fewer emotional symptoms, fewer eating/digestive problems, improved body image and vitality, better emotional and social functioning, and less treatment burden for those with CF (Flewelling et al, 2019). Overall, social support appears to be good for you.

Four commonly discussed types of social support (Uchino, 2004) are emotional, tangible, informational support, and companionship. Emotional support involves empathy, love, and warmth. Tangible support (also called instrumental support) refers to help with finances or material goods. Informational support involves advice or guidance. And companionship involves contact with others with whom you can share activities and emotions. The key might be to figure out who you can go to for each type of support.

Are There Support Groups for My Family Members?

Yes! Support groups are available for family members (and for close friends of those who have CF). They can be in person, or they can be virtual (by telephone or internet). The CF Foundation has different options for family members and caregivers. Here's the link for locating support through the CF Foundation: https://www.cff.org/.

Other resources exist, as well, including, but not limited to the following:

- https://clairesplacefoundation.org/programs/outreach-program/

- https://www.cfroundtable.com/partners/cf-resources/

- https://cysticfibrosisnewstoday.com/caring-for-a-family-member-with-cystic-fibrosis/

- https://www.lung.org/lung-health-and-diseases/lung-disease-lookup/cystic-fibrosis/living-with-cystic-fibrosis.html

When and How Might I Tell My Romantic Partner About My Having CF?

This is an excellent question and it can be somewhat tricky to answer. Although it would be helpful if we could say, "Tell them on your third date," unfortunately, there is a lack of research on this topic and no definitive answer. Experts have discussed the important need for better understanding of how persons with chronic illnesses navigate romantic relationships (Helgeson et al, 2015; Maslow et al, 2011). For people with CF, disclosing their disease to a romantic partner is crucial for several reasons. First, it has an impact on day-to-day activities (ranging from time-consuming breathing treatments to frequent hospitalizations). Second, CF can significantly decrease one's life expectancy. Finally, it can affect the decision whether to have children (or how many) and how that would happen.

A recent paper explored aspects of disclosing CF-related information to a romantic partner (Broekema and Weber, 2017). Researchers conducted in-depth interviews with adults living with CF to learn more about their experiences. Four themes emerged from the discussions. First, these patients were concerned with weighing the risks and benefits of sharing CF-related information. One individual did not want to experience rejection (risk) but was motivated by a feeling of wanting acceptance (benefit). A second theme had to do with privacy and a significant change in health status. The course of CF can be unpredictable, at times requiring unplanned hospitalizations. These types of events might necessitate disclosure. The third theme these individuals discussed was the motivation behind a disclosure—why they decided to share certain information at the time they did? Many times, it was out of a feeling of the need for social support in a given moment. Finally, the theme of reactions from outsiders (family of a significant other) was discussed.

To summarize, there is no "one size fits all" approach to deciding when to disclose personal health information to friends or romantic partners. Instead, a person should think about the potential risk and benefits of sharing information and the reason (motivation) behind sharing personal information. Ultimately, to achieve a close personal relationship, important information about oneself (including health!) will probably need to be shared. But the decision about when to share it is up to the individual.

WHICH PSYCHOLOGICAL INTERVENTIONS MIGHT HELP ME MANAGE MY CF?

Emily Muther, PhD and Alexandra Quittner, PhD

CHAPTER

In This Chapter

- Why Might I Need Psychological or Social Support?
- How Might Virtual Group Therapy Be of Help to Me?
- How Can Individual Therapy Be Helpful for Me?
- What Types of Stress Management Interventions Might I Try?
- How Can I Take Advantage of Virtual Peer Mentoring?
- How Can My CF Care Team Help Me Maintain Emotional Wellness?
- Should I Seek Professional Counseling or Psychiatric Care?
- How Can I Get a Referral in My Community?

Why Might I Need Psychological or Social Support?

Given the many challenges of managing cystic fibrosis (CF) each day, you need to have people around you who can provide you with both psychological and social support. Psychological support can include talking to someone who is a good listener, seeking suggestions and input from others, and identifying people who can provide emotional support. This type of support can come from family, friends, co-workers, or others in your social network. You might also elicit support from online "chat" groups that provide peer-to-peer support. A recent international study of depression and anxiety in those with CF and their parent caregivers revealed how common and challenging these symptoms can be (Quittner et al, 2014). Thus, seeking professional psychological support can also be helpful.

A key theme in addressing mental health challenges is this: "There is no health without mental health," a statement made by the first director of the *World Health Organization*, (WHO) who served from 1948 to 1953 (Prince et al, 2007). Thus, as Figure 14-1 illustrates, the goal is to focus on the "whole person" to integrate the treatment of physical and mental health. Recent studies have shown that depression affects physical health and causes *inflammation* in the body (Abbott, 2018; Stuart and Baune, 2012). Thus, treating *symptoms* of depression can reduce inflammation, infections, and adverse health outcomes.

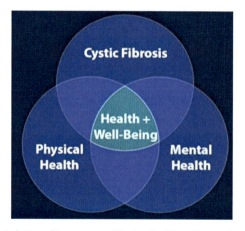

Figure 14-1: Relationship among CF, physical health, and mental health.

Several studies have indicated that individuals with CF and their parent caregivers are at risk for symptoms of depression and anxiety (Quittner et al, 2014). In fact, this is true for everyone (and their parents) who has a chronic condition. This is a "normal" response to challenging situations and thus it is critical for you to pay attention to how you are feeling physically and psychologically and to realize that help is available. Depression and anxiety can also affect how you manage your CF. Studies have also shown that depression negatively affects self-care, including adherence to CF treatments and attendance at CF clinics. Therefore, if you are feeling down, overwhelmed, or lacking in energy, you might have more difficulty motivating yourself to complete your treatments. Anxiety can also provoke avoidance of things that feel stressful, thereby making it more difficult to face things that need to be done to manage your CF and to live your life.

In addition, rates of depression and anxiety were found to be two to three times higher in those with CF and their parent caregivers in nine countries (accounting for more than 6,000 people with CF and 4,200 parents) than in community samples without CF (Quittner et al, 2014). This was a wake-up call for the CF community; it led to a growing awareness of the importance of assessing and treating psychiatric symptoms. This is happening all over the United States, Europe, Canada, and Australia!

Recently, with support of the *Cystic Fibrosis Foundation (CF Foundation)*, mental health screening has been conducted at more than 135 CF centers across the United States. The CF Foundation funded *mental health coordinators* (MHC), who can be *psychologists, psychiatrists*, or *clinical social workers*, for 3 years in these CF centers with the hope that the centers can sustain this effort after the funding ends. Each year, beginning at age 12, all individuals with CF and parent caregivers of children less than 17 years of age will complete a 5-minute screening to assess symptoms of depression and anxiety. This will facilitate brief support and counseling in the clinic and referral to appropriate community practitioners.

Given that symptoms of depression and anxiety are common and that *evidence-based treatments* can result in symptomatic improvement, those with CF and their parent caregivers with psychiatric symptoms should seek psychological support and/or medications to treat psychological distress. If you start an *antidepressant*, be aware that this class of medication can interact with medications used for management of CF. It is important to discuss this with your CF team (see Chapter 5 for more information regarding antidepressant use).

Having a social support network can provide a buffer from some of the adverse effects of stress. Whereas emotional support improves daily functioning, instrumental support (e.g., organizing medications in a pill box) also fills a critical need. Lack of access to in-person peer-to-peer support is often a problem for those with CF. Due to infection-control guidelines, people with CF should not be in the same room and should not socialize in group settings (e.g., support groups, family education days). However, there are creative ways to access this type of support, such as participating in online chat groups and group therapy via telehealth. Many CF centers introduce a newly diagnosed individual and their family to a more experienced parent caregiver who can provide a variety of supports (see Table 14-1).

Social isolation is a common issue for both adolescents and adults with CF; it can lead to loneliness and depression. Thus, social support accessed through family, friends, teachers, and activities (e.g., sports teams, classes, church) is important for maintaining your well-being.

Table 14-1: Types of Social Support

Emotional	Expressions of empathy, concern, affection, love, trust, and caring
Instrumental	Tangible aid and service (e.g., providing meals, giving a ride to the clinic)
Informational	Advice, suggestions, and information
Companionship	Type of support that gives someone a sense of social belonging

How Might Virtual Group Therapy Be of Help to Me?

There is an increasing need to improve access to mental health and other supportive services, especially for those living with and affected by a chronic illness. Barriers to receiving support and/or therapy include time constraints, limited financial resources, issues with insurance coverage, limited options, long commutes and transportation issues, and extended waitlists before visits.

Group therapy and support groups have been used by health care providers to provide psychotherapy, education, and assistance with challenges such as managing daily CF care, reducing stress associated with medical symptoms, and improving quality of life and social support. Groups provide opportunities to meet others with similar health issues or social challenges. You can learn from others, develop self-awareness, give and receive feedback, and recognize that others face similar challenges. Participation in these sessions can reduce feelings of isolation (Smith et al, 2016). Groups can help to eliminate some of the challenges of seeking therapy, by reducing the cost and by increasing the number of those who can receive support. Additionally, using web-based, or *virtual group therapy* can help to reduce barriers and improve access to support and therapeutic interventions.

Virtual support groups provide a range of therapeutic benefits that are like in-person support groups (Shoebotham and Coulson, 2016); online therapeutic interventions have also improved health outcomes (Heinicke et al, 2007). Virtual group therapy often addresses emotional and physical concerns and helps to improve overall coping and well-being. Within the CF community, virtual support groups exist for both patients and caregivers/family members through *Cystic Fibrosis Research Inc.* (CFRI) (www.cfri.org). CF-specific support groups are especially helpful for connecting with someone who understands what you are going through. Because of the limitations on face-to-face connections for those living with CF (due to infection-control guidelines), joining an online support community can be crucial for reducing isolation and stress related to coping with the illness.

How Can Individual Therapy Be Helpful for Me?

Evidence-based interventions that focus on treating depression and anxiety can also reduce the impact of stress. These interventions can be utilized both in the clinic settings and in more traditional outpatient mental health visits.

Cognitive-Behavioral Therapy

Cognitive-Behavioral Therapy (CBT) is an intervention that teaches you skills that can help you to cope with challenging situations. These skills include problem solving, *relaxation training*, cognitive restructuring (i.e., identifying negative thoughts and reframing them in more balanced ways), and use of guided imagery and *progressive muscle relaxation* (PMR) to reduce emotional distress. It also focuses on identifying and recognizing the links between your thoughts and your emotions. For example, if you are having negative thoughts about your health, these thoughts can trigger anxiety or depression (e.g., frequent worries). In this case, you might focus on changing or reframing your negative thoughts in a more positive or normative way—for example, "everyone has some challenge to deal with"—so that the emotional trigger does not happen as often. A CF-specific CBT intervention for those with CF is currently being developed. CBT sessions can be conducted in groups or individually.

Problem-solving is a component of CBT that focuses on identifying problems, such as adhering to a prescribed treatment, followed by brainstorming possible solutions that are personalized and collaborative (Quittner et al, 2012; Quittner and Li-Rosi, in press). The advantages of problem-solving are that it is brief (10–15 minutes), it can be conducted in a specialty clinic for CF, and it can be implemented by a variety of health care providers (e.g., social workers, nurses, *respiratory therapists*). Quittner and colleagues developed and tested a problem-solving intervention for adolescents with CF based on the IMPACT model (Interactive Model of Personalized and Collaborative Treatment; DeLambo et al, 2004; Quittner et al, 2012), which involves educational remediation of knowledge and skills, provision of a written Prescribed Treatment Plan (PTP), followed by problem solving to find a solution for the problem (see Figure 14-2 and Table 14-2). It has been useful in children, adolescents, adults with CF, and parent caregivers.

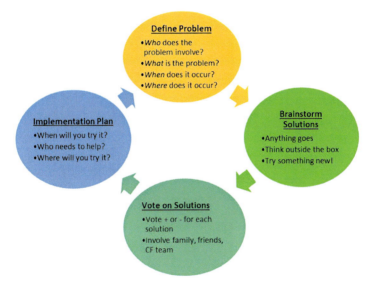

Figure 14-2: Steps of problem solving.

Case Vignette

Kevin, a 19-year-old with CF, had just completed his first year of college and had not told many of his classmates or friends that he had CF. He was planning to go out for pizza at the end of the week with college friends and did not want to take his enzymes in front of his peers. How can problem solving help him take his enzymes before eating (to benefit his health) without having to disclose his CF to anyone?

Table 14-2: Problem-Solving Steps

Steps of Problem-Solving	Description
Step 1: Define the problem	"I don't want to take my enzymes in front of my new friends, but I also don't want to end up with a stomach ache later." Who?—college friends; What?—not wanting them to see me taking enzymes and ask me why; When?—Friday night; Where?—pizza place.
Step 2: Brainstorm solutions	Kevin starts with the first solution, and then he and his respiratory therapist take turns generating solutions (writing several of them on sticky notes). Solutions: 1) Go to the restroom and take them with water 2) Excuse yourself to make a phone call, and then take them out of view (in your car, bathroom) 3) Put them in a can of mints and take them as if they were mints 4) Say you forgot your phone in your car, take your enzymes in the car, and then return 5) Take them at table before the pizza arrives; if someone asks, tell them that they are "probiotics to help with digestion"
Step 3: Vote on solutions	Solutions 1, 2, and 4 get all + votes; solution 3 and 5 are "voted down by Kevin." Kevin chooses which to try first. He selects "1," and the other solutions that received all + votes can be kept in his "back pocket" in case that solution did not work (or if he wants to mix it up!).
Step 4: Implementation plan	Kevin planned to go out to eat with his friends this Friday. He does not need help implementing it; it's up to him. He will try it at the local pizza place.

Motivational Interviewing (MI)

Motivational interviewing (MI) is a counseling approach that facilitates behavioral change, such as doing more prescribed treatments for CF. It was originally developed to treat addiction and smoking cessation (Miller, 1983), but it is now being applied to adherence issues in CF and other chronic conditions. MI is a menu of strategies that elicits a person's views and explores discrepancies between one person's beliefs and behaviors (e.g., on the one hand, you want to fit your airway clearance in more often, but on the other hand, it means that you might miss out on social activities with friends). MI is typically administered in individual sessions in which the discussion focuses on building awareness of how an issue affects you, considering the pros and cons of changing your behavior, setting goals for behavioral change, and avoiding confrontation in which the clinician is "convincing you" that you need to change (Channon et al, 2007). Evidence of efficacy has been found for MI in several adult and pediatric conditions, including diabetes and childhood asthma (Duff and Latchford, 2010; Borrelli et al, 2007; Doherty and Roberts, 2002). Although as of this writing there are no large studies that have tested MI in those with CF, it is being evaluated for improving adherence in CF.

In Denmark, a *randomized, controlled feasibility study* tested a life-coaching model in adults with CF that overlapped with principles of MI (Knudsen et al, 2017). Feasibility ratings were positive; however, they found no significant differences in health outcomes between the intervention and control groups. One small pilot in the United Kingdom showed promise for improving adherence to use of *colistin*; however, few details of that trial were published (Quinn et al, 2004). More evidence is needed to determine whether MI is effective in changing adherence behaviors in CF.

Acceptance and Commitment Therapy

Acceptance and Commitment Therapy (ACT) is a newer intervention that promotes psychological flexibility, which facilitates acceptance and committed action reflecting "values-based living." It is a behavioral intervention that focuses on your values and goals. "This therapy is about letting go, showing up for life, and getting yourself moving in directions you want to go" (Bennett et al, 2017). ACT has improved symptoms of depression and *anxiety*, and it might also be useful for improving adherence to CF treatments. ACT invites people to be open to unpleasant feelings, to learn how not to overreact to them, and to face situations in which these feelings arise.

Interpersonal Therapy

Interpersonal Therapy (IPT) is an evidence-based intervention for depression that is conducted in individual sessions. Interpersonal conflict, difficulty with changes in identity and self-esteem, and experiences of loss are well-known risk factors in the development of symptoms of depression or significant stress. IPT helps you to solve an interpersonal crisis to improve your life and to relieve your distress. It does so through a range of techniques and increases access to social support (Lipsitz and Markowitz, 2013). It helps you understand your emotions as social signals, improve your relationships, and mobilize your social supports. As your interpersonal relationships and social supports improve, further reductions in your psychological symptoms should follow.

What Types of Stress Management Interventions Might I Try?

The amount of stress we feel is altered by how relaxed we feel, by what we pay attention to, and by what we tell ourselves. When we are tense, our bodies become hyperalert and hypersensitive and we become more stressed. Several techniques such as *mindfulness training*, progressive muscle relaxation training, and *guided imagery* can be practiced at home to reduce stress and relieve anxiety. These approaches treat a variety of conditions and symptoms (e.g., stress, anxiety, pain, insomnia).

Mindfulness Training

Mindfulness is the psychological process of bringing your attention to experiences that are occurring in the present ("be here now") and focus on positive things in the present. "Mindfulness" means maintaining a moment-by-moment awareness of your thoughts, feelings, bodily sensations, and environment, through a gentle, nurturing lens. It is often combined with *meditation* or *yoga* practices that enable you to limit distractions and "tune in" to your inner thoughts and feelings. This is particularly helpful given that we are living in a world that moves quickly and we can be inundated with electronic communications and experiences in the digital world (e.g., phone calls, emails, social media). It is a way to quiet the mind and relax the body and it can reduce worries and obsessive thoughts.

Relaxation Training

Both the body and the mind can relax. The more we can teach ourselves to relax, to learn about our distress, and to encourage ourselves to cope, the less stress we will experience. The *relaxation response* is a state of deep rest that changes our physical and emotional responses to stress (e.g., decreases our heart rate, blood pressure, rate of breathing, muscle tension). Although relaxation techniques are simple, they require regular practice, just like any skill.

Progressive Muscle Relaxation

PMR is a technique used to help you learn how to control tension and to relax various muscle groups throughout your body, which can lead to an enhanced relaxation response and to reduced physical and emotional stress. Through PMR you learn how to pay close attention to your feelings of tension and relaxation to understand how your body feels when it is tense and how it might feel differently when your muscles become relaxed.

One type of PMR relaxation exercise uses Jacobsen's muscle-relaxation training method (Bernstein et al, 2000; Lehrer, 1982). It takes 15 to 20 minutes and you can do it lying down or sitting comfortably in a chair. It begins with several deep breaths to calm the body and the mind. Then, relax your feet and move the sensation slowly upward until relaxation reaches your head. At each step, you should tense and then relax your smallest muscle groups three to four times, alternating with deep breaths. For example, you might begin with your feet and tighten-hold-then-release your feet several times. After taking a deep breath, you might clench and release your calves several times, accompanied by deep breathing. The sensations you feel indicate that your body is becoming more relaxed, and that you have reached a deep state of relaxation. Achieving this state of relaxation can be helpful when you are not feeling well, when you are feeling stressed, and when you are having trouble stopping repetitive or negative thoughts. You might also enjoy listening to quiet music during relaxation training.

Guided Imagery

Guided imagery is a relaxation exercise in which you think of a restful and relaxing place (e.g., sitting on the beach, listening to birds in a forest) in which you can imagine feeling deeply relaxed, feeling calm, and slowing down worrisome thoughts. There are many apps that you can access on your phone that talk you through a guided-imagery exercise, often paired with peaceful music. A host of highly rated apps are easy to use and effective in reducing distress and increasing relaxation (e.g., "Simply Being"). Several apps are free and offer various types of relaxation techniques: guided imagery, PMR, mindfulness and meditation, and deep-breathing exercises (see Table 14-3).

Table 14-3: Relaxation Apps

	App	Cost
	Insight Timer	Free
	Ten Percent Happier	Free
	Calm	Free
	Breathe2Relax A portable stress management tool.	Free
	Headspace Personal trainer for the mind. Offers 10-minute meditations lessons to target health, performance and relationships.	Free
	Simply Being	Free
	Breethe	Free
	MindShift CBT Teaches relaxation skills, develops new thinking and suggests healthy activities.	Free
	Mindfulness Coach Developed to help people learn how to practice mindfulness and increase relaxation.	Free

How Can I Take Advantage of Virtual Peer Mentoring?

Peer support is based on the belief that people who have faced, endured, and overcome stressors and/or challenges can offer useful support, encouragement, hope, and mentorship to others in similar situations (Davidson et al, 2006). Peer support and mentoring is an approach that has been used for weight loss, career changes, and improving health across many illness groups; it is a useful way to increase support. Peer mentors who have similar experiences can add additional emotional and informational support and reduce loneliness and isolation. Additionally, peer mentors can serve as role models or informal coaches by drawing on personal experiences to help you overcome barriers to improving health or addressing emotional stressors (Ford et al, 2013; Gale et al, 2018).

The CF Foundation offers *CF Peer Mentoring Program* (www.cff.org) that provides support to those 16 years of age and older living with CF as well as to family members and spouses of people living with CF. Although this mentoring program is not considered a support group, it provides virtual support through one-on-one connections. Everyone is matched with a mentor for one-on-one connections through email, phone, or video calls. The goal of the CF Peer Mentoring Program is to help those who want support and guidance about living with CF connect with someone who has been through a similar situation. This virtual mentoring program allows those affected by CF to talk with someone who understands what it's like to live with, or to love someone with, the illness. You should talk with your CF care team or visit www.cff.org if you are interested in learning more about the peer-mentoring program.

The CF Foundation also offers other virtual events that are designed for young adults with CF who want to connect with others and share experiences about living with CF while facing challenges and life changes as well as becoming more independent. These events are called *CF BreatheCon* and *CF MiniCon*. BreatheCon is a two-day virtual event designed by and for people with CF who are 18 years or older and who want to connect and share experiences about life with CF. Conversations among participants are open and honest and the event includes interactive presentations, panel discussions, social activities, group chats, and small group breakout sessions.

The CF MiniCon allows young adults to experience presentations, group chats, and small group video breakout groups on a variety of topics related to living with CF, including talking about CF in new friendships and relationships, managing health and work/school, and maintaining mental health and wellbeing. These events focus on lifestyle and well-being and are not specifically related to medical topics.

How Can My CF Care Team Help Me Maintain Emotional Wellness?

The CF Foundation has funded more than 135 CF centers to implement annual screening of psychological symptoms and to provide brief interventions in clinic or referrals in the community for treatment. You should ask your CF Team if it is doing annual screening and if it has a MHC. Often this is a licensed social worker or a clinical psychologist. This annual screening is like taking your temperature, measuring your height or any other standard check-in the team does for your health. You can always share with your CF care team if you are not doing well emotionally and ask for advice, guidance, and appropriate referrals.

Should I Seek Professional Counseling or Psychiatric Care?

Professional mental health treatment can be helpful and effective for managing symptoms of depression and/or anxiety, or when you are struggling to cope with stress. A bevy of evidence-based interventions are effective in treating depression, anxiety, and other emotional symptoms. You should not let embarrassment or shame interfere with talking to your family, friends, and CF care team about how you are feeling or with talking with a trained mental health provider. When support from family and friends and positive lifestyle changes don't seem to be enough to resolve negative changes in your mood, thoughts, or behaviors, it might be time to seek help from a mental health professional.

Both *psychotherapy* and medications can effectively treat psychological symptoms; depending on the severity, nature, and length of your symptoms, a combination of the two might be needed. In therapy you will learn a variety of tools to improve your mood and to help you feel more motivated to take the necessary actions to feel better. Therapy can also impart skills that lead to better insight into the connections and triggers for your thoughts and feelings and ways to prevent symptoms from returning or intensifying. Psychiatric medications can be helpful to treat more intense or chronic symptoms, and they can relieve many of the symptoms of depression and anxiety. Even though medication can be helpful and important in alleviating emotional distress, it is important to develop an awareness about the potential triggers for your distress and to learn behavioral strategies to improve your mood and functioning.

Because many CF centers in the United States now actively screen those with CF and their caregivers for symptoms of depression and anxiety, it can be an easy way to talk with CF care providers about emotional health and options for working with a mental health provider in your community. The mental health screening tools (e.g., *Patient Health Questionnaire-9* and *Generalized Anxiety Disorder-7*) are meant to assess risk for depression and anxiety, and they can serve as a guide to when it might be an appropriate time to seek mental health treatment. If you notice that your scores on either of these measures are 10 or higher, or if your scores are higher than what is typical for you, you will likely benefit from working with a mental health professional. Your CF care team should also be able to provide you with additional information about resources in your community and what to expect.

How Can I Get a Referral in My Community?

Your CF care team can assist with making a referral to a therapist, *psychiatrist*, or another mental health professional in your community. The social worker and/or MHC on your care team will be able to guide you toward the resources available where you live. Your care team might have a list of mental health providers who have worked with others with CF or chronic illnesses, and who have openings to work with new patients. There are many reasons to seek the support of a mental health provider. If you think you would like to work with a mental health provider, it will be important to understand what your insurance will cover; this can guide the options available. In addition to your care team, you can often receive a list of mental health resources through your insurance carrier, which will include providers and resources that are considered in-network with your insurance provider. Often, these outside mental health professionals use a sliding-scale fee based on your income.

Many states and local communities have mental health centers with clinicians who work with children, adults, and families. These community mental health centers often accept all types of insurance, including Medicaid/Medicare as well as private insurance. For individual and group therapy referrals, there are online resources that allow you to search mental health providers in your community and to select additional specialties, locations, or other characteristics you are looking for in a therapist. For online resources for therapy referrals and other mental health resources, see Table 14-4.

Table 14-4: CF Psychosocial Resources

Resources to Obtain Mental Health Services in the Community	
www.psychologytoday.com	A website with individual and group psychotherapy providers who you can search by location, insurance, and specialty.
Virtual Mental Health Resources	
www.betterhelp.com	An online worldwide counseling platform.
www.mentalhealth.gov	Provides information and resources for people experiencing symptoms of any mental health issue.
www.nami.org	Information on mental health conditions, resources for social support, and other online tools.
Cystic Fibrosis Research Inc. www.cfri.org	Many psychosocial resources for individuals living with CF and their family members.
	Caregivers Support Groups: third Tuesday of every month.
	Living Mindfully with CF: Mindfulness-based stress reduction techniques, taught by Julie Desch, MD, who has CF.
Cystic Life www.cysticlife.org	Online community with blogs, resources, and reading materials relating to living with CF.

CF Foundation Resources	
CF BreatheCon *CF MiniCon* *CF FamilyCon* cff.org/BreatheCon	Virtual events created by and for the CF community. These events are typically 1 to 2 days and provide an opportunity to connect, share and learn from others living with or affected by CF.
CF Peer Connect	National peer-mentoring program for individuals 16 years and older as well as family members and partners of those with CF.
Online Relaxation Websites	
www.meditationoasis.com	
www.innerhealthstudio.com	

HOW CAN MY PAIN BE MANAGED?

Bethany Bartley, MD; Lara K. Dhingra, PhD; Saida Hussain, PhD;
Julie Balzano, PhD; Alexandra L. Quittner, PhD;
Elisabeth P. Dellon, MD, MPH; and Anna M. Georgiopoulos, MD

CHAPTER

In This Chapter

- Why Might I Have Pain from CF?

- What Can Relieve My Short-Term Pain?

- What Side Effects Could Result from Using Pain Medications?

- What Strategies Are Available to Prevent and Treat My Pain from Medical Procedures?

- What Can Improve My Chronic Pain?

- How Can the Mind–Body Connection Affect Chronic Pain?

- What Are Some Mind–Body Strategies That Can Help Me Cope with Chronic Pain?

Why Might I Have Pain from CF?

Many individuals with cystic fibrosis (CF) have pain related to their disease. Most often, pain will be brief; however, chronic pain can develop and require a dedicated and individualized pain management plan. The purpose of this chapter is to provide information and basic skills for managing pain to those with CF and their families. It includes brief descriptions of, and instructions for, effective mind–body approaches and medications for managing pain. An integrated team approach to pain management is important to simultaneously address the multiple ways that pain can affect you (e.g., physically, psychologically, socially, spiritually). We encourage you to have an ongoing conversation with members of your health care team about your pain so that it can provide you with the most appropriate and comprehensive care possible.

CF affects the function of many bodily organs and systems, and dysfunction of these systems can result in pain. Chest pain and abdominal pain are common and can result from a variety of conditions. Any new or worsening pain should be discussed with your CF provider.

Chest Pain

Respiratory symptoms in CF include persistent cough due to infections of your lungs with bacteria. Forceful coughing can cause painful injuries of your bones, muscles, or *cartilage* in your chest wall. This type of pain is referred to as *musculoskeletal chest pain. Rib fractures* (small breaks in the ribs) can occur during severe coughing episodes or with a chronic cough that lasts many weeks. Rib fractures typically occur on the sides of your chest (Hanak et al, 2005), and can cause pain overlying the affected rib. The pain often worsens with deep breathing, coughing, or moving (such as when rolling over in bed or reaching overhead).

More commonly, musculoskeletal chest pain is due to *inflammation* of the cartilage in the chest, which is the flexible connective tissue that connects your ribs to your breastbone. This specific pain and inflammation is called *costochondritis* and it is also often a result of frequent coughing. Costochondritis typically leads to diffuse soreness in the front of your chest along the sides of your breastbone. Such pain is usually reproduced by pressing on this area of the chest; it typically worsens with coughing, deep breathing, or exercising.

Inflammation inside of the chest wall also causes pain. This pain may be due to *mucus plugging* in the airways or bacterial growth deeper in the lungs, which causes inflammation to extend to the lining of the lung surface. Unlike musculoskeletal pain, this pain typically is not worsened by pressing on the chest, but it can be worsened by deep breathing.

Lung collapse, known as *pneumothorax*, can cause sudden chest pain that is often accompanied by shortness of breath. A pneumothorax occurs when air leaks out from the lungs into the space between the lungs and the chest wall. Chest pain due to a pneumothorax is typically one-sided and sharp; however, shortness of breath is commonly present. Fortunately, this complication is rare. If there is concern for a pneumothorax, you should be evaluated in the emergency department (ED).

Chest pain or discomfort can also be related to *gastroesophageal reflux disease* (GERD). GERD is very common in those with CF; it occurs in nearly 40% of children and adults

(CF Foundation Registry Annual Data Report, 2017). It is described as the abnormal backflow of stomach contents and acid into the *esophagus*, which is the tube that connects your mouth and stomach. Associated symptoms include *heartburn*, or a burning sensation in the chest, and regurgitation of food or a sour taste in the back of the throat.

It is also important to note, especially for older adults, that chest pain can be related to a *heart attack* or another heart-related and non-CF-related medical problem. Any chest pain or chest tightness that travels to your neck, jaw, shoulder, back, or arms should be evaluated promptly in the ED. In children and adolescents, heart disease is much less common than it is in adults; however, any chest pain that is accompanied by a fever, or chest pain that becomes worse with exertion should also be evaluated immediately.

Sinus Pain

Most adults living with CF develop *sinus disease*, and it affects nearly one-fourth of individuals with CF who are younger than 18 years of age (CF Foundation Registry Annual Data Report, 2017). The sinuses are air-filled spaces that surround the nose and produce a mucus layer to moisturize the inside of the nose. Your sinuses can become clogged in individuals with CF; this leads to chronic nasal congestion and sinus inflammation, called *sinusitis*. Headaches can also occur, most often experienced as a pressure type of pain in the forehead or mid-face surrounding the nose.

Abdominal Pain

Gastrointestinal (GI) issues such as constipation, fecal impaction, and pancreatic disease are common in CF. In most individuals with CF, the *pancreas* cannot make adequate *digestive enzymes* at birth. Digestive enzymes are proteins in the gut that are necessary to break down food for absorption of nutrients. Individuals with CF who cannot make enough digestive enzymes are diagnosed as having *pancreatic insufficiency* (PI) and require *pancreatic enzyme replacement therapy* (PERT). Of those with pancreatic sufficiency at birth, many develop PI requiring PERT later in life.

Constipation is also very common in CF. Constipation occurs when stooling becomes infrequent and the stool is often hard, small, and difficult to pass. Symptoms can be subtle and people, particularly children and adolescents, might not notice that they are having smaller or less-frequent bowel movements. Over time, the backup of stool leads to abdominal fullness and sometimes to pain, which is typically left-sided, though it can be diffuse throughout the abdomen. The abdominal discomfort related to constipation typically comes in waves and improves with a bowel movement. It can usually be managed at home by drinking extra fluids and using laxatives recommended by the CF care team; however, when vomiting occurs, urgent evaluation is necessary.

Distal intestinal obstruction syndrome (DIOS) is another condition that leads to having difficulty moving your bowels; it is unique to CF. DIOS is a blockage of bowel by stool that typically occurs where the small bowel meets the large bowel in the lower-right abdomen. This blockage can be partial or complete. Pain is often described as cramping and it tends to worsen in severity over time. This condition requires close medical attention, particularly when vomiting occurs. The cause of DIOS is not completely understood; however, it is much more common in those with PI, and inadequate doses of PERT can contribute (Andersen et al, 1990). Constipation can occur in both pancreatic sufficient and insufficient individuals, and PERT doses appear to be less related to constipation (Baker et al, 2005).

Inflammation of the pancreas, known as *pancreatitis*, can be a complication of CF; it causes pain in the upper abdomen that extends through to the back. Pain is persistent and typically severe. Pancreatitis occurs in less than 2% of individuals with CF (CF Foundation Annual Data Report, 2017), but is more common in those who are pancreatic sufficient (De Boeck et al, 2005). Some people experience a decline in pancreatic function following an episode of pancreatitis and they become pancreatic insufficient thereafter (De Boeck et al, 2005).

Kidney stones and *gallstones* can also occur more frequently in CF and lead to abdominal pain. Kidney stones, known as *nephrolithiasis*, can block the passage of urine from the kidney to the bladder and lead to severe pain in the lower back that extends around to the lower abdomen on the affected side. Blood can also be seen in the urine. Overall this complication is rare, occurring in 1.3% of adults with CF, and less often in children or adolescents (CF Foundation Registry Annual Data Report, 2017). The pain of gallstones, known as *cholelithiasis*, is typically crampy and located in the upper-right abdomen. Pain often worsens with meals. When gallstones are passed and become stuck in the bile ducts, complications like inflammation of the gallbladder *(cholecystitis)*, pancreatitis, or infection of the bile ducts *(cholangitis)* can occur and lead to serious illness. However, in general, gallstones and their complications are quite rare. *Gallstone* complications that require a surgery or a procedure occur in less than 0.5% of individuals with CF (CF Foundation Registry Annual Data Report, 2017).

Joint Pain

Many chronic conditions are associated with inflammation in the joints, known as *arthritis*. A CF-associated joint disease known as *CF arthropathy* exists, though is relatively uncommon (occurring in less than 10% of those with CF) (CF Foundation Registry Annual Data Report, 2017). It is characterized by episodes of pain and joint swelling. These episodes can occur during a pulmonary exacerbation or independent of exacerbations. Small joints of the hands and feet, as well as larger joints (like the knees, shoulders, and elbows) can be involved (Roehmel et al, 2019).

What Can Relieve My Short-Term Pain?

Musculoskeletal pain due to inflammation, such as costochondritis in the chest and arthritis in the joints, typically responds well to *non-steroidal anti-inflammatory drugs* (NSAIDs). Medications in this drug class include *ibuprofen* (brand name: *Advil*®, Motrin®) and *naproxen* (brand name: *Aleve®*, *Naprosyn®*). The choice of NSAID and the dose recommended depends on many factors, so it is best for you to consult with your CF provider. Physical therapy can also be helpful for musculoskeletal pain.

Chest pain due to a *rib fracture* might respond well to NSAIDs and/or to *acetaminophen* (brand name: *Tylenol®*). Alternative therapies include topical therapies such as heat or a medicated patch (i.e., a *lidocaine patch*). Using a pillow at night to support the sensitive side of the chest can also be helpful. Rest will help healing, though this can be challenging, as coughing is desired for optimized airway clearance in the setting of a pulmonary exacerbation. In these cases, if pain is not well controlled with NSAIDs, acetaminophen, and/or topical therapies, a trial of *opioid* medications (e.g., *oxycodone*) might be considered for some individuals before *chest physical therapy* for a short period until pain improves and it is no longer hindering airway clearance. NSAIDs, acetaminophen, and topical lidocaine patches are available over the counter, without a prescription, whereas opioid medications require a prescription. Use of pain medications should be discussed with and taken under the guidance of a health care professional.

Lower abdominal pain in CF is most often related to constipation. The pain of constipation routinely improves with use of products like *polyethylene glycol* (brand name: *MiraLAX®*) or *lactulose*, which are non-absorbable substances that draw water into the digestive tract to allow for the easier passage of stool. Polyethylene glycol is available at pharmacies without a prescription, whereas lactulose requires a prescription. More severe abdominal pain requires evaluation by a health care professional because it might represent DIOS, pancreatitis, kidney stones, or gallbladder disease, and these conditions pose the risk of significant complications.

GERD is typically managed with medications (such as *proton-pump inhibitors* [PPIs]) that decrease stomach acid. Many stomach acid–reducing medications are available over the counter; however, some PPIs require a prescription. Diet changes can also help to prevent GERD.

For new-onset pain, opioid pain medications or *intravenous* (IV) NSAIDs might be used to treat severe pain related to pancreatitis or kidney stones. DIOS is managed with oral hydration, laxatives, and, occasionally, *enemas*. Though rare, surgery might be required for severe cases of DIOS or gallbladder disease. Pain associated with any procedure or surgery involving the abdomen interferes with coughing and airway clearance, which is of utmost concern to those with CF. Postsurgical pain is typically treated with a combination of acetaminophen and opioids, with particular attention paid to adequate pain control to allow for an effective cough.

Sinus pain and pressure in CF typically responds well to sinus rinses as well as to use of acetaminophen and/or ibuprofen, as needed. In certain cases, pain in the sinuses and chest is related to bacterial infection and it improves with antibiotic therapy. Your CF provider will help to determine which therapies are indicated and what the risks and benefits are of each pain treatment option.

What Side Effects Could Result from Using Pain Medications?

Pain management should be individualized to you and your problem. Multiple treatment options are often used, so it is important to speak openly with your provider about pain and to offer feedback if a treatment option is working well, or not well enough.

NSAIDs are commonly used to treat a variety of short-term and long-term pains. Those with kidney problems should use these agents with caution, and when you are taking other medication that are cleared by the kidneys (e.g., certain IV antibiotics). Additionally, short-term use of NSAIDs can cause stomach upset; long-term use can cause *stomach ulcers* and bleeding from the stomach. NSAIDs can also "thin" the blood (and reduce the ability of the blood to clot); therefore they are often stopped when you are coughing blood, known as *hemoptysis*, during a pulmonary exacerbation. Although NSAIDs rarely harm the liver, those who have liver disease should use acetaminophen with caution.

Topical therapies (like heat and medicated patches) are generally well tolerated. Medicated patches such as lidocaine patches can cause redness or irritation at the site of their application. Temporary skin redness following application is not worrisome; however, if rashes or irritation of the skin develops, you should discuss this with your doctor before using medications.

Opioid medications are an important class of medication to treat pain; however, you must use them carefully due to their potential for unintended abuse, addiction, and overdose-related deaths. In addition to their addictive potential, those with CF need to use opioids with caution because it can cause severe constipation and intestinal blockage as well as *respiratory depression*. Respiratory depression refers to breathing that is suppressed— either not fast enough or deep enough—to maintain adequate exchange of oxygen and carbon dioxide in the lungs. Symptoms include sleepiness, confusion, and headache; this condition can be life-threatening and it requires medical attention. Safe prescribing and appropriate use of opioids should prevent respiratory depression.

What Strategies Are Available to Prevent and Treat My Pain from Medical Procedures?

Certain therapies, like *antibiotics*, might need to be given intravenously, or directly into a vein to treat pulmonary exacerbations in CF. To access the vein, a small *catheter*, sometimes called an IV, can be placed in the hand or arm. These small IVs can last for only a few days. For longer-term IV therapy, a *peripherally inserted central catheter* (PICC) can be placed in the arm. PICC lines are typically used for a single course of IV antibiotics and then removed after therapy is completed (which typically takes a few days or weeks).

Alternatively, an implantable device called a *port* can be placed under the skin on the chest and accessed when needed for those who often require IV therapies. Ports are designed to be used for many years. With all of these options, some individuals experience pain when a needle is used to pierce the skin to access the vein or an implanted port. Blood clots can also occur with PICC lines and lead to pain and swelling in the arm.

Statements issued by the *World Health Organization* (WHO) and the International Association for the Study of Pain (IASP) declared that, "The relief of pain should be a human right" (WHO, 2004). However, a recent study found that the worst pain reported by hospitalized patients was caused by *needle sticks* (Friedrichsdorf et al, 2015). Painful experiences with needles can lead to both negative short-term and long-term consequences. In the short term, needle-related distress can lead to *anxiety*, anticipatory worry, insomnia, and fear. In the long run, these issues can lead to poor adherence to treatments, avoidance of clinic visits, and *needle phobias* (Blount et al, 2003; Kennedy et al, 2008; Young, 2005). Roughly one-fourth of adults develop phobias, which can come from childhood fears (Guideline Statement Journal of Paediatric Health 2006; Hamilton, 1995).

One study at a large children's hospital found that three-fourths of children experienced pain in the past 24 hours, mostly related to procedures such as needle sticks, IV and PICC line insertions, and other procedures; unfortunately, procedure-related pain was often under-recognized and undertreated. Anxiety and fear that precedes procedures is referred to as "*procedural distress.*" Less is known about procedural distress specifically in those with CF. However, in another study of children and adolescents with CF, 93% reported needle-related distress (Ayers et al, 2010). These high levels of distress, which can lead to avoidance of clinic visits and poor adherence to treatments, have a negative impact on people with CF and members of their families. Fortunately, there are very simple, evidence-based strategies that can be used to reduce procedural distress (Birnie et al, 2014; see Table 15-1).

Children's Minnesota developed the "Comfort Promise" model to reduce needle-related pain and procedural distress in children and adolescents (Friedrichsdorf et al, 2015). This program, among others, strongly suggests four strategies to reduce or eliminate procedural pain: numb the skin; give *sucrose* or breastfeed infants 0 to 12 months; encourage comfortable positions; and, provide age-appropriate distractions.

Table 15-1: Strategies to Reduce or Eliminate Pain

	Infants* (0–24 Months)	Preschool (2–5 Years Old)	School Age (6–12 Years Old)	Adolescence (13–18 Years Old)	Emerging Adults (19–25 Years Old)
Numb pain	• Use 4% lidocaine cream (or similar) 20–30 minutes before	• Use 4% lidocaine cream (or similar) 20–30 minutes before	• Use 4% lidocaine cream (or similar) 20–30 minutes before • Use nitrous oxide	• Use 4% lidocaine cream (or similar) 20–30 minutes before • Use nitrous oxide	• Use 4% lidocaine cream (or similar) 20–30 minutes before • Use nitrous oxide
Comfort positioning	• Provide swaddling • Use cuddling • Position chest to chest	• Position back to chest—in chair • Have parent hold arm	• Side by side • Position with back to chest straddle	• Side by side • Place chair next to bed	
Age-appropriate intervention(s)	• Use soothing voice • Provide a shaking toy	• Use active distraction: • Read a book • Provide a kaleidoscope • Watch cartoon videos • Blow bubbles • Provide a pinwheel	• Squeeze a stress ball • Play virtual reality games • Listen to music via headphones • Use hypnosis • Use guided visual imagery • Encourage muscle relaxation • Adopt a needle plan	• Listen to music via headphones • Play virtual reality games • Squeeze a stress ball • Encourage progressive muscle relaxation • Use guided imagery • Adopt a needle plan	• Encourage progressive muscle relaxation • Adopt a needle plan
Preventative strategies		Use play kits to introduce them to the process, step by step.	Develop a fear *hierarchy* for the individual child and use exposure-response prevention.**	Develop a fear *hierarchy* for the individual child and use exposure-response prevention.**	Develop a fear *hierarchy* for the individual child and use exposure-response prevention.**

* Breastfeeding, sucrose, pacifier for 0–2 months only. **See the section "Exposure-Response Prevention" in this chapter.

Exposure-Response Prevention

Cognitive-behavioral therapy (CBT) offers another effective strategy for addressing procedural distress; however, it requires some discussion, and practice is needed ahead of time. CF treatments begin early in life, so these strategies need to be taught early on. *Exposure-based therapy* starts by identifying a child's fears (from the least scary to the scariest) related to specific procedures (a fear *hierarchy*). For example, the least scary activity might be checking into the CF clinic and seeing the lab technician in her "white coat," whereas seeing the needle that will be used might feel scarier. Strategies to reduce *anxiety* at each step are practiced, including distraction, muscle relaxation, and listening to music.

Resources

- Be Sweet to Babies: http://www.cheo.on.ca/en/BeSweet2Babies
- Children's Comfort Promise. Children's Minnesota: https://www.childrensmn.org/services/care-specialties-departments/pain-program/childrens-comfort-promise/
- ChildKind: http://childkindinternational.org/
- HELPinKids&Adults: http://phm.utoronto.ca/helpinkids/index.html
- It Doesn't Have to Hurt: https://itdoesnthavetohurt.ca/#

What Can Improve My Chronic Pain?

Chronic pain is ongoing or frequent pain that lasts beyond the normal course of acute illness or injury, or for more than 3 to 6 months (Treede et al, 2019). Chronic pain that has already been evaluated by your CF provider and that has not become worse, and for which you are being treated, usually does not require immediate medical attention; this is a familiar pain. In comparison, acute pain is usually from an identifiable cause, such as an injury or tissue trauma, that resolves when healing occurs (Berry et al, 2001). Individuals with CF can experience both chronic pain and acute pain for various reasons. It is important to know the difference between chronic and acute pain because this will help you and your CF provider work together to develop the best care plan to manage your pain.

Pain that is frequent can have a negative impact on the quality of your life (Hayes et al, 2011). Chronic pain often makes you less likely to participate in everyday activities and activities you normally enjoy, and less likely to interact with family and friends. Some individuals experience overall distress, poor sleep quality, fatigue, and limited physical activity (Havermans et al, 2013). People with CF can find it difficult to participate in prescribed CF treatments when their pain is severe (Havermans et al, 2013).

When pain is not improving, it is important to communicate with your CF team about what you are experiencing and how it is affecting you (Allgood et al, 2018) so that all contributing factors and treatment options are carefully considered and reassessed over time. In some instances, the same strategies that are used to treat acute pain can be used for chronic pain. However, long-term use of medications such as NSAIDs or opiates can increase the risk of side effects. Additional classes of medication, such as *antidepressants* and anticonvulsants, can be helpful for chronic pain that involves dysregulation of the nervous system (ACPA, 2019). When treatments are providing little relief, usually a plan should be made to discontinue them safely. When pain has been persistent, a combination of approaches might be recommended to improve your quality of life and ability to be active and productive while minimizing side effects (ACPA, 2019).

Coping with chronic pain along with other life stressors can feel difficult or overwhelming. One study of adolescents living with CF found that certain kinds of emotional responses to pain, including rumination (such as trouble stopping frequent thoughts about pain), magnification (strong feeling that pain is unbearable or will not get better), and helplessness were associated with higher ratings of pain (Lechtzin et al, 2016). CBT and other psychological interventions can teach coping skills that make it easier to regain function while experiencing pain (ACPA, 2019). Additional modalities, such as massage therapy (Zink et al, 2019), exercise, physical therapy (Lee et al, 2009), yoga (McNamara et al, 2016), and acupuncture (Lin et al, 2005) can be useful for some kinds of CF-related pain. In the sections that follow, we describe some simple, evidence-based strategies that can help you to cope with your pain along with suggestions for integrating them in your day-to-day life.

How Can the Mind–Body Connection Affect Chronic Pain?

The biopsychosocial model (Figure 15-1) includes some of the factors that affect, and are affected by, pain (Turk et al, 2002). Pain can lead to many changes in your behaviors and thoughts; some of these changes are helpful and necessary (e.g., modifying activities), whereas others are not (e.g., isolation and depression):

- It is important to identify some of the ways that pain has affected your life. This will help you identify what you would like to focus on and improve and which coping skills you want to learn and apply.

- It is important to identify specific activities, thoughts, and feelings that might help pain or make it worse. This can help you to identify specific triggers (things that increase your pain) and learn how to manage them so that you can keep these strategies in your coping skills toolkit (Otis, 2007).

- Start your own personalized plan for pain management (see Table 15-2).

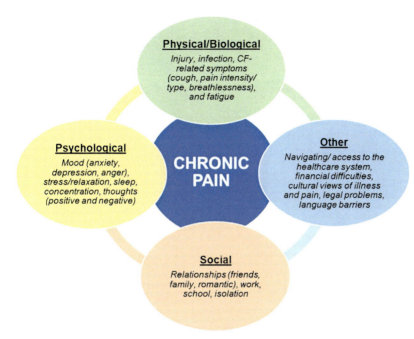

Figure 15-1: The biopsychosocial model in chronic pain.

What Are Some Mind–Body Strategies That Can Help Me Cope with Chronic Pain?

Several strategies that can be useful for coping with pain are listed below. These are most effective when practiced regularly (at least once per day, for 5–10 minutes), even when you are not experiencing pain, so that you can strengthen the skill.

If you feel discouraged early on, remember that these skills will become easier with practice. Different coping strategies work for different people. If you feel that a particular strategy is not helpful (even after you have tried it a few times) or causes you increased discomfort or pain, discontinue it.

Table 15-2: Personalized Plan for Pain Management

How Does Pain Affect Me?

Social: Pain can limit your activity level and type (you might cancel social events, stay in bed, or call-out from work) and your relationships.

What activities and/or relationships have been affected by your pain?

Psychological: Pain can affect your thoughts ("I will never get better," difficulty concentrating, slowed thinking), feelings (depressed, anxious, hopeless, angry), and sleep (restless, disrupted). Negative thoughts and feelings can increase your focus on pain.

How have your thoughts, feelings, and sleep been affected by your pain?

Physical: Pain varies in intensity, duration, pattern (e.g., constant, occasional, irregular), quality (numbness, tingling, aching), and location. Chronic pain is also associated with other bodily responses (e.g., muscle tightness, fatigue).

How does your pain affect you physically?

Other: Pain can make other life stressors feel more intense and overwhelming (e.g., completing CF treatments/participating in medical recommendations, school, work, legal/financial/relationship issues). Factors such as culture, primary language spoken, and access to health care can make it difficult to seek care for your pain.

What other stressors in your life are affected by your pain?

What Affects My Pain?

Identifying specific triggers (e.g., social, psychological, physical) that increase or decrease your pain can help you recognize what you might have control over and be able to change.

What increases your pain (e.g., too much physical exertion, increased coughing, stress/tension, focusing on your pain, depression, anger, boredom)?

What decreases your pain (e.g., participating in activities you enjoy, exercise, eating healthy food, medication, relaxation, appropriate amount of activity, spending quality time with family and friends, laughter)?

Adapted from: Otis, 2007.

Start a Pain Diary

A pain diary can help you to identify specific patterns related to your daily activities (e.g., thoughts, feelings, stressors that can be changed to better manage your pain. Feel free to track additional factors that you think might affect your pain (e.g., constipation, rest, exercise, nutrition, medication use) (American Chronic Pain Association, 2010).

In your diary, write the date and note the following every day for at least 1 week (Adapted from American Chronic Pain Association, 2010):

- **Pain Level** (0=None to 10=Worst)
- **Stress Level** (0=None to 10=Worst)
- **Exercise** (0=None to 10=Daily)
- **Activity Level** (0=None to 10=Typical)
- **Sleep Quality** (0=Poor to 10=Well rested)
- **Mood** (0=Calm to 10=Stressed, depressed)
- **Interaction** (0=No interaction to 10=Interact often)

Schedule Pleasant Activities

Increasing pleasurable activities improves mood, function, and well-being, and can even help you deal with pain. In Figure 15-2, identify the activities that you enjoy and would like to spend more time doing. Try doing at least three of these activities each week. When you do these things, you might be surprised to find that your body feels more comfortable—even with pain.

Figure 15-2: Which activities give you the most pleasure?

Schedule an achievable activity (once each week) during a realistic time when you are likely to follow through with your goal. Keep track of whether you did your pleasant activity, and your pain and stress levels, either in your Pain Diary or create a chart similar to Table 15-3.

Table 15-3: A Pain Diary

Activity	M	Tu	W	Th	F	Sa	Su	Pain (0 = No pain; 10 = Most pain)	Stress (0 = No stress; 10 = Most stress)
Walking			X					7	5

Find a quiet, comfortable place where you can be undisturbed for about 10 minutes.

1. Place one hand on your chest and the other above your belly button.

2. Close your eyes and breathe in slowly through your nose for a count of four, focusing on gently making your belly bigger and relaxing your body.

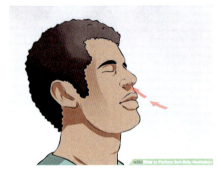

3. **Hold** for a second...and then slowly **breathe out through your mouth for a count of four**. As you breathe out, feel your muscles become looser and more relaxed. Your belly will become smaller when you let go of your breath.

4. **Hold** for a second . . . and then begin again, breathing in this relaxing way for 5-10 minutes.

Figure 15-3:   Soft-belly breathing (diaphragmatic breathing) for people with CF. Soft belly breathing techniques (Public domain). (Retrieved from: https://www.wikihow.com/Perform-Soft-Belly-Meditation.)

Breathing Tips . . .

Getting the Most from Soft Belly Breathing (Diaphragmatic Breathing):

- Breathe this way every day (or three to five times weekly) to lower your daily stress and tension, including stress caused by pain (Figure 15-3).

- Listen to your body—sit or lay down—whatever is comfortable. Gently straighten your back and relax (or drop) your shoulders.

- Try taking long breaths into the belly so that the hand on your chest hardly moves, while the hand on your belly rises and falls with the breath, like blowing up and letting the air out of a balloon.

- If you don't like the counting, try repeating to yourself "soft" on the inhale and "belly" on the exhale, or other words that comfort you and remind you to use this time to rest and relax.

- Make this a regular habit to keep stress from building up or to lower the stress and tension that you already feel.

- Check in with yourself throughout the day. If you begin to feel the discomfort of stress or pain, take a few moments to do five or six soft belly breaths.

- Complete the chart in the next section to see the benefits of relaxed breathing.

Breathing Practice Chart

1		2	3	4	5	6	7	8	9	10
Totally relaxed/ comfortable										Extremely tense/ uncomfortable

Write down which days you practiced your soft-belly breathing. How tense or relaxed are you before and after you give yourself time to breathe? Are there any changes you notice in your pain?

Date	Before Breathing	After Breathing	What Did I Notice?
Monday _____			
Tuesday _____			
Wednesday _____			
Thursday _____			
Friday _____			
Saturday _____			
Sunday _____			

WILL I NEED A TRANSPLANT?

Andrea Jonas, MD; Laveena Chhatwani, MD, MSc;
Eirik Gumeny, BA; and Yelizaveta Sher, MD

CHAPTER

In This Chapter

continued

- How Do I Decide Whether I Am Interested in Organ Transplantation?

- How Should I Proceed If I Want to Pursue Organ Transplantation?

- What Is It Like Waiting for an Organ Transplant? What Is It Like Getting "The Call"?

- What Might My Feelings Be Like About Organ Transplantation?

- When Is Retransplantation Considered?

- Can I Be an Organ Donor?

Introduction

Out of 29,887 individuals registered in the 2017 *Cystic Fibrosis Foundation (CF Foundation) Registry*, 1,712 people with cystic fibrosis (CF) reported that they had received a lung, kidney, heart, or *liver transplant* (although transplant recipients are likely to be under-represented in the CF Foundation Registry). Most of these individuals (1,548) received a lung transplant; of those, 250 reported having a lung transplant in 2017. In fact, those with CF accounted for approximately 16% of all lung transplants and nearly half (44%) of all people under the age of 50 years who underwent lung transplantation (Snell et al, 2017). This chapter focuses on lung transplantation, although we also discuss liver transplantation and multi-organ transplantation, which are much less common.

What Is Lung Transplantation?

Lung transplantation is a life-saving intervention for those with *end-stage lung disease* due to a variety of lung diseases, including CF (Weill et al, 2015). Lung transplantation is a complex surgical procedure that is followed by a lifetime of intense medical care, due to the need for chronic *immunosuppression. Immunosuppressive medications* help to prevent your *immune system* from rejecting or injuring the donor lungs that it detects as being "foreign" or "non-self."

Following lung transplantation, during which the native (old) lungs are removed and the donor (new) lungs are implanted, the lung transplant recipient is followed closely by a team of specialists dedicated to the care of lung transplant recipients after discharge; for follow-up, and for a lifetime. Although treatment can seem overwhelmingly complex, you are not alone on this journey; in fact, you are surrounded by transplant professionals who are dedicated to your care.

What Is Liver Transplantation? What Is Living Donor Liver Transplantation?

Liver transplantation is a treatment considered for those with severe *end-stage liver disease* (ESLD) from a variety of liver conditions. Approximately 1 in 4 individuals with CF have some degree of *CF Liver Disease* (CFLD) (van de Peppel et al, 2017; Freeman et al, 2019). In the most cases, CFLD is mild and might show up only as abnormal *liver function tests* (LFTs). In 5% to 10% of cases, CFLD can progress to *cirrhosis* (damage to the liver resulting in scarring *[fibrosis]*) (Freeman et al, 2019). This occurs almost exclusively in those with CF who are younger than 20 years of age. Severe cirrhosis and complications of *liver failure* can lead to consideration of liver transplantation in those with CF. Individuals with CFLD are carefully monitored by CF physicians in concert with a liver specialist, to watch for signs of worsening disease. If needed, the CF team will refer you to a liver transplant center.

In contrast to lung transplantation for CF, which is performed mostly in adults, liver transplantation in those with CF peaks in adolescence and is uncommon after 35 years of age (Freeman et al, 2019). Thus, the decision to undergo liver transplantation is more frequently made by, or for, children or adolescents with CF as compared to older individuals with CF who undergo lung transplantation. In rare cases, combined lung-liver transplantations have been performed in those with very severe CF lung disease and CFLD with liver failure (Snell et al, 2017).

A liver transplant is a medical procedure in which the failed liver is removed and replaced with a healthy *donor liver*. Some people can receive a piece of a liver from a *living donor*, a process called *living liver donation*.

What Is Multi-Organ Transplantation?

Multi-organ transplantation is uncommonly performed; it involves transplantation of more than one donor organ. Such an approach increases the complexity and the risk of the operation and can result in a longer wait for organs. *Combined lung-liver transplantation* has been performed in a small number of individuals with severe CFLD and severe CF lung disease.

Although CF does not affect the kidneys directly, some individuals with CF develop kidney disease due to repeated courses of antibiotics, infections, or other kidney-damaging interventions (e.g., use of *intravenous* [IV] *contrast* needed for *imaging studies*). If such a person needs a lung transplant for advanced CF lung disease, a discussion with the *nephrologists* (kidney specialists) is held to assess whether their kidneys would be able to tolerate the stress of a lung transplant operation or whether the individual should be considered for a combined lung-kidney transplant. In some cases, *kidney transplantation* occurs after lung transplantation, when years of immunosuppression has accelerated kidney damage.

Though CF does not directly affect the heart, on rare occasions an individual in need of lung transplant for severe CF lung disease might present with heart disease. *Heart-lung transplantation* has also been performed rarely.

Who and What Will Determine Whether I Will Benefit from a Lung Transplant?

Lung transplantation is considered for those whose lung disease is very severe and in those who have a high (greater than 50%) risk of death within 2 years (Weill et al, 2015). Predicting outcomes (including survival with CF lung disease) can be challenging (Morrell and Pilewski, 2016). It requires careful thought by CF physicians and lung transplant physicians to consider an individual's overall clinical course, including baseline lung function, rate of lung function decline, the number of CF exacerbations that have required hospitalization, and other factors. Certain features of CF lung disease identify individuals at high risk of death from CF lung disease (including *hemoptysis* [coughing blood], *pneumothorax* [lung collapse], low oxygen levels or high carbon dioxide levels on blood tests, and high pressures in the lung circulation) (Ramos et al, 2017; Ramos et al, 2019).

Early referral to a lung transplant center is recommended for those with severe CF lung disease (Ramos et al, 2019). This allows adequate time to educate and prepare you and your family for transplantation and to take care of any medical or psychosocial concerns that might be identified during the evaluation process. One measure to assess whether you are nearing the point of requiring a lung transplant is to track your *forced expiratory volume in the first second* (FEV1) (Morrell and Pilewski, 2016). When the FEV1 drops below 50%, your doctors might begin discussing lung transplantation (Ramos et al, 2019). If the FEV1 drops below 30%, your doctors might refer you for evaluation by a lung transplant center.

After you are referred to a lung transplant center, an extensive medical and psychosocial evaluation with a variety of tests and consultations is pursued (Morrell and Pilewski, 2016). Detailed patient education sessions are a part of the process, and you will have plenty of opportunities to ask questions.

After your clinic visit with the lung transplant specialist, the specifics of your case will be discussed at a Lung Transplant Selection Committee meeting, consisting of transplant physicians (e.g., *pulmonologists*, surgeons, *psychiatrists*), nurse coordinators, *pharmacists*, *social workers*, and *dietitians*. The Committee carefully considers all aspects of your case to determine whether you are a good transplant candidate (likely to benefit from transplant and to have a good outcome) and whether it is reasonable to proceed with active listing for a transplant now or later.

Ultimately, the decision as to whether to pursue an organ transplant is personal. The transplant and CF teams strive to provide you with every opportunity for transplantation if this is a treatment that is aligned with your values and preferences. Your medical team is there to provide you with all of the necessary information to help you with this important decision. If you decide you do not want to pursue transplant, you will be supported in this decision, as well. CF teams are dedicated to caring for you whether you choose to pursue a transplant or not. Some additional information to help you make your decision is provided later in this chapter.

What Is a 6-Minute Walk Test and What Can Be Learned from It?

A *6-minute walk test* is a non-invasive medical test performed in your doctor's office. The test is performed to keep track of your exercise capacity. During the test, a *respiratory therapist* (RT) will place an *oxygen saturation probe* on your finger or earlobe to monitor the oxygen saturation of your blood as well as your heart rate. The oxygen saturation probe is non-invasive, meaning it can monitor your oxygen level and heart rate without the use of needles. The respiratory therapist will ask you to walk as far as you can on flat ground in 6 minutes. If you become tired, you can take a break. It is important that you walk as far as you can during that time to give your doctors an accurate understanding of what your body is capable of. During the test, the respiratory therapist will monitor your oxygen level. If your oxygen level falls below a certain threshold, they will pause the test, and provide *supplemental oxygen* that you can use for the remainder of the test. After the test, the respiratory therapist will wait with you for your heart rate to return to normal.

The results of your 6-minute walk test helps your doctors to monitor your exercise capacity, providing an overall idea of your heart and lung function. The 6-minute walk test results are combined with your other test results (such as *pulmonary function testing* and laboratory testing) to keep track of the health of your lungs. The 6-minute walk test might be repeated once a year or more frequently to monitor changes in your health. The results of the test are also used to help determine if you might benefit from a lung transplant.

What Is a Right Heart Catheterization and What Can Be Learned from It?

A *right heart catheterization* is a medical procedure used to test the function of your heart. It is performed in the hospital, commonly in the *cardiac catheterization laboratory*. Your doctors will give you a light sedative so that you do not experience discomfort during the procedure. The procedure entails inserting a thin *catheter*, or tube, into a small incision site in your leg or arm. From there, the doctor is able to direct the catheter into the right side of your heart. When the catheter is inside of your heart, it can measure the pressure, the rate of blood flow, and the oxygen levels in your heart. When all of the information has been collected, the doctor removes the catheter. Recovery is generally quick, and you will be discharged home from the hospital the same day.

The information from the right heart catheterization helps your team of doctors understand the function of your heart. For instance, some people with CF might have high pressures in their heart, either due to chronically low oxygen levels, or due to liver disease. Others might have weakened heart muscles or might have small defects in their heart. The right heart catheterization allows your team of doctors to test you for all these possibilities. This testing is especially important for those being considered for a lung transplant.

If you are older than 40 years of age, your transplant center will likely also request a *left heart catheterization (coronary angiogram)* that allows for the visualization of the arteries that supply blood to your heart and the evaluation of any abnormalities. If someone with a weakened heart receives a lung transplant, the surgery and new lungs could place too much stress on their heart and cause it to fail. Your doctors will want to evaluate your heart to ensure that it is healthy enough to withstand lung transplantation.

What Does Lung Transplantation Involve?

During lung transplantation, you are taken to the operating room where you are placed under *general anesthesia* so that you do not feel anything and do not remember the surgery. The operation usually lasts from 6 to 8 hours, but you will likely be in the operating room for much longer. A *heart-lung bypass machine* or other invasive equipment might be used during the procedure. Transplant surgeons remove your lungs (native lungs) through an incision in your chest and replace those lungs with new donor lungs. The new lungs are then attached to the airways and to their blood supply. By the end of the operation, your new lungs have taken over the function of providing oxygen to your body.

After the operation, you will be cared for in the *intensive care unit* (ICU). A breathing tube is placed and connected to a *mechanical ventilator* (a breathing machine) helping your new lungs to breathe. Depending on your recovery, the breathing tube might be removed in 6 to 8 hours after your arrival to the ICU, although this might be delayed by several days in some cases. In a small proportion of cases, the breathing tube and mechanical ventilator might be needed to support the transplanted lungs even longer, while they establish optimal function.

You will also have *chest tubes* placed after the surgery. These chest tubes function to drain excess fluid that might accumulate around your new lungs; these tubes are generally removed within a week after surgery. While in the ICU, pain and anxiety are continually assessed and treated. Multiple medications, including *antibiotics* (to prevent infection after a complex operation) and immunosuppressive agents (to control the immune system from rejecting or injuring the donor lungs that it recognizes as "foreign" or "non-self") are initiated. A multi-disciplinary team of doctors, nurses, physical therapists, dietitians, pharmacists, psychiatrists, and social workers ensure that all of your needs are met during your recovery.

What Are the Risks and Benefits of Lung Transplantation?

The precise risks and benefits of lung transplant surgery are unique to each individual (Garrido and Dhillon, 2019). The transplant team will offer listing for an organ transplant only when the team's assessment is that the benefits of the transplant outweigh its risks in your situation. This assessment should then be taken into consideration with your values and preferences. Although your team will provide information and recommendations, your family and friends might offer to help you make your personal choice to pursue a transplant.

The main benefit of lung transplantation is the opportunity to live longer with advanced CF lung disease (Morrell and Pilewski, 2016). Along with living longer, your quality of life should improve and make you feel stronger. You might feel as though you have a new lease on life after transplantation.

The risks of lung transplantation are significant. Death occurs in 10% to 15% by the end of the first year after lung transplantation (Garrido and Dhillon, 2019). With regard to long-term outcome, median survival (time from transplant when 50% of individuals are alive) for those with CF undergoing lung transplantation is 9.52 years. However, there are a number of people with CF who continue to do well 10 to 15 years after lung transplant, although they currently are in the minority (Savi et al, 2018). Lung transplant outcomes overall, and specifically in CF, are improving. In fact, individuals with CF have some of the best outcomes compared to those who undergo lung transplantation for other lung diseases.

Additional risks include early complications, such as requiring extra time on the breathing machine. Other complications can develop further down the road. For instance, some degree of *organ rejection* (when an organ recipient's immune system considers the donor organ as a threat) can occur within the first weeks to months (Garrido and Dhillon, 2019). Immunosuppressants, although crucial to prevent rejection of the transplanted organ, lower your immune system's defense response, leaving you at a greater risk of infection and/or cancer (Garrido and Dhillon, 2019). In particular, skin cancer and colon cancer are more common in CF lung transplant recipients (Snell et al, 2017). In addition, diabetes is common after lung transplant, with 25% to 30% of individuals developing it in the first-year post-transplant and up to 40% at 5 years (Garrido and Dhillon, 2019). Finally, *reversible kidney dysfunction* is common immediately after transplant. However, over the long-term, 25% of those who survive lung transplantation develop severe kidney dysfunction at 3 years, and up to 40% develop it by 10 years (Garrido and Dhillon, 2019).

Several neuropsychiatric and psychological risks complicate organ transplantation (Sher et al, 2017; Sher, 2019). The neuropsychiatric complications that occur postoperatively include *delirium* (Sher et al, 2017) (characterized by confusion and disorientation) and *seizures*, likely due to immunosuppressants penetrating the *blood–brain barrier* and developing more frequently in CF lung transplant recipients (Snell et al, 2017). Longer-term emotional complications can include symptoms of *post-traumatic stress disorder* (PTSD) (Sher, 2019).

You should discuss your concerns with your team of doctors; they can provide you with more detailed information about your unique benefits and risks.

What Does the Recovery from Transplantation Involve?

Everyone's recovery from transplant surgery is different, and some people recover more quickly than others. Chances are that you have never had a major operation like transplant surgery before, and it is normal to feel nervous about the surgery. Do not be discouraged if you have a few setbacks as you are making your recovery. The recovery process requires a team approach, and you will have plenty of support from your transplant care team and from your family.

Everyone who undergoes an organ transplant requires time to recover in the ICU, where life-support machines (including a breathing machine) support your body through its recovery. While on the breathing machine, you will be unable to speak or to eat, and your doctors will keep you in a sleepy and comfortable state. Though you will be unable to speak while on the breathing machine, your family can visit with you, and most people are awake enough to interact with them. Usually the time spent on the breathing machine lasts only few hours to a few days. Excess fluid will be drained from the surgery site via chest tubes, which are then removed.

Pain after the surgery is expected. The incision site on your chest will likely take several weeks to recover, and it is normal to have some pain throughout the recovery period. Your doctors can manage your pain with medications, which they will gradually decrease as your pain improves.

Remember that the post-surgery period will require work. You can assist and hasten your recovery by doing the exercises your care team will teach you. This will include breathing exercises and physical therapy exercises. These exercises help you to regain your strength after surgery and help to prevent *pneumonia* from affecting your new lungs.

Transplant recipients are most at risk of infection during the first year following surgery, and therefore, you must take significant precautions to avoid becoming ill. These include wearing an approved filter mask anytime you are outside of your home and staying away from noticeably sick persons—including family members and loved ones. There will also be some food restrictions during this first year—mostly involving cooking and cleaning foods thoroughly—as the risk of illness from under-prepared food will be highest.

What Is the Typical Course Following Transplantation?

The expected course after transplant varies from person to person. An example of the postoperative course follows. You should discuss your unique circumstances with your doctor to understand how this sample trajectory might apply to you.

In-hospital recovery

Recovery starts in the ICU, where a breathing machine and other life-support measures are provided in the post-surgical phase. Typically, after 1 to 2 days, you will be able to be weaned from the breathing machine and to breathe comfortably on your own. Through physical therapy, you will start to mobilize, first sitting up in bed, then standing at the edge of the bed, and finally taking short walks in your hospital room. After you have gained enough strength, you will be transferred out of the ICU (often within 2 to 4 days after surgery), and to a general hospital ward. On the general hospital ward, you will continue your recovery: gradually taking longer and longer walks with physical therapy, increasing your nutritional intake, and weaning from pain medications.

During this time, your transplant doctors will continue to educate you and your family about your new organ, the new medications that you must take, the side effects that you should expect, and *symptoms* to look out for after you leave the hospital. You will be given a timetable for when all of your new transplant medications should be taken, and a schedule of appointments after you are discharged home.

When you are strong enough to walk and to eat full meals and have completed your in-hospital education, you will be discharged. The average duration of your hospital stay is approximately two weeks, although there are circumstances in which you might need to stay for many weeks and, less commonly, several months, if the post-transplant course has had complications.

Post-discharge recovery

After undergoing an organ transplant, it is important that you stay close to your transplant center for at least three months. If you live far away, you will need to temporarily move to live close to your transplant center. This proximity makes it easier for you to come for your frequent doctor's visits as well as to the hospital should you have any issues. After transplantation, most people will see their doctor 1 to 2 times per week for the first month, then once every two weeks, and, finally, once a month for the first several months after transplant. After the hospitalization, there will also be several weeks of physical rehabilitation.

Nearly everyone who receives an organ transplant will experience some complications. Though usually a minor complication, it is very common for people who have had a transplant to be re-admitted to the hospital at some point during the three months after transplantation.

Precautions will need to be taken every time you go into a public space; this will most often include general precautions, as well as the wearing of a filter mask and the use of antibacterial hand sanitizer. An exercise regimen will also be suggested.

Will I Still Have CF After Transplantation?

Yes. Because CF is a *genetic condition* that affects the entire body, it cannot be cured through transplantation. For instance, lung transplantation in a person with CF means that their new lungs would no longer be affected by CF, but the CF would still affect their other organs. You will also still follow up with your CF team in addition to your lung transplant doctors.

How Will My Medications/Treatments Change After Transplantation?

Transplant patients must take immunosuppressant medications diligently to prevent *rejection* of the transplanted organ (Ivulich et al, 2018). The doses will vary over time, depending on how your organ is functioning and how long ago your transplantation was performed. You will need to have laboratory tests to monitor medication levels in your blood. Because your immune system will be suppressed, you must also take preventative *(prophylactic) antibiotics*, antivirals, and *antifungals*, to prevent infections from setting in. Even though you may not require breathing treatments and nebulizers after transplantation, you will instead be adhering to a strict medication regimen to keep your new organs healthy. Depending on your weight gain following surgery, you might not need a feeding tube or nutritional supplements.

You will continue to take other medications to manage your CF, such as medications for your *pancreas* and GI tract, as well as to continue with sinus treatments.

What Are the Side Effects of Medicines I Might Take After Transplantation?

Side effects are common, particularly given the number of medications that you will be required to take after undergoing an organ transplant (Gamboa and Ferrando, 2019). Fortunately, the side effects are usually mild, and can be managed by your team of doctors. The side effects will depend on the type of medicine you are on. It is important to be knowledgeable about medication side effects.

Steroids

Steroids are commonly-used medications to suppress the immune system. Everyone who undergoes transplantation requires steroids. Common side effects include weight gain, water retention, high blood sugars, high blood pressure, easy bruising, irritability, and mood lability. Steroids can cause notable mood swings, a quickness to anger, and insomnia. These side effects are related to the dose of steroids you are on (i.e., the higher the steroid dose, the more likely you are to experience side effects) (Dubovsky et al, 2012). Most often, side effects can be managed by reducing the steroid dose.

Other immunosuppressive medications

In addition to steroids, your lung transplant team will put you on other immuno-suppressive medications to avoid rejection of your transplanted organ (Garrido and Dhillon, 2019). *Tacrolimus* is a commonly-used medication, and its side effects include kidney injury, headaches, tremors, high blood pressure, and diarrhea. *Mycophenolate mofetil* is another commonly-used immunosuppressive medication, and its side effects include decreased blood cell counts, diarrhea, and an upset stomach. If you are on these medications, your doctors will do routine blood work to make sure that your dosing is correct and to monitor you for any side effects.

Both immunosuppressants and steroids lower your resistance to infections. In the long term, the use of immunosuppressants results in an increased risk for cancer, particularly skin cancer (Ivulich et al, 2018). Thus, meticulous dermatology examinations at least once each year and age-appropriate cancer screening are an important part of post-transplant care.

Prophylactic antimicrobials

Prophylactic antibiotics are required after transplantation to protect you from infections (Garrido and Dhillon, 2019). *Bactrim®* (sulfamethoxazole/trimethoprim) is a commonly used antibiotic that is very well tolerated. Some patients develop increased *sun sensitivity* or a rash while on Bactrim®.

Other medications used include *valganciclovir*, which protects against viral infections. Its common side effects include nausea, diarrhea, and low blood counts.

How Can I Improve My Candidacy for Organ Transplantation?

If you are being recommended for an organ transplant, there is a reasonably good chance that you're already a good candidate for the procedure. The best thing, then, would be for you to continue doing what you're already doing: taking medications and adhering to all of your treatments, exercising as best as you can, and not smoking or using recreational drugs or alcohol.

Adherence to all medications and treatments is one of the most important contributors to successful transplant, yet it can be understandably difficult. If this is problem area for you, engage your CF team and be proactive in working with it to improve your adherence. Of course, use of tobacco, alcohol, and recreational substances can worsen your health and can interfere with multiple medications, and thus this is something transplant programs will evaluate. If you struggle with these areas, talk to your physicians early on, well before the transplant, and work on rehabilitation. If you use cannabis, talk to your providers; your transplant teams might advise you against it and come up with a plan to address this.

Additionally, candidacy can be improved by you being open to your medical team's input and suggestions. Your doctor might want to perform additional tests or start new treatments and medications, even after you are listed. In addition, honesty with your transplant team is important even if some topics are difficult for you. Remember, your team wants to know your unique circumstances to make its best recommendations regarding how the transplant can benefit you and what is the best way to improve your candidacy and post-transplant outcome.

Keeping up your weight is also an excellent way to improve your transplant candidacy. Potential recipients should continue to take their supplements and be receptive to the option of having a feeding tube (often an abdominal *PEG* or *G-J tube*) placed, if this has not already been done.

Finally, having a support system is a key element in successful organ transplantation and transplant programs; in fact, you might be required to have at least two people fully available to you for at least 3 months after transplantation. Nobody can go through transplant on their own; ensuring that you have a robust and functional support system is very important. Make sure that you know who your support system will be well ahead of your transplant evaluation, engage your identified support people in conversations about transplantation, bring them to your appointments, and make sure that they understand what is involved and are fully on board.

How Do I Decide Whether I Am Interested in Organ Transplantation?

People with CF should understand that if they are being considered for transplantation, there's probably a good reason behind it. End-stage CF doesn't leave a lot of options, and doctors wouldn't suggest such a surgery if they didn't need to.

Beyond that, consider that your quality of life will most likely improve afterward. Although a lung transplant is not a "cure" for CF, and post-transplant care involves intense medical follow-up and a lifetime of immunosuppression, life post-transplant can be markedly easier and better than life many years before. For one thing, you will most likely be able to breathe without supplemental oxygen and to be more active. You will probably no longer need to do airway clearance or nebulized treatments.

Transplant surgery is not easy, and you will participate in rehabilitation afterward. You can consider making a pros and cons list if you struggle making a decision regarding a transplant. You can envision your life before and after the surgery and consider all options available, including transplantation and *palliative care*.

Here are some things to consider while you are making your decision:

- What is your idea of good quality of life? Ask yourself whether you are able to do the things that bring meaning to your life. Will a lung transplant allow you to engage in those activities?

- Who in your life can provide support to you? Organ transplantation is a life-changing decision; it is not something that you can do alone. Ask yourself who in your life can be there to help you, whether it's with driving to appointments, keeping track of medications, talking to insurance companies, or helping you recover from your surgery. Discuss with these people how undergoing an organ transplant can transform both of your lives.

- Are you willing to take medications every day for the rest of your life? Understandably, taking medicine every day can be a daunting task, and is not for everyone. Ask yourself whether you're the type of person to skip days of your medicine when you are not feeling up to it. Is that a pattern that you are willing to change?

- What do you expect from an organ transplant? It is important to remember that organ transplantation does not provide a cure. People who have had transplants are still required to take medications, have frequent doctors' appointments, and, at times, be admitted to the hospital for complications that arise. Ask yourself whether continuing frequent doctors' visits is acceptable to you should you decide to proceed with a transplant.

How Should I Proceed If I Want to Pursue Organ Transplantation?

The decision as to whether to pursue an organ transplant is a personal one and is assessed on a case-by-case basis to adapt to your unique circumstances. A first step is often to discuss transplantation with your CF doctors. Tell them what you have read and learned; ask any questions you might have. They can help you to understand what transplantation might mean to you and to your family, what the benefits and risks might be, and how it will affect your life. Your doctor will help you decide whether pursuing an organ transplant is right for you and, if it is, when the referral and evaluation are warranted.

The next step is getting referred to the transplant team, which will perform extensive testing to assess your candidacy for an organ transplant (Ramos et al, 2019). That will likely include blood work, pulmonary function testing, cardiac catheterization, imaging, and exercise testing. The team will also evaluate your social situation to ensure that you have the support you will need going into and after transplantation. Lastly, it will assess your medical insurance to verify that you have the insurance coverage you need to get the treatments you will require and offer financial advice, if needed. Often, a lung transplant candidate will require help with medical insurance authorization, and the lung transplant coordinator and social worker will be able to assist you.

After an evaluation, the team will offer you their comprehensive recommendations. Some patients are told that they are "too well" to undergo transplant, meaning that their current lung function is good enough that it is not worth proceeding with the risk of a lung transplant yet. Others are told that they need to work on certain things (e.g., gaining weight, undergoing pulmonary rehabilitation to improve strength, or working on their support system) before they can be considered for transplant, to improve their success.

When the time comes, you and your doctor will decide whether to proceed with lung transplant listing. After you are accepted into the program, you are placed on the "*wait list,*" which is a computerized list that keeps track of everyone across the country who is waiting for an organ. While on the organ waiting list, you will continue to follow with your CF and the transplant teams to maintain your lung function.

What Is It Like Waiting for an Organ Transplant? What Is It Like Getting "The Call"?

Waiting for an organ transplant, especially a lung transplant, can be stressful (Flynn et al, 2014). You and your doctors often do not know in advance when "The Call" will come, and an accurate timetable cannot be given (The Call is the colloquial term for the phone call from the hospital letting you know that they have found donor organs for you). Your medical team might be able to let you know your allotment score on the transplant list and the average wait time, but, often, anything more specific and actionable than that is unknowable.

Occasionally, there might also be a "dry run," wherein you receive a call that donor organs are available, only to discover that sometime between The Call and the surgery, something has changed, and the organs are no longer available or are not a good match. This is often due to additional information about donor organs that had not been immediately available to the medical team—either a test result that shows worsening organ quality or concerns identified at visualization of the organs by the *surgeon* in the donor operating room. Sometimes this will happen after you are already under *anesthesia*. A dry run, however, as difficult as it might seem, is always in your best interests, albeit the emotional strain can be a lot to handle.

While on the transplant wait list, you might become sicker given that CF is a progressive disease. Depending on the wait time for the transplant, you might find your lung function declining or your weight more difficult to keep on. Activity levels will also often diminish.

Anxiety might also be worsening while waiting for the transplant, due to both physiological (e.g., having more shortness of breath, requiring more oxygen) and psychological reasons. It is understandable that you might worry when and if you will receive The Call and how it will be for you, while also worrying about growing sicker or keeping up the weight. Waiting on the list might also bring up existential questions for you: while preparing for The Call, the surgery, and post-transplant life, at the same time you might be faced with your mortality and possibility of dying before the transplant. This of course creates anxiety and fears. Some people cope with these existential questions by ensuring that they are prepared for either situation as much as they can be.

You will be required to keep your phone with you and on, at all times, awaiting The Call, which can come at any time of the day or night. Getting The Call is amazing and everything happens fast after it.

After you receive The Call, you will be required to get to the transplant hospital as fast as possible. When you arrive, you will be admitted immediately and preparation for the transplant will begin. There can sometimes still be several hours between The Call and the actual surgery, but the time will most likely seem to fly by, due to the anticipation and the pre-transplant activity.

What Might My Feelings Be Like About Organ Transplantation?

Depending on your lung function, and how early you are recommended for an organ transplant, there will most likely be some feeling of being conflicted regarding the surgery. You might think you can continue as you are, without the transplant, or that you have done just fine so far without one. This is understandable, though it is important to remember that doctors don't recommend organ transplantation without a reason and that CF is a progressive and often terminal disease.

You might also experience denial, convincing yourself that you do not need an organ transplant. Your doctors may also tell you that you will die without a transplant, and hearing that can be difficult to process. Facing your mortality is difficult, and some pushback against the notion is understandable.

In addition, you may tell yourself that the surgery is too risky, or that new CF drugs could alleviate their symptoms without the transplant. Feelings of depression or *anxiety* are not out of the question considering an organ transplant is an exceptionally stressful endeavor, and it can take some time to make a decision. This is all completely normal and understandable.

Afterward, you might also have *survivor's guilt*, wherein you might feel a burden about receiving and surviving an organ transplant, whereas others you know have not.

If you have difficulty processing or experiencing any of these feelings, reach out to your medical and mental health professionals and they can help you with additional supports during this difficult time.

When Is Retransplantation Considered?

Although lung transplantation is an effective way to treat *end-stage manifestations* of CF, it is not perfect. Despite advances in immunosuppressive medications, organ rejection is a very common occurrence. Everyone who undergoes lung transplantation will have an episode of rejection at some point. Most often, your doctors can treat organ rejection with medications. In most cases, the treatment is successful in reversing the rejection and allowing the organ to continue functioning. Over time, however, many people develop chronic rejection of the lung. *Chronic lung rejection* (*Chronic Lung Allograft Dysfunction* or *CLAD*) remains the main barrier to extended survival after lung transplantation (Garrido and Dhillon, 2019).

In select individuals who experience worsening respiratory symptoms and develop lung failure due to CLAD, *re-do lung transplantation* might be considered. Re-do lung transplant is associated with higher risks and a more difficult recovery than a first-time transplant and, hence, is appropriate in only a few selected circumstances; however, people with CF do better with re-do transplantation as compared to lung transplant recipients for other indications (Snell et al, 2017). Often, re-do transplantation is not feasible, due to other medical conditions that might have arisen since the initial transplant.

Can I Be an Organ Donor?

Contrary to popular belief, people with CF can safely donate organs and/or tissues (such as a cornea, heart, liver, kidney) to others. There is no risk of the transplanted organ transmitting CF. Evaluation of donated organs is done on a case-by-case basis, and people with CF have successfully donated tissues and corneas. There is no barrier to signing up to be on the donor registry, which you can do at www.organdonor.gov. Also, let your family and caregivers know about your wishes.

WHAT IS PALLIATIVE CARE?

Elisabeth P. Dellon, MD and Isabel Stenzel Byrnes, LCSW, MPH

CHAPTER

In This Chapter

- Is Palliative Care Useful Only When I Become Very Ill?

- How Can Palliative Care Help Me Manage My CF?

- Should I Stop My CF Treatments If I Am Working with a Palliative Care Specialist?

- What Kinds of Treatment Are Available If I Become Critically Ill?

- How Will I Decide What Kinds of Treatments to Receive?

- Who Should I Include in Discussions About My Wishes?

- How Can I Make Sure That My Treatment Team Knows My Wishes Regarding Health Care?

- What Can I Do to Prepare for Becoming Sicker or Nearing the End of My Life?

- Are My Spiritual Needs Being Met?

- How Can I Prepare Emotionally If I Am Approaching the End of My Life?

- How Will My Family and Friends Cope When I Die?

Is Palliative Care Useful Only When I Become Very Ill?

"Palliative care" is a familiar but often poorly understood term. The *World Health Organization* (WHO) defines palliative care as, ". . . an approach that improves the quality of life of patients and their families facing the problems associated with life-threatening illness, through the prevention and relief of suffering by means of early identification and impeccable assessment and treatment of pain and other problems, physical, psychosocial, and spiritual." (WHO, 1998) To help clarify what palliative care means in the context of cystic fibrosis (CF), individuals with CF, family caregivers, CF care team members, and palliative care specialists collaborated to create a more specific definition: "Palliative care focuses on reducing physical and emotional symptoms and improving quality of life for people with CF throughout their lives. Palliative care occurs alongside usual treatments and is individualized according to the unique goals, hopes, and values of each person with CF." (Dellon et al, 2018)

Individuals with CF endure bothersome *symptoms*, daily treatments and medications, and hard choices about medical therapies. As such, it is important to establish open communication with health care providers, with special attention paid to goals, hopes, worries, and symptoms. Medical decisions are ideally shared among individuals with CF, their caregivers, and their health care providers. This becomes particularly important as CF progresses and the choices become more difficult.

Palliative care can be provided by your CF care team, so called *"primary palliative care."* If more complex issues with symptoms or treatment decisions arise, palliative care specialists might be available to partner with you and your CF team to ensure that you receive the best possible care, and that your medical decisions are aligned with your goals for medical care. Although many people equate palliative care with *hospice*, it is important to understand that hospice care is intended for people who are believed to be in the last 6 months of their life with no curative/life-extending treatment pursued. It is focused on quality of life, living well for the time one has left to live, having a good death, and ensuring that loved ones of a dying person are well supported. Palliative care, on the other hand, should be an integral part of care throughout the life of those with chronic conditions like CF.

How Can Palliative Care Help Me Manage My CF?

Palliative care coincides with your usual CF therapies to help you feel as well as you can each day. Individuals with CF have numerous symptoms, physical (e.g., cough, pain in the chest and abdomen, shortness of breath, headache, nausea, and fatigue) and emotional (e.g., anxiety and depressed mood), due to their CF.

Your CF team considers your CF symptoms and makes recommendations for how best to treat them. Although many of your usual CF therapies improve your symptoms on most days, some symptoms might not be adequately treated. You might find that it's difficult to address all of your concerns during your CF clinic visits, or at times your CF care team isn't certain about how best to manage your symptoms and concerns. This is not because the team doesn't want to help you; rather, many symptoms of CF are difficult to treat.

Palliative care specialists are trained to investigate your symptoms in a way that complements the assessments of your CF care team. They don't understand CF in the same way that your CF care team does; however, because they treat people with a broad range of medical conditions, they are often able to recommend new medications and therapies. Some people associate palliative care with use of *opioids* or *narcotic* medications, like morphine. These medications are prescribed by palliative care specialists and other health care providers, when appropriate, but they are rarely first-line treatments. In the case of CF, opioids can be recommended for moderate to severe acute pain after a procedure or surgery and/or with illness exacerbations, for severe chronic pain that limits the ability to participate in CF therapies, for shortness of breath in those with advanced CF lung disease, and for pain and/or shortness of breath near the end of life. For emotional distress, in addition to partnering with your CF care team to recommend counseling and, when needed, medications, palliative care specialists address bigger worries that come with living with CF (e.g., questions like, "Why me?" and worries about how your CF symptoms affect your loved ones).

Should I Stop My CF Treatments If I Am Working with a Palliative Care Specialist?

CF treatments are essential to maintaining your health and to treating exacerbations of lung disease or *gastrointestinal* (GI) problems. Even though your treatments may be modified over time as your condition changes and as new therapies for CF become available, your CF care team will continue to recommend therapies that are tailored to your specific needs. Your palliative care team might recommend treatments in addition to your usual CF therapies that should help to relieve bothersome physical and emotional symptoms. Ideally, these recommendations will be made in collaboration with your CF team. A palliative care specialist or team will not take over your CF care; instead, it will provide expert consultation on distressing symptoms and help with communication about your goals, medical decisions, and wishes for your medical care.

What Kinds of Treatment Are Available If I Become Critically Ill?

As your lung disease worsens, you might be faced with decisions about embarking on different types of treatments to help you breathe. In addition to your typical CF therapies, oxygen and other types of respiratory support might be recommended by your CF team. Sometimes, these treatments are used over the long term, and at other times they are considered only in emergencies, as with a very severe illness. Some treatments can be used at home, some only in the hospital, and some only in an intensive care unit (ICU). It can be helpful to learn about these treatments from your CF team before facing decisions about their use so that you can gather information and ask questions. Following are some important terms to know.

Supplemental oxygen

Delivered by a small tube with prongs that sits below the nose or by a face mask. This is intended to help deliver oxygen to your vital organs and to help you breathe more comfortably. Some people use supplemental oxygen only when they're sick, during exercise, or during sleep, whereas others use it all the time (https://www.thoracic.org/patients/patient-resources/resources/oxygen-therapy.pdf).

Bi-level Positive Airway Pressure (BiPAP) or Continuous Positive Airway Pressure (CPAP)

These "*non-invasive ventilation* (NIV)" devices help push air into your lungs to support your breathing and reduce the work of your breathing. Pressure is delivered through a mask or nasal prongs. Some people use BiPAP or CPAP during sleep, some use it only when they are sick, and some use it more for comfort and to support their breathing.

Ventilator

This is a machine used to help someone breathe when their lungs are too impaired to breathe on their own. Using a ventilator involves *intubation*, a process of placing a breathing tube through the mouth into the trachea. The tube is then connected to a ventilator. Ventilators are used to help a person breathe during surgery or procedures; this is a different situation than when using a ventilator during a severe illness. Many doctors prefer to avoid intubation and use of ventilators in those with CF whose lungs are very impaired because some people with lung disease become dependent on the ventilator. Most people require medications to keep them drowsy ("sedated") to tolerate the breathing tube and the ventilator. Ventilators are used only in the ICU (https://www.thoracic.org/patients/patient-resources/resources/mechanical-ventilation.pdf).

Extracorporeal membrane oxygenation (ECMO)

ECMO is a life-support machine that replaces the function of the lungs and heart. It can be used for short periods to support someone through a very severe lung infection, and to help people continue living until a *lung transplant* can be performed. ECMO is used only in the ICU. Not everyone whose lungs are very impaired will benefit from ECMO, and not every hospital is able to treat individuals with ECMO. It is a high-risk treatment that requires careful monitoring and ongoing conversations about whether the benefits outweigh the risks (https://www.thoracic.org/patients/patient-resources/resources/what-is-ecmo.pdf).

If you are sick enough that these treatments are even considered, you should have frequent communication with your health care providers about your goals for medical care. Because some of these treatments can be offered only in the hospital, choosing them can limit your ability to return home. Sometimes decisions are made to try these treatments, and then goals change or problems arise and decisions are made to discontinue them. Your CF care team and other health care providers should talk to you about your goals, address your worries, and make recommendations for treatment that align with your goals. Although not every treatment will allow you to live longer when you are very ill, it is always possible to make you comfortable and make your quality of life with loved ones a priority.

How Will I Decide What Kinds of Treatments to Receive?

Individuals with CF face a bevy of decisions about their medical care. Many of these decisions about medical treatments are very personal. Everyone has their own approach. Some people like their health care providers to make recommendations; others prefer to seek advice from family members or from others with CF; some people weigh the pros and cons and do what feels right to them; and still others like a mixture of all of these approaches. Here are some questions that you might ask yourself when you have important decisions to make:

- Do I feel confident that I know what choices are available to me?

- What matters most to me when it comes to my medical care?

- Do I understand the possible benefits and possible risks of each option?

- Do I know about the risks and benefits and which risks would matter most to me?

- Do I have enough support and advice to make a decision?

- Am I comfortable asking my health care providers about my treatment options?

If you find yourself needing more information, worrying about the choices you're facing, or simply not knowing what to do, it's important to let your loved ones and your CF care team or other trusted health care providers know that you need more support and information. It is normal to have trouble making decisions from time to time. Sometimes, none of the options feel good to you, and you might worry about the outcomes of any of the choices you might make. For these reasons, and because most people need to consider the opinions of others before they make choices, making decisions can be emotional. The more your CF care team helps you to anticipate the decisions you might face, the less rushed you should feel about decision making.

Who Should I Include in Discussions About My Wishes?

Individuals with CF have a variety of people who care for them. When you think of your support network, imagine a series of concentric circles, with you in the middle. The closest circle around you may be occupied by your parents, siblings or a partner. The next circle might include friends or extended family members. The circle around that might be co-workers, school friends, or neighbors. Where your CF care team fits depends on your relationship to it.

It's up to the person with CF to decide who to include about your wishes for the future. In whom do you confide when you have a problem? Is there someone who has always been there for you, who understands you, and who knows your priorities? It's important to choose a person to make decisions for you if you are unable to decide for yourself. This is called a *power of attorney for health care*, or surrogate, agent, or *proxy*. This person should be in your closest circle and should really know you. This person should know your wishes and have access to any documents (such as an *advance directive*) that you've filled out indicating your wishes. You should specify an alternate, as well, in case your first choice is not available. You should also tell your CF team who this person is and have this list documented in your chart.

When discussing your wishes for your future, you will need someone who can handle uncertainties. It is natural to want to protect your loved ones from difficult emotions like grief or *anxiety*. Nevertheless, having these conversations before a crisis arises will prepare them and spare them from having to "guess" what you'd want if you become critically ill. Ideally, you might want someone who can support you during difficult times and who can respect your wishes above their own. It can also be helpful to discuss your wishes with someone who understands the medical world and can speak up as your advocate, if necessary.

How Can I Make Sure That My Treatment Team Knows My Wishes Regarding Health Care?

Your CF care team wants to know what you value and what your health care wishes are. Even though your doctors or social worker are often the ones to talk with you about your wishes, it's okay to choose any member of the team. It can take time, possibly over several visits and conversations, to clarify your wishes.

Sometimes, your CF care team will ask you to fill out important documents, such as an advance directive or *POLST* (sometimes called *POST*, *MOST*, or *MOLST*, depending on the state where you live [https://polst.org/]). These are documents that ask you to write down what you'd want for your health care if you cannot speak for yourself or if you become critically ill and are unable to engage in a goals-of-care discussion. They also help the CF care team learn who is serving as your agent or power of attorney. The CF team might ask you to complete these, and it might catch you off guard. Just because they are asking you to fill them out does not mean you are going to become sicker! Rather, they want you to understand your treatment options and to document your wishes so that they will be clear if a crisis arises. These documents also help to provide you with peace of mind by having others know what kinds of treatments you want and what you don't want. This assures that there won't be significant disagreement between your CF team and your family regarding your care decisions. Make sure these documents are scanned and accessible in your electronic medical record. You should keep a hardcopy of these documents and place it somewhere accessible in your home, such as on your refrigerator or in your medical file.

What Can I Do to Prepare for Becoming Sicker or Nearing the End of My Life?

It takes courage and strength to prepare for the difficult times that might lie ahead because of your CF. However, doing so will save energy for you and for your loved ones at challenging times. There are many ways in which you can prepare for becoming sicker or nearing the end of your life (e.g., you can update and clarify your wishes in your advance directive). Here are some strategies:

- Designate a power of attorney for finances, which might be the same person as your power of attorney for health care. Be sure to include names and contacts for any professionals you've worked with (e.g., as your accountant or lawyer).

- Prepare a living will or trust (and designate a trustee or executor of your estate and choose beneficiaries and heirs for your estate).

- Prepare a list of passwords for your online accounts for use by your agent or proxy.

- Prepare paperwork for your bank accounts, life insurance, social security, disability insurance, retirement funds, investments, property, business affairs, and taxes for your agent or proxy.

- Prepare a list of charities that you'd like your agent to donate to, from your estate or memorial contributions.

- Prepare in writing wishes for the distribution of your belongings (such as jewelry, collectibles, or other valuables).

- Prepare your wishes for your funeral (such as the location, music, who will speak).

- Document your wishes for your body after death. Would you like to donate your tissues and organs? Would you want to be cremated or buried? Would you want your body to go to science? Where would you like your remains to be laid to rest?

- Plan on designating a guardian for your pets or your children, if it will be someone other than your spouse.

- Plan to write your eulogy and obituary, or leave videos or letters behind for people you love to mark your legacy.

Many of these tasks will consume your time and energy, which can be limited at any stage by CF. Tackling tasks one at a time will help to conserve your physical energy while completing these chores. It will also help to lessen the amount of emotional energy you will expend confronting these difficult realities. Having a team of supporters, including family and friends, to bounce ideas off of can make these tasks less daunting. This effort is a generous gift to your loved ones to guide them to respect your wishes after you die.

Are My Spiritual Needs Being Met?

Palliative care recognizes the physical, emotional, social, and spiritual aspects of a person dealing with serious illness. Just as your physical suffering is treated, your spiritual symptoms of suffering also need to be addressed. Many palliative care teams have a designated interfaith chaplain who serves as a sounding board and counselor for patients and family members. Spiritual care does not mean religious practice; chaplains are trained to support you wherever you are in your spiritual path. A chaplain can offer non-judgmental listening to your concerns around facing the end of life. Some of those concerns might include the following:

- Why me? Why do I have CF and why am I at this stage of illness?

- Where is God in my suffering with CF?

- What can I hope for now that my disease is advanced?

- What comes after this life?

- What is the meaning of my life and the meaning of having CF?

- Have I lived a good enough life? What is my legacy?

- What do I do with my regrets, guilt, or resentment that I have for others?

- How can I spend my remaining days with dignity, without being a burden to my family?

- Will I survive a transplant? Why should I live while my donor dies?

Although chaplains and other health care team members might not have the answers to these questions, they can help guide you in your own reflection and discovery to help you find peace and serenity with the life you are living.

How Can I Prepare Emotionally If I Am Approaching the End of My Life?

CF can be a cruel disease, despite all our efforts to stay well. Facing this reality can be really difficult. It is not fair to have to deal with end-of-life issues, especially at a much younger age than normal. We need to grieve the things this disease often takes from us. It's okay to cry, and to feel angry, afraid, hopeless, lonely, anxious, guilty, and depressed. Grieving is a normal and acceptable response to loss. Grieving means yearning for what isn't, wishing for more, and dreaming about the "what-if's" in life. The grief process moves from intense sorrow to acceptance; it can take years to fully grieve the losses this disease has caused.

Grief takes energy and it can affect your physical health, as well. Finding ways to cope with these feelings will affect your quality of life. Sharing your feelings with others, writing down your feelings in a journal, creating art, playing music, being in nature, practicing meditation and prayer, or engaging in physical activity, as tolerated, can help manage difficult emotions. Getting to know other people with CF through the internet can help you feel less alone. It can help to talk to your CF care team and learn about what to expect as the end approaches. This knowledge can reduce your fear. A *psychotherapist* can also help you to explore and understand your feelings.

Another way to deal with your emotions is to take turns looking at and looking away from your reality. It's okay to find distractions that bring you joy, beauty, laughter, and fun. Denial is a natural response to overwhelming painful emotions. It is healthy as long as it doesn't prevent you from taking proper care of yourself. Accepting where you are in your CF journey can also reduce the energy it takes to protest—psychologically and physically—your reality so you can spend your energy in more productive ways. Many people refer to CF as a "fight." Reaching the end of CF does not mean you've lost your battle or that you've given up. It means CF is taking over against your will. Talking to yourself in compassionate ways, such as saying to yourself, "I've done my best with the life I was given," can be helpful. Living with CF requires living with hope. At the end of life, it's important to hold onto hope. Yet, hope can shift from living longer to living better—and dying with peace and comfort.

Sometimes, our experience with difficult emotions can open up the possibility for personal growth and maturity. We might communicate more openly with others, make amends, and share wisdom with family and friends. Telling stories and reviewing your life can bring solace. Recognizing the good things in your life, despite poor health, can promote gratitude and appreciation. There are times when facing death can help you think about the way you want to live. What is left on your bucket list and how can you pursue what you love? Shifting your focus from sorrow to empowerment can help you set your priorities and focus on how to live the best life you can in the time that you have remaining.

How Will My Family and Friends Cope When I Die?

Separation from our loved ones is often the biggest concern people have about death. Many parents and other family members have dedicated their lives to caring for you and your CF. Your death will leave a deep hole and it will take time for them to adjust to your absence. Like you, your family will need to do the work to grieve their loss, to see that they did their best to keep you alive, and that your death is not a failure on their part. CF has probably trained your family and friends to cope with loss; they will need to use all they've learned for their grieving process.

Even though it is natural to worry about how your friends and family will manage after your death, worrying about it can consume precious energy. It can also keep people holding on at the end of life for longer. Letting go means trusting that your loved ones will be okay without you. When people reach the end of life, they don't always have the energy to express what they want to say to their loved ones. It's important to say what needs to be said much earlier. Your courage to do so will give permission for your loved ones to open up to you about these difficult conversations. What can help your loved ones' grief in the long term is for you to give them permission to be happy again, to marry again, to follow their dreams, or to honor you by living fully. Sharing your belief system about how you will stay connected to your family and friends can also provide immense comfort.

A good death can ease the grief experience for family and friends. You have a role in preparing for that good death through your end-of-life paperwork, clear medical decisions, and your openness to honest conversations. Your relationships with your health care team and your own coping with your dying will also influence the coping of your loved ones.

Palliative care extends beyond your death. Most palliative care programs offer grief support or referrals to bereavement care. Your family and friends will be most comforted by remembering you and how you lived your life. Their memories of you will be with them forever. They have been permanently changed by knowing and loving you. You must find a way to trust that your loved ones will continue living their lives, as best as they can, without you in physical form. They will always continue to love you emotionally and spiritually.

WHAT MIGHT BE THE FUTURE OF CF PREVENTION AND TREATMENT?

Lael M. Yonker, MD; Christine M. Roach, RN, BSN;
Frances H. Kiles; and Isabel P. Neuringer, MD

CHAPTER

In This Chapter

- What Is a Clinical Trial and Why Do Such Trials Exist?
- What Types of Clinical Trials Are Being Conducted to Manage CF?
- What Are the Phases of Clinical Trials?
- What Are the Potential Benefits and Risks of Participating in a Clinical Trial?
- Who Is Eligible for a Clinical Trial?
- Why Should I Enroll in a Clinical Trial?
- What Is Informed Consent?
- What Is a Placebo and Could I Receive It?
- Where Are Clinical Trials Conducted?
- Who Pays for a Clinical Trial?
- What Questions Should I Ask Before Joining a Clinical Trial?
- What Happens When a Clinical Trial Is Completed?
- How Can I Learn More About Clinical Trials?

What Is a Clinical Trial and Why Do Such Trials Exist?

A *clinical trial* is a study that tests the full effects of an intervention on a selected population or is an *observational study* that follows patients who are already on a *United States Food and Drug Administration* (FDA)-approved medication. The intervention might be a medical therapy, a survey, or questionnaire about *symptoms*, or a *prospective* or *retrospective study*. Clinical trials in cystic fibrosis (CF) often involve medications, like antibiotics, mucolytics or *cystic fibrosis transmembrane conductance regulator* (CFTR) *modulators* to restore CFTR function, augment mucociliary clearance, reduce *inflammation*, treat infections, and improve nutrition or digestive health.

A clinical trial must pass through several steps before it enrolls participants. First, during the process of drug discovery, researchers identify an area of investigation or an unmet clinical dilemma, formulate the initial concept and *hypothesis*, and test the hypothesis in a *pre-clinical phase* using *in-vitro* or *in-vivo* models. Investigators then submit a proposal that includes the study design, inclusion and exclusion criteria, *informed consent* process, study tests planned, study end-points, and statistical analyses to the study site institution's *Institutional Review Board* (IRB). The study plan includes a *Data Safety Monitoring Board* (DSMB) that is composed of physicians, academics, legal experts, and members of the community. The IRB examines the proposal with a focus on safety and appropriate informed consent. Before clinical research can commence on a new drug, an *Investigational New Drug* (IND) application must be submitted to the FDA so that it can ensure the safety and proper oversight of the trial. This submission must include animal study data and toxicity data, manufacturing materials, clinical protocols, prior data from human subjects, and the investigator's profile. After IND approval, the trial can proceed through several phases.

What Types of Clinical Trials Are Being Conducted to Manage CF?

Current clinical trials in CF involve restoring CFTR function, promoting mucociliary clearance, reducing inflammation, fighting infection, and augmenting nutritional and gastrointestinal (GI) function. Studies aimed at restoring CFTR function include the CFTR modulators that promote correction of protein mis-folding (correctors) and potentiate *chloride channel* opening (potentiators). *Potentiators* can be used alone or in combination with a *corrector*. Although Kalydeco® is a commercially available potentiator, and Orkambi® and Symdeko® are commercially available potentiator–corrector combinations, many additional potentiator–corrector combinations are under evaluation, in conjunction with an *amplifier* that increases the total amount of CFTR protein. Although corrector and potentiator therapies are *mutation-specific*, amplifiers are *mutation-agnostic*, meaning that they do not rely on a specific CFTR mutation to work. The majority of these studies are now in Phase 2 and 3 clinical trials. Inhaled therapies aimed at the repair of CFTR-encoded *messenger RNA* (mRNA) are currently underway as Phase 1 and 2 clinical trials. Pre-clinical studies continue to elucidate additional pathways of restoring CFTR function. Clinical trials addressing *mucociliary clearance* include an inhaled *osmotic agent*, which pulls water into the airways to provide enhanced clearance, and compounds that decrease mucus thickness or block *sodium channel*–induced water loss from the airways.

Trials aimed at inflammation include reduction of *pro-inflammatory leukotriene B4* (LTB4), induction of anti-inflammatory products, *retinoids*, and inhibition of *neutrophil elastase*. Anti-infective trials include inhaled *levofloxacin*, inhaled *vancomycin*, inhaled *nitric oxide*, *intravenous* (IV) and inhaled compounds that limit bacterial growth through inhibition of iron metabolism, protection from *aminoglycoside toxicity*, restoration of airway surface liquid antimicrobial function, and disruption of biofilms. Lastly, nutritional and GI clinical trials involve *antioxidant* compounds, and new *pancreatic enzyme* formulations. In addition to these studies, many additional investigator-led studies are in progress within the United States and around the world. Looking toward the future, recent advances in genome editing have re-opened the possibility of repairing the *DNA* defect, using technologies such a *CRISPR-Cas9 technology*. This technique involves locating the mutation within the cell, excising the mutation, and then repairing the DNA from a corrected template using the cell's own DNA repair apparatus.

What Are the Phases of Clinical Trials?

Clinical trials typically have four phases:

Phase 1 trials primarily focus on determining whether a medication is safe and well tolerated, or whether there are any unwanted side effects. Typically, Phase 1 trials are first done with a small number of healthy volunteers, with the goal of looking at safety and tolerability.

Phase 2 trials are slightly larger and include only individuals for whom the treatment is targeted. For clinical trials involving a therapy designed to treat CF, only individuals with CF would be included. The goal of Phase 2 trials is to determine the ideal dose of a medication, and to begin to assess the benefit of the therapy. There are no set guidelines for the goals or format for Phase 2 trials. These trials primarily serve to determine the ideal study design for Phase 3 trials.

Phase 3 trials are *double-blinded placebo-controlled trials* that involve a larger number of participants, with the goal of determining the efficacy of a medication. After this trial is completed, the results are expected to be presented to the FDA to determine whether an investigational treatment can be approved for clinical care.

Phase 4 trials are performed on medications that are already clinically approved. These trials are termed "*post-market clinical trials*" and assess long-term side effects or long-term outcomes related to a treatment. Participants often don't need to come in for study visits for this type of trial. Instead, after a consent form has been signed, medical records and reports are tracked by the company.

In general, these four phases of clinical trials only include adults. However, this can vary. For example, many of the CFTR-modulator clinical trials included individuals ages 12 and older. If positive results are seen in clinical trials in this older population, trials are repeated in younger children, and then in toddlers and infants. However, medication dosing and trial design can change, adapting to be age-appropriate. After a medication receives FDA approval, following a successful Phase 3 clinical trial, it is only approved for the age range that was studied.

Table 18-1 provides a summary of the clinical trial phases.

Table 18-1: Characteristics of Clinical Trials

Clinical Trial Type	Overview
Phase 1	Small number of participants. Assess safety and tolerability of a medication.
Phase 2	Moderate number of participants. Assess for effectiveness of a medicine in a small population.
Phase 3	Large number of participants. Compare effect with "*gold standard*" of clinical care.
Phase 4	Post-FDA approval. Monitors for long-term *side effects* and outcomes in "real-world" use. Typically, no study visits are required.

What Are the Potential Benefits and Risks of Participating in a Clinical Trial?

Being part of a clinical trial can provide you with the following benefits:

- You might get a new treatment for CF before it is available to everyone with CF.

- You can play a more active role in your own health care by deciding whether to participate.

- You will be seen more frequently by the *research team* and will have individualized care with your research team as part of your study sessions.

- You might have the chance to help others get a better treatment for CF and you might help researchers further their understanding of CF (NIH, 2017).

Risks of taking part in a clinical trial include the following:

- The new treatment might not work or it might not be better than the standard treatment you or your child were previously receiving for CF.

- Side effects that are generally mild and temporary but can be unpleasant. However, with routine medical care, side effects are rare.

- You might not be part of the treatment group that gets the new treatment; instead, you might be assigned to the no-treatment (i.e., *placebo*) group or to standard-of-care medication.

- It can be inconvenient. Medical appointments are more frequent, some visits can be lengthy.

- You might have more testing (including sweat tests, blood tests, urine tests, spirometry testing, and other study-specific testing) done than you are used to having.

- You or your child of child-bearing age might need to use birth control while on the clinical trial (NIH, 2017).

Who Is Eligible for a Clinical Trial?

The design of the study will determine the eligibility criteria for that particular study. Some studies will offer participation to healthy volunteers as well as those who have the clinical condition and might benefit from enrollment. Inclusion and exclusion criteria outline who can participate; usually these factors include your age, gender, characteristics of disease, and co-morbidities that would increase the risk of participation and potentially lead to exclusion from the study. Inclusion and exclusion criteria aim to standardize the study population and to protect their safety, without excluding candidates who would qualify.

In general, the study eligibility can examine patient populations of certain ages; for example, older than 18 years. Certain vulnerable populations might be excluded or require the assent of the patient with the consent of a caregiver, if younger than 18, or if disabled and unable to verbalize consent. In CF, certain *mutations, forced expiratory volume in the first second* (FEV1) below 40%, liver disease, transplant status, and *colonization* with certain pathogens might be criteria for exclusion.

Why Should I Enroll in a Clinical Trial?

The advantages of participating in a clinical trial include early access to a potentially beneficial medication, close follow-up, and frequent contact with your CF team. Most important, though, participation allows medical care to advance and to improve. For this reason alone, participation is essential and extremely beneficial to the CF community.

A medication cannot make it through all phases of research and ultimately reach patients in need without enrolling study participants. To improve medical care for the future, participation in clinical trials is critical. Although a study cannot promise any benefit to an individual during study participation, participation can be of benefit in the future— for example, if or when a new therapy becomes FDA-approved and clinically available, and participation can benefit the larger community of CF patients.

In all diseases, including CF, clinical trials offer hope for better treatments. However, it is important to understand that a clinical trial cannot promise that an individual study participant will achieve better outcomes during their participation in the trial. One reason for this is because many trials will have patients randomly assigned to take a placebo, or sugar pill, rather than the active study medication. This allows the researchers to better understand the effects of a medication on a patient population. Another reason that research studies cannot guarantee benefit for an individual participant is that the true benefits of the treatment are not yet known.

There might be exciting pre-clinical studies or promising early-phase studies, but until the treatment completes all phases of research and is proven to be safe and effective, it cannot be approved by the FDA to be offered as a treatment to patients. However, in Phase 3 trials, in which a medication is expected to be presented to the FDA following the completion of the study, pharmaceutical companies will occasionally offer an *open-label clinical trial* for participants until the medication is clinically approved. In this setting, there is some short-term benefit of early access to a treatment.

Additionally, study visits provide closer follow-up and easier access to your medical team. If you are taking better care of yourself and are under the watchful eye of your care team, even if you are on a placebo, it is likely that you will have some symptomatic improvement.

What Is Informed Consent?

Informed consent is a process in which, in this setting of clinical trials, the clinical trial is described in full so that you can understand the study and what would be expected of you if you choose to participate in the study. Potential participants have the right to know everything about the study, including what the goal of the study is; why you have the option to participate; what the potential risks and benefits are; what the procedures and visits will entail; what would be expected of you or your child as a participant; how your personal information will or will not be used; how long the study will last; what other options exist for you or for your child; whether it will cost you anything to be in the study or whether study participation will be billed to your insurance; what would happen if you or your child were injured as a result of being in the study; who to contact if you have any questions or want more information about the study; and whether you will be compensated or reimbursed for your time related to the study or the expenses you'd incur at a study visit (e.g., parking or mileage or transportation).

Generally, it is ideal to be able to get the informed consent form ahead of a scheduled screening visit so that you can review all of the details at a comfortable pace and come prepared to ask any questions that you might have. In person, the study doctor or *research coordinator* will review the written consent form (page by page) with you in person. You will then sign the consent form, assuming all questions are asked and answered to your satisfaction and understanding. You will be given a copy of the document signed by you, for your records.

It is every person's right to choose whether they want to participate; no one will hold it against you or your child if you decide not to participate in the study. If throughout the study there is new information that might affect your health or your willingness to participate, you will be asked to re-consent after going through the informed consent process addressing those changes or new information. If initially you chose to enroll in the study and signed the consent, you can always change your mind and notify the study team that you no longer want to participate. In this case, you might be asked to return for a final visit, to return study medication, and to complete final study assessments. This possibility would have been discussed during the informed consent process.

Because children are not legally able to give a consent until they turn 18, local regulations might require an assent form be given to your child. An assent form is a simplified consent form, in language the child can understand, that allows the child to be part of the decision process and to agree or disagree to take part in the study. To take part in the *assent process* your child should be mature enough to understand the study and what they will be expected to do during the study. The assent process, like the informed consent process, is meant to be an ongoing conversation between the child and the research team. The child is encouraged to ask questions.

When assenting or consenting to a research study it is important to know your rights as a research participant:

- A study team member should explain the research study to you.

- Whether you participate is up to you.

- You can choose not to take part in the research.

- You can agree to take part and later change your mind.

- Your decision not to participate will not be held against you.

- You can ask all the questions you want before you decide about participation.

What Is a Placebo and Could I Receive It?

Some studies use a placebo during a clinical trial. A placebo is an inactive drug or treatment that is identical in appearance to the study drug or treatment and it is given in place of the active study drug or treatment for all or part of the study. A placebo or inactive treatment is used in a trial so that participants taking the placebo can be compared to participants who take the active study medication or treatment. Almost always, to reduce bias, the investigator and the study team and you or your child will not know whether you are assigned to the active study medication or to the placebo. This is called *blinding*, and it allows for both the researchers and participants to be objective when evaluating whether the study medication is working.

Some clinical trials do not use a placebo; instead, they might compare the active study medication with a standard-of-care medication. Either way, the informed consent form will spell out whether a placebo could be used and what the chance is that you could receive a placebo. Some sponsors will ultimately tell you after the study data has been analyzed whether you were assigned a placebo. Many CF clinical trials that use a placebo when studying the effectiveness of a study medication will then offer a follow-up clinical trial with active study medication for all participants, allowing them to collect safety data on the longer-term effects of the medication.

Where Are Clinical Trials Conducted?

Some CF clinical trials are large, *multi-center studies*, enrolling at centers nationwide, or even worldwide. Others are smaller studies, enrolling at one or two hospitals.

In the United States, many of the larger, multi-center trials are conducted at CF *Therapeutic Development Centers* (TDCs). All TDCs are accredited CF Care Centers, although not all CF Care Centers run clinical trials. TDCs are often integrated in the clinic, and individuals with CF might be informed of study activities during their clinical visits. TDCs are part of the highly organized *Therapeutic Development Network* (TDN) and are supported by the *Cystic Fibrosis Foundation (CF Foundation)*. The TDN coordinates enrollment of CF patients into high-priority clinical trials. The TDN reviews proposals for clinical trials, determines the feasibility of the trial, and assesses any safety concerns. If the

TDN feels that the research is well founded and that it has met all pre-clinical require-ments for safety, the TDN will alert TDCs of this upcoming trial, and TDCs can then participate.

Not all clinical trials participate in the TDN review process. Companies can contact the CF Care center or TDC independently and offer participation. The best way to know whether a clinical trial is TDN-sanctioned is to ask the research coordinators or CF care team involved in the clinical trial.

Some clinical trials are not multi-center trials. Many early-phase clinical trials can occur at a single hospital, which might have a TDC. These clinical trials are usually *investigator-initiated trials*, which means they are designed by a CF researcher at an aca-demic hospital and not by a pharmaceutical company. These trials are often in early stage of development but can lead to important advances in CF care.

Research visits for a clinical trial are often conducted in a designated research area within the hospital or clinic site, although this can be highly variable between centers. Research visits can be coordinated to occur around the time of regular clinic visits to increase participation.

Who Pays for a Clinical Trial?

Clinical trials are paid for by the sponsor of the study. Sponsors can be a company (e.g., a pharmaceutical company), a governmental agency (e.g., the National Institutes of Health), medical institutions or research foundations, or an individual. Sponsors might pay for some or all of the study depending on whether the procedure is normally part of your general routine health care. Informed consent should detail who is paying for the clinical trial and if there are any costs that are not covered by the sponsor.

What Questions Should I Ask Before Joining a Clinical Trial?

The most important questions to ask are: Why is the study being done? What are the specific goals? What do the investigators hope to achieve? and What are the study end-points? After qualifying for the study, it is critical to determine potential risks and benefits of participation because the results can lead to future—but not necessarily immediate—individual benefit. Information to learn includes: the planned duration of the study, the frequency of study visits, and testing that might include blood work, spirometry, imaging, sweat testing, and quality-of-life assessments and questionnaires. For those already on a complex medical regimen that is optimized for their heath, it is important to ensure that there will be no changes to the current medical regimen. Compensation for transportation, time, and commitment to the study is routinely provided and should be reviewed.

What Happens When a Clinical Trial Is Completed?

After all individuals have completed participation in a clinical trial, the data is finalized and the database is locked. The data from the study is then analyzed to determine whether the medicine worked. Investigator-initiated studies, or studies that were designed and run by a CF researcher at an academic hospital, might have their findings published. *Pharmaceutical company-sponsored trials* will also likely publish their findings, but they will also issue press releases that share the key findings from their trial. These findings are also shared and reviewed with the full research team.

Participants are typically notified as to whether they were on placebo or the investigational medication after the study has been finalized. After a Phase 3 trial is completed, the data supporting the investigational drug are presented to the FDA. The FDA will then determine whether a medication is sufficiently effective and safe to warrant approval. If approved by the FDA, a medication becomes eligible for clinical prescription and insurance coverage. Studies of long-term use of a medication (Phase 4) outside of a clinical trial are also required following FDA approval.

How Can I Learn More About Clinical Trials?

Your CF team members are a great resource for clinical trials that are ongoing at your CF center. Ask your doctor what trials are available at your center and get to know your CF research coordinators. Ask about upcoming studies. Clinical trials, especially for new modulator therapies, fill enrollment quickly; if you want to be part of them it is best to make this known to your team. The CF research team often knows people who participated in the lower-profile observational studies, and these people tend to be approached first when clinical trials are actively enrolling.

Often a research team will adapt your study visits to your work schedule or your child's school schedule if the study allows for various times of days for study visits. Don't discount a study because of time commitments.

If your CF center does not participate in clinical research or if it does not offer something that is specific to you or your child's CF mutation, it might be aware of research being done at alternate centers in the country. Often, CF centers are looking for participants from other centers and would pay for travel for a clinical trial.

Information can be obtained about ongoing clinical trials for CF. It is now a requirement for all clinical trials in the United States to be posted on https://ClinicalTrials.gov. Searching on this website for terms like "cystic fibrosis" can provide relevant clinical trial information.

The CF Foundation also has a *Clinical Trial Finder* within its user-friendly website at https://www.cff.org/trials/finder. The search engine on this site is geared toward individuals with CF and is an excellent resource for all the trials being conducted in North America. Specific filtering allows for the input of you or your child's age, zip code, distance you are willing to travel, FEV1% predicted number, you or your child's genetic mutation and the type of trial you might be interested in. Cost should not be a barrier when deciding whether to travel. Sponsors will generally cover all associated travel costs to study centers at your own center site or sites far from your home and reimburse you for mileage, tolls, parking, plane, hotel stay, meals, and other associated travel costs.

WHERE CAN I TURN FOR ADDITIONAL INFORMATION ON CF AND ITS TREATMENT?

Meg Dvorak, LCSW; Chris Kvam JD, MPP; and
Mary Shannon Fracchia, MD

CHAPTER

In This Chapter

- How Can I Become an Expert on CF?

- Where Can I Go for Reliable Information About CF?

- What Internet Sites Can I Use to Learn More About CF?

- What Resources and Organizations Are Available to Those with CF?

How Can I Become an Expert on CF?

Receiving the diagnosis of cystic fibrosis (CF) can be overwhelming, and the initial reaction for most patients and parents is to "google." Often, the diagnosis is given either prenatally or in the newborn period, a particularly vulnerable time for new parents. As hopes and emotions are fragile, the information flooding the internet can be too much to handle. Literally thousands of websites pop up with information about CF that are not necessarily credible or based on any legitimate evidence. Parents are reading about life expectancies and lung transplants when they haven't had a chance to understand what CF even is. People with CF should be cautious about receiving information from sources not provided to them by their medical team.

The best way to become an expert about CF is through good communication with a medical provider whose expertise is CF. You can learn the most by visiting an *accredited CF center*. The initial visit is usually a comprehensive overview of what CF is, what symptoms and signs are expected with CF, what treatment options are available, and what the overall life trajectory looks like for those with CF. Expert clinicians empower their patients to understand and to become comfortable with all of the information. This first visit is not the only time to ask questions. Quarterly visits are recommended for medical check-ups and to encourage continued understanding and autonomy. The rest of this chapter provides additional ideas for becoming an expert on CF.

Where Can I Go for Reliable Information About CF?

Although going to your primary CF team is the best way to gather information, being social media savvy can increase your knowledge and support when done correctly. The first step is finding committees and organizations that promote *evidence-based guidelines*. When researching medical issues on CF, medical societies and journals provide the best information. *Pediatrics* and the *Journal of Pediatrics* have published age-specific guidelines on managing CF. The disease evolves as children age and different recommendations apply. For adult care, *Chest* has published consensus guidelines, which you also can find on the *American Thoracic Society* website.

What Internet Sites Can I Use to Learn More About CF?

Living with CF can be undeniably isolating. For very good reasons associated with infection control, people with CF cannot congregate and form bonds of personal support in the same way that people living with other chronic illnesses can and often do. The age of the CF camp has passed. However, the arrival of social media and the internet has offered some new and exciting opportunities for support and relationships within the CF community, not only for people with CF, but also for their parents and for other concerned members of your extended community. Navigating this online world takes skill; awareness of the potential trade-offs (good and bad) is necessary for healthy participation in these spaces. It is easy to find incredible examples of the power of friendships with other people who have CF. However, it is important to recognize that not every CF online community is a healthy place, and that there are trade-offs to use of social media.

There are several types of online spaces. These include online journals, newsletters, and blogs—many written by people with CF, with varying amounts of interactive conversation; forums that allow registered users to discuss specific topics (CF-related or not) with one another; and social media platforms such as Facebook, Instagram, Twitter, and Snapchat that offer a variety of public or non-public posting options, groups, and private messaging.

People with CF, or anyone interested in online spaces, should ask themselves several questions as they navigate them. Here are some useful tips and questions to consider as online content is consumed. First, what is the reader or consumer looking to get out of those resources? Are they looking for unbiased, data-driven, validated medical information? Are they looking to learn from what other people with CF have been willing to share online? Are they looking for friendship or connection with others who have CF (or parents, siblings, spouses of people with CF)? Second, who is the author of the content being consumed? Are they creating content for the CF community, the world at large, or themselves? How is your data being used? Does the curator of the forum or content sell registered user information? Does the author have an agenda? Is anything being marketed or sold to consumers? Consumers might not always be able to answer all of these questions, but they are still worth considering when evaluating any particular online source of CF information.

Social media has its share of pitfalls. The face of CF is diverse, and an array of disease experiences can be easily viewed. Nothing highlights the wide spectrum of CF like social media. #CysticFibrosis on Instagram provides thousands of images of those with end-stage CF, hemoptysis, and pain. It also provides images of people with CF running marathons, graduating from college, getting married, and living amazing lives. Each member/consumer should consider whether they are prepared to see both the life-affirming accomplishments that many people with CF share on social media as they overcome challenges as well as the more difficult stories of people declining due to the natural progression of the disease. Having hundreds of friends with CF on Facebook guarantees that one will regularly watch some of those friends become very sick, possibly die, and see their page convert into a tribute. How does a member of Facebook deal with that reality? Blocking or unfriending people with CF who have passed can save you from daily reminders that pop up on newsfeeds, but it can also generate a host of negative feelings. You would do well to consider whether the collective effect of seeing these images, and "meeting" people online, whether you actually ever converse, across the spectrum of the disease, is a net positive or net negative on your emotional ability to deal with your own case of CF, or your child's case of CF. Remember that your own outcome is not tied to anyone else's disease experience.

CF-related social media is not immune to the ills that plague social media today. Public and private/secret Facebook groups might not be mediated well, or moderators can have individual biases that influence how conversation flows in groups. Trolling can occur on message boards or groups and might not be well addressed. Confronting the misinformation and negativity that can exist in these spaces requires time and energy. Consumers should consider to what extent they are prepared, if at all, to engage in that world. Some people have found these places to be positive vents for frustration, or ways to deal with very real and otherwise untreated depression and other issues. You can think about whether people who are living full lives with CF, with jobs, children, and spouses, are well represented in these spaces, and whether a newcomer or parent with a newly diagnosed child is seeing a balanced view of life with CF.

If an online forum thread, blog, Facebook group, or Instagram hashtag only instills fear in parents of newly diagnosed children or feeds depression and *anxiety* in adolescent and young adult members, it is absolutely appropriate to disengage and to determine that life is better off-line. If participating in social media makes you feel as though you are missing out or are inferior because of the impact CF has had on your abilities to live a full and active life, or guilty because you are not experiencing the disease progression of some of your peers, do not ignore those feelings. Take a critical look at online usage. Do not hesitate to discuss how this virtual world is affecting your life with real friends and care teams.

Children with CF are growing up with this technology and might understand it better than their parents do. Responsible usage should be encouraged. Try to make sure that children and adolescents see all sides of CF. If they have Facebook friends who are very sick or who pass away, make sure they have also seen examples of positivity, like *The CF Roundtable*—a Quarterly publication by CF adults for the CF community; the *WindSprints Podcast* by Jerry Cahill of the Boomer Esiason Foundation; and the *CF Lifestyle Foundation Blog*. Children and adults with CF need to understand that their own case of CF is not defined by the experience of others.

Parents with CF also need to evaluate how they portray their young child's diagnosis online. Asking questions of peers in an online forum about issues such as a child's dietary issues, or challenges with repeated infections is reasonable, and a very empowering resource. Is that the same as creating an Instagram account and documenting your young child's journey with CF for the world to see? Who is that account for? What purpose does it serve? Is it about the toddler in a fish mask, or an unmet need of the parent for empathy? That public persona and constant documentation of disease will have an effect on your young child. Parents should consider this as they grow up.

There are no easy answers to the dilemmas presented by social media and the internet age. However, as we enter the second decade of Facebook, do not hesitate to step back and assess with clearer eyes the obvious positives as well as the subtle negatives of this new-found connectivity.

What Resources and Organizations Are Available to Those with CF?

In addition to medical experts, internet sites, journals, lectures, podcasts, and peer engagement, various organizations can provide people living with CF and their families additional information, guidance, and assistance.

The *Cystic Fibrosis Foundation (CF Foundation)*, accessed at www.CFF.org, is the gold-standard for the most reliable, up-to-date, and evidence-based source of information on CF. The CF Foundation was established in 1955 by a group of parents who were determined to save the lives of their children with CF. The CF Foundation has been at the forefront of funding vital research and creating a network of CF care centers throughout the United States to provide accredited, standardized treatment to people with CF. Over the years, the CF Foundation has broadened its scope to include a multitude of educational and support programs to assist the larger CF community.

The CF Foundation website is easy to navigate and it contains helpful links for almost everything related to CF, from the most basic, "What is CF?" to more complex questions about research and treatment. Each of the six tabs on the home page contains detailed menus to guide your search. Given that CF has evolved into a lifelong chronic disease across a variety of cultures, the CF Foundation includes resources from birth to older adulthood.

The *Compass Program*, one of the CF Foundation's highly utilized services, provides individualized confidential case management services for a variety of needs that can arise while living with CF. Services include assistance with selecting insurance plans, finding covered providers, troubleshooting medical bills, finding resources for basic living expenses, and problem-solving life issues. The Compass Program is a free service to individuals and families living with CF as well as to providers. Highly trained and knowledgeable case managers are on hand to take real-time phone calls Monday through Friday between 9 am and 7 pm EST.

The CF Foundation *Peer Connect Program* offers topic-based peer mentoring for people with CF and their family members, ages 16 and older. The mentors in this program are vetted and trained, and connections are made over video, phone, email, or text. Peer mentoring not only facilitates a relationship, but provides for education and information sharing among those who share a similar disease experience. Requesting a mentor is an easy four-step process that is done online through the CF Foundation website. The CF Foundation also hosts regular virtual events called "*BreatheCons*" and "*MiniCons*" that allow individuals with CF to connect with peers in real time using virtual chat rooms.

The CF Foundation's *CF Legal Information Hotline* and *CF Social Security Project* (CFSSP) are vital programs to address the myriad legal needs of individuals and families living with CF. Staffed by attorneys with many years of experience, these programs provide reliable information about selection of insurance plans, social security and disability benefits, education and employment concerns, and government insurance programs, such as Medicare and Medicaid. The CF Social Security Project provides free representation to people with CF in applications to Social Security Administration benefits or a continuing disability review. The easiest way to connect with the attorneys is via email at CFLegal@sufianpassamano.com or referral through *Compass*.

Every year in the fall, The CF Foundation hosts the *North American Cystic Fibrosis Conference* (NACFC) where CF professionals from around the world promote the exchange of information and best practice models for delivery of care. Only select individuals with CF can attend this event due to infection guidelines; however, many sessions at the conference are live-streamed and can be viewed in real time or via recordings at www.NACFC.org.

Cystic Fibrosis Research Incorporated (CFRI), accessed through www.CFRI.org, is a non-profit organization established in 1975 and devoted to serving the needs of the CF community and finding a cure for CF through research, advocacy, education, and sustainability. In addition to funding research, CFRI has innovative support programs for those touched by CF. CFRI publishes a quarterly educational newsletter and weekly email announcements about research, events, and support programs.

CFRI hosts an Annual Education Conference in July in Northern California. This small conference is attended by individuals and families living with CF as well as industry and CF center professionals and researchers. The conference includes support groups that facilitate connections and important discussions about the emotional impact of CF. CFRI also hosts monthly educational podcasts on a wide range of topics across the disease spectrum.

CFRI recognizes that beyond finding a cure, individuals and families living with CF need support programs for day-to-day living. The monthly caregiver support groups (for both pediatrics and adults) provide a topic-based group that is available both via Zoom Video conference or in person. The annual *Mother's Retreat* offers a healing environment to honor the unique journey of the CF mother. There are multiple live-streamed wellness sessions, such as yoga and mindfulness, offered at very low cost or free throughout the year. To address the mental health needs of the CF community, CFRI offers financial support for a limited number of counseling sessions with a therapist of your choosing. The availability of support programs is subject to funding through CFRI's community and industry partnerships.

The *European Cystic Fibrosis Society* (ECFS; www.ECFS.eu) is an international community of scientific and clinical professionals devoted to improving the quality of life and survival of people with CF. The ECFS is based in Denmark and, along with CF Europe, which represents people and families from 39 European countries who are living with CF, has a similar function to the CF Foundation. The ECFS publishes the *Journal of Cystic Fibrosis* (JCF), which includes six issues per year of original scientific articles, case reports, and editorials on CF. Additionally, the ECFS hosts an annual conference in Europe, establishes a network of care centers throughout Europe, and maintains specialist "working groups" to maintain the highest standards of care. Memberships to the ECFS are available at different levels starting at 120 €.

Another well-established organization is the *Adult Cystic Fibrosis Association Incorporated* (USACFA). The USACFA, established in 1990, publishes a quarterly newsletter called the "*CF Roundtable*" which is a 60-page document that includes not only thoughtful and humorous personal stories, but also educational information about a variety of topics related to living with CF in adulthood. The subscription is free (donations are welcome) and can be delivered in printed or emailed form (www.cfroundtable.com).

You can find many educational and assistance resources at the state and local level. CF centers accredited by the CF Foundation offer annual *Family Education Days*, with speakers, break-out sessions, and access to local industry professionals. Education days are often recorded or live-streamed for those who are not able to attend in person. CF-center staff can provide specific information about education days, center newsletters, and other local events, including *Great Strides Walks* or regional CF Foundation fundraisers.

The *CF Center Social Worker* is an excellent resource for up-to-date information and referrals to local support programs and government entitlements, such as Medicaid, in-home support services, and food stamps. The social worker can facilitate referrals to organizations that assist with rent, transportation, or out-of-pocket medical expenses.

Another resource that is worth mentioning is the *HealthWell Foundation* (www.HealthWellFoundation.org) which provides financial assistance to eligible applicants who are underinsured by filling in the gap to help cover co-pays, premiums, deductibles, and other out-of-pocket medical expenses. Comprehensive CF care is expensive, and insurance plans seldom cover everything. HealthWell Foundation can arrange for direct billing with providers as well as payment cards for the pharmacy. The application process is easy and can be done online or over the phone. Applicants are notified almost instantly of approval.

Given that people with CF are living longer, fuller lives, multiple organizations have been created to help people achieve various fitness and wellness goals.

The *CF Lifestyle Foundation* (CFLF; www.CFLF.org) provides education and inspiration on maintaining an active lifestyle while living with CF. The CFLF provides generous recreation grants to eligible applicants fund an activity of their choosing, from yoga to surfing, to a gym membership. Recreation grants are for up to $500 and can be applied to either physical, social, or emotional activities. Educational materials are available in print or video through the website.

The *Cystic Fibrosis Fitness Institute* (CFFI; www.cffitness.org) aims to help individuals with CF to attain fitness goals or to start a new exercise program, regardless of disease status. Using focused breathing techniques and a combination of strength, endurance, and flexibility training, CFFI can create individualized workout programs to improve your quality of life through fitness. Endorsed by both experts in the field and adults with CF, CFFI recognizes the importance of physical fitness, not only for enhanced well-being, but for slowing down the progression of disease.

Attain Health (www.attainhealth.org) offers integrative performance and health coaching to empower individuals with CF and their caregivers to optimally manage all aspects of the disease. Attain has a three-pronged program which includes virtual pulmonary rehab, CF-Related Diabetes (CFRD) education and coaching, and peer support groups for all ages. The virtual pulmonary rehab offers clients a functional movement assessment and tracks work-outs on a mobile app. The CFRD coaching offers cohorts of 10 to 20 clients a 3-month program of rigorous diabetes education and management. Referrals can be made through clinic providers or individually through the website.

In addition, many books have been written about CF from different perspectives from childhood through adulthood. There is even a book written from the perspective of a spouse, which has become more common as people live longer with CF. Whatever your journey might include, there is likely a well-written memoir to supplement your learning. There are too many books to list here, but you can request a "*CF Bibliography*" from your CF care team.

GLOSSARY

504 Plan: A plan developed to ensure that a child attending an elementary or secondary school and who has a disability identified under the law receives accommodations ensuring their academic success and access to the learning environment. This is a provision of a civil rights law in Section 504 of the Rehabilitation Act.

6-foot rule: The infection control rule created by CF Foundation to decrease risk of cross-contamination between individuals with CF. It recommends that people with CF need to maintain distance of at least 6 feet between each other.

6-minute walk test: A test that determines how far you can walk in 6 minutes and measures your pulse, blood pressure, and oxygen levels during the test. It can help to determine whether your endurance has changed over time and whether treatments are effective.

Abdominal X-ray: A two-dimensional radiologic image of the structures of the abdomen, including the stomach, spleen, and the intestines.

Acamprosate: A medication that when combined with counseling can be used to treat alcohol addiction.

Acapella®: The brand name of a common positive expiratory pressure airway oscillating device used for airway clearance.

Acceptance and Commitment Therapy (ACT): Developed within a coherent theoretical and philosophical framework, ACT is a unique empirically based psychological intervention that uses acceptance and mindfulness strategies, together with commitment and behavior change strategies, to increase psychological flexibility.

Accredited CF center: A treatment facility that delivers care to people with CF in accordance with CF Foundation policies and guidelines.

Acetaminophen (brand name: Tylenol®): A type of drug that is used to reduce fever or mild to moderate pain.

Acetylcysteine: A medication used in CF to loosen thick mucus; it can be administered orally or via inhalation. Acetylcysteine is an antioxidant and it has also been used to treat acetaminophen overdose.

Acid reflux: The condition when acid flows backward from the stomach up the esophagus, or "food pipe," causing a burning sensation in the chest, referred to as heartburn.

Acid-fast bacilli: A group of microorganisms, such as mycobacterium, that can be detected in CF and other lung diseases. These bacteria have mycolic acids in their cell walls, which resist laboratory staining, thus showing up red under the microscope.

Acini: The functional unit of the pancreas that produces the digestive enzymes.

Active cycle of breathing techniques (ACBT): A cycle of techniques used to loosen airway secretions. These techniques include breathing control, thoracic expansion exercises, and forced expiratory technique.

Acute respiratory tract exacerbation: A flaring symptom of any chronic lung disease, usually caused by infection and resulting in increased coughing or production of mucus. It is also referred to as pulmonary exacerbation.

Adoption: When a person or couple assume parenting responsibilities and legal duties for a child that is not their biological offspring.

Adult Cystic Fibrosis Association Incorporated (USACFA): An independent, non-profit corporation whose goals include to foster a nationwide network of support groups for adults with CF, sponsor/collaborate on regional conferences in the United States for the exchange of information between the medical and research community and adults with CF, and to publish the quarterly newsletter "CF Roundtable."

Advance care planning: A process of thinking ahead about your wishes for medical care. It is intended to align your goals of care with treatment decisions. Specific wishes can be documented and revised as needed over time.

Advance directives: Products of advance care planning. These include legal documents or legally-documented verbal statements that specify surrogate decision makers and/or treatment decisions. They include a power of attorney for health care (aka surrogate, agent, or proxy), oral or written living wills, and specific orders to limit intensive treatments, like cardiopulmonary resuscitation and intubation. They also can be included in a specific type of provider orders, known as Physician Orders for Life-Sustaining Treatment (POLST) or Medical Orders for Scope of Treatment (MOST or MOLST).

Aerobic capacity: A measure of the ability of the heart and lungs to distribute oxygen to the body.

Aerobic exercise: Brisk exercise of mild to moderate intensity, also known as cardio exercise, that increases circulation of oxygen through the blood, increases respiration and heart rate, and strengthens heart and lungs.

Aerobika®: The brand name of a common positive expiratory pressure airway oscillating device used for airway clearance.

Aerosolizes: Turns the liquid in the nebulizer cup into a fine mist.

Affordable Care Act (ACA): A comprehensive law enacted in March 2010 to make affordable health insurance available to more people. The law provides people with subsidies known as "premium tax credits" that lower costs for households with incomes between 100% and 400% of the federal poverty level (FPL). In addition, it provided for an expanded Medicaid program to cover all adults with income below 138% of the FPL; however, not all states have expanded their Medicaid programs.

Airway reactivity: The ability of the lungs to exchange oxygen and carbon dioxide.

Airway clearance techniques (ACTs): Methods to clear the mucus from your lungs. All ACTs involve coughing or huffing, and many use percussion (clapping) or vibration to loosen mucus from the airway walls.

Airway hydrators: Inhaled medications that help to pull water out of cells into the airways, helping to loosen mucus. A commonly prescribed example is hypertonic saline.

Airway oscillating device (oscillatory PEP): A pneumatic oscillating positive pressure device that you exhale into to aid in the clearance of mucus from your lungs.

Alanine amino transferase (ALT or SGPT): Blood test that checks for liver damage.

Albumin: Protein made by your liver; it is checked to ensure proper liver function.

Albuterol: An inhaled medication in the class called beta-agonists, which helps to relax the airways, thus relieving shortness of breath caused by the airway spasms.

Alcohol use disorder: A medical condition that is manifested by a pattern of problematic alcohol consumption characterized by several of the following: drinking more than intended; being preoccupied with alcohol; inability to stop drinking despite problems with health, relationships, or work; drinking more and more alcohol to achieve the same response; and experiencing withdrawal (e.g., tremors, anxiety, insomnia, confusion, vital sign instability) when abruptly stopping.

Alkaline phosphatase: A protein made in liver, bones, and other tissues. When it is elevated, it might indicate liver or bone disease.

Allele: One of two alternative forms of a gene, each inherited from one biologic parent, found in the same place on the same chromosome.

Allergen: A substance that is recognized by the immune system triggering an immune reaction.

Allergen-specific IgE: Antibodies produced by the immune system; overproduced in case of an allergy. In that case, IgE travels to different cells and releases chemicals leading to an allergic reaction.

Allergic bronchopulmonary aspergillosis: An allergic reaction to a common environmental mold that can lead to difficulty breathing in individuals with CF.

Allergist: A doctor specializing in the diagnosis and treatment of allergies.

Alpha-2 agonists: A group of medications that is thought to affect receptors in the brain in a way that improves attention-deficit hyperactivity disorder (ADHD).

American Academy of Pediatrics (AAP): An American professional association of pediatricians.

Americans with Disabilities Act (ADA): A 1990 civil rights law that prohibits discrimination against people with disabilities under certain circumstances in all areas of public life including but not limited to work and school.

Aminoglycoside toxicity: Negative side effects of aminoglycoside antibiotics, which can include hearing loss and kidney damage.

Aminoglycoside: Antibiotic medications that treat Gram-negative bacteria, such as *Pseudomonas aeruginosa*.

Amniocentesis: A medical procedure in a needle is used to sample amniotic fluid from the uterus in the early stages of pregnancy. This procedure can be used to test for genetic conditions in the fetus.

Amniotic fluid: The fluid surrounding a fetus in the uterus.

Amphetamine: A type of stimulant medication that speeds up the messages traveling between the brain and the body. These medications can be used to treat conditions such as ADHD.

Amplifier: A compound that amplifies, or increases, the amount of CFTR that is produced within a cell.

Anemia: A lack of red blood cells that causes reduced oxygen flow in the body. Signs and symptoms include fatigue, dizziness, and abnormally pale skin.

Anesthesia: Administration of medication to prevent pain and discomfort during a surgical procedure.

Anthropometric data: Data related to the size, weight, and proportion of the human body.

Antibiotics: Medications given either by mouth or intravenously to combat bacterial infection.

Antibodies: Proteins made by the immune system in response to bacteria, viruses, and other foreign bodies.

Antidepressants: Medications that can relieve symptoms of major depression, anxiety disorders, seasonal affective disorder, and dysthymia (mild chronic depression), as well as other conditions.

Antifungals: Medications that destroy or slow the growth of fungal organisms.

Anti-inflammatories: Medications that are taken to reduce inflammation (e.g., ibuprofen and azithromycin).

Antimicrobial sensitivity: Laboratory test used to determine which medication is effective in preventing the growth of bacteria or fungi.

Antioxidant: A compound that inhibits oxidation, which is a chemical process that can damage cells.

Anti-rejection medications: Also called immunosuppressants. These drugs are used by someone who has had an organ transplant to reduce the chance of their body rejecting the new organ.

Anxiety: An emotional response to a feeling of preoccupation or fear.

Arterial blood gas (ABG): A test of pulmonary function that uses blood to measure levels of oxygen and carbon dioxide in the blood.

Artery: A blood vessel that carries oxygenated blood away from the heart to parts of the body.

Arthritis: Inflammation in the joints.

Arthropathy: Joint disease, including arthritis (inflammation of one or more joints) and joint pain.

Artificial insemination: An assisted reproductive technology method in which sperm is introduced into the uterus to cause pregnancy.

Ascites: Fluid build-up in the abdominal cavity.

Aspartate amino transferase (AST or SGOT): Blood test that checks for liver damage.

Aspergillus: A common environmental fungus that can colonize the lungs of patients with CF causing chronic cough, mucus production, and allergies, which can create symptoms similar to those of asthma.

Aspergillus fumigatus: A fungus in the genus or category of *Aspergillus*. It is the most common *Aspergillus* species to cause disease.

Aspergillus IgE: A blood test that detects an antibody to this fungus and that checks if a person is allergic to Aspergillus.

Assent process: Process of agreeing to take a part in a research project.

Assisted reproductive technology (ART): Medical fertility treatment in which both the woman's eggs and the embryo are handled. This includes *in-vitro* fertilization in which the eggs are surgically removed from the ovaries, mixed with sperm in a laboratory, and the resultant embryo is then implanted into the uterus.

Asthma: A chronic lung disease that causes inflammation and narrowing of the airways, at times also producing mucus.

Atomoxetine (Strattera®): A medication used to treat ADHD. It belongs to a group of medicines called selective norepinephrine re-uptake inhibitors.

Attain Health: An integrative health and performance coaching program for people with CF.

Attention deficit hyperactivity disorder (ADHD): A chronic mental health condition that usually starts in childhood; it is characterized by inattention, hyperactivity, and sometimes impulsivity.

Autism spectrum disorders: Developmental disorders affecting communication and behavior.

Autogenic drainage (AD): An airway clearance technique that helps to clear secretions by breathing at different lung volumes.

Autoimmune: A condition in which your body recognizes itself as foreign and attacks healthy cells.

Autosomal recessive condition: An inheritance pattern in which two copies of an abnormal gene need to be present for a disease to manifest. This means that if a child has an autosomal recessive disease, he or she needs to inherit a copy of the defective gene from each parent.

Azithromycin: An antibiotic that is used for its anti-inflammatory effects in CF.

Azole antifungals: A class of medications used to treat fungal infections.

Aztreonam (Cayston®): An antibiotic used to treat Gram-negative organisms, to include, but not limited to *Pseudomonas aeruginosa* species.

Bacterial colonization of the airway: The presence of bacteria in the airway at all times, even in the absence of active disease.

Bactrim®: An antibiotic that is commonly given to prevent infections, such as *Pneumocystis* pneumonia (PCP), in patients who have undergone a transplant and are, therefore, immunosuppressed. Bactrim can also be used to treat certain infections (e.g., urinary tract infections).

Basic metabolic panel (BMP): A blood tests that checks your glucose, electrolyte levels, and kidney function.

Behavioral sleep medicine specialist: A health care provider, most commonly a psychologist, who focuses on the evaluation and treatment of sleep disorders by addressing behavioral, psychological, and physiological factors that interfere with sleep.

Benzodiazepine: A medication class that is used to treat anxiety. Lorazepam (Ativan®) is a fast-acting benzodiazepine that can be used for the short-term relief of anxiety associated with medical procedures in individuals living with CF.

Bethkis: A brand name formulation of nebulized tobramycin.

Bile: A liquid produced in the liver and stored in the gallbladder that assists with digestion.

Bile ducts: The small tubes that connect the liver to the gallbladder and the small intestines through which bile travels.

Bi-level positive airway pressure (BiPAP): A form of positive airway pressure ventilation that uses a higher pressure of oxygen when you breathe in, and a lower pressure when you breathe out. The alternating pressures encourage the lungs to operate more efficiently.

Bilirubin: Orange-yellow substance that is produced by break-down of the red blood cells, processed by the liver, and excreted from the body. High levels of bilirubin can indicate liver disease.

Bisphosphonate therapy: Bisphosphonates are a group of medications used to treat osteoporosis, also called brittle bone disease. These medications work by reducing the turnover of bone to help preserve bone density. Therapy can either be with pills or through an infusion.

Blinding: Procedure during clinical trials when patients, or clinical trial administrators, or both do not know what arm of the experiment the patients are in (active arm or control arm). It is done to ensure that participants are not biased to reported results.

Blood sugar level: The level of glucose in the blood.

Blood-brain barrier: The natural barrier present in your body that separates the central nervous system (brain and spinal cord) from the bloodstream. In some circumstances, your doctors will consider whether certain medications you receive are able to cross the blood–brain barrier.

Blood urea nitrogen (BUN): A test that measures the amount of urea nitrogen in blood. High levels can indicate kidney disease.

Bone mass: A measure of the amount of minerals (mostly calcium and phosphorous) contained in a certain volume of bone.

Body mass index (BMI): A measurement used to assess nutritional status and growth calculated by dividing a person's weight (in kilograms) by their height (in meters squared).

Bone mineral density (BMD): A measure of the strength of bones. This number is used to diagnose osteopenia or osteoporosis, or varying degrees of brittle bone disease.

Bowel obstruction: A blockage of the small or large intestine that prevents digested food or liquid from passing through; this can be a serious medical condition.

BreatheCons: Live virtual events for people with CF to learn more about a specific topic.

Breathing control (BC): Focusing on controlling your breathing so that you can take long, deep, breaths rather than fast, shallow, breaths.

Bronchial artery: The arterial blood supply that brings oxygen to the lungs. Usually, there are two bronchial arteries supplying the left lung and one bronchial artery supplying the right lung.

Bronchial arterial embolization: A minimally-invasive procedure in which an enlarged bronchial artery is located and blocked off to prevent bleeding.

Bronchiectasis: A chronic condition in which the walls of the bronchi, or airways, are thickened or dilated from inflammation and infection. People with this condition, of which CF is one cause, suffer from flare-ups with increased cough, mucus production, and breathing difficulty.

Bronchodilator: A type of medication that opens the airways making it easier to breath.

Bronchoscope: A flexible, fiber-optic tube that is passed through the mouth and airway during bronchoscopy that enables viewing of the airways of the lungs.

Bronchoscopy: A procedure that uses a thin tube attached to a camera to examine the airways of the lungs.

Bronchospasm: This occurs when the small airways of the lung (bronchi) contract and narrow, making it more difficult for air to be exhaled. Symptoms commonly include cough, wheezing, chest tightness, and shortness of breath. Various inhaled medications can reduce these symptoms.

Bupropion (Zyban®): A prescription medication that can be used to assist in quitting smoking.

Burkholderia cepacia complex: A group of Gram-negative bacteria that can cause chronic infections in the lungs of people with CF.

Caloric intake: The number of calories a person consumes daily.

Cannabis use disorder: A mental health/medical disorder defined as continued use of cannabis despite impairment and complications related to its use.

Capillary: A very small branch of larger blood vessels.

Carbon dioxide: A colorless, odorless, gas that is present in the air in the small amounts; it is expelled from the lungs through breathing.

Cardiac catheterization laboratory: A room in the hospital where cardiac catheterization, a heart test, is performed. In cardiac catheterization, doctors insert a small catheter into your heart to test your heart's function (e.g., contractility, blood pressure, oxygen level).

Cardiovascular system: The heart and blood vessels, also known as the circulatory system.

Carrier: Someone who carries a single copy of a mutated gene for a condition, trait, or mutation, but does not have that condition, trait, or mutation.

Carrier rate: The proportion of individuals in a population who have a single copy of a specific recessive gene mutation.

Carrier status: Genetic status determining whether a patient has the disease, is a carrier of the mutation without having the disease, or has no disease or defective genes. A person with one non-functional copy of the gene is a carrier. Persons who are CF carriers have one normal gene and one affected gene; they have no CF symptoms but can pass the non-functioning gene on to their children.

Carrier testing: Genetic testing to identify whether a person is a carrier of a particular genetic mutation.

Cartilage: Flexible connective tissue; for example, the tissue that connects the ribs to the breastbone.

Catheter: A hollow plastic tube. A catheter can be used for many purposes in the hospital setting, including administering medications (central venous catheter), draining urine (foley catheter), and providing diagnostic information to doctors (cardiac catheter).

Catheterization: Insertion of a thin tube into a large blood vessel and threaded to small ones used both for diagnosis and therapy. In the case of bronchial artery embolization, the catheterization procedure is what allows release of small particles to block off the abnormal vessel.

Cavitary lesions: Gas-filled spaces surrounded by thick walls.

Cell: Cells are the unit of organization for all living things. A single bacterium is made up of one cell and a human is made up of trillions of cells.

Cell membrane: Each cell is contained by a cell membrane, keeping the components of that cell contained inside the cell.

Central nervous system (CNS): The CNS is part of the nervous system, which is the control center for the body. It includes the brain and spinal cord.

Centrally implanted catheter: A line usually implanted in the chest, such as mediport, for administration of medications.

CF arthropathy: Arthritis associated with CF.

CF "clean out:" Another name for the treatment of a CF pulmonary exacerbation.

CF Bibliography: A list of books and memoirs written for or about CF.

CF BreatheCon: A virtual event that is sponsored by the CF Foundation and held for adults with CF. The goal is for adults with CF to connect, share, and learn from others with CF through open and honest dialogue. Includes guest speakers, discussion panels, small-group video breakouts, group chats, activities and workshops. *See also* BreatheCon.

CF carrier: A person who carries one copy of a non-functioning CFTR gene. This person does not have disease but has the potential to pass this gene to their children.

CF center social worker: A person who holds a master's degree in social work whose job is to provide social work services to people with CF.

CF Connect: Hosted by the United States Adult Cystic Fibrosis Association (USACFA), Incorporated, this Facebook group is designed to connect individuals with CF and parents of children with CF.

CF FamilyCon: A virtual event similar to BreatheCon, but geared towards people with CF and their family members to provide an opportunity to connect, share, and learn from each other.

CF Foundation Patient Registry: The CF Foundation Patient Registry collects information on the health status of people with CF who receive care in CF Foundation-accredited care centers and agree to participate in the Registry. This information is used to create CF care guidelines, assist care teams in providing care to individuals with CF, and guide quality improvement initiatives at care centers. Researchers use the Patient Registry to study CF treatments and outcomes and to design CF clinical trials.

CF Foundation Peer Connect Program: A peer-mentoring program for people with CF via the CF Foundation.

CF Legal Hotline: Sponsored by the CF Foundation, the CF Legal Information Hotline provides free information about the laws that protect your rights and can answer questions about health insurance, disability, government benefits, employment, and school.

CF Lifestyle Foundation: A non-profit organization that provides recreation grants to people with CF.

CF MiniCon: A virtual event for adults living with CF and their family members similar to BreatheCons, but focused on specific topics (e.g., transplant, reproductive health, self- care, relationships).

CF modulator therapy: A medication for people with CF that is designed to fix the problems caused by a mutated CFTR gene.

CF Peer Connect: A peer-support program that matches people with CF (16+ years) and their family members with a peer mentor who has faced a similar circumstance, such as work decisions, dating, or caregiver balance. This program is supported by the CF Foundation.

CF Peer Mentoring Program: Program through CF Foundation that provides support to those 16 years of age and older living with CF as well as to family members and spouses of people living with CF. Although this mentoring program is not considered a support group, it provides virtual support through one-on-one connections.

CF Screening Positive Inconclusive Diagnosis (CFSPID): Individuals who have a positive newborn screen but have either a normal sweat chloride with one CFTR mutation of unclear significance or an intermediate range sweat chloride test and one or fewer CF-causing genetic mutations.

CF Social Security Project (CFSSP): A legal service to assist with Social Security benefits.

CF transmembrane conductance regulator (CFTR): A protein that sits in the cell surface. This protein functions as a channel to transport chloride and other molecules across the cell surface, either from the inside to the outside, or the outside to the inside. CFTR is found in many organs in the body. Dysfunctional CFTR leads to the clinical manifestations of CF.

CF transmembrane conductance regulator (CFTR) gene: The genetic code for the CFTR protein that a cell transcribes, or reads, to make the CFTR protein. If this gene is altered or dysfunctional, it will code for a protein that is altered or dysfunctional.

CF transmembrane conductance regulator (CFTR) protein: A protein that sits in the cell wall. This protein functions on both sides of the wall, both inside the cell and outside the cell, to transport chloride across the wall.

CF-causing mutation: A change in the usual DNA sequence of the CFTR gene that leads to the production of a dysfunctional CFTR protein.

CF-related diabetes (CFRD): A type of diabetes specific to people with CF with components of both insulin resistance and insulin deficiency due to damage to the pancreas. It is diagnosed through blood tests and, if not treated, can cause weight loss and poor lung function. Not all people with CF will develop CFRD, but all should be screened for it starting by early adolescence.

CF-related metabolic syndrome (CRMS): Individuals who have a positive newborn screen but have either a normal sweat chloride with one CFTR mutation of unclear significance or an intermediate range sweat chloride test and one or fewer CF-causing genetic mutations.

CF-related osteoporosis: Bone disease in patients with CF due to higher risk of osteopenia, decreased mineral concentrations in the bones. Thus bones with people with osteoporosis are weaker and more likely to fracture.

CFTR modulator: A broad class of drugs that improve the function of CFTR protein, thus restoring effective transport of chloride across the cell surface. The goal of CFTR therapy is to improve or prevent the clinical manifestations of CF.

Chest physical therapy (CPT): In CPT, manual percussion and vibration are applied to the chest wall in various positions to mobilize and drain mucus from the lungs. It needs to be performed by a trained individual, but most family members can learn this technique easily.

Chest physiotherapy: Respiratory treatments that help to remove mucus from the airway. This can include various positive airway pressure breathing exercises, percussion chest therapy, high-frequency chest wall oscillation (vest) therapy, or postural drainage.

Chest tube: A thin, hollow, tube that is inserted in between the ribs into the pleural space (the compartment surrounding the lungs and underneath the chest wall) to remove either fluid, blood, or air. Chest tubes are necessary after a transplant surgery to drain excess fluid that accumulates in the post-operative period.

Chest X-ray: An imaging technique that uses small amounts of radiation to produce pictures of the chest; it is used to detect abnormalities or diseases of the airways, blood vessels, bones, heart, and lungs.

Chlamydia: A common sexually-transmitted infection that can be prevented by using condoms or treated with antibiotics.

Chloride: Derived from the element chlorine, a negatively-charged atom with the symbol Cl–. This is a major constituent of salt in the body and is one of the atoms that is transported through the CFTR protein. Chloride is formed when the element gains an additional electron, generating a negative charge.

Chloride channel: A channel on cell membranes that transports chloride from one side of the cell to the other. In people with CF, these channels do not work correctly.

Cholangitis: Inflammation of the bile duct system, which carries bile from your liver and gallbladder into the first part of your small intestine.

Cholelithiasis: A medical condition, also known as gallstones, in which gallstones form in the gallbladder. When symptomatic, they typically cause cramping pain in the upper-right abdomen that often worsens with meals.

Cholesterol: A waxy substance created in the liver or consumed in many foods that is essential for normal cell function, but when consumed in high levels can cause heart disease.

Chorionic villus sampling (CVS): A medical procedure in which a small sample of the chorion (part of the placenta) is taken in the early stages of pregnancy. This procedure can be used to test for genetic conditions in the fetus. It can be performed slightly earlier in the pregnancy than amniocentesis.

Chromosome: A thread-like structure composed of nucleic acids found in the nucleus, or center, of most living cells. These groups of nucleic acids carry an individual's genetic information in units called genes.

Chronic lung rejection (Chronic Lung Allograft Dysfunction or CLAD): In chronic lung rejection, the transplanted lung is recognized as "foreign" by the recipient's immune system. The immune system attempts to reject the lung and can cause damage to the airways or lung tissue. Over time, the chronic rejection can make it so that the transplanted lung is no longer able to function normally.

Chronic obstructive pulmonary disease (COPD): A chronic lung disease, caused by inflammation, that causes obstructed airflow from the lungs. It is usually accompanied by shortness of breath, coughing, and mucus production from the lungs.

Chronotherapy: In the context of a circadian rhythm disorder, chronotherapy is aimed at moving a person's bedtime and rising time later and later each day until a person is sleeping on a normal schedule.

Ciprofloxacin: An antibiotic belonging to the fluoroquinolone class of antibiotics, frequently used to treat *Pseudomonas aeruginosa* lung infections in CF.

Circadian rhythm disorder: Circadian rhythm disorders are disruptions in a person's circadian rhythm—a name given to the "internal body clock" that regulates the (approximately) 24-hour cycle of biological processes in animals and plants. Key features of circadian rhythm disorders are either continuous or occasional disruption of sleep patterns resulting from a malfunction in the "internal body clock" or a mismatch between the "internal body clock" and the external environment regarding the timing and duration of sleep.

Cirrhosis: A condition in which the function of the liver is impaired due to excess scar tissue (called fibrosis) in the liver tissue.

Citalopram (Celexa®): A medication used to treat depression and anxiety. It belongs to a group of medicines known as selective serotonin re-uptake inhibitors that work by increasing the activity of a chemical called serotonin in the brain.

Citrate: Low levels of this chemical in urine is associated with a higher risk of kidney stones. Citrus foods, such as lemon, contain high levels of citrate, which can be used to alkalinize urine by increasing the urinary pH and to block new kidney stone formation.

Clinical social work: A specialty practice area of social work that focuses on the assessment, diagnosis, treatment, and prevention of emotional and behavioral disturbances. Social workers who provide individual, group, and family services are required to be licensed, certified, or supervised at the clinical level in their state of practice.

Clinical Trial Finder: A tool created by the CF Foundation to facilitate finding clinical trials for which an individual might be eligible (https://www.cff.org/Trials/Finder).

Clinical trial/interventional trial: An investigation or research that involves one or more human subjects, and assesses/evaluates the safety and effectiveness of a medication or medical device.

Clonidine: A medication that belongs to a group of medications called alpha-2 receptor agonists that treat many medical conditions, including high blood pressure and ADHD.

Clubbing: Referring to nail clubbing, which is a change in the structure of the nail at the nailbed leading to the appearance similar to an upside-down spoon. This can occur due to many different health conditions, including chronic lung disease.

Codon: A group of three nucleotides in a gene, which, together, provide instructions for the protein product. For instance, a "stop codon" is a group of three nucleotides that instruct the cell to stop making the final protein product.

Cognitive-behavioral therapy (CBT): A counseling intervention that aims to improve mental health by identifying and changing unhelpful thoughts, beliefs, or attitudes and improving emotional control by building healthy coping strategies.

Cognitive-behavioral therapy for insomnia (CBT-I): An evidence-based treatment aimed at changing sleep habits, scheduling factors, and misconceptions about sleep and insomnia that perpetuate sleep difficulties.

Co-insurance: The cost that the policy holder shares with the health insurance company for covered services, calculated as a percentage. For example, if the policy holder has an office visit that costs $100 before insurance, and the plan's co-insurance requirement is 20%, the policy holder would pay $20. The health insurance plan would then pay the remaining 80%, or $80.

Colistin: An antibiotic used to treat Gram-negative bacilli organisms. It is used intravenously or via inhalation to treat some CF-related infections.

Colon: The large intestines.

Colonization: A process in which bacteria become permanent residents of an airway or sinus surface.

Colonize: When referring to airways, it is the inhabiting of organisms in the CF airway; colonization does not usually cause active infection.

Colonoscopy: A procedure during which a fiber-optic scope (similar to bronchoscope) enables viewing of the rectum and colon to inspect the tissue of the large intestine and to look for cancer of the colon.

Colorectal cancer: Cancer affecting the colon and the rectum.

Combined lung-liver transplantation: A medical procedure in which the patient's lungs and liver are removed and replaced with donated lungs and liver. This procedure is performed for people who have both end-stage lung disease and cirrhosis at the same time.

Compass Program: A case management service for people with CF.

Complete blood count: Blood test that measures concentration of red blood cells, white blood cells, and platelets.

Comprehensive metabolic panel (CMP): An expanded blood test that measures electrolyte levels, glucose, kidney function, and liver function.

Compressor: A machine that puts out air at high pressure; when connected to nebulizers filled with fluid, the compressed air streams the liquid in mist form for inhalation.

Computed tomography (CT) imaging: An imaging technique that uses computer-guided X-rays or ultrasound to display a cross-sectional image through the human body.

Congenital: Often inherited medical condition, that occurs before or at birth.

Congenital bilateral absence of the vas deferens (CBAVD): Absence of the sperm canal presenting from birth which is a common finding in males with CF. The vas deferens is the tube that carries sperm out of the testes to be incorporated in semen. Although the testes function normally, the absence of this tube often renders a male unable to father children without the assistance of reproductive technologies.

Consolidated Omnibus Budget Reconciliation Act (COBRA): A form of employer-based coverage that gives employees and their families the option to extend their insurance if they lose job-based health coverage, such as by leaving their job or being laid off.

Constipation: Describes the condition in which stool is infrequent and/or difficult to pass; over time this can lead to pain in the lower-left abdomen that is relieved with a bowel movement.

Continuous alternating therapy: The use of different inhaled antibiotics in alternating sequence.

Continuous glucose monitoring (CGM) device: A computerized device that is inserted under the skin via a tiny sensor wire that tracks glucose levels throughout the day. It transmits real-time blood glucose data wirelessly to a receiver for the patient to view the information.

Continuous positive airway pressure (CPAP): A form of positive airway pressure ventilation that applies mild air pressure on a continuous basis to keep your airways continuously open. It can be used to treat sleep apnea, respiratory failure, newborns with difficulty breathing, and pneumonia.

Contraception: Device, medication, or method that prevents pregnancy. Also known as "birth control."

Contrast material: A material that has a different opacity from the internal organs, which when administered through the vein allows visualization of the organs on radiography or computed tomography scans.

Co-pay/co-payment: A fixed dollar amount that the policy holder pays for covered health care service. In most cases, co-payments do not count toward the deductible but do count toward the out-of-pocket maximum. Co-payments vary between plans and may apply to different health care services, such as urgent care, office visits, or medications.

Cor pulmonale: A condition that causes the right side of the heart to fail.

Coronary angiogram: A medical test in which a catheter is inserted into the heart vessels and dye is injected. The test allows doctors to check for blockages (stenoses) in your heart vessels.

Corrector: A drug that alters cellular processing of CFTR, allowing for an increased amount of CFTR to reach the cell surface.

Corticosteroids: A class of medications with strong anti-inflammatory properties.

Cost/benefit analysis: An approach to review and weigh the strengths (benefits) and weaknesses (costs) of a decision you need to make. This analysis helps you to make an informed decision by ensuring the weaknesses or costs are as low as they can be.

Costochondritis: Inflammation of the flexible connective tissue that connects the ribs to the breastbone in the chest; often due to frequent coughing and causing diffuse tenderness to the front of the chest.

CRISPR-Cas9 technology: A technology aimed at gene editing, allowing for non-mutated CFTR production.

Cross-sectional images: Images in the form of a plane through the body with the structures cut across.

Cyanosis: A discoloration of the skin, usually blue or purple, caused by poor circulation of blood or not enough oxygen in the blood.

Cystic changes: Architectural distortion leading to the formation of abnormal sac-like structures filled with either mucus or air. In CF, these changes most commonly occur in the pancreas and lungs.

Cystic Fibrosis Fitness Institute: A non-profit organization to address fitness goals with people with CF.

Cystic Fibrosis Foundation (CF Foundation): The leading organization in CF clinical care, research, and community support. It is a non-profit organization in the United States whose mission is to cure CF and provide all people with the disease the opportunity to lead full, productive lives by funding research and drug development; promoting individualized treatment; and ensuring access to high-quality, specialized care. (https://www.cff.org).

Cystic Fibrosis Foundation (CF Foundation) Registry: A patient registry of people with CF maintained by the CF Foundation. The registry allows CF centers to pool their patient data to understand better how to treat people with CF.

CF Liver Disease (CFLD): Liver disease affecting about one-third of individuals with CF. Liver inflammation is caused by thickened liver secretions blocking the liver ducts.

CF nurse: A registered nurse who has specialized knowledge in the nursing care related to CF, associated with the CF center, and often works as a CF center coordinator.

CF-related diabetes (CFRD): In CFRD, the thick sticky mucus that accompanies CF scars the pancreas and prevents the pancreas from producing normal amounts of insulin, which affects health and nutrition.

Creatinine: Protein measured to estimate kidney function.

Cystic Fibrosis Research Inc. (CFRI): A non-profit organization founded in 1975 that funds innovative CF research and offers education, advocacy, and psychosocial support programs and services to those with CF as well as their families and caregivers.

Cystic fibrosis transmembrane conductance regulator (CFTR): A membrane protein and chloride channel that is controlled by the CFTR gene. This protein functions as a channel to transport chloride and other molecules across the cell surface, either from the inside to the outside, or the outside to the inside. Dysfunctional CFTR leads to the clinical manifestations of CF.

Cystic fibrosis transmembrane conductance regulator (CFTR) mutations: Mutations are abnormalities in the DNA sequence of a gene. CFTR mutations are the genetic abnormality seen in CF, leading to creation of abnormal CFTR protein.

CYSTIC-L: A discussion group and email-based forum devoted to providing support to CF patients as well as information on new medical advances and treatments.

Cytochrome P450 (CYP450): A group of proteins found primarily in the liver that serve to break down many medications.

Data Safety Monitoring Board (DSMB): A committee that reviews safety data of a clinical trial routinely throughout the duration of the study.

Deductible: A fixed dollar amount that the policy holder must pay before the insurance company starts to make payments for covered medical services. Some insurance plans have both individual and family deductibles, while some family health insurance plans may have only a family deductible. Deductibles may apply only to specific services and may not apply to office visits or prescription medications. Under the Affordable Care Act, deductibles do not apply to preventive care (such as annual exams and immunizations) and routine gynecological visits.

Delirium: A disturbance in mental abilities characterized by confusion and decreased awareness of the environment, resulting from underlying medical, surgical, or medication-related effects. People with delirium may have abrupt changes in their mood, psychomotor activity, and might report seeing or hearing things that others do not hear or see. It is treated with correction of underlying medical condition and at times additional psychiatric medications.

De-oxygenated blood: Blood returning from the body to the heart that has lower oxygen levels compared to oxygenated blood that is pumped to the body from the heart.

Deoxyribonucleic acid (DNA): The genetic make-up of human cells. This material acts as the main constituent of chromosomes and is the source of inherited genetic information.

Depression: A mood disorder that causes feelings of sadness and a lack of interest or pleasure in daily activities that is severe enough to interfere with working, studying, sleeping, and enjoying life.

Dexlansoprazole: A medication in a class called proton-pump inhibitors that serves to reduce the amount of acid in the stomach.

Diabetes: A condition in which the level of glucose in the blood is too high, either due to lack of insulin or insulin resistance.

Diabetic ketoacidosis (DKA): A dangerous complication of diabetes in which the body is unable to use glucose due to a lack of insulin and thereby starts to break down fat, which leads to high levels of ketones. The excess ketones cause the blood to become too acidic which leads to electrolyte disturbances that can be fatal.

Dialysis: A medical procedure through which toxins are removed from the body of those who have kidney failure. A dialysis machine can artificially take over the function of the kidney.

Diaphragm: A dome-shaped muscle separating chest from the abdomen in mammals and playing a major role in breathing.

Diaphragmatic breathing: Deep breathing that is done by contracting the diaphragm, which is the muscle located horizontally at the base of your ribs under your lungs. During this type of breathing, your chest should not rise and your belly expands as air enters the lungs.

Dietitian: A clinician who is a part of the multi-discplinary CF team responsible for dietary guidance and education to ensure that the patient receives the proper caloric, protein, vitamin, and mineral content in their diet. The dietitian works closely with the pulmonologist to provide adequate enzyme dosing and to assess and treat gastrointestinal manifestations and endocrine complications.

Diffusion capacity: A type of pulmonary function test, used to measure the transfer of oxygen and carbon dioxide between the lungs and the blood.

Digestive enzymes: Proteins released from the pancreas to help with digestion. Naturally occurring digestive enzymes are often deficient in people with CF, requiring the use of medications that serve the same purpose.

Disease-causing mutations: A change in the genetic code that can result in a certain disease or disorder. If a person inherits such a mutation, development of a disorder is more likely but not guaranteed.

Distal intestinal obstruction syndrome (DIOS): A partial or complete blockage of bowel by stool or thickened mucus that occurs in some individuals with CF and typically causes pain in the lower-right abdomen.

Disulfiram (Antabuse®): A prescription medication that can facilitate alcohol abstinence by making you feel sick when you drink alcohol.

Donor liver: A healthy liver that comes from a deceased person. The healthy liver is then transplanted into someone who has end-stage liver disease and requires a transplant.

Dornase alpha (Pulmozyme®): An inhaled solution of recombinant human deoxyribonuclease I (rhDNase), an enzyme that breaks down mucus DNA. In CF, dornase alfa is inhaled into the airway to thin sticky mucus to help with clearance.

Double lumen: A lumen is a hollow space within a tube or vessel. When referring to single or double lumen with central intravenous lines, it refers to the number of hollow tubes or lines available to the patient for use. A single lumen has one line, and a double lumen has two lines.

Double-blinded placebo-controlled study: A study that includes both an investigational drug and a placebo, but neither the participants nor the researchers know which the participant is receiving.

Drug formulary: A list of prescription medications covered by a health insurance plan. Formularies can be open (little or no limitation on the medications covered), closed (coverage is limited to the medications contained in the formulary), or restricted (some flexibility in medication choice).

Dual-energy X-ray absorptiometry (DEXA, DXA) scan: An X-ray imaging test used to evaluate bone density.

Ducts: Tube-shaped structures that are present in many organs and are used to transport fluids in the body.

Dyspnea: Shortness of breath or difficulty breathing.

Edibles: Foods infused with cannabis/marijuana.

Egg donor: A person who donates one of their eggs to someone who cannot produce or use their own.

Ejaculate: Fluid that's discharged from a penis during sexual climax.

Ejaculatory duct: The ducts that allow sperm to travel from the vas deferens to the urethra where it is able to be expelled during ejaculation.

Elastase: An enzyme produced in the pancreas that breaks down proteins.

Elaxacaftor-tezacaftor-ivacaftor (Trikafta®): A triple medication combination of CFTR modulators used in some people with CF.

Electrocardiogram (EKG): A recording of the electrical activity of the heart or heartbeats using wire conductors attached to the patient's skin.

Electrode: A conductor through which electricity enters or leaves an object.

Embryos: One of the stages of development between an egg and a fetus. This term is used from the second to the eighth week of pregnancy.

Employer-based disability: A disability program offered by an employer and intended to replace some of a working person's income when a disability prevents that person from working.

Encoded: Literally, "to represent complicated information in a simple or short way." In genetics, instructions for cells on how to build proteins are encoded in DNA in the form of genes.

Endocrine: An endocrine gland will release substances directly into the bloodstream.

Endocrinologist: A doctor who diagnoses and treats disorders of the endocrine glands and hormones, such as diabetes, thyroid conditions, and growth disorders in children and adolescents.

Endoscopic exam: A non-surgical procedure using an endoscope, a flexible tube with a light and camera at the end, to inspect the nasal cavity or digestive tract. The video and pictures of the procedures are displayed on a monitor for viewing.

End-stage liver disease (ESLD): A medical condition in which the liver is so damaged that it has stopped functioning. Most patients with ESLD will also have cirrhosis (scar tissue) in the liver.

End-stage lung disease: Most severe form of lung disease, when lung function is seriously compromised.

End-stage manifestations: When a disease process affects an organ so much so that the organ is no longer able to carry out its regular function.

End-stage renal disease: A medical condition in which the kidneys are so damaged that they are no longer able to carry out their regular function of clearing toxins from the blood. People with end-stage renal disease may require dialysis.

Enema: An injection of liquid and/or medication into the rectum, sometimes used to treat constipation or distal intestinal obstruction syndrome (DIOS).

Enzyme replacement therapy: Referring to pancreatic enzyme replacement therapy, this is treatment with external forms of pancreatic enzymes (lipase, amylase, proteases) taken before meals to aid in food digestion. Usually, pancreatic enzyme therapy is done through pill form, but there are also digestive cartridges used for digestion of formula.

Enzymes: Proteins that catalyze a chemical reaction. In CF, pancreatic enzymes catalyze the digestion of fat and are taken by mouth with meals to prevent fat malabsorption and malnutrition.

Eosinophils: A type of white blood cells that are most frequently released or elevated in response to parasites, cancer, or an allergic reaction.

Epididymis: A duct, or tube, which connects the testis to the vas deferens to transport sperm.

Equal Employment Opportunity Commission (EEOC): A federal agency that administers and enforces civil rights laws against workplace discrimination.

Escitalopram (Lexapro®): A medication used to treat depression and anxiety. It belongs to a group of medicines known as SSRIs that work by increasing the activity of a chemical called serotonin in the brain.

Esomeprazole: A medication in a class called proton-pump inhibitors that serves to reduce the amount of acid in the stomach.

Esophageal varices: Enlarged blood vessels in the esophagus due to portal hypertension.

Esophagus: The tube that connects the mouth and stomach.

European CF Society (ECFS): A European organization dedicated to improving the survival and quality of life for people affected by CF by promoting research, education, and care.

Evidence-based guidelines: Integrating the best available external clinical evidence.

Evidence-based treatments: Treatments based on research science, often listed as "best practices" and "preferred approaches."

Exercise oximetry testing: A non-invasive pulmonary function test that measures the level of oxygen in blood when the patient is walking. It is often used to determine whether a patient needs oxygen.

Exocrine: An exocrine gland, such as the pancreas, releases substances through a duct to another surface, such as the GI tract.

Exocrine pancreatic insufficiency (EPI): The failure of the pancreas to secrete sufficient digestive enzymes into the intestine to effectively digest food that has been eaten. This complication is observed in 85% of people with CF.

Exposure-based therapy: A technique in therapy used to treat anxiety disorders that involves exposing the patient to the source of anxiety without intending to cause danger.

F508del: The most common mutation of the CFTR protein in people with CF.

Facemask: A mask covering the nose, mouth, and sometimes the eyes.

Family Education Days: An annual education event at a CF treatment center.

Family Medical Leave Act of 1993 (FMLA): A United States labor law requiring covered employers to provide employees with job-protected and unpaid leave for qualified medical and family reasons.

Famotidine: A medication in a class called histamine-2 receptor antagonists that serves to reduce the amount of acid in the stomach.

Fat malabsorption: Inability to absorb and wasting of dietary fat.

Fatty acid metabolism: The complex process in the body that takes cholesterol and fat and turns them into forms needed to for normal cell function.

Fear hierarchy: A list of triggers of fear, ranked from least to most anxiety provoking.

Feeding tube: A medical device used to provide nutrition directly to the stomach or small intestine via a tube that is either inserted into your nose or your abdomen. Feeding tubes are used in those who cannot obtain nutrition by mouth, are unable to swallow safely, or need additional nutrition supplementation beyond what they can take in by mouth.

Fertile: Having the ability to produce offspring. Fertility is based on many factors, for men and women, and include the production and release of sperm or eggs.

Fertility specialist: A medical professional who specializes in helping people who have fertility issues to reproduce.

Fibrosis: Scar tissue. Fibrosis can form in any part of the body because of injury, inflammation, or infection.

Flexibility exercise: Exercises to promote range of motion throughout the joints of the body, such as stretching or yoga activities.

Fluoroscopy: A type of medical imaging allowing for continuous X-rays, which helps localize anatomy, such as arteries and veins.

Fluoxetine (Prozac®): A medication used to treat depression and anxiety. It belongs to a group of medicines known as selective serotonin re-uptake inhibitors that work by increasing the activity of a chemical called serotonin in the brain.

Flutter device®: The brand name of a common positive expiratory pressure airway oscillating device used for airway clearance.

Food and Drug Administration (FDA): A federal agency that oversees all food and drug-related matters, including drug development.

Forced expiratory technique (FET): An airway clearance technique sometimes called "huff coughing" that consists of one to two huffs from mid-to-low lung volumes with the back of the throat open.

Forced expiratory volume in the first second (FEV1): The maximal amount of air that can be forcibly exhaled in one second. It provides a measure of lung function in people with CF. The FEV1 can decline due to acute sickness (such as a CF exacerbation), or the FEV1 might decline gradually over time due to permanent loss of lung function.

Forced vital capacity (FVC): The total volume exhaled from the time of forceful exhalation until the end of the maneuver.

Fostering: When a person or couple assume temporary parenting responsibilities and legal duties for a child that is not their biological offspring.

Fracture: A partial or complete break of a bone.

Full lung volumes by plethysmography: A plethysmograph is an instrument used for measuring volume changes within the lung. A full-volume study provides data about absolute volumes of air in the lung that a simple spirometry test cannot provide; thus, it is a more accurate measure of lung volumes. For this particular test, the patient sits inside an airtight box and inhales or exhales to a particular volume while calculations are made by the computer.

Fungus: A type of the microorganism that includes molds and yeasts. Candida is an example of a fungus that can infect human beings.

Gallbladder: A small pouch under the liver. During digestion, it receives and stores bile before releasing into the intestine, to digest fats.

Gallstone: Stone-like formation of non-digestible material, usually cholesterol or bilirubin. Most gallstones are passed without symptoms. Gallstones can sometimes become stuck in the bile ducts leading to cholecystitis, or inflammation of the gallbladder, and it can result in a colicky abdominal pain in the upper-right side of the abdomen.

Gallstones: *See* cholelithiasis.

Gastric reflux (heartburn, gastroesophageal reflux): *See* gastroesophageal reflux disease.

Gastric tube, gastrostomy tube (G-tube): A surgically placed catheter that enters the stomach (or in some cases the small intestine, referred to as a "J-tube") and allows people to take medications and nutrition without swallowing.

Gastric varices: Enlarged blood vessels in the stomach due to portal hypertension.

Gastroenterologist: A doctor who diagnoses and treats disorders of the stomach and intestines.

Gastroesophageal reflux disease (GERD) (also known as heartburn or gastric reflux): A physical condition in which gastric acid (acid from the stomach) flows backward, up into the esophagus, potentially causing heartburn and discomfort in the chest.

Gastrointestinal (GI): Referring or relating to the stomach and the intestines.

Gastroparesis: A condition in which the stomach slows down the normal emptying process of food into the small intestine. Symptoms include feeling full soon after eating small amounts of food, nausea, and vomiting.

General anesthesia: Medication administered in the operating room to induce a "sleep state." Under general anesthesia, patients don't feel or remember anything. Nearly all major surgeries require administration of general anesthesia for the duration of the procedure.

Generalized Anxiety Disorder-7 (GAD-7): A brief screening tool (with seven questions) to assess symptoms of anxiety as defined by diagnostic manuals. It takes less than 5 minutes and has very strong evidence of reliability and validity.

Genes: A sequence of nucleotides, or DNA, forming part of a chromosome. Genes are the basic unit of heredity. The DNA sequence in genes encodes for proteins. Simply, genes can be thought of blueprints or sets of instructions for the cell to follow when building proteins. They are passed from parent to offspring.

Genetic: Related to genes, heredity, or traits passed down from parent to offspring; a genetic disorder is a disorder that is inherited from your parents.

Genetic code: A set of rules used by living cells to convert information from the genetic material (DNA) into proteins. The genetic code is made up of nucleic acids, where a 3-nucleic acid group codes for a specific amino acid (a protein unit) which is added to the protein product in the sequence outlined by the DNA.

Genetic condition/disorder: A condition caused by abnormalities in a person's DNA. The abnormality can be as small as a single added nucleic acid to a gene or as large as the addition or deletion of an entire chromosome. These conditions are nearly always hereditary, meaning they are passed down from one generation to the next.

Genetic counselor: A clinician with special education and training to provide personalized information about genetic health including how inherited diseases and conditions can affect you or your family, likelihood of disease within a family, and which genetic tests a person should undergo. He or she helps to inform decisions about health, advises people on the risks and likelihoods of different genetic disorders, and helps them prepare for raising a child with a genetic disorder.

Genetic disease: *See* genetic condition/disorder.

Genetic disorder: *See* genetic condition/disorder.

Genetic malformations: *See* genetic mutation.

Genetic mutation: A permanent change in a DNA sequence of a gene in such a way that the gene is significantly different from what is found in most people. Mutations in one or more genes sometimes result in a condition or disease, like CF.

Genetic test: A medical test that identifies changes in a gene that may predispose an individual to a disease.

Geneticist: An expert in genetics, the science of genes, heredity, and variation of organisms.

Genotype: The specific genetic make-up of a person's genes.

Gestational diabetes: A type of diabetes that develops during pregnancy and usually goes away after birth. Women with CF have a higher risk of developing gestational diabetes than do women who do not have CF.

Gestational surrogacy: IVF is used to create an embryo, which is then implanted in a woman who has agreed to become pregnant on behalf of the future parents.

G-J (gastrostomy-jejunotomy) tube: A feeding tube inserted into the abdomen with two ports for feeding. The "G" port directly leads to your stomach; the other (the "J" port) leads to the second part of the small intestine, called the jejunum.

Glottis: The structure in the back of the throat that covers the opening of the trachea ("wind pipe") when you swallow to prevent food and secretions from entering the lungs.

Glucometer: A device used to measure the concentration of glucose (a type of simple sugar) in the blood.

Glucose: A simple sugar which is an important source of energy.

Gold standard: A diagnostic test to best identify the presence or absence of a particular condition or the best treatment.

Gonorrhea: A sexually transmitted infection that can be treated with antibiotics or prevented by using condoms when engaging in sexual activity.

Great Strides Walks: A fundraiser event for the CF Foundation.

G-tube: A gastrostomy tube; a tube inserted through the abdomen that delivers nutrition directly to the stomach.

Guanfacine: Belongs to a group of medications called alpha-2 receptor agonists that treat many medical conditions including high blood pressure and ADHD.

Guided imagery: A technique in which you are guided to imagine specific scenarios or scenery (often in nature, such as the ocean, forest, or park) in which you are able to breathe deeply, relax, and reduce symptoms of distress. With practice, guided imagery can be used in situations in which you feel anxiety or distress.

H_2O: The chemical description of water.

Haemophilus influenzae: A bacterium that can cause a variety of infections, including pneumonias.

Hallucinations: Perceptions that appear real but are created by your mind, most frequently hearing sounds or seeing things that are not there. These can be symptoms of a medical or psychiatric illness, or side effects of a medication or drug.

Health insurance marketplace: Also known as the Health Insurance Exchange, provides people a way to buy health insurance if they do not have access to group-based employer plans or do not qualify for Medicare or Medicaid. It was created as a result of the Affordable Care Act to help residents of the United States pay for health care.

Health maintenance organization (HMO): A type of health plan that provides for a set of pre-negotiated health services from a network of health care providers for a fixed annual fee. Out-of-network services are generally not covered in this model.

HealthWell Foundation: A non-profit organization that provides financial assistance to cover out-of-pocket health care costs.

Heart attack: A medical emergency that occurs when blood flow to the heart muscle is blocked. Common symptoms include chest pressure, tightness, pain, or a squeezing sensation that can spread to the neck, jaw, arms, or back, and can be accompanied by nausea, shortness of breath, and/or lightheadedness or sudden dizziness.

Heartburn: A burning sensation in the chest secondary to backflow of food or stomach contents and stomach acid into the esophagus.

Heart-lung bypass machine: A machine used in the operating room that can artificially take over the function of the heart and lungs. The heart-lung bypass machine can pump oxygenated blood throughout the body for a certain period. This machine is commonly used for people who are undergoing lung transplantation and allows the surgeons to safely remove the old lungs from the body and replace them with new lungs, without compromising oxygen delivery to the rest of the body.

Heart-lung transplantation: A medical procedure in which the heart and lungs are removed and replaced with healthy, donated organs.

Hemoglobin: A protein responsible for transporting oxygen in the blood. It is red, which is responsible for the color of blood cells.

Hemoptysis: Coughing blood or blood-stained mucus from the bronchi, larynx, trachea, or lungs.

Hepatitis B: A sexually transmitted virus that infects the liver. It can be prevented by receiving a vaccine or by using condoms during sexual activity.

Heterozygous: An individual with two different alleles of a gene, leading to variations in the alleles passed to their biologic children.

Hickman: A type of central intravenous line or catheter used for administering medications or drawing blood that can stay in the vein for a prolonged period.

Hierarchy: A system or organization in which groups are ranked according to status or importance.

High-altitude simulation test (HAST): A form of pulmonary function testing. A patient breathes air that has a low level of oxygen to determine whether they will need supplemental oxygen while flying.

High-frequency chest-wall oscillation (HFCWO): The creation of rapid changes in pressure on the chest wall by a vest that wraps around the body and quickly inflates and deflates to aid in airway clearance.

High-risk obstetrician: An obstetrician who has received additional training to evaluate and monitor pregnancies that are considered more risky or complicated than most pregnancies.

Histamine-2 receptor antagonists: A class of medications used to reduce the amount of acid in the stomach, commonly used to treat gastroesophageal reflux disease.

Home glucose monitoring meters: *See* glucometer. The home devices are usually smaller and more portable than those used in the hospital or doctor's offices.

Homebound Instruction (HBI): Delivery of educational services by school district personnel within a student's home due to the student's inability to attend school because of disability or health problems.

Homozygous: An individual with two identical alleles for a gene.

Hormones: Chemicals in the body that signal the organs of the body to work together.

Hospice: An approach to care and an insurance benefit for those whose goal is to maximize their quality of life. Referral to hospice is appropriate for those who are expected to live 6 months or less if their disease follows its expected course. People who enroll in hospice typically receive the support of a team of health care professionals and numerous other services. Most care is provided in the home, but some hospice care is provided in the hospital or in inpatient hospice facilities.

Huff cough: A type of coughing technique, letting air out of the lungs while whispering the word "huff," allowing air and mucus to be expelled from small airways.

Huffing (huff coughing): A technique that helps move mucus from the lungs, involving taking a deep breath, holding it, and then actively exhaling in a slow continuous but forceful fashion.

Human Immunodeficiency Virus (HIV): A virus that can be spread through unprotected sex, or sharing of hypodermic needles. HIV cannot be cured but can be managed with medication. It can be prevented by using protection during sex and by not sharing needles with other people.

Hypercapnia: Also known as hypercarbia and CO_2 retention; a condition of abnormally elevated CO_2 levels in the blood.

Hypercarbia: *See* Hypercapnia.

Hyperemesis syndrome: A condition in which severe and repeated bouts of vomiting occur in daily long-term users of marijuana.

Hypertension: High blood pressure.

Hypertonic saline: A solution of sodium chloride (salt) at a concentration higher than the concentration of salt found in human blood. In CF, hypertonic saline is inhaled into the airway to hydrate dry, thick mucus.

Hypertrophic osteoarthropathy: A rare bone condition specific to chronic lung disease, such as CF, which presents with clubbing, inflammation surrounding the bone, joint swelling, and pain.

Hypothesis: An idea that can be tested by a research study.

Hypoxemia: Abnormally low levels of oxygen in the blood, causing hypoxia, or low oxygen levels in the tissues of the body.

Hypoxemic: The state of having low oxygen levels.

Ibuprofen (Advil®, Motrin®): A drug in the non-steroidal anti-inflammatory drug (NSAID) class that reduces inflammation, fever, and mild to moderate pain.

Imaging: Visualizing parts, tissues, or internal structures of the body with X-rays, computed tomography (CT) scans, magnetic resonance imaging (MRI), nuclear medicine, positron emission tomography (PET), and ultrasound.

Imaging studies: Medical studies performed to better visualize a patient's organs and other body structures. Imaging studies can include an X-ray, a CT scan (or CAT scan), and an MRI, among others.

Immune system: Our body's defense system against infection.

Immune-reactive trypsinogen levels: An assay used as a screening test in many newborn screens for CF. The level of immune-reactive trypsinogen in the blood directly correlates with pancreatic duct obstruction and abnormal pancreatic enzyme release. A higher level is correlated with an increased risk of CF.

Immunoglobulins: Antibodies produced by our body's immune system, which usually rise when there is an immune response to an allergen.

Immunologist: A doctor who diagnoses and treats allergies, asthma, and immune deficiency disorders and autoimmune diseases.

Immunoreactive trypsinogen (IRT): An inactive precursor protein produced in the pancreas. Newborn infants have their blood tested for the level of this precursor protein to screen for CF.

Immunosuppression: The state of having a weakened immune system. Immunosuppression can be due to an underlying disease or, in the case of transplanted patients, immuno-suppression can be due to medications given to prevent organ rejection.

Immunosuppressive medications: Medicines that prevent the immune system from rejecting a transplanted organ. These medicines work by blunting the effect of the immune system, and have the side effect of making the immune system less able to fight infections.

Implantable vascular access device: A medical device that allows medicine to be directly delivered into large veins, usually at the neck or chest.

In utero: "In the uterus," related to the embryo in the womb.

Individual Education Plan (IEP): A formal plan that schools and families develop to provide people with disabilities like CF to have specialized education and services to meet their unique needs. This is a provision of federal education law in the Individuals with Disabilities Education Act (IDEA).

Individuals with Disabilities Education Act (IDEA): A federal law that makes available a free appropriate public education to eligible children with disabilities throughout the nation and ensures special education and related services to those children.

Induction: The process of speeding up a chemical reaction.

Infectious disease specialist: A doctor who diagnoses and treats infections caused by bacteria, viruses, fungi, and parasites.

Inflammation: A defense mechanism in the body that is activated when the immune system recognizes damaged cells, irritants, and pathogens, and begins the healing process. Inflammation can also become chronic in some conditions, such as CF. The cellular responses that generate redness, swelling, pain, and warmth at a site of infection.

Influenza: A seasonal respiratory virus that can cause pneumonia.

Informed consent: A process used by researchers to communicate the risks and potential benefits of participating in a clinical trial to potential and enrolled study participants.

Inherited: Passed from one generation to the next.

Inhibition: The process of slowing down a chemical reaction.

Insomnia: Persistent problems falling asleep, staying asleep, or waking up too early that interferes with daily functioning. People with insomnia can feel dissatisfied with their sleep and usually experience one or more of the following symptoms: fatigue, low energy, difficulty concentrating, mood disturbances, and decreased performance in work or at school.

Institutional Review Board (IRB): A committee that reviews the safety and ethical parameters of a study with the primary goal of protecting its human participants. A study cannot be performed without IRB approval.

Insulin pump: A device inserted just under the skin used to deliver insulin into the body for those with diabetes.

Insulin: A hormone that is responsible for allowing blood glucose to enter cells, providing them with the energy to function. Lack or ineffectiveness of insulin plays a key role in the development of diabetes and its replacement might be important in treating diabetes.

Intensive care unit (ICU): A hospital unit that cares for critically ill individuals.

International Committee on Mental Health in CF: A panel of experts assembled by the CF Foundation and the European CF Society that have created international recommendations regarding the screening and treatment of anxiety and depression in CF.

International normalized ratio (INR): An assay or a test to evaluate coagulation of the blood or how well or poorly it clots.

International Society for Pediatric and Adolescent Diabetes: A professional organization whose charge is to promote research, education, and advocacy related to diabetes in children, adolescents, and young adults.

Interpersonal Therapy (IPT): A form of psychotherapy in which the focus is on a patient's relationships with peers and family members and the way they see themselves and how these things affect our mood.

Interstitial lung disease (ILD): An umbrella term for a large group of disorders that cause scarring (fibrosis) of the lung tissue.

Intestinal blockage: Blockage of the passage of food or stool through the large or small intestines.

Intestines: Part of the digestive tract.

Intrapulmonary percussive ventilator (IPV): A pneumatic positive pressure device used to move mucus.

Intrathoracic pressure: The pressure inside the chest during inhalation and exhalation.

Intrauterine devices (IUDs): A small device that is inserted in the uterus to prevent pregnancy. There are two types of IUDs: hormonal and copper. Both are reversible, very effective, and last for several years.

Intrauterine insemination (IUI): A fertility treatment in which a small tube is used to inject sperm directly into the uterus.

Intravenous (IV): Situated in, or administered into the vein of the body.

Intravenous (IV) contrast: Medication that can be given as part of a medical imaging study. The IV contrast allows the doctors to see your blood vessels more clearly on a CT scan or MRI.

Intubation: A process of inserting an endotracheal tube to aid ventilation of the lungs.

Intussusception: Refers to a segment of the intestine that folds over itself, causing an obstruction in the intestine, usually where the small and large intestines meet.

Investigational New Drug (IND): A drug that is declared to be under clinical investigation, with the intent of going to market.

Investigator-initiated: A study driven by a researcher at your institution rather than by a pharmaceutical or biotech company.

In-vitro: In cell culture.

In-vitro fertilization: A method of assisted reproductive technology where an egg is combined with sperm outside the body and implanted after fertilization occurs.

In-vivo: In living animals, which can include mice, rats, ferrets, or other animals.

Ipratropium: A medication that opens up and relaxes airways; it is administered by an inhaler or nebulizer.

Ivacaftor (Kalydeco®): A modulator therapy drug used to treat some mutations of CF.

Jaundice: Yellowing of the skin due to bilirubin build-up in the blood from liver failure.

Journal of Cystic Fibrosis (JCF): A scientific publication about CF, published by Elsevier for the European Cystic Fibrosis Society.

J-tube: A tube that is inserted into the small intestine (jejunum) through the abdominal wall to provide extra calories or medications without needing to swallow.

Kidney stones: *See* nephrolithiasis. Hard deposits of minerals that form inside the kidneys. If the kidney stone is large enough, it can cause blockage of the ureter, the tube that connects the kidney to the bladder, leading to pain and blood in the urine.

Kidney transplant: Surgery through which a donated kidney is surgically inserted into a person with end-stage renal disease.

Lactulose: A non-absorbable sugar that is used as a gentle laxative to draw water into the digestive tract and treat constipation.

Lansoprazole: A medication in a class called proton-pump inhibitors that serves to reduce the amount of acid in the stomach.

Laxatives: Medications used to help with the passage of stool.

Layering: The addition of extra ingredients to meals to increase their caloric content.

Left heart catheterization: A medical procedure in which a catheter is inserted into the blood vessels of your heart. Dye is then injected into the blood vessels, which allows your doctors to check for blockages in the blood vessels of the heart.

Levalbuterol: A medication that opens up and relaxes airways; it is administered by an inhaler or nebulizer.

Levofloxacin: An antibiotic belonging to the fluoroquinolone class frequently used to treat *Pseudomonas aeruginosa* lung infections in CF.

Lidocaine patch: A topical adhesive patch containing the medication lidocaine, which treats pain in the area it is applied by preventing nerves from sending pain signals.

Linezolid (Zyvox®): An antibiotic used to treat methicillin-resistant *Staphylococcus aureus* (MRSA) infections.

Liver: The largest solid organ in the upper-right quadrant of the abdomen that serves many vital functions, including filtering the blood, detoxifying chemicals, metabolizing drugs, production and excretion of bile, metabolism of fats, proteins, and carbohydrates, storage of glycogen, and synthesis of important proteins (e.g., albumin, clotting factors).

Liver failure: A medical condition in which the liver has sustained so much damage it can no longer function normally. In some cases, the liver failure is reversible. In other cases, liver failure can lead to end-stage liver disease, or irreversible loss of liver function.

Liver function tests (LFTs): Blood tests that relate to the liver that can detect liver damage or measure how well the liver is working.

Liver transplant: A surgical procedure in which a healthy, donated, liver is transplanted into a person with end-stage liver disease.

Living donor: A live donor who is a healthy person undergoing an elective surgery to remove an organ (a kidney) or a part of their organ (a liver lobule) to donate to another person.

Living liver donation: Donation of a liver lobule or part by a healthy volunteer. Since liver re-generates, this is possible.

Loperamide: An opioid medication used to treat diarrhea.

Lubiprostone (Amitiza®): A medication used to treat constipation that works by activating chloride channels in the gastrointestinal tract.

Lumacaftor-ivacaftor (Orkambi®): A combination of two CFTR-modulator medications.

Lumen: Opening.

Lung capacity: The volume of air associated with the different phases of inhalation and exhalation.

Lung transplant: Surgery that is done to replace diseased lungs with healthy lungs, usually from a donor who has recently died. Individuals with CF might consider a lung transplant if their lung function is very low and their quality of life is suffering related to this.

Major depressive disorder (MDD): A major mental health condition characterized by feeling depressed, not enjoying daily activities, feeling hopeless or helpless, struggling with sleep, appetite, and energy, and possibly thoughts about dying of wanting to die for at least two weeks. MDD impairs a person's functioning.

Malabsorption: When nutrients are not absorbed in the small intestine in CF, usually caused by loss of function of the pancreas.

Malnutrition: A non-specific physical condition wherein the body does not obtain enough of one or more nutrients to perform normal functions.

Mannitol (Bronchitol®): The inhaled form of a medication that draws water into the airways by osmosis, which makes the mucus thinner.

Manual chest percussion: An airway clearance technique that is applied to the chest wall in various positions to mobilize and drain mucus from the lungs. It needs to be performed by a trained individual, but most family members can learn this technique.

Manual chest physiotherapy (CPT): A method of clearing the airways of mucus in which a care provider hits the back with cupped palms to create vibrations in the lungs.

Maternal-Fetal Medicine (MFM): A medical specialty focusing on high-risk pregnancies.

Measles, Mumps, and Rubella (MMR): A combination vaccine that prevents three common infections that can cause fevers, rash, sore throat, and pneumonia.

Mechanical ventilator: A machine that can breathe for a person who is too sick to breathe on their own. Mechanical ventilation is performed through a breathing tube inserted into the patient's trachea (wind pipe).

Meconium: Meconium is the first feces, or stool, of a newborn infant known for being very thick.

Meconium ileus: Meconium ileus occurs when meconium obstructs, or blocks, a child's intestines. This usually occurs only if the child has an underlying condition that makes their secretions very thick and is usually seen only in children with CF. It often requires surgical intervention. It is the first presentation in about 20% of people with CF.

Medicaid: A health care program funded jointly by the federal government and state governments. Medicaid provides free or low-cost health care coverage for low-income individuals and people meeting certain eligibility requirements.

Medical marijuana: In some states it is legal to purchase and use marijuana to treat symptoms related to chronic illnesses.

Medicare: A federally administered health insurance program for people older than 65 who are receiving benefits from the Social Security Administration or the Railroad Retirement Board (RRB), people younger than 65 who are receiving Social Security Disability Insurance (SSDI), or people receiving certain disability benefits from the RRB.

Mediport®: A surgically implanted device that allows easy access to a patient's veins, used for medication administration and blood draws. Also referred to as a port or port-a-cath as well as by many other brand names.

Meditation: The act of giving your attention to only one thing, either as a religious activity or as a way of becoming calm and relaxed.

Melatonin: A naturally occurring hormone that regulates our sleep–wake cycle.

Mental health coordinator (MHC): A member of the CF care team who is responsible for services that include, but are not limited to, providing annual anxiety and depression screening and follow-up, coordinating evidence-based treatment for depression and anxiety, developing and maintaining a referral network of community-based mental health practitioners, and serving as an educator and liaison for mental health care for the CF center, hospital or institution, community practitioners, and payers.

Messenger RNA (mRNA): A single-stranded RNA, which is complementary to one of the DNA strands. It leaves the nucleus of the cell and goes into the ribosome to provide the blueprint for the production of the proteins.

Metabolize: A normal chemical process in the body in which substances are broken down.

Methacholine bronchial challenge testing: A test used to diagnose asthma in which a patient breathes in a medication called methacholine.

Methicillin-resistant Staphylococcus aureus (MRSA): A common bacterium that can cause skin, blood, and lung infections. It is a common chronic lung infection in people with CF.

Methylphenidate: A medication used to treat attention-deficit hyperactivity disorder. It belongs to a class of medications called CNS stimulants.

Microbiology lab: A laboratory that studies small microbes, such as bacteria, viruses, and fungi.

Microbiology tests: Lab tests that look at microorganisms in the body and help decide on appropriate antibiotic treatment.

Microscope: A laboratory instrument used to view very small objects, such as microbes and cells, under high magnification.

Mindfulness training: Teaching or learning of practices designed to help participants increase their ability to live fully in the present and accept certain feelings or situations.

Mineral: An element essential for normal growth and nutrition.

Mini-Cons: Live virtual events for smaller groups on a specific topic related to CF.

Moon facies: A rounded appearance due to fat deposits on the sides of the face.

Mother's Retreat: An annual weekend event for mothers of children and adults with CF.

Motivational interviewing (MI): A strategy to help people address ambivalence or inaction to changing unhealthy actions by identifying and validating internal motivations and strengths.

Mucociliary clearance: Removal of particles from the airways as the result of the movement of the mucus coating due to the beating of the underlying cilia.

Mucolytics: Medications that help with clearing of the mucus from the upper and lower airways.

Mucus: A gelatinous substance produced by mucosal glands in various organs in the body. Mucus functions to lubricate and protect exposed surfaces in the body. In CF, mucus is dehydrated, thick, and sticky.

Mucus plugging: A partial or complete blockage of the airway by mucus.

Multi-site (centers) study: A clinical trial that involves multiple clinical centers.

Muscle relaxation: A method that aims to relax the muscles to block anxiety.

Musculoskeletal chest pain: Pain due to injury or inflammation of the bones, muscles, or cartilage in the chest wall.

Musculoskeletal system: The bones, muscles, tendons, and ligaments of the body.

Mutation: A permanent alteration in the genetic sequence of nucleic acids such that the person's genetic sequence is different than what is found in most people.

Mutation-agnostic: The effect of the compound does not depend on the type of CF mutation.

Mutation-specific: The effect of the compound depends on the type of mutation.

Mycophenolate mofetil: A medication that works to suppress the immune system and is commonly given to transplant recipients to help prevent organ rejection.

Naltrexone: A prescription medication that blocks the effect of opiates in the brain. It is used to treat opiate and alcohol use disorders to prevent the euphoric effects of these drugs and decrease the desire to use them.

Naproxen (brand name: Aleve®, Naprosyn®): A drug in the non-steroidal anti-inflammatory drug (NSAID) class that reduces inflammation, fever, and mild to moderate pain.

Narcotic: Technically defined as a drug or other substance that affects mood or behavior and is sold for non-medical purposes, but this term is casually used (even in health care settings) to describe opioid pain medications like morphine.

Nasal cannula: A small lightweight tube placed in the nostrils to deliver supplemental oxygen.

Nasal polyps: Small groups of inflamed tissue in the nose due to chronic inflammation.

Nasal potential difference (NPD): A test in which the voltage across a mucus membrane, or lining, of the nose is measured. This test measures the function of the CFTR protein.

Nasogastric (NG) tube: A thin tube that is used for short-term nutrition support. It is placed through the nose and into the stomach.

National Society of Genetic Counselors: A professional association of genetic counselors.

Nebulized: The process of turning liquid medications into tiny droplets, which are then inhaled for direct delivery to the lungs.

Nebulizer: A device that changes liquid medication into a fine mist, allowing for inhalation of the medication.

Needle phobias: Fear of needles and needle procedures.

Needle sticks: A puncture of the needle into the vein for IV placement or blood draw.

Neonatal intensive care unit (NICU): A special part of a hospital for the care of newborns who are ill or born prematurely.

Neonatal period: The newborn period, usually referring to the first month of life.

Nephrolithiasis: Also known as kidney stones. When symptomatic, they block the flow of urine from the kidney to the bladder and typically cause back pain that extends around to the lower abdomen on the affected side.

Nephrologists: Physicians who focus on the diagnosis and treatment of kidney disease.

Neutrophils: The most common type of the white blood cells, that are essential for the immune system response.

Neutrophil elastase: A component that is released by inflammatory cells called neutrophils during immune responses with the intent of killing bacteria; it can also damage airway cells.

Newborn screening test: A public-health program in which infants are tested shortly after birth for a list of conditions that are treatable but might not be evident at the time of birth.

Nicotine replacement: Prescription and non-prescription medications (e.g., gums, patches, lozenges, vaping devices) that contain nicotine without the negative health effects of cigarette smoke; used to help quit smoking.

Nitric oxide: A chemical compound released by cells that causes dilation of the blood vessels; it can also have anti-microbial effects.

Nocturnal feeds: Nutrition support through a feeding tube that is delivered at night (generally when sleeping) to provide additional calories and/or to allow time away from the feeding tube pump during the day.

Nocturnal oximetry: A common test that uses a pulse oximeter worn on your index finger at night to continuously record your blood oxygen level during sleep.

Non-invasive ventilation (NIV): Administration of breathing support without using an invasive artificial airway, such as an endotracheal or tracheostomy tube. Examples of non-invasive ventilation include continuous positive airway pressure (CPAP) or bi-level positive airway pressure (BiPAP).

Non-steroidal anti-inflammatory drugs (NSAIDs): A class of drug that reduces pain and inflammation and can also be used to decrease fever and to prevent blood clots.

Non-tuberculosis mycobacterial (NTM) infections: A type of bacterial infection caused by non-tuberculous mycobacteria that are found naturally in water and soil. Lung infection by this type of bacteria is caused by inhaling the organism from the environment. It does not cause disease in most people, but for some susceptible individuals, such as those with CF, a slowly progressive disease/infection can occur.

North American Cystic Fibrosis Conference (NACFC): Annual conference devoted to educating the CF community, organized by CF Foundation.

Nortriptyline: A prescription medication that is commonly used to treat depression.

Nutrient: Components of foods that provide energy and the building blocks for growth and tissue repair: protein, fat, carbohydrate, water, vitamins, and minerals.

Nutritional status: Health status in terms of the nutrients in a person's diet.

ObamaCare: A federal law whose formal name is the Patient Protection and Affordable Care Act, passed in 2010. Among other provisions, this law enhanced patient protections, expanded Medicaid eligibility, prevents health plans from creating exclusions due to pre-existing conditions, allows people to stay on a parental health insurance plan until age 26, and mandated health coverage for every individual, reliant on states creating marketplaces for individual health plans.

Obesity: Excessive amount of body fat, defined as a BMI of greater than or equal to 30.

Observational study: A study in which different groups of people are observed, without intervention, over time to assess the effect of an exposure(s) or risk factor(s).

Obstetrician/Gynecologist: An obstetrician is a doctor who delivers babies. A gynecologist is a doctor who diagnoses and treats diseases of the female reproductive organs.

Obstructive lung disease: A type of lung disease characterized by airway inflammation and easily collapsed airways. This is due to blockage of airflow either by narrowed airways due to inflammation, or mucus impaction.

Obstructive sleep apnea (OSA): Intermittent or irregular airflow blockage during sleep that is caused by collapse of the structures in the back of the throat.

Omeprazole: A medication in a class called proton-pump inhibitors that serves to reduce the amount of acid in the stomach.

Open-label clinical trial: A trial in which the participants and researchers know that the participants are receiving study drug.

Opioid: A medication like morphine that is used to treat pain or shortness of breath.

Optimal nutritional status: The goal weight and body mass people should aim to achieve to stay in good health.

Oral contrast: A solution that is swallowed to help enhance X-ray or CT images of the esophagus, stomach, or intestines.

Oral glucose tolerance testing (OGTT): A test assessing a person for the presence of diabetes. A person drinks a sweet drink and blood glucose is measured several times at difference time points.

Organ rejection: The condition in which a transplant recipient's immune system has recognized the transplanted organ as "foreign" and has begun to attack the organ. Organ rejection can range from mild to severe and is treated in the hospital setting with medications.

Oropharynx: The back of the throat, specifically the back-third part of the tongue, the soft palate, or roof of the mouth, and the side and back walls of the throat.

Oscillatory vest: A device that delivers high-frequency vibrations via a vest that the patient wears. This is a common therapy for mucus clearance.

Osmosis: A process by which liquid moves from an area of high particle concentration to an area of lower particle concentration, serving to make the concentrations more equally distributed.

Osmotic agent: A drug that pulls water into the airway, increasing the water content and decreasing the density of sputum, making it easier to cough out.

Osteopenia: A decrease in bone mass or strength.

Osteoporosis: A condition in which bone is abnormally thin, thus increasing the risk for fracture.

Otorhinolaryngologist: An ear, nose, and throat doctor.

Out-of-pocket (OOP) maximum: The maximum amount that the policy holder can spend for covered services in a set coverage period. After the out-of-pocket maximum is reached, the health insurance plan pays for all covered services for the remainder of the coverage period.

Ovarian hyperstimulation syndrome: A condition that can sometimes occur as a result of taking fertility medications. Rarely this condition can result in serious illness or death.

Overnight sleep study: More formally called polysomnography (PSG), an overnight sleep study typically uses a series of electrodes placed on your head to measure brain waves during sleep to determine what stage of sleep you are in, a device to measure your breathing, and a pulse oximeter to measure your blood oxygen levels throughout the night.

Over-the-counter (OTC): Medications that are available to consumers without a clinician's prescription.

Oxaclobacter formigenes: Bacteria that is found in the colon and has been shown to be beneficial to humans. These bacteria break down oxalate, a major contributor to kidney stones.

Oxalate: The most common type of kidney stones are made of calcium oxalate, which forms when calcium binds to oxalate. Oxalate, found in many types of foods, can lead to high levels of this chemical in your urine that can increase the risk for kidney stones.

Oxycodone: A drug in the opioid class of medications that reduces moderate to severe pain.

Oxygen saturation: The percentage of oxygen that is bound to or saturated with hemoglobin.

Oxygen saturation probe: A non-invasive medical device placed on the fingertip that can check your oxygen level.

Palliative care: The provision of medical care focused on symptom relief and quality of life. Palliative care clinicians are a group of specialists who focus entirely on symptom relief for patients. Palliative care can be implemented at any stage of a disease process: from initial diagnosis, up until the time of death.

Palpitations: The sensation of extra heartbeats or a fluttering feeling in the chest.

Pancreas: An organ located in the abdomen that helps in both digestion of food (exocrine function) as well as regulation of blood glucose (endocrine function).

Pancreatic: Related to pancreas.

Pancreatic beta-cell: The cells of the pancreas that produce insulin.

Pancreatic ducts: The ducts that connect the pancreas to the small intestines that allow for delivery of pancreatic enzymes that help in food digestion.

Pancreatic enzyme replacement therapy (PERT): Medication used in people with exocrine pancreatic insufficiencies containing digestive enzymes (amylase, protease, lipase) that allow for proper digestion of protein, fat, and carbohydrates in food. The necessary digestive enzymes are taken in the form of a capsule with meals.

Pancreatic enzymes: Digestive enzymes (lipase, amylase, proteases) produced by the pancreas that break down fats, proteins, and carbohydrates.

Pancreatic insufficiency: A condition in which the pancreas is unable to produce the chemicals needed to digest fats, proteins, and carbohydrates (sugars).

Pancreatic juices: Liquids secreted by the pancreas that contains pancreatic enzymes, sodium bicarbonate, and water.

Pancreatitis: Inflammation of the pancreas, causing persistent upper abdominal pain.

Pantoprazole: A medication in a class called proton-pump inhibitors that serves to reduce the amount of acid in the stomach.

PaO2: Stands for partial pressure of arterial oxygen, one of the components measured in the arterial blood gas (ABG) test.

Parenteral: Administration through a vein, such as an IV.

Partial thromboplastin time (PTT): An assay or a test to evaluate coagulation of the blood or how well or poorly it clots.

Particulate: Very small separate particles; dust is considered a particulate.

Patient Health Questionnaire-9 (PHQ-9): A self-administered screening tool, consisting of nine questions, to assess symptoms of depression, which map onto diagnostic criteria. It is highly reliable and well validated.

PEG tube: Percutaneous endoscopic gastrostomy tube inserted into the abdominal cavity to provide nutrition.

Percussion: The action of gently slapping the back and chest as if you were playing a drum.

Periostitis: Inflammation surrounding bone.

Peripheral IV (PIV): A small intravenous catheter that is inserted in small veins, used to administer medication, fluids, or blood products.

Peripherally inserted central catheter (PICC): A type of intravenous line that is inserted in the upper arm with a catheter extending into a large vein near the heart. This can be used for infusion of medication, fluids, or blood productions, as well as withdrawing blood. PICC lines can remain in place for a prolonged period.

Pessaries: Flexible devices that can be placed into the vagina to help support the pelvic organs, such as the bladder, uterus, or rectum to prevent pelvic organ prolapse and urinary incontinence.

pH: A chemical calculation used to describe how acidic or alkaline a solution is.

Pharmaceutical company-sponsored trials: Trials that are paid for by pharmaceutical companies.

Pharmacist: A health care professional who is licensed to prepare and dispense prescription drugs and counsel patients regarding their effects and proper use.

Phase 1 trial: A trial aimed to assess the safety and tolerability of a medicine.

Phase 2 trial: A trial aimed to assess the efficacy of a medicine.

Phase 3 trial: A trial aimed to define the effect of a medicine, compared with the "gold standard" of clinical care.

Phase 4 trial: An observational trial aimed to assess long-term side effects and outcomes of a medicine, post-FDA approval.

Photosensitivity: A medication side effect that can cause you to become sunburned or develop rashes more easily when exposed to the sun. It is important to wear sunscreen when taking these medications.

Physical therapist (PT): A clinician responsible for the assessment of the musculoskeletal, cardiovascular, and pulmonary systems, including muscle fitness, balance and coordination, and aerobic capacity. The PT can coach individuals with CF regarding posture, exercise, and physical activity to improve their outcomes and overall physical health.

Pilocarpine: A chemical used to stimulate sweat glands. This drug can have many other effects on the body depending on where or how it is applied.

Placebo: An inactive substance or treatment that looks the same and is administered in the same way as an active study drug or treatment being studied.

Placenta: In a pregnant woman, this is an organ sac that is attached to the fetus by the umbilical cord, providing oxygen and nutrients.

Pneumonia: An infection involving the lungs, which can be bacterial, fungal, or viral.

Pneumonia vaccine: Refers to two vaccines, PPSV23 and PCV13, which are given at least 1 year apart to prevent infections in the lung, brain, and blood caused by the *pneumococcus* bacterium. Although called the "pneumonia vaccine," it only prevents infection by this bacterium and not all infections that cause pneumonia. It is usually given to adults older than 65 years of age, but people with CF should get it after the age of 2.

Pneumothorax: Lung collapse caused by air leaking out from the lungs into the space between the lungs and chest wall, sometimes causing chest pain and shortness of breath. Depending on the severity of the lung collapse, someone with a pneumothorax might require a chest tube to re-expand their lung.

POLST (aka POST, MOST, MOLST): Physician Orders for Life-Sustaining Treatment (POLST) or Medical Orders for Scope of Treatment (MOST or MOLST) are types of advance directives. Each state has its own official document that includes options for life-sustaining treatments in the event of emergencies or a decline in health. This form gives medical orders to emergency personnel based on your current medical situation. You can work with a health care provider and loved ones to complete this form, if you wish.

Polyethylene glycol 3350 (MiraLAX®): A minimally absorbed substance that is used as a gentle laxative to draw water into the digestive tract and treat constipation.

Polyps: Small abnormal and inflammatory tissue growths in the shape of small, flat bumps or mushroom-like stalks. Polyps in the colon are the most common, but it's also possible to develop polyps in the ear canal, nasal passages, throat, and, in females, the cervix. Most are benign, but some can be pre-cancerous with potential to develop into cancer.

Port: Also called a port-a-cath; an implanted device and attached catheter (tube) typically in the upper chest that is used to access a vein for medications or blood draws.

Port-a-cath: *See* mediport or port.

Portal hypertension: Abnormally high pressures in the blood vessels of the liver, often a sign of liver disease.

Portal vein: The largest vein supplying the liver.

Positive expiratory pressure (PEP): A force that is applied by different devices (airway clearance devices and ventilators) to keep the small airways of the lung open during exhalation.

Positive expiratory pressure (PEP) device: A small, portable device that the patient exhales into, creating small pressures in the lungs to open collapsed airways and to help clear the airways of mucus. Some common brands are Flutter®, Acapella®, Quake®, Aerobika®.

Post-market clinical trials: Clinical studies that are performed after a drug has been FDA-approved.

Postpartum depression: Depression that occurs in the mother shortly after the birth of a child.

Postpartum period: The first 6 weeks after childbirth.

Post-traumatic stress disorder (PTSD): A mental health condition that's triggered by experiencing or witnessing a terrifying event (e.g., natural disaster, war/combat, rape, traumatic medical experience). People might experience intrusive thoughts about the event, flashbacks, nightmares, severe anxiety, and might be drawn to avoid objects/situations/people reminding them of this trauma.

Postural drainage (PD): Usually done with manual CPT, in which the patient lies in different positions to allow for better drainage of mucus from the lungs.

Potentiator: A drug that changes the 3-dimensional shape of the CFTR channel to improve chloride transport across the cell membrane.

Power of attorney for health care (aka surrogate, agent, or proxy): An assignment of the power to act in your place to make decisions for you if you become incapacitated, meaning unable to make decisions for yourself. Choosing someone to hold your power of attorney for health care is one type of advance directive.

Power ports: *See* mediport. Power ports have the capability of withstanding high-pressure infusions, such as contrast dye used for certain imaging techniques.

Pre-clinical phase: Research performed on a drug before it is deemed safe to study in humans.

Pre-diabetes: A serious health condition where blood sugars are elevated, but not yet to the levels of being diagnosed with diabetes. It predicts developing CF-related (or another form of) diabetes in the next 3 to 4 years.

Predicted values: Expected normal values.

Prednisone: A corticosteroid medication given to suppress inflammation or a response from the immune system.

Pre-existing condition clause: Prior to the Affordable Care Act, health insurance companies had the ability to deny coverage for an individual who had a medical diagnosis before seeking insurance coverage with the plan.

Preferred provider organization (PPO): A type of health plan in which a network of medical professionals, including hospitals, arrange to provide services to subscribed clients at reduced rates. In such an arrangement, care received by non-participating providers (those "out-of-network") might not be covered.

Pre-implantation genetic diagnosis (PGD): A procedure that can be used during in-vitro fertilization in which embryos are screened for a specific condition, disease, or genetic mutation prior to being implanted in the body.

Premature: Refers to a birth occurring more than 3 weeks prior to the due date.

Premature stop codons: When a cell is reading the nucleic acids of a gene, the nucleic acids are read in groups of three, where each triplet is called a codon. After the protein product is made, the final triplet of nucleic acids will signal to the cell that the protein is complete with a codon called a "stop codon." A premature stop codon is a mutation in which the genetic sequence signals to stop making a protein too soon before the final protein product has been completed.

Premium: A monthly amount paid by the policy holder to purchase a health insurance plan for a specific benefit period. A premium must be paid to keep the coverage active, regardless of whether the policy holder seeks care. Failure to pay the premium by the due date may result in termination of the health insurance policy. It is helpful to note that for employer-sponsored group plans, the employer pays a portion of the premium and the remainder is deducted from the employee's (policy holder's) paycheck. Most insurers require employers to contribute at least half of the premium cost for covered employees.

Prenatal: The period after conception but before birth.

Prenatal genetic testing: Testing that is done before birth to identify genetic conditions in a fetus.

Prenatal screening: Tests to detect problems in a fetus. Some of these tests can be used to detect chromosomal or genetic conditions, such as Down syndrome, CF, or Tay-Sachs disease.

Prescription medications: All medications that need a physician's approval to purchase. These are different than over-the-counter medications that can be purchased without a physician's approval.

Pre-term delivery: Delivery before the predicted due date of the baby.

Prevalence: In epidemiology, the proportion of a population with a specific disease or characteristic.

Primary care provider (PCP): A physician who provides basic medical care, regularly follow ups with the patient, and coordinates their care with specialty physicians.

Primary osteoporosis: Disease of the bone affecting its mass and structure, that is age related, often occurring in later adulthood, and affecting women after menopause more than in men; it is not due to another condition.

Primary palliative care: Palliative care that is provided by one's primary medical team rather than a palliative care specialist. In the case of someone with CF, primary palliative care might be provided by their CF care team.

Prior authorization: A formal review and approval process conducted by your insurance company before it will agree to cover a service, medication, or prescription refill.

Private or commercial insurance: Health insurance that is not administered by the federal or state government. Costs are often shared between the insurance company and the person who is insured.

Procedural distress: Pain, distress, and/or fear associated with needles or medical procedures.

Prognosis: The likely course of the disease.

Progressive muscle relaxation training: A relaxing and effective technique for reducing overall body tension as well as psychological stress. By tensing your muscles before relaxing them, you can relax them more thoroughly after you release, letting go of physical tension more effectively.

Pro-inflammatory leukotriene B4 (LTB4): An inflammatory eicosanoid, or fatty acid metabolite, that plays an important role in neutrophil inflammatory responses.

Prophylactic antibiotics: Medications that are taken to prevent infection in people who are taking immunosuppressive medications. These medicines prevent opportunistic infections, or infections that take advantage of someone with a suppressed immune system, from setting in.

Prospective study: A study that follows a group of individuals over time to assess the effect of an intervention.

Proteins: Complex molecules made up of amino acids that are produced by cells to perform specific biological functions.

Prothrombin time (PT): *See* INR/PT above.

Proton-pump inhibitors (PPIs): A group of drugs that decrease stomach acid production and are used to treat GERD.

Proxy: A person designated to represent the wishes of someone else. If someone becomes too ill to speak on their own behalf, a proxy can make decisions for them.

Pseudomonas aeruginosa: A Gram-negative bacterium that commonly infects the lungs of people with CF.

Pseudomonas cepacia: An older and no-longer used name for the bacterium *Burkholderia cepacia complex.*

Psychiatrist: A licensed, medical doctor who has extensive training in diagnosing and treating psychiatric disorders. Psychiatrists are licensed to prescribe medications for psychiatric disorders and symptoms.

Psychologist: A non-medical doctor who diagnoses and treats emotional and mental suffering with behavioral interventions.

Psychosocial intervention: Educational, interpersonal, or behavioral intervention targeted at mental health or substance use disorders.

Psychotherapist: Mental health professional who treats emotional symptoms and disorders using treatments, or therapies that do not involve medications but can complement medications when medications are felt to be needed. Psychotherapists treat conditions like anxiety and depression and can help people learn ways to cope with stressors.

Psychotherapy: A general term for treating mental health problems by talking with a psychiatrist, psychologist, or other mental health care provider. During psychotherapy, you learn about your condition and your moods, feelings, thoughts, and behaviors.

Psychotic symptoms: Symptoms of psychosis, such as delusions (believing things that are not true), experiencing hallucinations (seeing or hearing things that are not real), or having a thought disorder (illogical thinking).

Puffer: Synonym for inhaler, which is a device designed to turn a medicine (usually a liquid or powder) into an aerosol that is breathed into the lungs.

Pulmonary: Relating to the lung or respiratory system.

Pulmonary arterial pressures: The pressure in the main vessel of the heart that brings blood to the lungs so that it can receive oxygen. Chronic lung diseases like CF can cause this pressure to increase.

Pulmonary exacerbation: Acute worsening of respiratory symptoms (such as increased cough, sputum production, or shortness of breath), associated with a decline in lung function that requires treatment.

Pulmonary function lab: A laboratory where pulmonary function tests are performed.

Pulmonary function tests (PFTs): A general term referring to a variety of non-invasive diagnostic tests used to measure how one's lungs are working; they measure the speed at which air leaves the chest (spirometry), the size of the lungs (plethysmography) and how well the lungs put oxygen into the blood (diffusion capacity).

Pulmonary hypertension: A type of high blood pressure that affects blood flow from your heart to your lungs.

Pulmonary system: The system in the human body that enables us to breathe. It includes the upper respiratory tract (nose, mouth, and the beginning of the trachea) and the lower respiratory tract (the trachea, the bronchi, broncheoli, and the lungs).

Pulmonologist: A doctor who diagnoses and treats lung diseases.

Pulmozyme®: A cough medicine that makes mucus thinner and looser.

Pulse oximetry: A test that measures the saturation of oxygen in the blood using a sensor typically attached to a finger, toe, or ear.

QT-interval: One of many specific parts of the cardiac cycle that is measured on an electrocardiogram.

Quake®: The brand name of a positive expiratory pressure airway oscillating device used for airway clearance.

Qualitative interviews: Interviews during which researchers ask questions and participants answer.

Radial artery: A major artery in the human forearm. An artery is a large blood vessel, usually carrying oxygenated blood.

Radiologist: A doctor who diagnoses diseases with medical imaging procedures (exams/tests) such as X-rays, computed tomography (CT), magnetic resonance imaging (MRI), nuclear medicine, positron emission tomography (PET), and ultrasound, and who may perform image-guided procedures.

Randomized, controlled feasibility study: A randomized study is a research design in which participants are assigned to a treatment or control group; in a feasibility study the goal is to evaluate whether the treatment is effective and practical in the "real world."

Ranitidine: A medication in a class called histamine-2 receptor antagonists that serves to reduce the amount of acid in the stomach.

Rectal prolapse: A condition in which the rectum, or last part of the large intestines, drops down outside of the anus.

Red blood cells (RBCs): Cells in the blood that carry oxygen.

Re-do lung transplantation: Lung transplantation that is done after the originally transplanted lungs fail.

Registered Dietitian (RD): Trained nutrition clinician who has passed necessary certification.

Rehabilitation Act of 1973: A law that prohibits discrimination on the basis of disability in programs conducted by federal agencies, in programs receiving federal financial assistance, in federal employment and in the employment practices of federal contractors.

Rejection: A medical condition in which the immune system has recognized a transplanted organ as "foreign" and is attacking the transplanted organ.

Relaxation response: Your personal ability to release chemicals and brain signals that make your muscles and organs slow down and increase blood flow to the brain.

Relaxation training: Relaxation training is any method, process, procedure, or activity that helps a person to relax; to attain a state of increased calmness; or otherwise reduce levels of pain, anxiety, stress, or anger.

Repaglinide (Prandin®): An oral medication used in diabetes that works by stimulating the pancreas to release more insulin.

Research coordinator: A person responsible for coordinating and conducting clinical trials using good clinical practice, under the direction of a principal investigator.

Research team: A group of people working together toward a common research goal. Clinical research team members often have direct contact with study participants, have contact with participants' identifiable or biological samples, or have access to participants' personal information. Often in CF research, the team will be your standard-of-care team members, as well.

Resistance exercise: Exercises targeted to an individual muscle or group of muscles to increase their size and strength. Resistance training can use free weights, weight machines, resistance bands, or even one's own body weight to increase the size and strength of the targeted muscle.

Respiration: The action of breathing.

Respiratory depression: Hypoventilation, or slow, shallow breathing that is ineffective for adequate exchange of oxygen and carbon dioxide between the lungs and the blood.

Respiratory failure: Refers to failing of the function of the lungs usually from an underlying cause affecting normal exchange of oxygen and carbon dioxide.

Respiratory therapist (RT): A medical care provider who specializes in giving breathing treatments, performing breathing tests (pulmonary function tests), and managing ventilators in the hospital setting. Respiratory therapists work closely with the team of doctors in ensuring that patients receive the highest quality care. The RT evaluates the effectiveness of respiratory therapies and techniques and educates the individual with CF and their family about respiratory care.

Restorative sleep: The combination of deep sleep and rapid eye movement (REM) stage of sleep that we enter each night. These stages of sleep are thought to be where our bodies and minds undergo the most renewal.

Restrictive lung disease: Chronic lung conditions that limit the ability of a person's lungs to expand during inhalation. Examples include interstitial lung disease and sarcoidosis.

Retinoids: A class of chemical compounds that are related to vitamin A and are believed to play a role in epithelial cell growth.

Retrospective study: Studies that are performed by looking at events that have already occurred. Typically, the data is obtained by chart-review.

Reversible kidney dysfunction: Temporary loss of kidney function due to an acute problem (such as active infection). Reversible kidney dysfunction generally improves with treatment of the underlying problem. Rarely, people with reversible kidney dysfunction will require dialysis while waiting for their kidney function to return.

Rib fracture: A small break in a rib bone of the chest wall that often causes pain on the side of the chest wall.

Rifampin: An antibiotic that can be used to treat a wide range of infections.

Right heart catheterization: A medical test to study the function of the heart. During the test, a doctor will insert a thin catheter into the heart to measure the blood flow and oxygen levels.

Right heart dysfunction: The condition when the right side of the heart has difficulty pumping deoxygenated blood through the pulmonary artery and into the lungs.

Salt supplementation: The practice of adding extra salt to the diet of people with CF to replace that lost in sweat.

Scedosporium species complex: A fungal organism that can causes a wide variety of infections in humans and animals.

School avoidance: Refusal to go to or delaying going to school due to negative there experiences.

Screening test: A screening test is intended as a preventative test used in a population of people to identify those at risk for a disease. This test, if positive, often requires a confirmatory test to make a diagnosis.

Secondary osteoporosis: Osteoporosis developing due to another disease, such as CF.

Seizures: A sudden disturbance in brain's electrical activity leading to abnormal movements, feelings, and behaviors, as well as possible loss of consciousness.

Selective serotonin re-uptake inhibitors (SSRIs): A medication class used to treat depression and anxiety. They work by increasing the activity of a chemical called serotonin in the brain.

Septum: A partition that separates two chambers; humans, for example, have a septum in the heart between the chambers as well as a septum in the nose separating the nares.

Serotonin: An important chemical and neurotransmitter that the body produces. It has a wide variety of functions including helping to regulate mood, appetite, and sleep.

Serotonin syndrome: This occurs when too much serotonin accumulates in the body. Serotonin syndrome can lead to fever, confusion, agitation, tremor, sweating, and diarrhea.

Sertraline (Zoloft®): A medication used to treat depression and anxiety. It belongs to a group of medicines known as selective serotonin re-uptake inhibitors that work by increasing the activity of a chemical called serotonin in the brain.

Sexually transmitted infections (STIs): A group of infections that can be transmitted through sexual contact. This group includes, HPV, herpes, chlamydia, gonorrhea, HIV/AIDS, syphilis, and trichomoniasis.

Shunting: When blood bypasses the lung and does not pick up oxygen to carry to the rest of the body.

Side effects/adverse events: An unfavorable change in the health of a study participant, including abnormal laboratory findings, that happens during a clinical trial or within a certain amount of time after a clinical trial, whether or not it is caused by the study or the study medication.

Sign: An objective, observable, or measurable evidence of disease (e.g., crackles on listening to the chest; obstruction on pulmonary function testing).

Single lumen ports: *See* double lumen port.

Sinus disease: Any of a number of medical conditions that can affect the sinuses, which are normal air-filled cavities within the face. The sinuses are frequently infected and inflamed in CF.

Sinuses: Air-filled spaces surrounding the nose and within the facial bones that aid in the humidification and purification of the air that we breathe.

Sinusitis: Inflammation of the mucus layer lining the sinuses around the nose, often leading to nasal congestion and facial pain and pressure.

Sleep apnea: A type of sleep disorder characterized by repeated interruption in the normal breathing pattern.

Sleep hygiene: Recommended behavioral and environmental practices intended to promote better quality sleep.

Social Security Administration (SSA): The agency in the United States federal government that administers Social Security, a social insurance program consisting of retirement, disability, and survivors' benefits.

Social Security Disability Income (SSDI): Income available to workers who have accumulated a sufficient number of work credits.

Social worker: A clinician who provides access to resources, coordinates services to help with the financial and legal aspects of living with a chronic illness, assesses the psychological impact of the disease on the patient and their family, helps with parenting issues, and promotes self-management and quality of life. A social worker will assess and counsel you on the emotional, social, and financial aspects of living with CF as well as provide guidance to help navigate health insurance, work, school, and life transitions.

Sodium channel: A channel on cell membranes that transports sodium from one side of the cell to the other.

Spasmodic cough: A coughing fit.

Spirometer: A machine that records the airflow of your breaths.

Spirometry: The measuring of breath using a spirometer.

SpO$_2$: Stands for peripheral capillary oxygen saturation, which is an estimate of the amount of oxygen in the blood.

Sponsor: An individual, company, institution or organization that takes responsibility for the initiation, management, and/or financing of a clinical trial.

Sputum culture: A test used to detect the presence of microbes in the sputum.

Stage of change: A model of counseling that helps providers identify where a patient is on their journey to behavior change and be able to tailor the support or advice provided to the patient's needs and motivations at that time.

Standardized care guidelines: A set of standardized terms that record a person's physical exam findings, circumstances, events, and interventions in detail to inform a standardized approach to clinical care, decision making, research, and quality improvement.

Staphylococcus aureus: A Gram-positive, round-shaped bacterium that is often found on the skin and respiratory tract.

Steatorrhea: Fat in stool, either observed or measured in the laboratory.

Stenotrophomonas maltophilia: A Gram-negative bacterium that is uncommon but difficult to treat.

Steroid: A medication given to suppress the immune system and commonly used to prevent rejection in transplant patients. Common side effects include weight gain, high blood pressure, high blood sugars, and restlessness/anxiety.

Stigma: Attitudes experienced and expressed by certain people viewing you in a negative way because you have a distinguishing characteristic or personal trait that's thought to be, or actually might be, disadvantageous.

Stimulant medications: A group of medications used to treat attention-deficit hyperactivity disorder.

Stomach ulcers: Typically painful sores that can develop on the lining of the stomach.

Stool: Food waste that is passed through the rectum.

Stool elastase testing: A laboratory test used to evaluate the digestive function of the pancreas.

Strengthening exercise: Exercises targeted to an individual muscle or group of muscles to increase their size and strength.

Sucrose: A common sugar.

Summary of benefits and coverage (SBC): An easy-to-read summary that lets the patient make apples-to-apples comparisons of costs and coverage between health plans. You can compare options based on price, benefits, and other features that might be of importance.

Sun sensitivity: A medication side effect in which a person has a higher chance of developing a sunburn. This can be avoided through avoiding sun exposure, wearing long-sleeved clothing and wide-brimmed hats, and applying sunscreen.

Supplemental oxygen: Also known as oxygen therapy. Your health care provider can order this therapy to provide your body with extra oxygen to support vital bodily functions. You will use an oxygen concentrator that delivers higher concentrations of oxygen than what is available in the air using a nasal cannula, CPAP, or BiPAP machine.

Supplemental Security Income (SSI): A United States federal welfare program that provides cash assistance to individuals residing in the United States who are either aged 65 or older, blind, or disabled.

Support Families Program: A peer-support program through Claire's Place Foundation Incorporated, in which newly diagnosed or isolated families can seek support and guidance from other families in the CF community. Families affected by CF can also become registered Support Families.

Surgeon: A doctor who performs operations to treat disease, injury, or deformity.

Surrogacy: When a woman agrees to become pregnant and give birth to a child on behalf of another person or couple who want to become parents.

Survivor's guilt: An emotional/mental health condition when someone feels guilty and as if they have done something wrong by surviving a traumatic event, when others have not survived.

Susceptibility testing: A test to determine which antimicrobial can kill a microbe, and how effectively.

Sweat chloride: A test to measure the amount of chloride in a person's sweat. This test serves to measure the function of a person's CFTR proteins.

Sweat gland: A tube-like structure, found in the deeper layers of skin, that secretes sweat.

Sweat test: A laboratory test in which the concentration of chloride in the sweat is measured. In individuals presenting with a positive newborn screen, clinical features consistent with CF, or a positive family history, a diagnosis of CF can be made if the sweat chloride value is greater than or equal to 60 mmol/L.

Sweat testing: A procedure that stimulates the sweat glands to make sweat and measures the amount of chloride (salt) in it as a way to diagnose CF. People with CF have more chloride in their sweat than people without CF.

Symptom: A subjective feeling related to a medical or emotional condition. Symptoms can be chronic (i.e., present most or all of the time), or acute (i.e., meaning sudden or new). Examples of common symptoms include shortness of breath, pain, and anxiety.

Symptom-free: The absence of symptoms.

Synovitis: Inflammation of fluid surrounding bone.

Syphilis: A sexually transmitted infection that can infect the entire body and cause serious problems if left untreated.

Tacrolimus: A medication given to suppress the immune system in a patient who has received an organ transplant.

Teratogenic: Drugs or medications that can be harmful to a developing fetus.

Testes: The oval organs located in the scrotum of the male reproductive system that produce and store sperm. The testes also produce testosterone.

Tetanus, Diphtheria, and Pertussis (TDaP): A vaccine that is usually given to children to prevent three bacterial infections. Pertussis is commonly referred to as "whooping cough."

Tetrahydrocannabinol (THC): The "psychoactive" agent in marijuana/cannabis that is responsible for the "high" sensation.

Tezacaftor-ivacaftor (Symdeko®): A combination of two CFTR-modulator medications.

The CF Roundtable: A quarterly publication by CF adults for the CF community.

Therapeutic Development Center (TDC): The CF Foundation-sponsored and accredited CF research center within a single CF center.

Therapeutic Development Network (TDN): A network of CF Foundation–sponsored research centers nationwide and a centralized coordinating center that helps shape, standardize, and ensure the forward progress of CF-specific clinical trials.

Therapy: Treatment.

Thoracic expansion exercises (TEE): Deep-breathing exercises with breath holds designed to help with airway clearance as a part of active cycle of breathing.

Thrombosis: Thickening of blood into a blood clot.

Tobi®: An antibiotic (nebulized tobramycin) used to treat lung infections.

Tobi Podhaler: A brand name formulation of tobramycin via inhaler.

Tobramycin: An antibiotic in the aminoglycoside class used to treat Gram-negative bacterial infections (e.g., *Pseudomonas* organisms). It is used intravenously or via inhalation to treat some CF-related organisms.

Trachea: The tube that connects the mouth to the lungs. It is the main airway of the body.

Traditional surrogacy: An uncommon form of surrogacy where a woman agrees to be inseminated and give birth to a child for another person or couple who want to become parents. In traditional surrogacy, the child is biologically related to the woman who becomes pregnant.

Triglycerides: A type of fat in the blood that is created when your body breaks down nutrients to store in fat cells, which are released later for energy between meals.

Tryptophan: An essential amino acid necessary for growth in infants and for nitrogen balance in adults. It is commonly found in meat, fish, spinach, bananas, eggs, oats, pumpkin seeds, and sesame seeds.

Type 1 diabetes: A type of diabetes in which the pancreatic beta cells are destroyed through an autoimmune process leading to no insulin production.

Type 2 diabetes: A condition in which the pancreas is able to make insulin, but the body is less responsive to it (i.e., insulin resistance) and therefore cannot control blood sugars.

Ultrasound: An imaging method that uses high-frequency sound waves to visualize structures within your body. These images can provide valuable information for diagnosing and treating many diseases.

Urinary incontinence: Involuntary leakage of urine.

Ursodiol (Actigall®): A medication used to improve bile flow and reduce inflammation in the liver.

Vaccine: An injection that causes the body to create protection against common infections through the production of antibodies.

Vaginal rings: A form of hormonal birth control, inserted into the vagina, which is used to prevent pregnancy.

Valganciclovir: An antifungal medication.

Vancomycin: An antibiotic medication that treats infections due to certain bacterial agents.

Vaping: Inhaling and exhaling the vapor produced by an electronic cigarette or similar device.

Varenicline (Chantix®): A prescription medication that can be used to help quit smoking.

Varices: Enlarged blood vessels often in the esophagus and stomach, due to portal hypertension.

Vas deferens: Part of the male reproductive system; the sperm canal that carries sperm from the testes to the ejaculatory duct.

Vasectomy: A form of birth control where a man's vas deferens are cut or blocked to prevent pregnancy. This procedure can sometimes, but not always, be reversed.

Vena cava: A large vein that carries deoxygenated blood back to the heart.

Ventilator: Machine used to help someone breathe when their lungs are too sick to breathe on their own. Requires an endotracheal tube (breathing tube inserted through the mouth or nose) or a tracheostomy (breathing tube inserted directly into the windpipe through the neck) for use. This is an "invasive" form of ventilation, as opposed to non-invasive ventilation (see the earlier definition).

Vest therapy: An airway clearance technique that uses an inflatable vest to loosen and mobilize secretions. The vest attaches by hoses to an air pulse generator producing pressures to about 50 cm H_2O at frequencies of 5 to 25 Hz.

Vibration: The application of manual shaking of the chest wall usually during exhale to help mobilize secretions.

Virtual group therapy: A type of group therapy session that can be conducted via the internet (e.g., Skype) or phone. Often delivered through telehealth services at hospitals, group therapy for individuals with CF eliminates concerns about cross-infection.

Vitamin: A compound essential for normal growth and nutrition.

Vitamin D: A fat-soluble vitamin important for bone metabolism.

Volvulus: A type of abdominal obstruction in which a loop of intestine wraps around itself. This can be quite painful and cause nausea, vomiting, abdominal bloating, constipation, and at times blood in stool.

Wait list: The list of patients who need an organ transplant and are waiting for an organ to become available. Patients on the wait list continue to see their doctors and the lung transplant team.

WindSprints Podcast: A series of videos produced by Jerry Cahill and the Boomer Esiason Foundation answering questions of general interest to the CF population.

World Health Organization (WHO): A specialized agency run by the United Nations that promotes the health of people worldwide.

X-ray guidance: Using X-rays to obtain real-time images of the internal structures of a person to allow for accurate identification and performance of various radiologic and surgical procedures.

Yoga: A series of postures and movements accompanied by deep breathing and relaxation. It aims to increase physical flexibility, mindfulness, and integration of physical and emotional health.

REFERENCES

1. Abbot A: Depression: The radical theory linking it to inflammation. *Nature*. 2018; 557: 663–634.

2. Abbott J, Morton AM, Musson H, et al: Nutritional status, perceived body image and eating behaviours in adults with cystic fibrosis. *Clinical Nutrition*. 2007; 26(1): 91–99.

3. Abraham JM, Taylor CJ: Cystic fibrosis & disorders of the large intestine: DIOS, constipation, and colorectal cancer. *Journal of Cystic Fibrosis*. Best Practices in the Management of the Gastrointestinal Aspects of Cystic Fibrosis, 2017; 16 (November): S40–49.

4. Accurso FJ, Sontag MK, Wagener JS: Complications associated with symptomatic diagnosis in infants with cystic fibrosis. *Journal of Pediatrics*. 2005: S37–S41.

5. ACPA Resource Guide to Pain Medications and Treatments: An Integrated Guide to Medical, Interventional, Behavioral, Pharmacologic and Rehabilitation Therapies, 2019 Edition. American Chronic Pain Association. Accessed on 5/27/19 at https://www.theacpa.org/wp-content/uploads/2019/02/ACPA_Resource_Guide_2019.pdf.

6. Adult Lung Transplants. Kaplan-Meier Survival by Major Diagnosis, International Society for Heart and Lung Transplantation. 2018.

7. Ahmad A, Ahmed A, Patrizio P: Cystic fibrosis and fertility. *Current Opinion in Obstetrics and Gynecology*. 2013; 25(3): 167.

8. Akbar M, Egli M, Cho YE, et al: Medications for alcohol use disorders: An overview. *Pharmacology Therapy*. 2018; 185: 64–85.

9. Allgood SJ, Kozachik S, Alexander KA, et al: Descriptions of the pain experience in adults and adolescents with cystic fibrosis. *Pain Management Nursing*. 2018 Aug; 19(4): 340–347. doi: 10.1016/j.pmn.2017.11.011. Epub 2018 Mar 1.

10. American College of Obstetricians and Gynecologists (ACOG). (2017). Cystic Fibrosis: Prenatal Screening and Diagnosis. Retrieved from https://www.acog.org/Patients/FAQs/Cystic-Fibrosis-Prenatal-Screening-and-Diagnosis?IsMobileSet=false#futures.

11. American Psychiatric Association: Diagnostic and Statistical Manual of Mental Disorders (5th ed.). Arlington, VA: American Psychiatric Publishing, 2013.

12. Andersen HO, Hjelt K, Waever E, et al: The age-related incidence of meconium ileus equivalent in a cystic fibrosis population: The impact of high-energy intake. *Journal of Pediatric Gastroenterology and Nutrition*.1990; 11(3): 356–360.

13. APA: *Diagnostic and Statistical Manual of Mental Disorders*, 5th ed. (DSM-5). Washington, DC, American Psychiatric Association, 2013.

14. Aslund C, Larm P, Starrin B, et al: The buffering effect of tangible social support on financial stress: Influence on psychological well-being and psychosomatic symptoms in a large sample of the adult general population. *International Journal of Equity Health*. 2014; 13(1): 1.

15. Assis DN, Freedman SD: Gastrointestinal disorders in cystic fibrosis. *Clinics in Chest Medicine*. 2016; 37: 109–118.

16. Aswani N, Taylor CJ, McGaw J, et al: Pubertal growth and development in cystic fibrosis: A retrospective review. *Acta Paediatrica*. 2003; 92(9): 1029–1032.

17. Ayers S, Muller I, Mahoney L: Understanding needle-related distress in children with cystic fibrosis. *British Journal of Health Psychology*. 2010; 16(2): 329–343.

18. Baker SS, Borowitz D, Duffy L, et al: Pancreatic enzyme therapy and clinical outcomes in patients with cystic fibrosis. *Journal of Pediatrics*. 2005; 146(2): 189–193.

19. Balfour-Lynn IM, Welch K: Inhaled corticosteroids for cystic fibrosis. *Cochrane Database of Systematic Reviews*. 2009:CD001915.

20. Barker DH, Quittner AL: Parental depression and pancreatic enzymes adherence in children with cystic fibrosis. *Pediatrics*. 2016; 137(2): e20152296.

21. Barker H, Moses J, O'Leary C: 'I've got to prioritise': Being a parent with cystic fibrosis. *Psychology, Health & Medicine*. 2017; 22(6): 744–752.

22. Barrett TW, Moran GJ: Methicillin-resistant Staphylococcus aureus infections among competitive sports participants—Colorado, Indiana, Pennsylvania, and Los Angeles County, 2000-2003. *Annals of Emergency Medicine*. 2004; 43: 43–47.

23. Bennett DS, O'Hayer CV, Wolfe W, et al: ACT with CF, reducing anxiety and depression among individuals with cystic fibrosis through Acceptance and Commitment Therapy: A treatment manual including adaptation for telehealth. *Unpublished Manual*. p. 6.

24. Bernstein D, Borkovec T, Hazlett-Stevens H: *New directions in progressive relaxation training: A guidebook for helping professionals.* 2000; Westport, CT: Praeger Publishers.

25. Berry PH, Chapman CR, Covington EC, et al, eds.: Pain: Current Understanding of Assessment, Management, and Treatments. National Pharmaceutical Council, 2001. Accessed May 30, 2019, at http://www.npcnow.org/publication/pain-current-understanding-assessmentmanagement-and-treatments.

26. Besier T, Born A, Henrich G, et al: Anxiety, depression, and life satisfaction in parents caring for children with cystic fibrosis. *Pediatric Pulmonology.* 2011; 46(7): 672–682.

27. Biazotti MC, Pinto Junior W, Albuquerque MC, et al: Preimplantation genetic diagnosis for cystic fibrosis: A case report. *Einstein (São Paulo).* 2015; 13(1): 110–113.

28. Biddick R, Spilker T, Martin A, et al: Evidence of transmission of *Burkholderia cepacia*, *Burkholderia multivorans* and *Burkholderia dolosa* among persons with cystic fibrosis. *FEMS Microbiology Letter.* 2003; 228: 57-62.

29. Birnie KA, Noel M, Parker JA, et al: Systematic review and meta-analysis of distraction and hypnosis for needle-related pain and distress in children and adolescents. *Journal of Pediatric Psychology.* 2014; 39(8): 783–808.

30. Bishay LC, Sawicki GS: Strategies to optimize treatment adherence in adolescent patients with cystic fibrosis. *Adolescent Health, Medicine and Therapeutics.* 2016; 7: 117–124.

31. Blount RL, Piira T, Cohen LL: Management of pediatric pain and distress due to painful medical procedures. In: Roberts MC, ed.: *Handbook of Pediatric Psychology.* 3rd ed. New York: Guilford Press; 2003: pp. 216–233.

32. Blubond-Langner M: *In the Shadow of Illness: Parents and Siblings of the Chronically Ill Child*, Princeton University Press; 1996.

33. Bombieri C, Claustres M, De Boeck K, et al: Recommendations for the classification of diseases as CFTR-related disorders. *Journal of Cystic Fibrosis.* 2011; 10 Suppl 2: S86–102.

34. Borowitz D, Robinson KA, Rosenfeld M, et al: Cystic Fibrosis Foundation evidence-based guidelines for management of infants with cystic fibrosis. *Journal of Pediatrics.* 2009; 155(Suppl 6): S73–S93.

35. Borrelli B, Riekert KA, Weinstein A, et al: Brief motivational interviewing as a clinical strategy to promote asthma medication adherence. *Journal of Allergy and Clinical Immunology.* 2007; 120(5): 1023–1030.

36. Borschuk AP, Everhart S, Eakin MN, et al: Disease disclosure in individuals with cystic fibrosis: Association with psychosocial and health outcomes. *Journal of Cystic Fibrosis: Official Journal of the European Cystic Fibrosis Society.* 2016; 15(5): 696–702.

37.   Bourdeau TL, Mullins LL, Carpentier MY, et al: An examination of parenting variables and child self-care behavior across disease groups. *Journal of Developmental and Physical Disabilities*. 2007; 19: 125–134.

38.   Boyd JM, Mehta A, Murphy DJ: Fertility and pregnancy outcomes in men and women with cystic fibrosis in the United Kingdom. *Human Reproduction*. 2004; 19: 2238–2243.

39.   Bradley JM, Moran F: Physical training for cystic fibrosis. *Cochrane Database of Systematic Reviews*. 2008: 1.

40.   Brinson GM, Peadar G, Noone MA, et al: Bronchial artery embolization for the treatment of hemoptysis in patients with cystic fibrosis. *American Journal of Respiratory and Critical Care Medicine*. 1998; 157(6): 1951–1958.

41.   Brochard L: Mechanical ventilation: Invasive versus noninvasive. *European Respiratory Journal*. 2003; 22: 31s–37s.

42.   Broekema K, Weber KM: Disclosures of cystic fibrosis-related information to romantic partners. *Qualitative Health Research*. 2017; 27(10): 1575–1585.

43.   Brown T: FDA Panel Recommends Mannitol Inhalation Powder for CF. May 9, 2019. Retrieved June 12, 2019, from: https://www.medscape.com/viewarticle/912853. UBuck H: 10 Things I Wish I Knew Before Coming to College. https://www.cff.org/CF-Community-Blog/Posts/2015/10-Things-I-Wish-I-Knew-Before-Coming-to-College/ 2015.

44.   Budev MM, Arroliga AC, Emery S: Exacerbation of underlying pulmonary disease in pregnancy. *Critical Care Medicine*. 2005; 33(10 Suppl): S313–318.

45.   Burden C, Ion R, Chung Y, et al: Current pregnancy outcomes in women with cystic fibrosis. *European Journal of Obstetrics & Gynecology and Reproductive Biology*. 2012; 164(2): 142–145.

46.   Button BM, Button B: Structure and function of the mucus clearance system of the lung. *Cold Spring Harbor Perspectives in Medicine*. 3: 2013.

47.   Canistro D, Vivarelli F, Cirillo S, et al: E-cigarettes induce toxicological effects that can raise the cancer risk. *Scientific Reports*. 2017; 7: 2028.

48.   Casey SC, Ellison O, Fulton J, et al: Cystic Fibrosis Foundation herbal products fact sheet: Use of herbal products in cystic fibrosis. 2010. Retrieved June 13, 2019, from: https://www.cff.org/PDF-Archive/Herbal-Products-Fact-Sheet/.

49.   Castellani C, Massie J, Sontage M, et al: Newborn screening for cystic fibrosis. *Lancet Respiratory Medicine*. 2016: 653–661.

50. Center for Pediatric Traumatic Stress at the Children's Hospital of Philadelphia and Nemours/Alfred I du Pont Hospital for Children, a partner in the National Child Traumatic Stress Network. https://www.chop.edu/conditions-diseases/pediatric-traumatic-stress.

51. Centers for Disease Control and Prevention (CDC). (2018). Contraception. Retrieved from https://www.cdc.gov/reproductivehealth/contraception/index.htm.

52. CF and Mental Health: Building Resilience – A Guide for Parents and Caregivers. 20193/29/2019.

53. *CFTR2 Mutation List History*. 2015. http://cftr2.org/mutations_history.php.

54. Channon SJ, Huws-Thomas MV, Rollnick S, et al: A multicenter randomized controlled trial of motivational interviewing in teenagers with diabetes. *Diabetes Care.* 2007; 30: 1390–1395.

55. Chavkin DE, Molinaro TA, Roe AH, et al: Donor sperm insemination cycles: Are two inseminations better than one? *Journal of Andrology.* 2012; 33(3): 375–380.

56. Cheng EY, Goss CH, McKone EF, et al: Aggressive prenatal care results in successful fetal outcomes in CF women. *Fibrosis, 5 SRC – BaiduScholar.* 2006: 85–91.

57. Cheng K, Ashby D, Smyth RL: Ursodeoxycholic acid for cystic fibrosis-related liver disease. *Cochrane Database of Systematic Reviews.* 2017: CD000222.

58. Chotirmall SH, Smith SG, Gunaratnam C, et al: Effect of estrogen on pseudomonas mucoidy and exacerbations in cystic fibrosis. *New England Journal of Medicine.* 2012; 366(21): 1978–1986.

59. Clarke EA, Watson P, Freeston JE, et al: Assessing arthritis in the context of cystic fibrosis. *Pediatric Pulmonology.* 2019: 1–8.

60. Claustres M: Molecular pathology of the CFTR locus in male infertility. *Reproductive Biomed Online.* 2005; 10(1): 14–41.

61. COBRA Coverage and Health Insurance Marketplace Options. HealthCare.gov. www.healthcare.gov/unemployed/cobra-coverage/.

62. Coffey M, Whitaker V, Gentin N, et al: Differences in outcomes between early and late diagnosis of cystic fibrosis in the newborn screening era. *The Journal of Pediatrics.* 2017: 137–145.

63. Cohen-Cymberknoh M, Tanny T, Breuer O, et al: Attention deficit hyperactivity disorder symptoms in patients with cystic fibrosis. *Journal of Cystic Fibrosis: Official Journal of the European Cystic Fibrosis Society.* 2018; 17(2): 281–285.

64. Cotten SW, Bender LM, Willis MS: Multiple positive sweat chloride tests in an infant asymptomatic for cystic fibrosis. *Laboratory Medicine.* 2012: 1–5.

65.   Cunningham JC, Taussig LM, eds. *An Introduction to Cystic Fibrosis For Parents and Their Families.* Bethesda, MD: Cystic Fibrosis Foundation; 2013.

66.   Cystic Fibrosis Foundation (2019, March). Caring for a child with CF. Retrieved from https://www.cff.org/Life-With-CF/Caring-for-a-Child-With-CF/.

67.   Cystic Fibrosis Foundation (2019, March). Drug development pipeline. Retrieved from https://www.cff.org/trials/pipeline.

68.   *Cystic Fibrosis Foundation Annual Patient Registry Report.* (2014). Retrieved from Bethesda, MD.

69.   Cystic Fibrosis Foundation Patient Registry 2017 Annual Data Report. Bethesda, Maryland. © 2018 Cystic Fibrosis Foundation.

70.   Cystic Fibrosis Foundation Patient Registry Highlights. 2017. www.cff.org/Research/ Researcher-Resources/Patient-Registry/2017-Cystic-Fibrosis-Foundation-Patient-Registry-Highlights.pdf.

71.   Cystic Fibrosis Foundation: 2012. *CF Care Guidelines: Nutrition & GI.* http://www.cff. org/treatments/CFCareGuidelines/Nutrition/.

72.   Cystic Fibrosis Foundation: 2012. *Consider Tube Feeding.* https://www.cff.org/Life-With-CF/Daily-Life/Fitness-and-Nutrition/Nutrition/Tube-Feeding-Another-Healthy-Option/Consider-Tube-Feeding/.

73.   Cystic Fibrosis Foundation: Drug Development Pipeline. Retrieved June 12, 2019, from: https://www.cff.org/Trials/Pipeline.

74.   Cystic Fibrosis Foundation: Nebulizer Care at Home. Retrieved June 12, 2019, from: https://www.cff.org/Life-With-CF/Treatments-and-Therapies/Medications/ Nebulizer-Care-at-Home/.

75.   Cystic Fibrosis Foundation: Vitamins. Retrieved June 13, 2019, from: https://www. cff.org/Life-With-CF/Daily-Life/Fitness-and-Nutrition/Nutrition/Getting-Your-Nutrients/Vitamins/.

76.   Davidson L, Chinman M, Sells D, et al: Peer support among adults with serious mental illness: A report from the field. *Schizophrenia Bulletin.* 2006; 32: 443–450.

77.   De Boeck K, Weren M, Proesmans M, et al: Pancreatitis among patients with cystic fibrosis: Correlation with pancreatic status and genotype. *Pediatrics.* 2005; 115(4): e463–469.

78.   Deighan M, Ash S, McMorrow R: Anaesthesia for parturients with severe cystic fibrosis: A case series. *International Journal of Obstetric Anesthesia.* 2014; 23(1): 75–79.

79.   DeLambo K, Ievers-Landis C, Drotar, D, et al: Association of observed family relationship quality and problem-solving skills with treatment adherence in older children and adolescents with cystic fibrosis. *Journal of Pediatric Psychology.* 2004; 29(5): 343–353.

80.   Dell B: CF is an inherently angry disease but we can't let it win: Part 1. 2019.

81.   Dell B: CF is an inherently angry disease but we can't let it win: Part 2. https:// cysticfibrosisnewstoday.com/2018/02/27/cf-is-an-inherently-angry-disease-but- we-cant-let-it-win-part-2-peace/ 2019.

82.   Dellon EP, Goggin J, Chen E, et al: Defining palliative care in cystic fibrosis: A Delphi study. *Journal of Cystic Fibrosis.* 2018; 17: 416–421.

83.   Diclemente CC, Prochaska JO, Fairhurst S, et al: The process of smoking cessation: An analysis of pre-contemplation, contemplation, and preparation stages of change. *Journal of Consult Clinical Psychology.* 1991; 59: 295–304.

84.   DiMatteo MR: Social support and patient adherence to medical treatment: A meta-analysis. *Health Psychology.* 2004; 23(2): 207.

85.   Doherty Y, Roberts S: Motivational interviewing in diabetes practice. *Diabetic Medicine: A Journal of the British Diabetic Association.* 2002; 19 (Suppl 3): 1–6.

86.   Dubovsky AN, Arvikar S, Stern TA, et al: The neuropsychiatric complications of glucocorticoid use: Steroid psychosis revisited. *Psychosomatics.* 2012; 53(2): 103–115.

87.   Duff AJ, Latchford GJ: Motivational interviewing for adherence problems in cystic fibrosis. *Pediatric Pulmonology.* 2010; 45(3): 211–220.

88.   Edenborough FP, Borgo G, Knoop C, et al: Guidelines for the management of pregnancy in women with cystic fibrosis. *Journal of Cystic Fibrosis.* 2008; 7 (Suppl 1): S2–32.

89.   Edenborough FP, Mackenzie WE, Stableforth DE: The outcome of 72 pregnancies in 55 women with cystic fibrosis in the United Kingdom 1977-1996. *BJOG.* 2000; 107(2): 254–261.

90.   Edinger JD, Carney CE: *Overcoming Insomnia: A Cognitive-Behavioral Approach – Therapist Guide.* New York, NY: Oxford University Press; 2015.

91.   Elphick HE, Mallory G: Oxygen therapy for cystic fibrosis. *Cochrane Database of Systematic Reviews.* 2013; 7. DOI: 10.1002/14651858.CD003884.pub4

92.   Engle JL, Mermelstein R, Baker TB, et al: Effects of motivation phase intervention components on quit attempts in smokers unwilling to quit: A factorial experiment. *Drug & Alcohol Dependence.* 2019; 197: 149–157.

93.   Ergan B, Akgun M, Pacilli AMG, et al: Should I stay or should I go? COPD and air travel. *European Respiratory Reviews.* 2018; 27: 1–13.

94. Evon DM, Burker EJ, Sedway JA, et al: Tobacco and alcohol use in lung transplant candidates and recipients. *Clinical Transplantation*. 2005; 19(2): 207–214.

95. Farrell PM, Kosorok MR, Rock MJ, et al: Early diagnosis of cystic fibrosis through neonatal screening prevents severe malnutrition and improves long-term growth. Wisconsin Cystic Fibrosis Neonatal Screening Study Group. *Pediatrics*. 2001: 1.

96. Farrell PM, Li Z, Kosorok MR, et al: Bronchopulmonary disease in children with cystic fibrosis after early or delayed diagnosis. *American Journal of Respiratory and Critical Care Medicine*. 2003: 1100.

97. Farrell PM, Rosenstein BJ, White TB, et al: Guidelines for diagnosis of cystic fibrosis in newborns through older adults: Cystic Fibrosis Foundation consensus report. *Journal of Pediatrics*. 2008: S4–S14.

98. Farrell PM, White TB, Ren CL, et al: Diagnosis of cystic fibrosis: Consensus Guidelines from the Cystic Fibrosis Foundation. *Journal of Pediatrics*. 2017: S4–S15.

99. Fauroux B, Pepin JL, Boelle PY, et al: Sleep quality and nocturnal hypoxemia and hypercapnia in children and young adults with cystic fibrosis. *Archives of Disease in Childhood*. 2012; 97(11): 960–966.

100. FDA Clinical Trial Glossary File. https://www.fda.gov.

101. Filigno SS, Strong E, Hente, et al: Promoting school success for students with cystic fibrosis: A novel empirically-based program. *Pediatric Pulmonology*. 2017.

102. Filigno SS, Strong E, Hente, et al: We have a lot to learn: School needs and school absences for student with cystic fibrosis. *Pediatric Pulmonology*. 2018.

103. Fink JB, Mahlmeiser MJ: High-frequency oscillation of the airway and chest wall. *Respiratory Care*. 2002; 47: 797–807.

104. Flewelling KD, Sellers DE, Sawicki GS, et al: Social support is associated with fewer reported symptoms and decreased treatment burden in adults with cystic fibrosis. *Journal of Cystic Fibrosis*. Epub ahead of print. 2019.

105. Flume PA, Mogayzel PJ Jr, Robinson KA, et al: Clinical Practice Guidelines for Pulmonary Therapies Committee: Cystic fibrosis pulmonary guidelines: Treatment of pulmonary exacerbations. *American Journal of Respiratory Critical Care Medicine*. 2009a; 180(9): 802–808.

106. Flume PA, Mogayzel PJ, Robinson KA, et al: Cystic fibrosis pulmonary guidelines. *American Journal of Respiratory and Critical Care Medicine*. 2010; 182(3): 298–306.

107. Flume PA, Robinson KA, O'Sullivan BP, et al: Clinical Practice Guidelines for Pulmonary Therapies Committee: Cystic fibrosis pulmonary guidelines: Airway clearance therapies. *Respiratory Care*. 2009b; 54(4): 522–537.

108. Flume PA: Pulmonary complications of cystic fibrosis. *Respiratory Care.* 2009; 54(5): 618–627.

109. Flynn K, Daiches A, Malpus Z, et al: A post-transplant person: Narratives of heart or lung transplantation and intensive care unit delirium. *Health.* 2014; 18(4): 352–368.

110. Ford P, Clifford A, Gussy K, et al: A systematic review of peer-support programs for smoking cessation in disadvantaged groups. *International Journal of Environmental Research and Public Health.* 2013; 10: 5507–5522.

111. Frayman KB, Kazmerski TM, Sawyer SM: A systematic review of the prevalence and impact of urinary incontinence in cystic fibrosis. *Respirology.* 2018; 23(1): 46–54.

112. Freeman AJ, Sellers ZM, Mazariegos G, et al: A multidisciplinary approach to pretransplant and posttransplant management of cystic fibrosis-associated liver disease. *Liver Transplantation: Official Publication of the American Association for the Study of Liver Diseases and the International Liver Transplantation Society.* 2019; 25(4): 640–657.

113. Friedrichsdorf SJ, Postier A, Eull D, et al: Pain outcomes in a US children's hospital: A prospective cross-sectional survey. *Hospital Pediatrics.* 2015; 5(1): 18–26.

114. Gale NK, Kenyon S, MacArthur C, et al: Synthetic social support: Theorizing lay health worker interventions. *Social Science & Medicine.* 2018; 196: 96–105.

115. Gallant MP: The influence of social support on chronic illness self-management: A review and directions for research. *Health Education Behaviors.* 2003; 30(2): 170–195.

116. Gamboa MC, Ferrando SJ: Psychopharmacology in transplant patients. In: Sher Y, Maldonado JR, eds. *Psychosocial Care of End-Stage Organ Disease and Transplant Patients.* Cham, Springer International Publishing; 2019: pp. 453–469.

117. Garrido G, Dhillon GS: Medical Course and Complications After Lung Transplantation. In: Sher Y, Maldonado JR, eds. *Psychosocial Care of End-Stage Organ Disease and Transplant Patients.* Cham, Springer International Publishing; 2019: pp. 279–288.

118. Georgiopoulos AM, Friedman D, Porter EA, et al: Screening for ADHD in adults with cystic fibrosis: Prevalence, health-related quality of life, and adherence. *Journal of Cystic Fibrosis.* 2018; 17(2): 276–280.

119. Georgiopoulos AM, Hua LL: The diagnosis and treatment of attention deficit-hyperactivity disorder in children and adolescents with cystic fibrosis: A retrospective study. *Psychosomatics.* 2011; 52(2): 160–166.

120. Gibney EM, Goldfarb DS: The association of nephrolithiasis with cystic fibrosis. *American Journal of Kidney Diseases.* 2003; 42(1): 1–11.

121. Gibson LE, Cooke RE: A test for concentration of electrolytes in sweat in cystic fibrosis of the pancreas utilizing pilocarpine by iotophoresis. *Journal of Pediatrics.* 1959: 545–549.

122. Gillet D, de Braekeleer M, Bellis G, et al: For the French Cystic Fibrosis Registry: *Cystic fibrosis and pregnancy Report from French data BJOG 91218, 109 SRC – BaiduScholar.* 1980–1999. 2002.

123. Gilljam M, Ellis L, Corey M, et al: Clinical manifestations of cystic fibrosis among patients with diagnosis in adulthood. *Chest.* 2004: 1215.

124. Giombi KD, Kosa KM, Rains C, et al: Consumers' perceptions of edible marijuana products for recreational use: Likes, dislikes and, reasons for use. *Substance Use & Misuse.* 2018; 53: 541-547.

125. Goss CH, Rubenfeld GD, Otto K, et al: The effect of pregnancy on survival in women with cystic fibrosis. *Chest.* 2003; 124: 1460–1468.

126. Green H, Jones AM: The microbiome and emerging pathogens in cystic fibrosis and non-cystic fibrosis bronchiectasis. *Seminars in Respiratory and Critical Care Medicine.* 2015; 36: 225–235.

127. Greene L: "You know you're a CF parent when…." 2016.

128. Greer SM, Goldstein AN, Walker MP: The impact of sleep deprivation on food desire in the human brain. *Nature Communications.* 2013; 4: 2259.

129. Grieve AJ, Tluczek A, Racine-Gilles CN, et al: Associations between academic achievement and psychosocial variables in adolescents with cystic fibrosis. *The Journal of School Health.* 2011; 81(11): 713–720.

130. Grosse SD, Rosenfeld M, Devine OJ, et al: Potential impact of newborn screening for cystic fibrosis on child survival: A systematic review and analysis. *Journal of Pediatrics.* 2006: 362.

131. Guiahi M, Davis A: First-trimester abortion in women with medical conditions. *Contraception.* 2012; 86(6): 662–630.

132. Guideline statement: Management of procedure-related pain in children and adolescents. *Journal of Paediatric Child Health.* 2006; 42(suppl 1): S1–S29.

133. Guo Y, Su M, McNutt MA, et al: Expression and distribution of cystic fibrosis transmembrane conductance regulator in neurons of the human brain. *Journal of Histochemistry and Cytochemistry.* 2009; 57(12): 1113–1120.

134. Gyi KM, Hodson ME, Yacoub MY, et al: Pregnancy in cystic fibrosis lung transplant recipients: Case series and review. *Fibrosis, 5 SRC – BaiduScholar.* 2006: 171–175.

135. Hadjiliadis D, Khoruts A, Zauber AG, et al: Cystic fibrosis colorectal cancer screening consensus recommendations. *Gastroenterology*. 2018; 154(3): 736–745.e14.

136. Hajek P, Phillips-Waller A, Przuij D, et al: A randomized trial of E-cigarettes versus nicotine-replacement therapy. *New England Journal of Medicine*. 2019; 380: 629–637.

137. Hamilton JG: Needle phobia: A neglected diagnosis. *Journal of Family Practice*. 1995; 41:169–175.

138. Hamosh A, FitzSimmons SC, Macek M JR, et al: Comparison of the clinical manifestations of cystic fibrosis in black and white patients. *Journal of Pediatrics*. 1998: 255.

139. Hanak V, Hartman TE, Ryu JH: Cough-induced rib fractures. *Mayo Clinic Proceedings*. 2005; 80(7): 879–882.

140. Hassanzad M, Eslampanah S, Modaresi M, et al: Pulmonary function and hospital admissions in patients with cystic fibrosis based on household second-hand smoking. *Tanaffos*. 2018; 17: 37–41.

141. Havermans T, Colpaert K, De Boeck K, et al: Pain in CF: Review of the literature. *Journal of Cystic Fibrosis*. 2013;12: 423–430.

142. Hayes M, Yaster M, Haythornthwaite JA, et al: Pain is a common problem affecting clinical outcomes in adults with cystic fibrosis. *Chest*. 2011;140: 1598-1603.

143. Heinicke BE, Paxton SJ, McLean SA, et al: Internet-delivered targeted group intervention for body dissatisfaction and disordered eating in adolescent girls: A randomized controlled trial. *Journal of Abnormal Child Psychology*. 2007; 35: 379–391.

144. Helgeson VS, Mascatelli K, Reynolds KA, et al: Friendship and romantic relationships among emerging adults with and without type 1 diabetes. *Journal of Pediatric Psychology*. 2015; 40: 359–371.

145. Helms SW, Christon LM, Dellon EP, et al: Patient and provider perspectives on communication about body image with adolescents and young adults with cystic fibrosis. *Journal of Pediatric Psychology*. 2017; 42(9): 1040–1050.

146. Heltshe SL, Godfrey EM, Josephy T, et al: Pregnancy among cystic fibrosis women in the era of CFTR modulators. *Journal of Cystic Fibrosis*. 2017; 16(6): 687–694.

147. Hilman BC, Aitken ML, Constantinescu M: Pregnancy in patients with cystic fibrosis. *Clinical Obstetrics and Gynecology*. 1996; 39: 70–86.

148. Hodges CA, Palmert MR, Drumm ML: Infertility in females with cystic fibrosis is multifactorial: Evidence from mouse models. *Endocrinology*. 2008; 149(6): 2790–2797.

149. Hodgkinson R, Lester H: Stresses and coping strategies of mothers living with a child with cystic fibrosis: Implications for nursing professionals. *Journal of Advanced Nursing*. 2002; 39(4): 377–383.

150. https://polst.org/. Accessed March 2019

151. Hubert D, Patrat C, Guibert J, et al: Results of assisted reproductive technique in men with cystic fibrosis. *Human Reproduction*. 2006; 21(5): 1232–1236.

152. Irwin S, Tecklin J: *Cardiopulmonary Physical Therapy: A Guide to Practice*. St. Louis, MS: Mosby, 2004.

153. Ivulich S, Westall G, Dooley M, et al: The evolution of lung transplant immunosuppression. *Drugs*. 2018; 78(10): 965–982.

154. Jones GH, Walshaw MJ: Potential impact on fertility of new systemic therapies for cystic fibrosis. *Paediatric Respiratory Reviews*. 2015; 16 Suppl 1: 25–27.

155. Jordan CL, Noah TL, Henry MM: Therapeutic challenges posed by critical drug-drug interactions in cystic fibrosis. *Pediatric Pulmonology*. 2016; 51: S61–S70.

156. Kang SH, de Tarso Roth Dalcin P, Bejzman Piltcher O, et al: Chronic rhinosinusitis and nasal polyposis in cystic fibrosis: Update on diagnosis and treatment. *Jornal Brasileiro de Pneumologia*. 2015; 41(1): 65–76.

157. Katz ES: Cystic fibrosis and sleep. *Clinics in Chest Medicine*. 2014; 35(3): 495–504.

158. Kazmerski TM, Sawicki GS, Miller E, et al: Sexual and reproductive health behaviors and experiences reported by young women with cystic fibrosis. *Journal of Cystic Fibrosis*. 2018; 17(1): 57–63.

159. Kempainen RR, Williams CB, Hazelwood A, et al: Comparison of high-frequency chest wall oscillation with differing waveforms for airway clearance in cystic fibrosis. *Chest*. 2007; 132(4): 1227–1232.

160. Kemper JA, Honig EG, Martin GS: Effects of marijuana exposure on expiratory airflow: A study of adults who participated in the U.S. national health and nutrition examination study. *Annals of the American Thoracic Society*. 2014; 12: 135–141.

161. Kennedy RM, Luhmann J, Zempsky WT: Clinical implications of unmanaged needle insertion pain and distress in children. *Pediatrics*. 2008; 122: 130–133.

162. Kessler RC, Adler L, Barkley R, et al: The prevalence and correlates of adult ADHD in the United States: Results from the National Comorbidity Survey Replication. *American Journal of Psychiatry*. 2006; 163(4): 716–723.

163. Kim P: Human Maternal Brain Plasticity: Adaptation to Parenting. *New Directions for Child and Adolescent Development*. 2016; 153: 47–58.

164. Kirk S, Milnes L: An exploration of how young people and parents use online support in the context of living with cystic fibrosis. *Health Expectations: An International Journal of Public Participation in Health Care and Health Policy.* 2016; 19(2): 309–321.

165. Klager S, Vallarino J, MacNaughton P, et al: Flavoring chemicals and aldehydes in E-cigarette emissions. *Environmental Science Technology.* 2017; 51(18): 10806–10813.

166. Knudsen KB, Pressler T, Mortensen LH, et al: Coach to cope: Feasibility of a life coaching program for young adults with cystic fibrosis. *Patient Preference and Adherence.* 2017; 11: 1613–1623.

167. Komp DM, Selden RF: Coagulation abnormalities in cystic fibrosis. *Chest.* 1970; 58(5): 501–503.

168. Konrad K, Thon A, Fritsch M, et al: Comparison of cystic fibrosis–related diabetes with type 1 diabetes based on a German/Austrian Pediatric Diabetes Registry. *Diabetes Care.* 2013; 36(4): 879–886.

169. Koscik RL, Farrell PM, Kosorok MR, et al: Cognitive function of children with cystic fibrosis: Deleterious effect of early malnutrition. *Pediatrics.* 2004: 1549.

170. Kurinczuk JJ: Safety issues in assisted reproduction technology. From theory to reality—just what are the data telling us about ICSI offspring health and future fertility and should we be concerned? *Human Reproduction.* 2003; 18(5): 925–931.

171. Ladores SI, Kazmerski TM, Rowe SM: Becoming pregnant while on targeted therapeutics for cystic fibrosis: A case report. *Journal of Obstetric, Gynecologic, and Neonatal Nursing.* 2016; 46(1): 72–77.

172. Lahiri T, Hempstead SE, Brady C, et al: Clinical practice guidelines from the Cystic Fibrosis Foundation for preschoolers with cystic fibrosis. *Pediatrics.* 2016; 137(4).

173. Lail, M: Sharing My CF With Colleagues. https://www.cff.org/CF-Community-Blog/Posts/2015/Sharing-My-CF-With-Colleagues/ 2015.

174. Langfelder-Schwind E, Karczeski B, Strecker MN, et al: Molecular testing for cystic fibrosis carrier status practice guidelines: Recommendations of the National Society of Genetic Counselors. *Journal of Genetic Counseling.* 2014: 5–15.

175. Lapin CD: Airway physiology, autogenic drainage, and active cycle of breathing. *Respiratory Care.* 2002; 47: 778–785.

176. Laude JR, Bailey SR, Crew E, et al: Extended treatment for cigarette smoking cessation: A randomized control trial. *Addiction.* 2017; 112: 1451–1459.

177. Lechtzin N, Allgood S, Hong G, et al: The association between pain and clinical outcomes in adolescents with cystic fibrosis. *Journal of Pain and Symptom Management.* 2016 Nov; 52(5): 681–687. doi: 10.1016/j.jpainsymman.2016.03.023. Epub 2016 Sep 29.

178. Lee A, Holdsworth M, Holland A, et al: The immediate effect of musculoskeletal physiotherapy techniques and massage on pain and ease of breathing in adults with cystic fibrosis. *Journal of Cystic Fibrosis.* 2009 Jan; 8(1): 79–81. doi: 10.1016/j.jcf.2008.07.002. Epub 2008 Aug 20.

179. Lee MS, Allen JG, Christiani DC: Endotoxin and (1→3)-β-D-glucan(1→3)-β-D-glucan contamination in electronic cigarette products sold in the united states. *Environmental Health Perspectives.* 2019; 127(4): 470008.

180. LeGrys VA, Applequist R, Briscoe DR, et al: *Sweat testing: Sample collection and quantitative chloride analysis; approved guideline.* Wayne: Clinical and Laboratory Standards Institute, 2009.

181. LeGrys VA, Yankaskas JR, Quittell LM, et al, Cystic Fibrosis Foundation: Diagnostic sweat testing: The Cystic Fibrosis Foundation guidelines. *Journal of Pediatrics.* 2007: 85–89.

182. Lehrer PM: How to relax and how to not relax: A re-evaluation of the work of Edmund Jacobson. *Behaviour Research and Therapy.* 1982; 20(5): 417–428.

183. Levin FR, Mariani JJ, Pavlicova M, et al: Dronabinol and lofexidine for cannabis use disorder: A randomized, double-blind, placebo-controlled trial. *Drug & Alcohol Dependence.* 2016; 159: 53–60.

184. Lin YC, Ly H, Golianu B: Acupuncture pain management for patients with cystic fibrosis: A pilot study. *American Journal of Chinese Medicine.* 2005; 33(1): 151–156.

185. Lipsitz, JD, Markowitz JC: Mechanisms of change in interpersonal therapy (IPT). *Clinical Psychology Review.* 2013; 33(8): 1134–1147.

186. LiPuma J, Dasen SE, Nielson DW, et al: Person-to-person transmission of *Pseudomonas cepacia* between patients with cystic fibrosis. *Lancet.* 1990; 336: 1094–1096.

187. Lyon A, Bilton D: Fertility issues in cystic fibrosis. *Paediatric Respiratory Reviews.* 2002; 3(3): 236–240.

188. Mahmoud MK, Punukollu D, Mahmood T: In vitro fertilization. *Obstetrics, Gynaecology Reproductive Medicine, 23 SRC – BaiduScholar.* 2013: 238–246.

189. Malfroot A, Adam G, Ciofu O, et al: Immunization in the current management of cystic fibrosis patients. *Journal of Cystic Fibrosis.* 2005; 4: 77–87.

190. Marconi A, Di Forti M, Lewis CM, et al: Meta-analysis of the association between the level of cannabis use and risk of psychosis. *Schizophrenia Bulletin.* 2016; 42(5): 1262–1269.

191. Marquette M, Charles S. Haworth CS: Bone health and disease in cystic fibrosis. *Paediatric Respiratory Reviews*, Royal Society of Medicine – The 29th symposium: Cystic fibrosis in children and adults, 17th November 2015; 2016; 20 (August): 2–5.

192. Maslow GR, Haydon A, McRee AL, et al: Growing up with a chronic illness: Social success, educational/vocational distress. *Journal of Adolescent Health*. 2011; 49: 206–212.

193. Matel J: Nutritional management of cystic fibrosis. *Journal of Parenteral and Enteral Nutrition*. 2012; 36(1): 60S–67S.

194. Mathiesen IH, Pressler T, Oturai P, et al: Osteoporosis is associated with deteriorating clinical status in adults with cystic fibrosis. *International Journal of Endocrinology*. 2018: 1–9.

195. McArdle JR, Talwalkar JS: Macrolides in cystic fibrosis. *Clinics in Chest Medicine*. 2007; 28: 347–360.

196. McIlwaine MP, Alarie N, Davidson GF, et al: Long-term multicentre randomised controlled study of high frequency chest wall oscillation versus positive expiratory pressure mask in cystic fibrosis. *Thorax*. 2013; 68(8):746–751.

197. McMullen AH, Pasta DJ, Frederick PD: Impact of pregnancy on women with cystic fibrosis. *Chest, 129 SRC – BaiduScholar*. 2006: 706–711.

198. Metcalfe A, Plumridge G, Coad J, et al: Parents' and children's communication about genetic risk: A qualitative study, learning from families' experiences. *European Journal of Human Genetics*. 2011; 19(6): 640–646.

199. Michel SH, Maqbool A, Hanna MD, et al: Nutrition management of pediatric patients who have cystic fibrosis. *Pediatric Clinics of North America*. 2009; 56(5): 1123–1141.

200. Miller WR: Motivational interviewing with problem drinkers. *Behavioural Psychotherapy*. 1983; 11(2): 147.

201. Milliken EJT: Cystic fibrosis in art. *Journal of the American Medical Association*. 2018; 320(12): 1224–1226.

202. Mogayzel PJ Jr, Naureckas ET, Robinson KA, et al: Pulmonary Clinical Practice Guidelines Committee: Cystic fibrosis pulmonary guidelines: Chronic medications for maintenance of lung health. *American Journal of Respiratory Critical Care Medicine*. 2013; 187(7): 680–689.

203. Mohr LC: The hypoxia altitude simulation test: An increasingly performed test for the evaluation of patients prior to air travel. *Chest*. 2008; 133: 839–841.

204. Moran A, Becker D, Casella SJ, et al: Epidemiology, pathophysiology, and prognostic implications of cystic fibrosis–related diabetes. *Diabetes Care*. 2010; 33(12): 2677–2683.

205. Moran A, Brunzell C, Cohen RC, et al: The CFRD Guidelines Committee: Clinical care guidelines for cystic fibrosis–related diabetes. *Diabetes Care.* 2010; 33(12): 2697–2708.

206. Moran A, Doherty L, Wang X, et al: Abnormal glucose metabolism in cystic fibrosis. *Journal of Pediatrics.* 1998; 133(1): 10–17.

207. Moran A, Pillay K, Becker D, et al: ISPAD Clinical Practice Consensus Guidelines 2018: Management of cystic fibrosis-related diabetes in children and adolescents. *Pediatric Diabetes.* 2018; 19(S27): 64–74.

208. Moran A, Pillay K, Becker D, et al: Management of cystic fibrosis related diabetes in children and adolescents. *Pediatric Diabetes.* 2014; 15 (suppl 20): 65–76.

209. Moreau NL, Dennis GL, Ames E, et al: Electrocardiogram (EKG) guided peripherally inserted central catheter placement and tip position: Results of a trial to replace radiological confirmation. *Journal of the Association of Vascular Access.* 2010; 15(1): 8–14.

210. Morrell MR, Pilewski JM: Lung transplantation for cystic fibrosis. *Clinics in Chest Medicine.* 2016; 37(1): 127–138.

211. Morrison L, Agnew J: Oscillating devices for airway clearance in people with cystic fibrosis. *Cochrane Database of Systematic Reviews.* 2009: CD006842

212. Moukarzel S, Dyer R, Innis S: Complex relation between diet and phospholipid fatty acids in children with cystic fibrosis. *Journal of Pediatric Gastroenterology and Nutrition.* 2017; 64: 598–604.

213. Muchekehu RW, Quinton PM: A new role for bicarbonate secretion in cervico-uterine mucus release. *Journal of Physiology 588Pt 13 SRC – BaiduScholar.* 2010: 2329–2342

214. Munck A, Alberti C, Colombo C, et al: International prospective study of distal instestinal obstruction syndrome in cystic fibrosis: Associated factors and outcomes. *Journal of Cystic Fibrosis.* 2016; 15: 531–539.

215. Neill AM, Nelson-Piercy C: Hazards of assisted conception in women with severe medical disease. *Human Fertility Camb, 4 SRC – BaiduScholar.* 2001: 239–245.

216. Nevitt SJ, Thornton J, Murray CS, et al: Inhaled mannitol for cystic fibrosis. *Cochrane Database in Systematic Reviews.* 2018, CD008649.

217. NIH: US National Library of Medicine. https://clinicaltrials.gov/ct2/about-studies/glossary.

218. Nippins M: Personalizing exercise and physical activity prescriptions. In: Watson R, ed. *Diet, Food, Nutrition and Exercise in Cystic Fibrosis.* 2014. Elsevier: 38.

219. Nixon P, Orenstein D, Kelsey S, et al: The prognostic value of exercise testing in patients with cystic fibrosis. *New England Journal of Medicine*. 1992; 327: 1785–1788.

220. Norris AW, Ode KL, Merjaneh L, et al: Survival in a bad neighborhood: Pancreatic islets in cystic fibrosis. *Journal of Endocrinology*. February 1, 2019. pii: JOE-18-0468. R1. doi: 10.1530/JOE-18-0468. [Epub ahead of print] Review. PMID: 30759072.

221. O'Sullivan BP, Freedman SD: Cystic fibrosis. *The Lancet*. 2009; 373(9678): 1891–1904.

222. Oermann CM, Swank PR, Sockrider MM: Validation of an instrument measuring patient satisfaction with chest physiotherapy techniques in cystic fibrosis. *Chest*. 2000; 118: 92–97.

223. Oliver KN, Free ML, Bok C, et al: Stigma and optimism in adolescents and young adults with cystic fibrosis. *Journal of Cystic Fibrosis: Official Journal of the European Cystic Fibrosis Society*. 2014; 13(6): 737–744.

224. O'Neil S, Leahy F, Pasterkamp H: The effects of chronic hyperinflation, nutritional status, and posture on respiratory muscle strength in cystic fibrosis. *American Review of Respiratory Disease*. 1983; 128: 1051–54.

225. Ortega-García JA, Perales JE, Cárceles-Álvarez A, et al: Long-term follow-up of a Tobacco Prevention and Cessation Program in cystic fibrosis patients. *Adicciones*. 2016; 28(2): 99–107.

226. Ortega-García JA, Trinidad López-Fernández M, Llano R, et al: Smoking Prevention and Cessation Programme in Cystic Fibrosis: Integrating an environmental health approach. *Journal of Cystic Fibrosis: Official Journal of the European Cystic Fibrosis Society*. 2012; 11(1): 34–39.

227. Otis JD: *Managing Chronic Pain: A Cognitive-Behavioral Therapy Approach*. Oxford: University Press, 2007.

228. Paul L: Is bronchoscopy an obsolete tool in cystic fibrosis? The role of bronchoscopy in cystic fibrosis and its clinical use. *Journal of Thoracic Disease*. 2017; 9(suppl 10): S1139–S1145.

229. Peebles AD: Physiotherapy. In: Hill CM, ed.: *Practical Guidelines for Cystic Fibrosis Care. 1st Edition*. 1998. London: Churchill Livingstone.

230. Pegues DA, Carson LA, Tablan OC, et al: Acquisition of *Pseudomonas cepacia* at summer camps for patients with cystic fibrosis. *Journal of Pediatrics*. 1994; 124: 694–702.

231. Perin C, Fagondes SC, Casarotto FC, et al: Sleep findings and predictors of sleep desaturation in adult cystic fibrosis patients. *Sleep and Breathing*. 2012; 16(4): 1041–1048.

232. Pinquart M: Body image of children and adolescents with chronic illness: A meta-analytic comparison with healthy peers. *Body Image*. 2013; 10(2): 141–148.

233. Prince M, Patel V, Saxena S: No health without mental health. *Lancet.* 2007; 370(9590): 859–877.

234. Quinn J, Latchford G, Duff A, et al: Measuring, predicting and improving adherence to inhalation therapy in individuals with CF with CF: Randomised controlled study of motivational interviewing. *Pediatric Pulmonology.* 2004; 38(s27): 360.

235. Quittner AL, Abbott J, Georgiopoulos AM, et al: International Committee on Mental Health in Cystic Fibrosis: Cystic Fibrosis Foundation and European Cystic Fibrosis Society Consensus Statements for Screening and Treating Depression and Anxiety. *Thorax.* 2016; 71(1): 26–34.

236. Quittner AL, Alpern AN, Blackwell LS: Treatment adherence in adolescents with Cystic Fibrosis. In: Castellani C, Elborn S, and Heijerman H (eds.), *Health care issues and challenges in the adolescent with cystic fibrosis.* 2012; 77–91. Oxford, UK: Elsevier Inc.

237. Quittner AL, Goldbeck L, Abbott J, et al: Prevalence of depression and anxiety in patients with cystic fibrosis and parent caregivers: Results of the International Depression Epidemiological Study (TIDES) across Nine Countries. *Thorax.* 2014; 69(12): 1090–1097.

238. Quittner AL, Li-Rosi A: Cystic Fibrosis. In: Modi & Driscoll, eds., *Adherence and Self-Management in Pediatric Populations.* United Kingdom: Elsevier Publishing; in press.

239. Quittner AL, Opipari LC: Differential treatment of siblings: Interview and diary analyses comparing two family contexts. *Child Development.* 1994; 65: 800–814.

240. Rabin HR, Butler SM, Wohl ME, et al: Pulmonary exacerbations in cystic fibrosis. *Pediatric Pulmonology.* 2004; 37: 400–406.

241. Ramos KJ, Smith PJ, McKone EF, et al: Lung transplant referral for individuals with cystic fibrosis: Cystic Fibrosis Foundation consensus. *Journal of Cystic Fibrosis.* 2019; 18(3): 321–333.

242. Ramos KJ, Somayaji R, Lease ED, et al: Cystic fibrosis physicians' perspectives on the timing of referral for lung transplant evaluation: A survey of physicians in the United States. *BMC Pulmonary Medicine.* 2017; 17(1): 21.

243. Ratjen F, Bell SC, Rowe SM, et al: Cystic fibrosis. *Nature Reviews Disease Primers.* 2015; 1:15010.

244. Rigotti NA: Smoking cessation in patients with respiratory disease: Existing treatments and future directions. *Lancet Respiratory Medicine.* 2013; 3: 241–250.

245. Robinson NB, DiMango E: Prevalence of gastroesophageal reflux disease in cystic fibrosis and implications for lung disease. *Annals of the American Thoracic Society.* 2014; 11(6): 964–968.

246. Robson AG, Lenney J, Innes JA: Using laboratory measurements to predict in-flight desaturation in respiratory patients: Are current guidelines appropriate? *Respiratory Medicine*. 2008; 102: 1592–1597.

247. Rock MJ, Mischler EH, Farrell PM, et al: Immunoreactive trypsinogen screening for cystic fibrosis: Characterization of infants with a false-positive screening test. *Pediatric Pulmonary*. 1989: 42–48.

248. Roe AH, Traxler S, Schreiber CA: Contraception in women with cystic fibrosis: A systematic review of the literature. *Contraception*. 2016; 93(1): 3–10.

249. Roehmel JF, Kallinich T, Staab D, et al: Clinical manifestations and risk factors of arthropathy in cystic fibrosis. *Respiratory Medicine*. 2019; 147: 66–71.

250. Rohlfs EM, Zhou Z, Heim RA, et al: Cystic fibrosis carrier testing in an ethnically diverse US population. *Clinical Chemistry*. 2011; 57(6): 841.

251. Rowe SM, Clancy JP, Wilschanski M: Nasal potential difference measurements to assess CFTR ion channel activity. *Methods in Molecular Biology*. 2011: 69–86.

252. Rutherford AJ: Male infertility and cystic fibrosis. *Journal of the Royal Society of Medicine*. 2007; 100 (Suppl 47): 29–34.

253. Sachs J, McGlade E, Yurgelun-Todd D: Safety and toxicity of cannabinoids. *Neurotherapeutics*. 2015; 12: 735–746.

254. Safi C, Zheng Z, Dimango E, et al: Chronic rhinosinusitis in cystic fibrosis: Diagnosis and medical management. *Medical Sciences*. 2019; 7(2): 32.

255. Saiman L, Seigel JD, LiPuma JJ, et al: Infection prevention and control guideline for cystic fibrosis: 2013 update. *Infection Control & Hospital Epidemiology*. 2014; 35(S1): S1-S67.

256. Salm N, Yetter E, Tluczek A: Informing parents about positive newborn screen results: Parents' recommendations. *Journal of Child Health Care: For Professionals Working with Children in the Hospital and Community*. 2012; 16(4): 367–381.

257. Sanders DB, Bittner RC, Rosenfeld M, et al: Failure to recover to baseline pulmonary function after cystic fibrosis pulmonary exacerbation. *American Journal of Respiratory and Critical Care Medicine*. 2010; 182: 627–632.

258. Savi D, Mordenti M, Bonci E, et al: Survival after lung transplant for cystic fibrosis in Italy: A single center experience with 20 years of follow-up. *Transplantation Proceedings*. 2018; 50(10): 3732–3738.

259. Sawicki GS, Sellers DE, Robinson WM: Self-reported physical and psychological symptom burden in adults with cystic fibrosis. *Journal of Pain and Symptom Management*. 2008; 35(4): 372–380.

260. Sawicki GS, Tiddens H: Managing treatment complexity in cystic fibrosis: Challenges and opportunities. *Pediatric Pulmonology*. 2012; 47(6): 523–533.

261. Sawyer SM, Farrant B, Cerritelli B, et al: A survey of sexual and reproductive health in men with cystic fibrosis: New challenges for adolescent and adult services. *Thorax*. 2005; 60(4): 326–330.

262. Schindler T, Michel S, Wilson A: Nutrition management of cystic fibrosis in the 21st century. *Nutrition in Clinical Practice*. 2015; 30: 488–500.

263. Schmid K, Fink K, Holl RW, et al: Predictors for future cystic fibrosis-related diabetes by oral glucose tolerance test. *Journal of Cystic Fibrosis*. 2014; 13: 80–85.

264. Schmid-Mohler G, Caress AL, Spirig R, et al: Thrust out of normality-How adults living with cystic fibrosis experience pulmonary exacerbations: A qualitative study. *Journal of Clinical Nursing*. 2019; 28(1-2): 190–200.

265. School Avoidance: Tips for Concerned Parents. Retrieved 3/25/2019, from https://www.healthychildren.org/English/health-issues/conditions/emotional-problems/Pages/School-Avoidance.aspx.

266. Schoyer KD, Gilbert F, Rosenwaks Z: Infertility and abnormal cervical mucus in two sisters who are compound heterozygotes for the cystic fibrosis (CF) F508 and R117H/7T mutations. *Fertility and Sterility 1201, 90 SRC – BaiduScholar*. 2008: e19–22.

267. Schwarzenberg SJ, Hempstead SE, McDonald CM, et al: Enteral tube feeds for individuals with cystic fibrosis: Cystic Fibrosis Foundation evidence informed guidelines. *Journal of Cystic Fibrosis*. 2016; 15(6): 724–735.

268. Sermet-Gaudelus I, Girodon E, Roussel D, et al: Measurement of nasal potential difference in young children with an equivocal sweat test following newborn screening for cystic fibrosis. *Thorax*. 2010: 539–544.

269. Shearer JE, Bryon M: The nature and prevalence of eating disorders and eating disturbance in adolescents with cystic fibrosis. *Journal of the Royal Society of Medicine*. 2004; 97 (Suppl 44): 36–42.

270. Sher Y, Mooney J, Dhillon GS, et al: Delirium after lung transplantation: Association with recipient characteristics, hospital resource utilization, and mortality. *Clinical Transplantation*. 2017; 31(5).

271. Sher Y: Post-transplant Psychosocial and Mental Health Care of the Lung Recipient. In: Sher Y, Maldonado JR, eds: *Psychosocial Care of End-Stage Organ Disease and Transplant Patients*. Cham, Springer International Publishing; 2019: pp. 289–298.

272. Shifren A, Byers DE, Witt CA, et al: *Pulmonary Medicine Subspecialty Consult*. 2nd ed. Department of Medicine, Washington University School of Medicine; 2016.

273. Shoebotham A, Coulson NS: Therapeutic affordances of online support group use in women with endometriosis. *Journal of Medical Internet Research*. 2016; 18: e109.

274. Shrader Smith D: *Mallory's 65 Roses*. 1997.

275. Sly PD, Wainwright CE: Preserving lung function: The Holy Grail in managing cystic fibrosis. *Annals of the American Thoracic Society*. 2017; 14(6): 833–835.

276. Smith C, McNaughton DA, Meyer S: Client perceptions of group education in the management of type 2 diabetes in South Australia. *Australian Journal of Primary Care* 2015; 22 (4): 360-367.

277. Smith M: *Salt in My Soul: An Unfinished life*. United States of America: Spiegel & Grau, Random House; 2019.

278. Snell G, Reed A, Stern M, et al: The evolution of lung transplantation for cystic fibrosis: A 2017 update. *Journal of Cystic Fibrosis: Official Journal of the European Cystic Fibrosis Society*. 2017; 16(5): 553–564.

279. Sosnay PR, Siklosi KR, Van Goor F, et al: Defining the disease liability of variants in the cystic fibrosis transmembrane conductance regulator gene. *Nature Genetics*. 2013: 1160–1170.

280. Southern K, Merelle MME, Dankert-Roelse J, et al: Newborn screening for cystic fibrosis. *Cochrane Database of Systematic Reviews*. 2009.

281. Spicuzza L, Sciuto C, Leonardi S, et al: Early occurrence of obstructive sleep apnea in infants and children with cystic fibrosis. *Archives of Pediatrics & Adolescent Medicine*. 2012; 166(12): 1165–1169.

282. Stallings VA, Stark LJ, Robinson KA, et al: Evidence-based practice recommendations for nutrition-related management of children and adults with cystic fibrosis and pancreatic insufficiency: Results of a systematic review. *Journal of American Dietician Association*. 2008; 108(5): 832–839.

283. Steigerwald S, Wong PO, Cohen BE: Smoking, vaping, and use of edibles and other forms of marijuana among U.S. adults. *Annals of Internal Medicine*. 2018; 169: 890–892.

284. Stenbit AE, Flume PA: Pulmonary exacerbations in cystic fibrosis. *Current Opinion in Pulmonary Medicine*. 2011; 17: 442–447.

285. Stephenson AL, Mannik LA, Walsh S, et al: Longitudinal trends in nutritional status and the relation between lung function and BMI in cystic fibrosis: A population-based cohort study. *The American Journal of Clinical Nutrition*. 2013; 97(4): 872–877.

286. Stern RC, Byard PJ, Tomashefski JF, et al: Recreational use of psychoactive drugs by patients with cystic fibrosis. *Journal of Pediatrics*. 1987; 111(2): 293–299.

287. Stuart MJ, Baune BT: Depression and type 2 diabetes: Inflammatory mechanisms of a psychoneuroendocrine co-morbidity. *Neuroscience & Biobehavioral Reviews*. 2012; 36(1): 658–676.

288. Swisher A, Hebestreit H, Mejia-Downs A, et al: Exercise and habitual physical activity for people with cystic fibrosis: Expert consensus, evidence-based guide for advising patients. *Cardiopulmonary Physical Therapy Journal*. 2015; 26: 85–98.

289. Talwalkar JS, Koff JL, Lee HB, et al: Cystic fibrosis transmembrane regulator modulators: Implications for the management of depression and anxiety in cystic fibrosis. *Psychosomatics*. 2017; 58(4): 343–354.

290. Talwalkar JS, Murray TS: The approach to *Pseudomonas aeruginosa* in cystic fibrosis. *Clinics in Chest Medicine*. 2016, 37: 69–81.

291. Tan WC, Lo C, Jong A, et al: Marijuana and chronic obstructive lung disease: A population-based study. *Canadian Medical Association Journal*. 2009; 180: 814–820.

292. Tetrault JM, Crothers K, Moore BA, et al: Effects of marijuana smoking on pulmonary function and respiratory complications: A systematic review. *Archives of Internal Medicine*. 2007; 167: 221–228.

293. The American Chronic Pain Association. Live Better with Pain Log. 2010. Accessed May 30, 2019, at https://www.theacpa.org/wp-content/uploads/2017/08/Pain-Log-Rev-2010-V2.pdf.

294. Thiara G, Goldman R: Milk consumption and mucus production is children with asthma. *Canadian Family Physician*. 2012; 58: 165–166.

295. Thorpe-Beeston JG, Madge S, Gyi K: The outcome of pregnancies in women with cystic fibrosis-single centre experience. *BJOG 35461, 120 SRC – BaiduScholar*. 2013: 1998–2011.

296. Tierney S: Body image and cystic fibrosis: A critical review. *Body Image*. 2012; 9(1): 12–19.

297. Treede RD, Rief W, Barke A, et al: Chronic pain as a symptom or a disease: The IASP Classification of Chronic Pain for the International Classification of Diseases (ICD-11). *Pain* 2019; 160: 19–27.

298. Trimble D, Donaldson SH: Ivacaftor withdrawal syndrome in cystic fibrosis patients with the G551D mutation. *Journal of Cystic Fibrosis*. 2018; 17(2): e13–e16.

299. Truby H, Cowlishaw P, O'Neil C, et al: The long-term efficacy of gastrostomy feeding in children with cystic fibrosis on anthropometric markers of nutritional status and pulmonary function. *Open Respiratory Medical Journal*. 2009; 3: 112–115.

300. Truby H, Paxton AS: Body image and dieting behavior in cystic fibrosis. *Pediatrics*. 2001; 107(6): E92.

301. Turck D, Braegger C, Colombo C, et al: ESPEN-ESPGHAN-ECFS guidelines on nutrition care for infants, children and adults with cystic fibrosis. *Clinical Nutrition*. 2016; 35: 557–577.

302. Turk DC, Monarch ES: Biopsychosocial perspectives on chronic pain. In: Turk DC, Gatchel RJ (Eds.), *Psychological Approaches to Pain Management*. 2nd ed. New York: The Guilford Press; 2002: pp. 3–29.

303. U.S. Department of Health and Human Services. NIH. Clinical Trials: Benefits, Risks and Safety. https://www.nia.nih.gov/health/clinical-trials-benefits-risks-and-safety; May 2017

304. Uchino BN: *Social support and physical health: Understanding the Health Consequences of Relationships*. Yale University Press; 2004.

305. Ulph F, Cullinan T, Qureshi N, et al: Parents' responses to receiving sickle cell or cystic fibrosis carrier results for their child following newborn screening. *European Journal of Human Genetics: EJHG*. 2015; 23(4): 459–465.

306. van de Peppel IP, Bertolini A, Jonker JW, et al: Diagnosis, follow-up and treatment of cystic fibrosis-related liver disease. *Current Opinion in Pulmonary Medicine*. 2017; 23(6): 562–569.

307. van Staa AL, Jedeloo S, van Meeteren J, et al: Crossing the transition chasm: Experiences and recommendations for improving transitional care of young adults, parents and providers. *Child: Care, Health and Development*. 2011; 37(6): 821–832.

308. Vaz-Drago R, Custodio N, Carmo-Fonseca M: Deep intronic mutations and human disease. *Human Genetics*. 2017: 1093–1111.

309. Vertex pharmaceuticals. (2017). Lumacaftor-ivacaftor: Patient information. Retrieved from http://pi.vrtx.com/files/uspi_lumacaftor_ivacaftor.pdf.

310. Vertex pharmaceuticals. (2018). Tezacaftor-ivacaftor: Patient information. Retrieved from https://pi.vrtx.com/files/uspi_tezacaftor_ivacaftor.pdf.

311. Verwejj PE, Keremans JJ, Voss A, et al: Fungal contamination of tobacco and marijuana. *Journal of the American Medical Association*. 2000; 284: 2875.

312. Wage and Hour Division (WHD). FAQs: FMLA – Wage and Hour Division (WHD) – U.S. Department of Labor, www.dol.gov/whd/fmla/fmla-faqs.htm.

313. Wagener JS, Williams MJ, Millar SJ, et al: Pulmonary exacerbations and acute declines in lung function in patients with cystic fibrosis. *Journal of Cystic Fibrosis*. 2018; 17: 496–502.

314. Wang J: Cystic fibrosis and sinusitis. The Cystic Fibrosis Center at Stanford. September 2011. https://med.stanford.edu/cfcenter/teens/Sinusitis.html.

315. Wang TW, Gentzke A, Sharapova S, et al: Tobacco product use among middle and high school students – United States, 2011-2017. *Morbidity & Mortality Weekly Reports*. 2018; 67: 629–633.

316. Waters V, Ratjen F: Pulmonary exacerbations in children with cystic fibrosis. *Annals of American Thoracic Society.* 2015; 12 (Suppl 2): S200–206.

317. Weill D, Benden C, Corris PA, et al: A consensus document for the selection of lung transplant candidates: 2014--An update from the Pulmonary Transplantation Council of the International Society for Heart and Lung Transplantation. *The Journal of Heart and Lung Transplantation: The Official Publication of the International Society for Heart Transplantation.* 2015; 34(1): 1–15.

318. Weitzman ER, Ziemnik RE, Huang Q, et al: Alcohol and marijuana use and treatment nonadherence among medically vulnerable youth. *Pediatrics.* 2015; 13: 450–457.

319. West JB: *Respiratory Physiology – The Essentials.* Baltimore, MD: William & Wilkins; 1985.

320. White H, Morton AM, Conway SP, et al: Enteral tube feeding in adults with cystic fibrosis: Patient choice and impact on long term outcomes. *Journal of Cystic Fibrosis.* 2013; 12(6): 616–622.

321. Whiteman MK, Oduyebo T, Zapata LB, et al: Contraceptive safety among women with cystic fibrosis: A systematic review. *Contraception.* 2016; 94(6): 621–629.

322. Wilschanski M, Durie PR: Patterns of GI disease in adulthood associated with mutations in the CFTR gene. *Gut.* 2007; 56(8): 1153–1163.

323. Wilschanski M, Novak I: The cystic fibrosis of exocrine pancreas. *Cold Spring Harbor Perspectives in Medicine.* 2013; 3(5).

324. Wilson LM, Morrison L, Robinson KA: Airway clearance techniques for cystic fibrosis: An overview of Cochrane systematic reviews. *Cochrane Database Systematic Reviews.* 2019; 1:CD011231.

325. Withers AL: Management issues for adolescents with cystic fibrosis. *Pulmonary Medicine.* 2012: 134132.

326. Wolman RL: Osteoporosis and exercise. In: McLatchie G, Harris M, King J, et al, eds.: *ABC of Sports Medicine. 4th ed.* BMJ Publihing; 1999.

327. Wong MG, Heriot SA: Parents of children with cystic fibrosis: How they hope, cope and despair. *Child: Care, Health and Development.* 2008; 34(3): 344–354.

328. World Health Organization. 1998. Accessed March 2019. http://www.who.int/cancer/palliative/definition/en/.

329. World Health Organization. World Health Organization supports global effort to relieve chronic pain. 2004. Available at: http://www. who.int/mediacentre/news/releases/2004/ pr70/en. Accessed March 26, 2019.

330. Wuthrich B, Schmid A, Walther B, et al: Milk consumption does not lead to mucus production or occurrence of asthma. *Journal of the American College of Nutrition*. 2005; 24: 547S–555S.

331. Yankaskas JR, Marshall BC, Sufian B, et al: Cystic fibrosis adult care: Consensus conference report. *Chest*. 2004; 25(Suppl 1): 1S–39S.

332. Yen EH, Quinton H, Borowitz D: Better nutritional status in early childhood is associated with improved clinical outcomes and survival in patients with cystic fibrosis. *The Journal of Pediatrics*. 2013: 530–535.

333. Young KD: Pediatric procedural pain. *Annals of Emergency Medicine*. 2005; 45: 160–171.

334. Zuckerman JB, Zuaro DE, Prato BS, et al: Bacterial contamination of cystic fibrosis clinics. *Journal of Cystic Fibrosis*. 2009; 8: 186–192.

INDEX